International African Library 7
General editors: J. D. Y. Peel and David Parkin

I COULD SPEAK UNTIL TOMORROW

In affectionate memory of
Elvania and Pio Zirimu

International African Library

General Editors

J. D. Y. Peel *and* David Parkin

The *International African Library* is a major monograph series from the International African Institute and complements its quarterly periodical *Africa*, the premier journal in the field of African studies. Theoretically informed ethnographies, studies of social relations 'on the ground' which are sensitive to local cultural forms, have long been central to the Institute's publications programme. The *IAL* maintains this strength but extends it into new areas of contemporary concern, both practical and intellectual. It includes works focused on problems of development, especially on the linkages between the local and national levels of society; studies along the interface between the social and environmental sciences; and historical studies, especially those of a social, cultural or interdisciplinary character.

Titles in series:

1 Sandra T. Barnes *Patrons and power: creating a political community in metropolitan Lagos*†
2 Jane I. Guyer (ed.) *Feeding African cities: essays in social history*†
3 Paul Spencer *The Maasai of Matapato: a study of rituals of rebellion*†
4 Johan Pottier *Migrants no more: settlement and survival in Mambwe villages, Zambia*†
5 Günther Schlee *Identities on the move: clanship and pastoralism in northern Kenya*
6 Suzette Heald *Controlling anger: the sociology of Gisu violence*
7 Karin Barber *I could speak until tomorrow: oriki, women and the past in a Yoruba town**
8 Richard Fardon *Between God, the Dead and the Wild: Chamba interpretations of religion and ritual**

* *Published in the USA by the Smithsonian Institution Press*
† *Published in the USA by Indiana University Press*

Editorial Consultants

Kofi Agawu
Pierre Bonte
John Comaroff
Johannes Fabian
Paulin Hountondji
Ivan Karp
Sally Falk Moore

I COULD SPEAK UNTIL TOMORROW

Oriki, Women, and the Past
in a Yoruba Town

Karin Barber

EDINBURGH UNIVERSITY PRESS
for the INTERNATIONAL AFRICAN INSTITUTE, London

© Karin Barber 1991

Edinburgh University Press
22 George Square, Edinburgh

Set in Linotron Plantin
by Koinonia, Bury, and
Printed and bound in Great Britain by
CPI Antony Rowe, Chippenham and Eastbourne

British Library Cataloguing
in Publication Data
Barber, Karin
I could speak until tomorrow: Oriki, women
and the past in a Yoruba town. –(International
African Library. 7)
1. Nigeria. Yoruba. Cultural processes
I. Title II. Series
305.89633
ISBN 0 7486 0210 0

CONTENTS

MAPS, DIAGRAMS AND TABLES

ACKNOWLEDGEMENTS

It would be impossible to thank individually all the people who did me kindnesses in Okuku. Many of them are named in the following pages, as performers of *oriki* or as interpreters, explainers and tellers of history. However, there are some to whom I owe special gratitude. During the three years that I lived in Okuku, I stayed with the family of Mr G. A. Akindele. To all of the Akindeles I extend my heartfelt thanks for their generosity, hospitality and tolerance. I had the privilege of being made an honorary daughter of the late Olokuku, His Highness James Ọlaoṣebikan Oyewusi II. From the moment of my first arrival, in July 1974, to his untimely death in March 1980, the Olokuku showed me every kindness. Always entertaining, unfailingly gracious, he was also in his way a man of genius. It was an honour to be admitted into his confidence.

In 1977 I left Okuku to take up an appointment at the University of Ifẹ, but our connection did not come to an end, rather it expanded as our spheres of operation diverged. My parents, Charles and Barbara Barber, and my brother John visited Okuku at different times. The Olokuku also visited my parents in Leeds, where he liked to say he had been offered 'seventeen different kinds of meat, including zebra'. He made my Ph.D. graduation day at the University of Ifẹ memorable by attending it with an entourage of eight of the town chiefs, even though he was by then very ill. His successor, the present Olokuku, His Highness Samuel Oyebọde Oyelẹyẹ Oluronkẹ II, has continued the gracious tradition and made me feel as much at home in Okuku as ever. Our connection was symbolised and cemented through his kind action, supported by the chiefs and the Okuku Welfare Association, in conferring on me the chieftaincy title Iyamoye in 1984. As the Olokuku said, 'We want you to know by this that you can never leave us, except physically'.

I also owe special gratitude to Joseph Faramade Ajeiigbe, who helped me enormously with my research during my second and third years in Okuku. Not only did he transcribe almost all my recorded texts, he also went through them with me, word by word, commenting in Yoruba on local allusions, obscure meanings and poetic idioms. His guidance and contacts were also very helpful in the rest of my field work.

At Ifẹ, I was fortunate enough to be supervised in my Ph.D. research by Professor Richard Taylor and Professor 'Wande Abimbọla. I am also grateful to Professor 'Sope Oyelaran and Professor A. Akiwọwọ for many illuminating discussions over the years, first as a student and later as a colleague. Professor Ọlabiyi Yai has long been a formative influence in my thoughts about Yoruba literature. When I began the long drawn-out process of rewriting my thesis for publication, Jane Bryce and Ruth Finnegan gave me the benefit of detailed readings and comments on the first draft. John Peel has been a patient, constructive and encouraging critic throughout the production of the present version, and Chris Wickham also made many helpful suggestions. I owe most of all to Paulo Farias, who read all my numerous drafts with unfailing perceptiveness, and provided constant support and encouragement.

NOTE ON ORTHOGRAPHY

Yoruba is a tonal language, with three underlying pitch levels for vowels and syllabic nasals: low tone (indicated with a grave accent: kò, ˋn), mid tone (not marked: **le, n**) and high tone (indicated with an acute accent: **wí, ˊn**). Speech is characterised by continual glides between these levels.

The orthography adopted in this book is the modern standard style recommended by the Yoruba Orthography Committee. The following symbols are employed:

ẹ roughly as in English 'get' (cf. **e** as in French 'chez')

ọ roughly as in English 'pot' (cf. **o** as in French 'eau')

ṣ the sound written in English as sh

p the voiceless labio-velar sound kp where k and p are simultaneously pronounced.

Poetic texts in Yoruba are written with full tone markings. Lineation is partly subjective, but is based on a combination of the performer's breath-pauses and the linguistic structure of the text. Where the texts reveal features of the Ọṣun area dialect, these have been preserved, e.g. Enikoyi [for standard Yoruba Onikoyi], ṣègi [for standard Yoruba sègi], mid-tone third person possessive rẹ [for standard Yoruba low-tone rè].

When Yoruba sentences or phrases are quoted in passing, they are italicised and tone-marked. However, isolated Yoruba words are not tone-marked, because the frequency of their occurrence would cause problems for the typesetters. For reference, all such words are listed with full tone marks in the glossary. The word 'ọba' (king) is not italicised because it is used in English constructions such as ọba's, ọbas, ọbaship.

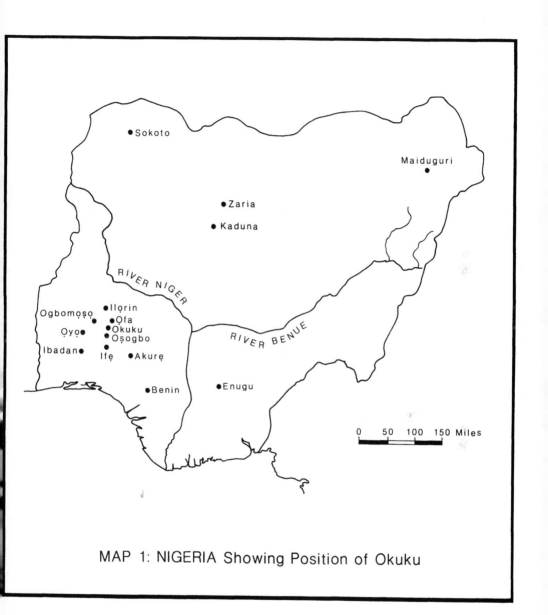

MAP 1: NIGERIA Showing Position of Okuku

1

ANTHROPOLOGY, TEXT AND TOWN

Literary texts tell us things about society and culture that we could learn in no other way. In this book I investigate what *oriki* tell us about Okuku and what Okuku told me about *oriki*.

Okuku is a town in the Ọyọ State of Nigeria, small by Yoruba standards, but an important political and cultural centre in its own area, the Odo-Ọtin district. *Oriki* are a genre of Yoruba oral poetry that could be described as attributions or appellations: collections of epithets, pithy or elaborated, which are addressed to a subject. In Okuku they are performed mainly by women.

Oriki are a master discourse. In the enormous wealth and ferment of Yoruba oral literature, they are probably the best-known of all forms. They are composed for innumerable subjects of all types, human, animal and spiritual; and they are performed in numerous modes or genres. They are compact and evocative, enigmatic and arresting formulations, utterances which are believed to capture the essential qualities of their subjects, and by being uttered, to evoke them. They establish unique identities and at the same time make relationships between beings. They are a central component of almost every significant ceremonial in the life of the compound and town; and are also constantly in the air as greetings, congratulations and jokes. They are deeply cherished by their owners.

The most conspicuous of the genres based on *oriki* are those performed by specialists, like the hunters who perform *ijala* chants, or professional entertainers like the travelling *egungun* masqueraders. Both men and women can make a name for themselves as public performers, by going wherever great celebrations are being held – and, nowadays, by appearing on television and making records. There is also, however, a less conspicuous but much more pervasive tradition of *oriki* performance carried on by ordinary women, the wives and daughters of the town's compounds, who learn and perform the *oriki* relevant to the individuals and groups with which they are associated. This less showy, more anonymous, but often more profound tradition of *oriki* chants performed by women is the central subject of this book.

Because *oriki* are crucial in making the relationships, human and spiritual, that constitute the Yoruba world, they reveal connections and hidden faces in society that would not otherwise be accessible. By attending to what people say themselves, through the concentrated and oblique refractions of *oriki* – and through what they say about *oriki* – we learn how people constitute their society. Texts like this can lead into the heart of a community's own conception of itself: without which, any description of social structure or process will remain purely external. In extended texts, better than in brief citations of lexical items, descriptions of physical artefacts, or artificially-constructed interview schedules, we find the possibility of entering into people's own discourse about their social world.

Malinowski knew the value of 'texts'. He collected them with avidity and spent a lot of his time in the field poring over them. But despite the modern dominance of interpretative approaches in anthropology, it is rather unusual for literature to assume its proper place at the centre of anthropological enquiry. Work like that of Fernandez (1982, 1986), Jackson (1982), Abu-Lughod (1986) and Beidelman (1986), where literary texts are used as a key diagnostic device, a thread leading into the inner aspects of a society's imaginative life, are still rather rare. Anthropology has on the whole been content to leave literature to the folklorists and oral historiographers, whose aims have been somewhat different.[1]

Anthropology, in fact, has tended to adopt interpretative techniques from literary criticism and apply them to almost anything *but* literary texts. Ritual symbolism,[2] spatial relations,[3] and culture itself[4] have been treated as texts whose metaphorical meanings can be 'read' like those of a work of literature. Semiotics and structuralism have attempted, with partial success, to show that the symbolic and classificatory systems of signification that anthropology has traditionally concentrated on are *homologous* to language. What is much more evidently true, however, is that they are *implicated* in language and dependent on it. Sooner or later, they are interpreted, amplified, or evaluated by a verbal commentary, and without this speech context they could not continue to operate. As Vološinov (or Bakhtin),[5] the great Russian literary theorist put it sixty years ago, speech is 'an essential ingredient in all ideological production'; ritual, music, visual art, not to mention day-to-day behaviour, are all 'bathed by, suspended in, and cannot be entirely segregated or divorced from the element of speech' (Vološinov 1973a, p. 15). And in Okuku – as in other places – literary texts function like nodal points in the flow of speech. They are salient and enduring landmarks in the field of discourse, reference points to which speakers orient themselves or from which they take their departure. It is often through literary texts that exegetical commentary is directed towards these other systems of signification.

The literary utterance is at once action in society and reflection upon society. That is, it talks about social process from within because it is part of it. Speech act theory has enabled us to ask what a speaker is *doing* in uttering certain words;[6] and what the performer of *oriki* is doing is a vital part of the social process. *Oriki* performance is involved in struggles for power as well as in the legitimation of the status quo. *Oriki* are used to swell the reputation of the person they are addressed to and to lay claim to membership of certain social groups. But *oriki* not only *are* a form of social action, they also *represent* social action: not of course as in a mirror image, but in a mediated and refracted discourse. Whether implicitly or explicitly, they offer a commentary on it: a commentary which is made up of heterogeneous and sometimes competing views.

Literary texts, whether written or oral, offer an especially valuable representation of ideology because of their concentrated, 'worked-on' character. Literary texts are often described as having involved greater thought or effort than other kinds of utterance, as being more premeditated, or as undertaking to exhibit a greater degree of skill.[7] They may articulate and give form to otherwise amorphous notions circulating in society. Because a literary text is more detached from the immediate context than other utterances, having the quality of repeatability and the capacity to be recreated in a variety of situations, it is compelled to put things into words which normally are left unsaid. Less of its content can be assumed from the immediate context of utterance. In this way, the text becomes, as Vološinov put it, 'a powerful condenser of unarticulated social evaluations – each word is saturated with them' (Vološinov 1973b:107). The text, furthermore, does not just represent an already-constituted ideological viewpoint; it is in the text that a viewpoint is constructed, in the process revealing more about the ideology implicit in daily discourse than could otherwise be discovered. The text itself says more than it knows; it generates 'surplus': meanings that go beyond, and may subvert, the purported intentions of the work. It has the capacity to pick up subterranean ideological impulses that are brought to realisation in no other discursive arena.[8]

Above all, literary texts are revealing because they are inherently discursive. Verbal forms lend themselves to verbal exegesis. There is a continuity between the object of discussion and the discussion itself which is conducive to detailed, active, conscious commentary by the people involved in its production and transmission. In Okuku, as in many other places, language, linguistic formulations, and especially literary texts, are intended and expected to be talked about, to be explained, expounded, and opened up so that the multiple meanings enclosed and compressed within them are revealed. Quoting an *oriki* often leads automatically to a historical narrative. It may also open out into a discussion of family taboos, the characters of the gods, or the composition and relations of social groups. The *oriki* are not just the trigger which sets off a separate discourse; they are the kernel of the discourse itself, which will not take place except with reference to the *oriki*. They are thus, in many cases, the only route into the subject. It is in literary texts that commentary on all spheres of experience is inscribed and from the starting point of literary texts that second-order discussion is instigated.

Not only are literary texts made to be interpreted; they are also accompanied by well-developed indigenous methods and techniques by which their interpretation is carried out. The decoding of *oriki* – as of other Yoruba oral texts[9] – relies on etymology, etiology, personal memory, and something like riddling. These techniques provide the outsider with a guiding thread, a certain limited access to the inner aspects of the discourse. The outsider contemplating ritual, art or cooking is seldom so fortunate.

Some literary texts are more central to social discourse than others. In the history of European literature, there have been periods when the role of the literary text has extended far beyond the boundaries we recognise today, organising fields of knowledge which now are assigned to discourses not defined as 'literature'.[10] In oral cultures, Ong suggests, the literary text always plays this kind of mnemonic and organising role (Ong 1982).[11] If literary form is what makes knowledge memorable and therefore transmittable, then all of inherited knowledge in oral cultures is 'literature'. It is in poetry and narrative that history, philosophy and natural science are encoded and through their forms that this knowledge is organised. It is certainly true that in Yoruba towns, oral literature is still an organising discourse. Even those who are functionally literate base a large part of their self-conception – their ideas about society and their place in it – on *itan* (narratives) and *oriki*.

Oriki commemorate personalities, events and actions that people consider important. They provide a way of thinking about social relationships within and between families, and a way of promoting and expressing the rivalry of ambitious individuals. They are the living link through which relationships with the *oriṣa*, the 'gods', are conducted. And it is in *oriki* that the past is encapsulated and brought into the present, where it exercises a continual pull. *Oriki*, then, are one of the principal discursive mediums through which people apprehend history, society, and the spiritual world.

This study traces the ways in which *oriki* enter into the construction of personal power and communal solidarity in Okuku, and how they implicate the past in the process. The guiding thread of *oriki* leads to some discoveries about the constitution of this Yoruba town. The way notions of kinship and town membership are articulated in *oriki*, and the way the *oriki* are actually used in daily life, reveal a complexity and negotiability in the composition of fundamental social units that existing accounts of Yoruba social structure do not prepare one for. The *oriki* of individuals also bring to view the central importance of the self-aggrandisement of 'big men', who within the chiefly hierarchy and between its interstices operate much in the manner of their New Guinean counterparts, building up a following and thereby creating a place for themselves in society. Though the phenomenon of patron–client relationships has been well described in the context of modern Yoruba city life,[12] the 'traditional political system' of Yoruba towns has always been presented much more in terms of the checks and balances between governmental institutions, or the 'representative' character of chiefship and the importance of competition between lineages rather than between individual big men. Personal *oriki* are the means by which a big man's reputation is established. Through them, we are afforded access to the dynamic process of self-aggrandisement and the values it generates. *Oriki* show that big men are a central and long-established feature of Yoruba social processes.

Oriki, however, do not represent the only way of apprehending social or spiritual realities. The other 'literary' discourses that coexist with *oriki* – notably Ifa divination poetry and *itan* or narratives – offer other ways, which converge with *oriki* along some dimensions and diverge along others. In some respects, they offer a different view of the world and are the means through which different social and spiritual relationships are established. These differences and convergences need to be mapped in future work. There is a particularly close, symbiotic relationship between *oriki* and *itan* which makes its presence felt throughout this study. But my focus is always on *oriki* and the models they provide for interpreting and intervening in social experience – without suggesting that these are the only models or that they are used in all contexts or equally by all members of the community. Indeed, it is precisely the element of 'bias', their aptness to express values from a particular angle, with particular ends in view, which makes them valuable as clues to social experience and social process.[13] *Oriki* are nothing if not partisan. Struggle is evident in these texts: rivalry, aspiration, self-promotion, an intensity of projection and volition that is almost beyond words.

If the reasons for studying a Yoruba town through *oriki* are self-evident, something more probably needs to be said about the reasons for studying *oriki* through the particular town of Okuku. Apart from the fact that I took an immediate liking to Okuku, and was treated from the moment I arrived as someone who belonged, there were some broad general reasons for staying there rather than in one of the numerous other places I visited during my first year in Nigeria. Okuku is culturally and politically an Ọyọ town – though with strong Ijẹsa influences and some features of dialect peculiar to the Ọsun area – and *oriki* are believed to be more highly developed in the Ọyọ area than in other parts of Yorubaland.[14] Okuku is also an old town, with an unusually important ọba ('king') for its size, and exceptionally strong ceremonial life. However, all Yoruba towns have their own traditions of performing arts and their own cultural specialities and peculiarities, and a study based in any one of them would have yielded equally interesting results. It would be impossible to select one place as being outstanding. On the other hand, it would be equally impossible to select a 'typical' place representative of the Yoruba small town, though there is a gap in the existing literature for this category.[15]

Scholars of Yoruba culture and society have always had to deal with the fact that there is no such thing as a 'representative' social unit. The concept seems inapplicable, in a place where there is, first, such regional diversity, and second, so many levels of organisation. It is not just that Yoruba are divided into recognised 'sub-groups' such as Ijẹbu, Ijẹṣa, Ọyọ or Ekiti, each of which has distinctive social and cultural features while possessing a common language and sharing fundamental social and cultural principles; but that even within any such Yoruba 'sub-group', different towns have different cultural traditions; different gods are prominent and different art forms are emphasised from one place to the next. At the same time, however, a town is not a discrete unit that can be treated in isolation. It is subordinate to a bigger town, overlord over smaller ones; it has economic and historical links with neighbouring towns. Members of every town also have their farm settlements, where they often spend more time than in the town proper. People have business connections, jobs and sometimes even property in other towns – and, for long periods, even in other countries. It is artificial to talk of any Yoruba town as if its people's interests and activities were confined within its boundaries. Culturally, too, no town is self-contained. While there are differences, there is also a great deal of overlap. The same cultural elements are found over wide areas, though they may appear in different configurations and with different meanings. What we are presented with could be described by Wittgenstein's famous notion of 'family resemblances', where a group of items share 'a complicated network of similarities overlapping and criss-crossing: sometimes overall similarities, sometimes similarities of detail', so that all somehow seem to go together, though there is no single diacritical feature which they all share (Wittgenstein, 1978, p. 32). Resonances and recognition combined with a feeling of strangeness, of displacement, are the experience of anyone who has lived in more than one place in Yoruba country.

Studies of Yoruba social structure have responded to this situation with local and comparative accounts of the varying forms found in different towns. P.C. Lloyd, in particular, has laid the groundwork for a systematic comparative overview of political and social organisation (Lloyd, 1954, 1958, 1960, 1962, 1965, 1968, 1971) and J.D.Y. Peel has provided an exceptionally full and penetrating social history of one town (Peel 1983). The study of culture, however, and especially of literature, has tended either to generalise prematurely, or to anthologise, synthesising elements taken from different places. The result has been a representation of 'culture' as a synthetic construct, occupying some ideal realm well above the concrete forms of real life. There are good reasons for generalising and synthesising. Much of the *oriki* I quote in this book will be recognised by people from other towns, and sometimes the interpretation given in one place will complement or enhance the one recognised in another. A broader view is ultimately inescapable. But this view can only be constructed on the basis of detailed, localised studies.

With *oriki*, the case for a locally-situated study becomes overwhelming. It is only in this way that all the various realisations of *oriki* can be seen together, as different points on a single spectrum of expressive acts, rather than as disembodied 'genres', treated as if they were unrelated. The truly extraordinary polymorphous adaptability of *oriki* and their fundamental importance in the culture only then become clearly apparent. Only a study that stays close to the ground is able to do justice to the anonymous, domestic, unnamed performances by 'household women', which are defined by the nature of the occasion on which they are performed. Even more importantly, only a localised study really permits detailed interpretation of these texts, for, as will become clear in the next chapter, they are rarely self-explanatory. Their exegesis is encoded in parallel oral traditions which are also localised. Some *oriki* are widely known, but even then, the exegesis offered in one town is likely to differ from that offered in another. And many *oriki* are composed in response to local events or to celebrate local personalities. In these cases, the *oriki* simply cannot be understood without detailed information drawn from the milieu in which the *oriki* are created and performed.

Above all, for an *oriki*-text to be apprehended as a text, it must be heard and seen in action. In a sense, as 'performance theory' has demonstrated,[16] all oral texts should be thought of as action rather than object, as process rather than pattern. They are fully realised only in the moment of performance. *Oriki* chants demand this approach more insistently than most forms of oral literature, however. There is a sense in which they are simply not accessible at all viewed as words on a page. They are not texts that 'speak for themselves'. Their obscurity goes beyond the opacity of particular verbal formulations or references. They are 'obscure' because it is what they are *doing* that animates them and gives them their form and significance. Detached from the scene of social action, laid out on the page they may appear to the untutored eye as little more than a jumble of fragments.

Rather than being representative, a study based in a particular town must be regarded as a starting point; a necessary basis for future comparative work that will draw on many more, similarly localised, case studies. I believe, however, from the evidence of existing work and from the experience of teaching and supervising students from all parts of the Yoruba-speaking area, that the underlying dynamics of social life in Okuku, and the part played in them by *oriki*, are widely shared. The implications of this analysis do go beyond the single small town in which it is located – though how far beyond, and with what qualifications, can only be discovered by future research.

In the course of learning what *oriki* can tell us about Okuku, then, Okuku will tell us how to interpret *oriki*. Texts are a 'way in' to understanding aspects of the life of a society. But at the same time, they are forms of art, with their own specific gravity and their own manner of existing as texts. What they can tell us about a society they can only tell us *through* their particular textuality.

They are not a source of 'data' that can be read straight; nor can their poetic properties be identified and set aside, so that the residue can be treated as data. They must be apprehended as art forms to be understood at all. And in the case of *oriki*, especially for an outsider, this is not easy. They are protean forms, elusive shape-changers, opaque, fragmented, and deliberately cryptic. They could hardly be more remote from the literary forms that conventional European criticism has grown up on. European literary theory has tended to generalise only from the literature that is least alien to its own culture and historical period, producing an ethnocentric and impoverished definition of literary form and value, which nonetheless usually pretends to be universal. To someone brought up in this mainstream, 'common sense' tradition of written literature, *oriki* are at first almost impossible to apprehend as texts. Yet what they tell us, they tell us by means of their textual properties. To begin to grasp how they work, the only way is to see them as they exist, in society. The society that produces them is not 'social background' but the very condition of their capacity to have meaning. It is only through Okuku (or another Yoruba town) that we can 'read' *oriki* at all.

The examination of *oriki* in Okuku, then, involves a perpetual going and return. If *oriki* illuminate aspects of social reality, they can do so only if we recognise, at a fundamental level, the textuality of *oriki*; their textuality – their properties as a verbal art – only reveals itself in its real social context. This book moves gradually outwards from the moment of performance itself, but always returns to look again at the textuality of the text in the light of widening rings of social context. Chapter 2 establishes the centrality of *oriki* among oral discourses in Okuku, and then presents the conundrum of *oriki*, the reasons for their perplexing opacity and the ways this affects our ability to apprehend them as 'literature' and as 'history'. Chapter 3 introduces the town as it is today, and then recreates its past as it is remembered in *oriki* and *itan*, showing how the textual mode of *oriki* conditions memories. After this rather lengthy scene-setting, we are in a position to return to the question of the baffling elusiveness of *oriki*, and to propose a first step towards making sense of it, by establishing the nature of the activity of uttering *oriki*. But if all *oriki* are animated by a common basic intent, their specific textual mode is determined by their context. After describing how women master the art of *oriki*, Chapter 4 goes on to describe in detail some characteristic contexts of performance, showing how the 'same' *oriki* take on new forms and significances according to the situation. Chapter 5 deals with *oriki orílè*, the *oriki* of people claiming the same place of origin, and shows how group identities are negotiated and affirmed through this medium. Chapter 6 is about big men and their personal *oriki*, in the nineteenth and twentieth centuries. It is a long chapter because Okuku's past offers such an array of diverse and compelling personalities. Finally, in the last chapter, I return to the textual properties of *oriki*, the way these properties enable the performance to do what it does, and the role of women in the constitution of the social world of Okuku. By this time, I hope, the fragmented shifting and elusive character of *oriki* texts will have begun to reveal its significance and make felt its eloquence.

2

THE INTERPRETATION OF *ORIKI*

1. THE PLACE OF *ORIKI* AMONG ORAL GENRES IN OKUKU

The position of *oriki* as a 'master discourse' can be seen immediately in the ubiquitous and manifold realisations of this genre in daily life. Continual performances bind together members of the community, those alive today and those receding into the past.

Okuku is a quiet town with an eventful history. In the eighteenth century it was sacked by the Ijẹsa and rebuilt. In the nineteenth century, after the fall of Old Ọyọ, it was in the middle of a battle zone. Several times, the town was overrun and evacuated to neighbouring towns. At the end of the nineteenth century it was resettled and began to expand again. In the early twentieth century colonial interventions altered the structure of government and transformed the local economy. There were great changes in the town's way of life as people took up cash-crop farming, first yams and then cocoa. Through all these dislocations of its history, however, Okuku has retained a sense of its own enduring continuity. The identity of the town is enshrined in the person of the ruler, the ọba, whose majesty is reaffirmed and recreated even today in cherished and highly charged ceremonial. But the sense of continuity is also remade by every household in the town in ceremonies connected with marriage, burial, and the propitiation of spiritual beings. In these ceremonies, the performance of oral poetry is virtually indispensable.

Oral performance of all kinds flourishes in Okuku. Old men know *itan*, stories about family and town history, and tell them when the occasion arises.[1] Until recently, every compound would have evenings telling *alọ* – folktales and riddles – in which both adults and children would join.[2] The *babalawo*, divination priests of the god Ifa, still master the great corpus of sacred, semi-secret Ifa verses, and perform them during consultations and cult meetings.[3] The annual Ifa festival opens with a night of vigil, during which all the *babalawo* gather at the palace to perform *iyẹrẹ Ifa*, a chant based on Ifa verses, in the presence of the ọba and a large audience of townspeople. Processional and dancing songs are sung at every funeral, festival and marriage. Prayers and incantations, as well as songs, are a vital part of the festivals of the *oriṣa*, the 'gods', which succeed each other round the calendar.

But it is performances of *oriki* that are most continually present to the consciousness and most highly valued by most of the population. While Ifa verses are esoteric and popular songs are ephemeral, *oriki* are both widely known and deeply cherished. People grow up hearing *oriki* every day. Mothers recite them to their babies to soothe them. Grandmothers greet the household with long recitations every morning. Friends call each others' *oriki* in the street in jocular salutation. Devotees invoke their *oriṣa* at the shrine every week with impassioned *oriki* chants. Some festivals include great set pieces of *oriki* chanting which townspeople will flock to hear whether or not they are involved in the cult of the *oriṣa* concerned. At funerals, each stage of the week-long ceremony requires *oriki* chanting, in a variety of styles, and for a variety of purposes. Every February, the season of marriage, girls are to be heard everywhere chanting *rara iyawo*, the bride's lament, in ceremonial progress around the town.

People remember that forty years ago, before the social and economic changes associated with colonial rule had weakened so many traditional cultural practices, there were many professional and specialist performers in Okuku. There was a band of *eleegun oje*,[4] the ancestral masqueraders who travelled as entertainers from town to town and made money from it, boasting in their *iwi* – the distinctive *egungun* chant – that they had no time or inclination for farming. There was the powerful hunters' guild, some of whose members were expert in chanting *ijala*, in honour of their *oriṣa* Ogun and to entertain an audience. Both *iwi* and *ijala* are specialised styles of chanting belonging to distinctive occupational and religious groups. Like so many other poetic 'genres' throughout the Yoruba-speaking area, however, they are made up mainly of *oriki*.[5] There also used to be a trumpeter who was part of the ọba's household. His duty was to wake the ọba before dawn every morning by saluting him on the trumpet, making it say:

Dìde, dìde, o bọ ṣòkòtò, ẹnìkan ìí fi iṣẹ́ ìgbọ̀nsẹ̀ rán ọmọ ẹni.

Get up, get up, put on your trousers, no-one can send someone else to shit for him.

After this rude awakening – so to speak – the ọba would be serenaded with the trumpeter's performance of *ọfọ* (incantations), *iwure* (blessings) and the royal *oriki*. Also in attendance were the drummers, who came every morning to sit at the palace doorway playing phrases from the ọba's *oriki* on their talking drums, and saluting the town chiefs when they arrived on their customary morning visit. There were 'praise-singers', specialists in the performance of *oriki* who would go to every social event in the neighbourhood and perform for money and gifts.

The *egungun* entertainers have now disbanded. The hunters' guild meets every month, but though the *ijala* chanters still entertain their fellow hunters during the meetings, *ijala* has become a genre that receives little general exposure in Okuku. There are no longer any trumpeters at the palace; the drummers come only on special occasions, and there is only one professional 'praise-singer' left in Okuku. But despite the decline in professional and specialist performance, *oriki* still flourish. The domestic tradition which underpins and informs the professional one is still vigorous and resilient. All women learn at least a few *oriki*, and in most compounds there are gifted women whose knowledge, though usually narrower than the specialist performers', is also deeper and more detailed. Some women know a great deal, not only of their own parents' *oriki* but also of their husbands' and husbands' mothers' and even grandmothers'. These women become known within the compound as experts and are called upon to lead the performance on ritual and festive occasions. But the other women participate too, repeating some chants line for line, singing a chorus to others.

Women are thus constantly involved in oral performance. This domestic tradition – which it is safe to assume exists in most other northern Yoruba towns too – has had very little attention in the considerable body of academic work on Yoruba oral literature. It does not lend itself easily to discrimination as a 'genre'; the women do not call it by any name or classify the great variety of their production according to style, subject matter or musical mode. It is difficult to detach, as an object of study, from the context of its performance. These women are not discovered by television presenters or asked to come and give public performances – as performers of *ijala* and *iwi* often are. They do not see themselves as entertainers or artists, but as the providers of the appropriate act of communication without which any ceremonial undertaking would be impossible.

2. *ORIKI*, DEFINITION AND THE TRANSCENDENCE OF TIME

The ubiquity of these performances arises from the fundamental ontological and vocative role of *oriki*. It is said that everything in existence has its own *oriki*. Subjects range from *orisa* and ancestors to living men and women, from elephants to palm trees, from the railway to *Ori*, the notion of destiny. Abstract ideas as well as concrete objects, the dead as well as the living, the absent as well as the present, can be addressed with their own *oriki*. The word *oriki* is used in Yoruba academic writing to translate the English word 'definition', for *oriki* are felt to encapsulate the essential qualities of entities. But *oriki* do more than define. They evoke a subject's qualities, go to the heart of it and elicit its inner potency. They are a highly charged form of utterance. Composed to single out and arrest in concentrated language whatever is remarkable in current experience, their utterance energises and enlivens the hearer. They are 'heavy' words, fused together into formulations that have an exceptional density and sensuous weight. An *oriki* can be a brief inscrutable phrase or an extended passage. Some *oriki* encapsulate in a laconic formula enormous public dramas, others commemorate little private incidents. All, however, are felt to evoke the essence of their subjects.

The *oriki* most commonly heard, and most extensive and elaborated, belong to three categories of subjects. First, there are the *oriki* of *orisa*, the gods, which will be dealt with in a separate study. Secondly, there are personal *oriki*, the *oriki* of individuals,[6] given in recognition of their outstanding or estimable characteristics. The most prominent citizens acquire the largest collections of epithets. These epithets allude, often in condensed, witty and oblique style, to the subject's achievements, sayings or qualities. And thirdly, there are *oriki orile*, the *oriki* by which large groups of people are identified through reference to common origin in an ancient, named town. Within any one present-day town, they tend to function as one of the distinguishing features of the *ile* – the 'houses' which are the primary political and social units in the town. They are the best known and the most highly esteemed of *oriki*. Many of the ancient towns of origin are now defunct, but the *oriki* which speak of them live on in vigorous profusion. *Oriki orile* usually circle around a few selected themes felt to be characteristic of the place concerned: the natural features of the area, the customs of the inhabitants, the *orisa* worshipped there, or memorable events in the town's ancient history.

These different categories of *oriki*, addressed to different kinds of subject, are not usually kept separate in performance. In most chants, the performer combines personal *oriki* with *oriki orile*, and in chants addressed to *orisa* she may combine all three types. Different chanting styles put emphasis on different kinds of *oriki*, but few chants are constructed entirely out of one type. In this way, different kinds of identity are brought together.

Though *oriki* are often called 'praise poetry', neither personal *oriki* nor *oriki orile* are wholly flattering to their subjects. Their point is rather to go to the heart of a subject's identity by evoking whatever is distinctive in it. If what makes a big man formidable is his violence, greed, or intemperance, these qualities will figure prominently in his personal *oriki*. In *oriki orile*, whole populations may be hailed – like the people of Ikoyi – for their skill at theft, or – like the women of Oko – for their rabid jealousy of their co-wives. Trivial incidents may be made much of. Precisely because they are peculiar, idiosyncratic or funny, these incidents are memorable: they imprint distinctive features on the smooth public face of the successful man. There exists, in fact, a kind of anti-*oriki* called *akija* ('provocative epithets') which deal exclusively with the shameful, painful, ridiculous and embarrassing incidents in a family's past. These epithets are worked artfully into daily conversation by old men, who are always looking for opportunities to tease each other. When one is successfully planted, the victim responds with mock outrage, and retaliates in kind. But even these insulting epithets can eventually become a mark of distinction, a source of pride, and can be incorporated into performances of *oriki* proper.[7]

But while *oriki* affirm the distinctiveness of their subjects, they are also agents of transcendence. As we shall show in the next chapter, it is in *oriki* that boundaries between entities are opened, even in the act of asserting the irreducible uniqueness of each. Through them, relationships are made and remade. In *oriki* of individuals and of social groups, this transcendence includes a transcendence of time. The past is reactivated in the present. The moment of a group's 'origin' is made present to consciousness as a contemporary sign of identity; prominent men of the past, predecessors of the living, are evoked in the midst of the activity of the present generation.

At the time of composition, each *oriki* refers to the here and now. They encapsulate whatever is noteworthy in contemporary experience. Epithets are composed as things happen, or as qualities in people emerge. But because they are valued, they are preserved, and transmitted for decades – sometimes even for centuries. They are then valued all the more for coming from the past, and bringing with them something of its accumulated capabilities, the attributes of earlier powers. In performance they are recycled and recomposed, but they also retain an essential core which is preserved even when its meaning has been forgotten. *Oriki* can thus be a thread that leads back into an otherwise irrecoverable social history.

Sometimes, listening to these texts in your mind's ear, you may have the sensation of a door opening onto a lost but still adjacent world: a world that may seem more substantial and more satisfying than the present. Through the condensed eloquence of *oriki* it is evoked and brought once more into view:

> Dáró-palé babaà mi, a-jí-fèlú-pàta
> Ó fijòkùn pagi àwọn àjà
> Abọ̀dẹ̀dẹ̀-gbọ́mọ-sánlẹ̀-láì-rẹ́ní
> Abigbangba-ilé-kunmọ-lóorun
> Pupáyẹmí abéyìnbó-dúró
> Bó ti ń dán ilée rẹ̀ ń dán
> Babaà mi wu Tápà lÉǹpe
> Ire lónìí oríì mi àfire.

> Gengele tí, tí ń jẹ ayé ò-jí-lù-pẹkẹ
> Ò-jí-mì-tìtì léyìn ìlẹ̀kùn
> Ènìyàn ì í mi irú ẹ̀ lásán
> Ẹni gbóge tẹ́ ẹ rí n ní í mi irú ẹ̀
> Bí ń tí ń dán nilé rẹ̀ ń dán
> Bàbáà mi wu Tápà lÉǹpe.[8]

One who makes indigo dye to decorate his house, my father, one
     who rises to paint his premises in dark blue

He uses dark green dye to paint the rafters
One whose passageways invite you to lie down without asking for
    a mat
One whose courtyards make you sleepy
'Fair-skin-suits-me', one who stands beside the European
As he glistens, so his house glistens
My father delights everyone as far as the Tapa at Enpe
May good luck attend me today.

A magnificent man, who revels in life, who rises to merriment
One who rises to shudder with splendour within his quarters
No-one quivers like that for nothing
It's only he, the handsome one, who quivers like that
As he glistens, so his house glistens
My father delights everyone as far as the Tapa at Enpe.

The sensuous conjunction of wealth, leisure, and wellbeing is almost palpable in this evocation of the well-decorated house and its personable owner, a man who lived in the early years of this century. The spacious, immaculate courtyards, the inviting corridors, the air of satisfying ease all create an extension of the personality being praised. The man himself is com-pacted of a magnificence so intense it makes him quiver. Domestic sufficiency and public fame are combined in imagery which is both condensed and accommodating, both laconic and gracious. Through its own qualities the verse brings to realisation the vanished glory of the town's *ọlọla*, those who are highly esteemed. *Oriki* like these evoke in concrete particularity the world that lies behind the visible surface of daily life, and that informs and animates it.

    Oriki, then, can open windows simultaneously onto the past and the present. They are the principal means by which a living relationship with the past is daily apprehended and reconstituted in the present. They are not 'history' in the sense of an overview or attempt to make sense of a sequence of events, but a way of experiencing the past by bringing it back to life. They represent the 'past in the present' (cf. Peel, 1984), a past which they have brought with them and which can be reopened and reactivated by their agency. But they also represent the 'present in the past', for through all the stages of their transmission they do not lose their relationship of contemporaneity to the events they refer to. They are not retrospective, nor are they subordinated to an overview of 'the past' as such. They are not thought to be *about* the past: they *are* fragments of the past, living encapsulated in the present. They still speak of the scandals of years ago with the same immediacy of reference as if it were today. In this way they do more than preserve a sense of continuity through the violent reversals of Okuku's history: they also keep 'the past' close at hand, at the heart of present concerns.

    This relationship with the past cannot be properly apprehended by treating *oriki* as a rather problematic and incomplete historical 'account'. How the past is experienced can only be grasped through seeing how relations in the present are constituted: by placing this evocation of 'the past' within the wider context of the mode of all *oriki*, which is simultaneously to define states of being and to transcend them.

3. ENCOUNTER WITH *ORIKI*

Through *oriki*, then, the essential attributes of all entities are affirmed, and people's connections with each other, with the spiritual universe, and with their past are kept alive and remade. In this fundamental sense, *oriki* are a master discourse. But they are also one that is extremely hard for outsiders to read. Hans Wolff in a seminal article (Wolff, 1962) has called *oriki* 'disjointed discourse'. They appear to be composed of fragments. They are labile, elliptical, allusive, and often deliberately obscure or incomplete. An *oriki* chant is a form that aims at high impact, high intensity, which it achieves through juxtaposing apparent opposites. Although they are so highly valued and so tenaciously preserved, *oriki* are also almost impossible to pin down. A corpus of *oriki* is said to be 'the same' whatever context the epithets appear in; but in fact they take on new shapes and even new meanings with every appearance.

When I first went to Okuku, I happened to arrive in the middle of the great annual Olooku festival. The ọba had just returned from an outing round the town. The chiefs, the elders of the royal family, and swarms of other townspeople were coming into the palace to congratulate him. Among them was a battered looking woman, elderly and shabby, who seemed to be going from person to person and screaming at them. 'What is she doing?' I asked. An obliging bystander explained: 'That is *oriki*'.

To me it was nothing but a meaningless jumble of sound. There was nothing in it that I could distinguish at all, despite my three years of studying Yoruba. It seemed to have no form: to be an unvarying and endless stream of utterances. The woman, I soon learned, was called Ṣangowẹmi, and was the town's only professional performer, to be seen at every festival and funeral. What was so striking was the intensity with which she focused on the person she was addressing, and the real avidity with which the person listened.

Even when, later on, I had transcriptions to look at, things were no better. Translation was very difficult. The schoolboy who first offered to help turned out to be baffled by much of it. What we did manage to translate seemed like the inside of an old knitting bag, a bundle of many-coloured scraps, a diversity of bits and pieces, with a lot of loose ends. I had begun with the text of a performance by Ṣangowẹmi. Later I found there were other styles of performance, more patterned and more coherent; but this was a matter of degree rather than of kind. They all had similar formal properties: or what seemed to me at the time to be an absence of properties. They seemed to have no shape, no centre and no inner cohesion.

I stayed three years in Okuku. During this time I experienced the intense pleasure of learning Yoruba, not only from books but from people who loved their language and never missed an opportunity to demonstrate its capabilities. People would produce choice phrases – proverbs, idioms or current slang – and then take endless pleasure in expounding their inner meaning. Daily life threatened to become a perpetual exchange of catchphrases. Fragments of *oriki* were treated the same way, like treasures brought out on view, though the explanations were not always so readily forthcoming. The hermeneutic habit was well established. I was given *oriki* myself: the *oriki* of the royal family, because I was 'adopted' by the ọba. Every day I would hear the same phrases ten or twenty times, recited by old women who never seemed to get tired of it: *'Àjíké Òkín, ọmọ olóòórò! Ọmọ aíbile! Ọmọ awayèjà! Ọmọ òpépé Ọládìlé, ọmọ akéré-fọba-súra!'* (Ajike Ọkin, child of the owner of the morning! Child of one who finds a place to be tough! One who seeks a space to fight! Child of the long-lived Ọladile, child of The-small-one-protected-by the-ọba!). Sometimes they would detain me for half an hour at a time while they recited long passages of *oriki*. The recitation was always an expression of affection, even when it was teasing. Like other people, I began to feel a pleasure in *oriki* independent of their meaning; and at the same time I began to discover the meanings upon meanings, the layers of allusion, so supple, laconic and ironical that I felt – rightly – I would never get to the bottom of them.

Here is a bit of one of the first texts I recorded, from a very long performance by Ṣangowẹmi:

> Ẹ è ní í fọdún èyí ṣàṣemọ
> Eésadẹ, ọmọ Owólabí èmi Àbèni n pè ọ́
> Ọmọ Mofómiké ọmọ Moyòsí ọmọ a-rílé-gbòfé-kùnrin
> Ọmọ abòòdèé kù bí òjò
> Mofómiké owó la fi ṣoge ó bá ọ gbélé orígun
> Ará Àrán ọmọ aṣòfélà
> Já a relée wa, Àrán-Òrin, ọmọ títé lewé ata
> Ọmọ Omíyọdé ọmọ Alari a-dá-ìdí-òro-lému-mu
> Bó o bá jí lónìí ọ júbà bàbáà rẹ Olúgbẹdẹ Ọtábílápó
> Ògún Àjàgbé tó rí kowéè jóògùn
> Kò rí n fún àlejò ó fi Fómiké tọrọ
> Ará Àrán ọmọ aṣòfélà, Àjàgbé tó wáá rí kowéè jóògùn
> Ṣá máa júbà babaà rẹ, ọ ọ́ fowó ìyókù womọ...

> This will not be the last festival you celebrate
> Eesadẹ, son of Owolabi, it is I Abẹni calling you
> Child of Mofomikẹ, child of Moyọsi, child of one who had a fine
>   house in which to receive slaves as gifts
> Child of one whose corridors reverberated like rain

Mofomikẹ, magnificence is acquired with money, money has
  made your house its headquarters
Native of Aran, child of one who gets rich on gifts
Let us go to our house, Aran-Ọrin, child of 'The pepper leaf spreads'
Child of Omiyọde, child of Alari, one who taps the base of the wild
  mango tree and gets wine
When you rise today pay homage to your father, Olugbẹdẹ
  Ọtabilapo
Ogun Ajagbe who got a *kowee* bird to make medicine
He had nothing to give the visitor so he made a present of Fomikẹ
Native of Aran, child of One who gets rich on gifts, Ajagbe who
  found a *kowee* bird to make medicine
Just make sure you pay homage to your father, you'll spend the rest
  of your money rearing children...

What was I to make of this? When I asked for explanations, the first thing
that struck me was that the performance was composed out of phrases or
passages that were apparently unconnected to each other. The words were
being addressed to Eesadẹ, a title-holder in the guild of hunters. Some of the
lines evoked the great wealth of one of Eesadẹ's forebears: 'child of one who
had a fine house in which to receive slaves as gifts', 'magnificence is acquired
with money, money has made your house its headquarters'. Others were
about knowledge of medicine: 'Ogun Ajagbe who got a *kowee* bird to make
medicine' (a *kowee* bird, I was told, is a harbinger of death, and medicine made
from it is very powerful). There was an allusion to an incident within the
family: 'He had nothing to give the visitor so he made a present of Fomikẹ'.
Some of the lines were personal *oriki*, belonging to particular individuals
connected with Eesadẹ. But others were fragments of *oriki orilẹ*. Eesadẹ's family,
I was told, is of Aran-Ọrin origin, and *oriki orilẹ* referring to the characteristics
and distinguishing features of this town are briefly quoted: 'Native of Aran,
child of one who gets rich on gifts/Let us go to your house, Aran-Ọrin, child
of "The pepper leaf spreads"'. Aran people, I learnt, 'get rich on gifts' because
they are a masquerading people whose performances are rewarded with
money, food and cloth. The pepper leaf is one of their emblems. All these
allusions and references were simply juxtaposed without explanation or
connection. There seemed to be no continuity between one reference and the
next; all seemed to have different origins as well as different contents.

Then, there was the obscurity of many of the allusions. This often seemed
not to be accidental, but the result of deliberate compression and truncation.
No reference seemed to be completed. The fragment of Aran *oriki orilẹ* makes
little sense unless the hearer already knows the context from which it has been
taken, where the themes of masquerading and the taboos and observances of
the Aran people are elaborated. The allusion to the man who 'had nothing to

give the visitor so he made a present of Fomikẹ' turns out to need the addition
of a second line before it can be understood: I was told that it goes on 'Fomikẹ
pulled a face and said he wouldn't go.' Then a story is needed to explain it.
An elder of the compound, Michael Adeọsun, the chief Ṣọbaloju, obliged:

> Olugbẹdẹ was a great man, a hunter, in the time of Oyewusi [the
> ọba who reigned c. 1888–1916]. Mofomikẹ was his younger brother
> by the same mother. Once they held a great hunters' meeting at
> his place. All the hunters came and saluted him, saluted him,
> saluted him [with *ijala* chanting]. He said he'd like to give them
> money, but money wasn't enough [to reward them for their
> chanting]; he'd like to give them cloth, but that wasn't enough
> either. He said he would give them Mofomikẹ, to go with them
> and become an entertainer like them. But Mofomikẹ refused point
> blank, he said he wouldn't go. It was all a joke.

Without this little *itan*, the words of the *oriki* can tell us nothing. As S. A.
Babalọla says of *oriki orilẹ*, 'These *oriki* ... are full of "half-words"; words that
you say to a sensible or knowledgeable person, and when they get inside him
or her, they become whole'.[9] The *oriki* supply half the message, but only a
knowledgeable hearer will know how to supply the other half.

Then, there was the impression given by this passage of an almost indistinguishable mix of references: to *oriki orilẹ* and to several different individuals
belonging to one family. There is a plethora of names, and attributions seem
to slide about within the text from one to another. Although Eesadẹ is the
recipient of the performance, he is addressed with the personal *oriki* of various
men – Mofomikẹ, Omiyọde, Alari, Olugbẹdẹ Ọtabilapo, Ogun Ajagbe – and
these are sometimes uttered in the same breath with *oriki orilẹ*: 'Native of Aran,
one who gets rich on gifts, Ajagbe who found a *kowee* bird to make medicine'.
One personal *oriki* also slides into another, and there are so many names that
it is hard to know who is being saluted at any moment.

Finally, the passage seems to be neither narrative nor descriptive. It is in
the vocative case throughout, and the utterance is clearly felt to be in some
way effectual. The act of addressing the subject is foregrounded by the singer,
who draws attention to her own role in the situation ('Eesadẹ child of Owolabi,
it is I Abẹni calling you'). The passage opens with a wish stated as an assertion
in the future tense ('This will not be the last festival you do'), a form of 'prayer'
felt to have the potential to affect the course of events. It ends with an
exhortation ('Just make sure you keep honouring your father so that you too
will have children to spend the rest of your money on'), which the hearer is
intended to heed. What the singer is in fact doing is saluting the man she is
addressing, Eesadẹ, by paying honour to his father (Mofomikẹ) and his father's
senior brother or – according to another account – his father's father
(Olugbẹdẹ). In doing so, she suggests, she is helping to ensure that Eesadẹ in
turn has children to honour him. *Oriki* are thus a principle of continuity

between the generations. By keeping alive the memory of your predecessors you ensure that your successors will keep alive the memory of you. The performance of *oriki* is an action which maintains connections and which can realign as well as reaffirm relationships within the social and spiritual economy.

To understand how *oriki* work we must first understand what it is that makes them seem initially so baffling. The root of the matter is their apparent internal disconnectedness. The nature of this disconnectedness must be grasped before we can understand the ways in which *oriki* chants do in fact attain their own kind of coherence – a theme to which I return in Chapter 7.

The performer has at her disposal a corpus of textual elements. These elements may all have had separate origins. They may have been composed by different people, at different times and with reference to different incidents or situations. The corpus of *oriki* attributed to a given subject is made up of items which are largely genetically separate. They therefore have no fixed or necessary relation to each other within the performance.

In the case of living subjects, the process by which independent epithets are accumulated can be seen to happen: more *oriki* are added to a person's repertoire as more of his or her qualities and actions become apparent during his or her life-time. Different people make them up: the drummers, members of the family, the town wits. Each one may allude to a separate incident or quality. With *oriki orilẹ*, the '*oriki* of origin', there are occasional clues in the texts themselves showing that something similar has happened over a much longer time-span. The compound of Ẹlẹmọsọ Awo, for instance, has *oriki orilẹ* which begin by identifying this group with Ijẹsaland, but then add references to Ọyọ:

> Ìjẹ̀sà ni mí, ilẹ̀ obì
> Ọmọ àtÈfọ̀n wáá sòògùn
> Tó lÓyọ̀ọ́ dùn
> Òun ò tún relé mọ́
> Àrẹmọ ni babaa wa wáá se fọ́ba
> Ẹ̀fọ̀n ló bí mi, Ọ̀yọ́ wò mí Ẹ́ ...

> I am an Ijẹsa, land of kola
> Child of one who came from Ẹfọn to make medicine
> Who said Ọyọ was so pleasant
> He wouldn't go home again
> So our ancestor became the maker of child-birth medicines for the
>   ọba
> I was born of Ẹfọn stock, brought up by Ọyọ people...

'I am an Ijẹsa, of the land of kola' is the core theme of the *oriki orilẹ* of all people claiming origin in Ijẹsaland. But – as this text itself explains – the *oriki* above belong to a particular group of Ijẹsa people who went to Ọyọ and settled there. The lines about Ọyọ were clearly composed by this group and added to their

Ijẹṣa *oriki orilẹ* some time after the latter had become established.

New *oriki*, then, are composed when something remarkable becomes evident, and are added to the existing corpus. Each corpus of *oriki* therefore contains a multiplicity of items from different historical moments, often accumulated over long periods. Each item is autonomous, referring to its own field of meaning and therefore capable of standing on its own. Each may point in a different direction. Each item is an internally coherent verbal formulation, but beyond that, different items may take very different shapes. They can be condensed or extensive, obscure or perspicuous, flattering or otherwise. *Oriki orilẹ* tend to be made up of long patterned passages, each of which is an internally coherent unit, while personal *oriki* tend more often to be composed of short items of one, two or three lines. A corpus, then, is a collection of items which are both autonomous and heterogeneous. In performance, the singer draws items from the corpus and assembles them rapidly, bringing them together into temporary conjunction.

To grasp a text like this involves not merely a problem of *information* (though to unravel a passage like Ṣangowẹmi's performance quoted above does require a great deal of circumstantial information), but a problem of comprehension. European academic disciplines prepare us for texts to work in certain ways. *Oriki*, it seems, work in quite other ways. Texts like this do not fit our mainstream conceptions, bred from European post-renaissance written texts, of what a literary text *is:* and though they are so much concerned with the past, they do not represent it in a way that is recognisable to us as 'history'.

4. *ORIKI* AS LITERARY TEXT

In Africa there are numerous genres of 'praise-poetry' that resemble *oriki* in their fluidity and internal indeterminacy. All of these forms are radically unlike the kind of 'literary text' which critics educated in the mainstream Euro-American literary tradition are used to dealing with – and this includes, at least in certain respects, most African literary scholars.[10] Perhaps this is why there really has been no adequate poetics of such forms. Instead, genre after genre has been documented, described, and placed against a social 'background'. Interesting and informative as these presentations are, they do not allow us to get to grips with the textuality of these poetic forms: how they work as texts and hence how they constitute meaning. It is striking that while there have been brilliant advances in the field of African narrative, analysis of *oriki*-type texts has remained almost unbroached. Oral narrative, as Scheub (1975), Cosentino (1982), Jackson (1982) and others have shown, is, like *oriki*, fluid and emergent, recreated in different ways in each performance. But each narrative has a discernible internal logic, a sequence of stages, a beginning and end, which can be grasped and described by the researcher. This inner formal coherence provides the firm ground from which the innovative studies mentioned above have been able to set out. *Oriki*-type texts, on the other hand, offer much more slippery and shifting ground; and European literary assumptions have tended much more to block the development of a suitable critical approach.

The disjunctiveness of an *oriki* chant is both the key to its textuality, and what makes it so difficult for outsiders to apprehend. Like the otter, you know not where to have it. The mainstream, 'common sense' view of literature in European culture – most clearly articulated in New Criticism which dominated English literary studies for more than half this century – has as its central postulate the notion that a work of literature is or should be a unity, in several senses. It has, or should have, *boundaries* and *closure*, which are achieved through the internal structure of the piece. Barbara Herrnstein Smith has written perceptively about 'poetic closure', Frank Kermode about 'the sense of an ending' (Smith, 1968; Kermode, 1967). As literary works unfold they perpetually defer closure and at the same time raise expectations of closure, so that the ending is produced from within the structure of the text. When the reader gets to the end, he or she experiences gratification, for the discourse has concluded rather than merely coming to a stop, and it can now be reviewed and experienced as a totality. According to mainstream criticism, a text also is, or should be, a unity in the sense of being a whole. It is supposed to be greater than the sum of its parts. 'The parts are nothing', Coleridge said. The Romantic formulation of organic wholeness in which all the parts 'interanimate' was succeeded by other metaphors: of a delicate mechanism held together by its inner tensions, as in British New Criticism; or a sentence which is more than the sum of its constituent words, as in linguistic criticism.[11] This view of the text takes it as axiomatic that each element has a determinate role to play which depends on its precise position within the text and its precise relations to the other parts. Move or remove a part and you have altered the whole. Apparent gaps and disconnections are significant in the same way as the perceptible links and ligatures in a text, for they signal that there is a *hidden* connection to be sought.[12] Finally, a literary text is seen as a unity in the sense of being the construct of single shaping consciousness, which draws on a literary tradition but recasts its materials to express an original and unique vision.

With these expectations, the outsider's inclination would be to look at an *oriki* text as a discrete object and seek significance in the precise arrangement of its constituent parts – to try to find a pattern even if a hidden one. But *oriki* chants are striking for the absence in them of boundaries, closure or an overall design. Since the units out of which an *oriki* chant is constructed are essentially autonomous, one unit does not arise out of its predecessor in the performance or give rise to its successor. Some studies have observed (not very surprisingly) that an *oriki* performance has a beginning, a middle and an end; but it does not have a 'sense of an ending'. It is true that many chants begin with an invocation of spiritual powers to assist the performer, or some other introductory device, and end with a song or other formula. There are also formulas to indicate that the performer is about to change her theme in the course of the chant. These formulas are like signposts in an essentially homogeneous and endless terrain. Any other element – including songs and the invocations appealing for spiritual support – can appear in any position in the text. The formulas are brought into play in response to external factors rather than produced out of internal structural ones. If the performer is addressing an important figure at a festive gathering, and an even more important person comes in, she may change to the newcomer's *oriki*.[13] As Olabiyi Yai has pointed out, this kind of shift cannot be regarded as 'deviation' within the text for there is no established centre from which the performer can deviate (Yai, 1972). The chant, in fact, has no centre in this sense of the word. The 'whole' is like a string of beads, a long chain of interchangeable parts, which can be extended or broken off at will without significantly altering its form. Eventually, the performer will stop – because she is tired, because the occasion does not require further performance, because she has exhausted her repertoire several times over, or because another performer wants to take over. She will signal her intention to stop by deploying a formula that says so, or by shifting from a chanting mode into a song, in which the audience will join. This marks the end of her performance but it does not produce closure, for the end does not arise out of what went before.

Similarly, the relations between the parts do not determine the significance of the text, nor can an *oriki* text be seen as a whole which is greater than the sum of its parts. The genetic autonomy of its constituent units means that unlike the organism, the mechanism or the sentence which provide metaphorical models for the 'whole' in mainstream criticism, the meaning of an *oriki* chant is not significantly affected by the removal of one part or the rearrangement of others. The internal relationships of a chant are indeterminate. There is no overall formal pattern to which units are subordinated and which assigns them a particular place in relation to the others. The performer enjoys considerable freedom – limited by habit rather than by rules of the genre – to string them together in whatever order and combination she wishes. Every performance of a particular subject's *oriki* will be similar, but the units will be to a greater or lesser degree differently selected and ordered, and sometimes differently worded. People will say it is the 'same' text each time. Many variations will not be noticed at all, precisely because they are not significant. Ostentatious variations may be appreciated – a performer who is clever at manipulating her material and producing novel effects from it will be admired[14] – but these variations are still not felt to affect the real significance of the text.

Studies of African oral narrative have looked closely at the relation between 'tradition' and the individual artist, and have shown how large a role the individual creative consciousness has to play in reshaping themes and motifs drawn from a common repertoire. The performer of *oriki*, likewise, has scope to recast her materials, recombine them and add new elements by borrowing, adapting and sometimes by fresh composition. However, unlike the tellers of oral tales discussed by Scheub (1975) and Cosentino (1982), the performer of *oriki* does not impose a unique vision or voice of her own upon her materials in such a way as to make them express her own distinctive personality. Or rather, she does so only partially. Each unit retains its own voice while being uttered in hers. And, as we shall see, there may be many different voices within a corpus of *oriki*, each speaking from a different position.

The European common sense view of the unity of the literary text derives in obvious ways from the formal properties made possible or necessary by writing – fixity, visible form, a material existence detached from both author and reader. There are other 'literary critical' views of the text that seem at first sight much more appropriate to *oriki* and to oral literature in general. Post-structuralist and deconstructive criticism, as I have argued elsewhere (Barber, 1984a), looked extremely radical when applied to written texts but would have seemed almost to be stating the obvious if they had been applied (though they never were) to oral ones. Intertextuality, the decentring of the text, the displacement of the author as the 'father' or creator of the text, the replacement of discrete autonomous literary works, as the object of analysis, with the interplay of literary codes:[15] all these notions effectively struck at common sense criticism just at the points where it was most deeply indebted to the assumption of writtenness. But at a deeper level post-structuralist criticism is inimical to oral texts. It immobilises the human agent at the same time that it empowers the text itself: texts interact, fructify, produce meaning; the human beings participate merely as *loci* or functions within a vast network of codes. Oral texts do not permit this evasion of the question of agency (ultimately a question of power) – of who is saying these things, to whom, in whose interests – for the speaker and the hearers are always visibly and concretely present, and text clearly has no existence apart from them.

And, more specifically, post-structuralist criticism does not apply to *oriki* and other oral texts like them because it was developed to deal with texts that are *intended* to be formal unities – though, according to post-structuralism, they can never actually achieve this. Gaps and flaws are significant because they are unintended, thrown up against the grain of the literary form, and they therefore reveal something which the text's conventions could not say. While conventional criticism presumes unity and therefore tries to find readings that will fill the gaps with significance, deconstructive criticism goes a step further and says that some gaps *cannot* be filled because, rather than being zero-signs within a code, they represent the limits of the code itself. But they are significant only because there is a presumption that they would have been avoided if this had been possible. Modernist texts that deliberately flout canons of formal unity depend, similarly, on the audience's expectation that they *will* be unified. In *oriki*, however, we have a text that seems to be made of gaps: a dazzling juxtaposition of fragments. There is no presumption of wholeness in the mainstream critical sense, no formal means of imposing such wholeness. The gaps are real gaps resulting from the separate genesis of the individual elements that make up the chant. As a technique for interpreting, the method that splits open the text from within seems redundant when the text is already so thoroughly, so fundamentally split in all directions.

Brilliant as performance theory and folklore studies have been at rehabilitating the orality of oral texts, reinstating the centrality of the express-ive resources and context of performance, and exploring the implications of Parry and Lord's crucial conception of 'composition in performance',[16] nonetheless, for texts like *oriki*, the shadow of the 'common sense' written-literature presumption of unity still seems to get in the way, to block off a full apprehension of how these texts work. Some scholars have emphasised their unity and down-played their disjunctiveness, while others have ignored their textuality altogether.[17]

However, as I shall indicate in the final section of this chapter, there has long existed the promise of a unified approach to literary texts, both oral and written, in the Marxist philosophy of language proposed by Vološinov/Bakhtin. New Criticism sees the literary text as an autonomous artefact. Structuralism and post-structuralism see it as the outcome of the operation of codes – that is, of virtually autonomous systems of signs, whose meaning is assigned by their relationships with each other *within* the system. Vološinov takes neither of these views. He foreshadows – and goes beyond – performance theory and speech act theory in seeing literary text as utterance, and utterance as attaining meaning only in and through the concrete contexts of real social existence. By asking precisely what kind of utterance *oriki* is, and in what social contexts its meanings are achieved, it becomes possible for us to see how the fluidity and fragmentation of the *oriki* text actually work. What makes Vološinov/Bakhtin even more interesting is that he sometimes writes exactly as if he had *oriki* in mind.

5. *ORIKI* AS A RELATIONSHIP WITH THE PAST

Oriki are *essentially* historical in the sense that they are one of the ways in which the relationship of the present with the past is constituted. But though it has often been suggested that they could provide a valuable source of historical data (see Biobaku, 1973, pp. 6–7; Law, 1977, pp. 19–20), *oriki* have in fact rarely been used in this way. Bọlanle Awẹ's historical analysis of Ibadan *oriki* (Awẹ, 1974, 1975) is the exception rather than the rule.[18] The genres on which leading oral historiographers understandably enough have focused their attention have been 'accounts' of the past which they assume to be very roughly comparable with the history produced by literate European historians

(Vansina, 1965, 1985; Miller, 1980): that is, narratives whose purpose is usually to explain by what chain of events things came to be as they are. The procedure adopted by most oral historians is directed towards the problem of separating the wheat of historical fact from the chaff of distortions introduced by political interests, literary conventions, mnemonic strategies, personal creativity and simple forgetfulness. In this way, it is hoped that nuggets of more or less factual information may be extracted. *Oriki*, however, seem to ask for an approach to 'oral history' that, like the fine discussions by Cunnison (1951), Bonte and Echard (1976), Peel (1984) and Sahlins (1987), concerns itself with the way the past is represented, and not only how this relates to what 'actually happened' but also how it conditions the way things happen next.

An *oriki* text, as we have seen, is not an 'account'. It is not narrative like a chronicle or consecutively ordered like a king-list. There is no necessary or permanent relationship between one item in an *oriki* chant and the next: each may refer to a different topic. There is therefore no narrative continuity between them. The discontinuity arises from the fact that each unit has its own historical moment in which it was composed and to which it alludes.

The span of time on which their separate originary points are located may be very wide indeed. Some *oriki* appear to date back many centuries; others came into existence within living memory. The *oriki* of ancient Ifẹ, recorded by S. A. Babalọla, contain lines referring to events presumed to have occurred in the twelfth or thirteenth century. Assuming that *oriki* then, like the ones composed within living memory, were contemporaneous with the events and personalities they refer to, we have examples of *oriki* that may have originated more than five hundred years ago.[19] Other *oriki* date themselves by references to specific historical personalities, for instance the Alaafin Abiọdun or 'Afọnja in Ilọrin', both late eighteenth century figures. Some *oriki* in Okuku refer to experiences or objects whose impact has been relatively recent: the presence of the European, or the use of iron sheets instead of thatching for roofs, introduced in the 1920s. The great majority of the *oriki* now being performed in Okuku appear, for reasons that will be discussed later, to have been composed between the second half of the eighteenth century and the middle of the twentieth. Few of them can be located very precisely in the past, but it is reasonable to suppose that a single performance often contains items composed as much as two hundred years apart.

Each corpus of *oriki* therefore contains a multiplicity of items from different historical moments, accumulated over long periods. This historical variegation in *oriki* usually remains invisible and uncommented on. The items from different historical moments are not usually arranged in chronological order, nor are the most ancient units separated from the newest ones; they may be performed in virtually any order and combination. This is not because a chronological ordering is beyond the scope of *oriki* performers – in certain circumstances, the *oriki* of all the successive ọbas of Okuku and those of the successive holders of the most senior chiefly title are performed in order[20] – but because *oriki* performances usually aim at something else. The past is recalled for a different purpose.

An *oriki* text taken as a whole is historically unlocatable in a double sense. Like all orally transmitted texts, it is historically mixed in the sense that it has passed through many stages of transmission, each of which has altered, however slightly, the 'original' material. In fact, in *oriki*, though there is an irreducible core in each unit which is supposed to be retained, there is a good deal of scope for the performer to recast them in her own way, and thus for the factors producing 'distortion' (in Vansina's terms) to enter them. So as it moves through time it accumulates layers of reinterpretation. But the text has the added complication of being, at any given moment in history, *internally* mixed, composed, like a patchwork, by juxtaposing pieces of diverse origin. Since the *oriki* are independent of each other, and, as we shall see, can be borrowed and migrate from one corpus to another, each in a sense has its own separate history of transmission and its own experiences of 'distortion'.

At the same time, however, *oriki* taken as a genre clearly has a history itself. Not only did certain historical periods apparently produce an efflorescence, an intensification of *oriki* production, but also, internal changes of form and style in *oriki* can be discerned. Despite the fluidity and malleability of each corpus and each unit within a corpus, definite expressive shifts corresponding to large-scale historical changes are sometimes evident. I have argued elsewhere (Barber, 1981a) that the new 'big men' of Ibadan in the second half of the nineteenth century called forth a new style in personal *oriki*; and that on the decline of these men's extraordinary capacity for expansion – that is, with the imposition of British rule – the new style lapsed and a version of the earlier type of *oriki* returned. No shifts as dramatic as this occurred in the history of Okuku, but the same ambiguity presents itself: on the one hand, *oriki* are fluid and malleable; on the other hand, they exhibit a kind of tenacity, a continued closeness to their moment of origin, which makes it possible for us to perceive through them the outlines of ideological change.

Since the units that make up an *oriki* text are genetically separate, each refers to its own field of meaning, which may be quite unrelated to the meaning of the unit which succeeds it in the performance. Furthermore, as we have seen, each of these meanings may be hidden, its interpretation found not *within* the text, but only in a tradition of explanation which exists outside the *oriki* themselves. As Babalola puts it, 'The *oriki* just hint fleetingly at histories; a full explanation can only be obtained by research and investigation' (Babalola, 1966b, p. 12).[21] Each formulation therefore gestures away from the text to its own, separate explanatory background. The explanation may turn out to be a full-blown narrative. It may consist of circumstantial information about the person for whom the *oriki* was composed, or it may just be an amplification or restatement of what the *oriki* says. And sometimes, not

unnaturally, it turns out to be no explanation at all: 'What does this mean?
Well, it's *oriki*'. The principle is the same in all cases, however: to know what
the *oriki* means, the hearer has to look for information which lies outside the
oriki tradition itself.

The exegesis of *oriki* reaches its fullest and most institutionalised form in
the genre called *itan*, 'narrative'. *Oriki* and *itan* are separate but symbiotic
traditions. They are institutionally separated, for while women are the
principal carriers of *oriki*, it is mainly old men who tell *itan*. And while *oriki*
are continually in the air, performed publicly and privately in innumerable
different contexts, *itan* are rarely told except when occasioned by a family
dispute, a chieftaincy contest or a direct request for information from a son
of the compound (or, of course, a researcher). If women are asked to explain
oriki, they may do so, especially when the explanation is anecdotal or of recent
provenance. They may even tell short *itan*, especially if male elders of the
compound are not within earshot. But they do not often sit down and relate
an extended past-oriented story. They tend rather to direct the enquirer to a
male elder of the compound. Despite the fact, however, that *itan* are
concentrated in the hands of the more powerful and prestigious members of
the house – the male elders – it does not seem to be the case that *itan* are regarded
as a more privileged, more 'historical' or truer evocation of the past than *oriki*.
The scholarly C. L. Adeoye seems to be articulating a commonly held view
when he states that on the contrary, it is *oriki* that bear the main responsibility
for recalling the past, and quotes Aristotle to the effect that *"Iwì kíké tàbí rárà
sísun tọ̀nà ju ìtàn lọ"* ("Poetry is truer than history")' (Adeoye, 1972, p. 58).

The relationship between *oriki* and the explanatory hinterland of *itan* to
which they point is complex. When people tell *itan* of a family or a town, they
often use the *oriki* as mnemonic staging posts. Each section of the narrative
may conclude 'And that is why the people of So-and-so are called Such-and-
such'. The telling of *itan* in these cases depends on the *oriki*. But not all tellers
of *itan* rely on *oriki* – some only touch on them here and there – and, conversely, not all *oriki* are to be explained by *itan*. *Oriki* and *itan*, then, are partly
complementary and symbiotic, but partly independent, traditions. One
cannot be reduced to the other, but nor can either function without the other.

Not only do the two traditions exist in a complex relationship, but the path
from the textual formulation to the explanatory background varies from one
unit of an *oriki* text to the next. In some the reference is direct, in some
oblique, metonymic, metaphorical or riddle-like. The 'sensible person' not
only has to recognise the *oriki* for a 'half word', he or she also has to know what
kind of completion it requires in each case. Babalọla is one of the few scholars
to have carried out in detail the investigation necessary to interpret extended
passages of *oriki*. His textual annotations in *Awọn Oriki Orilẹ* are a model of
minute and painstaking enquiry. Almost every syllable is unpicked to yield an
explanation, and the links between the words and their explanations are of

many kinds. There is the use of key words, which may appear completely isolated in the *oriki*, with no explanatory support; but each of which, to those who know, represents a central concept in an *itan*. Hearing the word is enough to trigger off memories of the whole story. Even more commonly, there are etymological links between *oriki* and explanatory hinterland. Obscure phrases are either restated to make a meaningful sentence which is then expounded, or they are placed in a narrative context where each of their syllables can be interpreted to fit somehow into the story. These cryptic phrases are not just traces or residues of a former, fuller expression. They are deliberately composed to be laconic, compressed and packed with hidden meaning. People take pride in their opacity. Although everyone can recognise an *oriki* as belonging to a particular person or group, only a few will know what story lies behind it; and there may even be layers of explanation, some of which are so private that their existence could not even be guessed from the text itself. Supplementary meanings may be added on to a well-known formulation from outside, so that only those in on the secret could decipher it.

The following passage can be taken as an illustration. It shows, first, that each successive unit in a performance of *oriki* may not only require narrative supplementation before it conveys any meaning, but that each one may require a different kind of supplementation, thus heightening the disjunctiveness of the text, and the disparateness of its constituent units. Secondly, it becomes clear that although the whole of the text is in a sense past-oriented, little of it actually yields historical narrative. What it yields is past-derived observations: emblematisation of a lineage's characteristics, gossip about contemporary figures, odd incidents within the family. And thirdly, it becomes evident that the function of any one of these references may be multiple, ambiguous or indeterminate. It is an excerpt from the text of a performance in honour of another Babalọla, of Ẹlẹmọsọ Awo's compound in Okuku, a group who call themselves *Enigbọori*. The performance, like many others of its type, mixes *oriki orilẹ* with personal *oriki* of past big men of the family:

Èmi náà lọmọ arùkú tí í torí baṣọ
Ìgbà n mo yẹgọ̀ nígbalẹ̀
Òkú yanhùnyan ó di gbọ́ngan
Ìdì n mo dirù kalẹ̀ lÁgurè
Ewú ọmọ Àlàó ọmọ ṣíṣẹ̀ ó wùyá   5
Babalọlá ọmọ ṣípá ọmọ́ wu baba
Irin ẹsẹ̀ ni babaà mi ń fi wu Ìyálóde
Enígbòórí ọmọ baba Báñlẹ́bu
Bénìyàn ò bá mi ní tìjòkùn
Yóò bá mi ní tajígẹ́ẹ̀lú   10
Enígbòórí, ni wọn ń ki baba Báñlẹ̀bu.

I am also the child of one who dons the masqueraders' costume
When I befit the costume in the sacred grove
A disruptive corpse was put a stop to
I tied my bundle up at Agure
Ewu, child of Alao, the first steps of the child delight its
    mother   5
Babalola, the child opens its arms, the child delights its father,
The way my father walks delights the Iyalode.
Enigboori, child of the father named Banlębu ['meet me at the
    dye-pits']
If people don't find me in the place where they boil *ijokun* dye
They'll meet me where we go early to pound indigo,   10
Enigboori, that's how they salute the father called 'Banlębu'.

The performer, an elderly sister of the Babalola being saluted, interpreted these lines for me. I went through my written version of her text line by line, asking her what each one referred to. Some lines she would accept as units, but with others she would continue the quotation with the line or lines which followed it before explaining them as a group. When I quoted 'I too am the child of one who puts on the masquerading costume', for instance, she immediately added 'When I befit the costume in the sacred grove' before she told me what these lines referred to. In other cases, she completed my quotation with lines that had not actually appeared in her performance. Thus she not only demarcated for me the units which in her view constituted the components of her chant, she also showed how fragments of text can stand for larger textual units not actually uttered but only implied. Throughout her whole exposition, which was of a much longer text than this excerpt, she never made any kind of links between two distinct units. Her method of interpretation thus did definitely suggest a conception of the performance as a collocation of separate units, each with its own hinterland of meaning, not necessarily, primarily or permanently related to the meanings of other units in the same performance. This is the gist of her interpretation:

(1) Unit 1 (lines 1–2):

I too am the child of one who puts on the masquerading costume
When I befit the costume in the sacred grove ...

This unit seems incomplete, but she didn't finish it. She said it was a reference to the fact that the lineage occupation was masquerading: the sacred grove was where the *egungun* priests went for three nights at the beginning of the biennial Egungun festival. The reference was thus a generalised one, alluding to a permanent characteristic of the lineage, not to a specific event.

(2) Unit 2 (line 3):

A disruptive corpse was put a stop to.

In her hands, this brief and obscure formulation unravelled into a complicated story about a real incident in the history of the family. The word *yanhùnyan* is apparently empty, and takes on a definite meaning only when one knows the story – and the only people likely to know it are the members of the small compound to which Babalọla belongs. One of the sons of the family was taken ill in the middle of a masquerading show. They thought he was dead – and to avoid disrupting the show they carried him into the house and hid him. But after the show was over he revived: thus a 'disruptive corpse' (*òkú yanhùnyan*) was 'put a stop to' (*ó di gbọ́ngan*). The reference is deliberately riddle-like, for not only does it use a word that has no ascertainable meaning until 'solved' by a specific application, it also seizes on the most puzzling moment of the whole affair – when the apparent corpse suddenly ceased to be a nuisance by coming alive – and alludes to that alone, without any explanation.

(3) Unit 3 (line 4):

I tied up my bundle at Agure

This might sound like a reference to another specific incident, but it turns out not to be. It is a fragment of a longer *oriki*, and will mean nothing to a listener who is not familiar with the rest of it. In full, it runs:

Ìdì n mo dirù kalẹ̀ lÁgurè
Nígbà tí n ò rẹ́ni tí yóò gbẹ̀rù mi
Ẹ bá n wá kékeré eégún kó gbé lé mi.

I tied up my load at Agure
Since I can't get anyone to lift my load for me
Find me a little *egungun* to lift it onto my head.

In the full version, it becomes clear that the 'load' is a bundle of masquerading gear, and that the point of the *oriki* is to emphasise the secret and exclusive status of the masqueraders' association. No-one is allowed to touch the gear except members, so a 'little *egungun*' has to be found, if there are no adult members about, to help to carry it. Like the first unit, this one turns out to be a generalised reference to the lineage occupation rather than an allusion to an actual event.

(4) Unit 4 (lines 5–7):

Ewu, child of Alao, the first steps of the child delight its mother
Babalọla, the child opens its arms, the child delights its father
The way my father walks delights the Iyalode [chief of the women].

The first two lines are a well-known formulation in praise of parenthood which can be used to salute any father or mother. But the third line turns it into a sly topical reference at Babalola's expense: it alludes to a clandestine love affair he was supposed to have been having with the Iyalode, the chief of the women.

(5) Unit 5 (lines 8–11):

> Enigboori, child of the father named 'Banlẹbu'
> If people don't find me in the place where they boil *ijokun* dye
> They'll meet me where we go early to pound indigo
> Enigboori, that's how they salute the father known as Banlẹbu.

This unit grows out of the subject's nickname 'Banlẹbu', which means 'meet me at the dye-pits'. This could suggest either that Babalola is himself the owner of the dye-pits and famous for his dye-making, or that he is the owner of rich-coloured robes and a marvellously decorated house (*ijokun* is a dark greenish dye used to paint the floors and walls inside the house, and *ẹlu* is the indigo used to dye cloth). This is a formulation which could be applied to anyone rich enough to have their clothes and house frequently and lavishly re-dyed. But Babalola's sister explained that to members of the family these lines have an additional, private meaning. They are made to refer to a family scandal caused by a daughter of the compound, married to Ọba Oyekunle (1916–34), when she ran off with a handsome travelling musician, only to be fetched back in disgrace by the ọba's messenger. The lines are interpreted by people in the family to mean 'If you don't find her in one place you'll surely find her in another' – in other words, in the house of *some* man or other! Here, then, is a meaning attached to the words by the 'owners' of the *oriki* for their own private amusement: it could not even be suspected by someone not in the know.

Each of these units, then, has to be supplemented by the hearer in a different way. To interpret the first unit, you have to know that it is a generalised reference to the lineage occupation, not a historical incident. In the second unit you have to know the whole story of a particular historical incident in order to be able to assign any meaning at all to the deliberately cryptic and obscure words. In the third unit you have to be able to complete the quotation to make sense of it. The fourth unit appears transparent, part of the common repertory of personal *oriki*, but the reference to the Iyalode can be understood at two levels – as a harmless conventional praise of someone's demeanour and gait, and as a scandalous topical allusion. To interpret the unit as the family do, you have to know that such a scandal was in the air at one time. And in the fifth unit, an extra meaning has been attached to a conventional formulation which would not even be suspected by people who had not heard of the escapade of Oyekunle's wife. Interpretation requires a different operation in each case. Each unit is to be understood – at least in the first instance – not in relation to the units adjacent to it in the performance, but in the light of its own domain of meaning: which, in each case, is reached by a different route.

Even if all these paths could be traced and all the explanatory stories surrounding a body of *oriki* could be recovered, they clearly would not add up to a narrative history, for each story has its own frame of reference and is self-sufficient; there is no attempt to place them within the borders of a single picture. When *itan* depend heavily on *oriki* as mnemonics, they too tend to take on an achronic, episodic quality, as will be seen in the next chapter. Furthermore, as we have seen, *oriki* are often not about significant historical events in the life of the town. They deal with qualities as much as with action, and with trivial and private episodes as much as with great public ones. In fact, many of the great events of Okuku's turbulent past are not recorded in the *oriki*, or are only occasionally and as it were inadvertently alluded to.[22] Rather than being organised into an 'account' of the past, the qualities, actions and events that *oriki* refer to are to be interpreted as *symptoms* of a state of being. *Oriki* encapsulate and embalm moments of experience, states of affairs, and remarkable incidents, not because they chronicle an earlier age but because they capture and in some way sum up the essential nature of the person or the lineage to whom they are attributed. Even when they seem trivial, they represent a larger condition. In the excerpt from the Ṣangowẹmi performance quoted in Section 3 above, the great hunter and medicine man Olugbẹdẹ was saluted as someone 'who had nothing to give the visitor so he made a present of Fomikẹ', and the explanatory story showed that this referred to a small family incident; but it was preserved because it captured in a humorous idiosyncratic act Olugbẹdẹ's essential quality as a jovial, generous, hospitable man. If the incident was a symptom of Olugbẹdẹ's *ọla* ('honour' or 'high esteem'), Olugbẹdẹ in turn has himself become a symptom of his descendants' glory. He has become symbolic property, for he represents the accumulated power and fame of the lineage.

But if *oriki* are not narrative history, neither is it easy to treat them as a series of portraits of historical personalities. Though they do yield a great deal of circumstantial information, particularly about nineteenth and early twentieth century figures, they are not always to be taken literally. *Oriki* do not describe people, they address them in a manner intended to enhance their standing. In the passage just referred to, there occur the lines 'child of one who had a fine house in which to receive slaves as gifts/Child of one whose corridors reverberated like rain/Mofomikẹ, magnificence is acquired with money, money has made your house its headquarters'. In this chunk of *oriki* text, the three lines, which go together, circle round a central idea: that Mofomikẹ has a wealthy and substantial household. It is full of slaves, presented to Mofomikẹ by his grateful friends and clients; it is so full of people that their footsteps make the house rumble; wealth itself has taken up residence there. These are vivid but conventional ways of attributing to a subject the desired state of social well-being, *ola*. It is an ideal state that is being evoked. There is no way of knowing from the evidence of the *oriki* alone how far, in reality, the historical Mofomikẹ attained the ideal. Furthermore, *oriki* that evoke a state of being, a status, or qualities of character are often transferred from one subject to another. What may begin as an allusion to a real, perceived situation may through such transference become a stylised or metaphorical attribution. An outsider cannot tell which is which, and after a certain amount of time has passed, neither can an insider.

A social history that attempted to use *oriki* to recover patterns of personal relations would meet with the same difficulties. *Oriki* do not record the genealogical relationships of the subjects commemorated in the *oriki*. In the Ṣangowẹmi passage, which is addressed initially to Eesadẹ, it is obvious that the relationships between Eesadẹ, Mofomikẹ, Olugbẹdẹ, Owolabi, Moyọsi, Omiyọde and Alari cannot be reconstructed from the information given in the text alone. Like other references, they depend for clarification on information transmitted outside the *oriki* tradition. Genealogical relationships, as we shall see, seem actually to be obscured, rather than clarified and preserved, by the *oriki*.

This does not mean, however, that *oriki* performed today should be regarded as fulfilling a purely synchronic function. Ulli Beier, in his study of the crowns of Okuku, observes that 'History, to Yoruba kings, praise singers and story tellers, is a means of explaining and justifying the present, rather than of enlightening the past' (Beier, 1982, p. 46), and it is true that the fluid and eclectic character of *oriki* makes them easy to modify in accordance with present-day interests. But at the same time, their disjunctive mode lends itself to the preservation of elements which do not 'fit in' with any immediate project. The inconvenient and the contradictory are retained and easily accommodated in the great, formless repertoire of the singers, and may be produced to serve a number of different purposes. This is a product of the most fundamental tendency in *oriki*, which is to maintain difference and insist on incompatibility even while keeping all the elements of experience in juxtaposition with each other. The past is not the present, but it must be kept alive in the present, contiguous and accessible to it. The occasional awkwardness of the past is perhaps valued as a sign of life in it. To explain *oriki* performances purely in terms of their function as charters to legitimate the present-day status quo, or as reflections of present-day interests, would be to miss what is to their practitioners their most profound significance – their capacity to transcend time.

6. PATHS TO INTERPRETATION

The disjunctiveness and lability of *oriki*, then, make them difficult for outsiders to apprehend either as literary texts or as historical documents. Nonetheless, *oriki* performances are brilliant, beautiful, evocative and moving verbal art; and *oriki* are steeped in the past. The important thing to acknowledge is that these qualities are attained not in spite of the chant's disjunctiveness but because of it, by means of it. The qualities of an *oriki* text that make it most baffling to outsiders are precisely what enable it to do the things it does. They are the foundations of its existence, the key to its 'literariness', the way it establishes itself as a text.

To understand the way *oriki* speak of human experience, constituting notions of social group, social origin, individual pre-eminence and relations with the spiritual world, we need to experience them from the inside. That is, we need to apprehend their meaning as it is constituted, by means of their disjunctive, labile form. To do this involves going beyond text. Not only does each *oriki* formulation lead outwards, as has just been demonstrated, to its own field of meaning carried in parallel traditions of anecdote and *itan*; but also, the way a text does constitute a 'performance' and does generate poetic excitement can only be understood by looking at the situation that occasions it. The *oriki* units performed in a funeral dirge will have a different significance from the 'same' units incorporated into a bride's lament or into festivities celebrating the opening of a new house.

Vološinov/Bakhtin suggested that the ways in which 'context' enters into text's meaning are both intimate and far-reaching: intimate in the sense that all words have only a highly plastic *potential* for signification until given a specific meaning by use in a concrete situation; far-reaching in the sense that the situation in question – that is, the common 'purview' shared by speaker and listener – includes not only their physical surroundings but the horizon of their shared knowledge, interests and assumptions. 'Context' therefore not only enters into utterance in an inescapable and constitutive way, but may also be as wide as society itself, or wider. According to this view, speech is the basis of social being. Literature rises out of a sea of innumerable 'little speech genres of internal and external kinds' which 'engulf and wash over all persistent forms and kinds of ideological creativity' [Vološinov (Bakhtin), 1973a, p. 19], and which register most sensitively the social changes which can be traced through many layers down to the economic base.

The apparently fragmented and shapeless *oriki* text assumes form, life and animation only when understood in its context, in both the narrowest and the widest sense. The deep contextualisation required to interpret this genre may make this study appear over-specialised, pursuing 'meaning' further and further down a literary cul-de-sac. I do not believe that this is the case, however. The literary properties of *oriki* constitute a challenge to conventional critical assumptions. They also, however, have extraordinary resonances with some of the propositions of recent critical theory. These resonances not only throw doubt on the notion of the wholly unprecedented and innovative character of certain European literary developments, but also show that

African oral texts go further, in some respects, than they do.[23] This suggests, at the very least, that one of the projects of future critical theory should be to widen the domain of 'literature' so as explicitly to include texts such as *oriki*. A comparative view, straddling the conventionally divided domains of 'literature' and 'oral literature', would, I believe, be productive of new critical thinking. Studies like the present one are a necesssary preliminary to such a comparative project.

For the purposes of the present analysis, there is one set of such resonances in the work of Vološinov/Bakhtin which is peculiarly illuminating to the study of *oriki*. Central to Vološinov/Bakhtin's philosophy of language was the notion of the dialogic. Utterance, he said, is dialogic in the sense that it is always oriented towards its reception. Utterance is not the creation or property of the utterer; on the contrary, it only has meaning because it inhabits the space *between* a speaker and a hearer. Language is 'a two-sided act. It is determined equally by *whose* word it is and for whom it is meant' [Vološinov (Bakhtin), 1973a, p. 86]. It is 'a border zone' between the speaker and the person spoken to, and it is in this border zone that human, that is social, consciousness is constituted. Thought, according to this view, is a stream of inner speech, and speech is learnt in dialogue. Thus consciousness and self-consciousness themselves are constituted dialogically. The 'self' cannot fix itself except by putting itself, through an act of the imagination, in the place of the other. This exchange is more than the interpersonal *gaze* proposed by Hegel and Sartre; for it is conducted above all through language. The words I utter are never fully my words, but I nevertheless to a certain extent manage to appropriate them. The process of interpersonal appropriation reaches its most developed form in literature, and Vološinov/Bakhtin thought that one way of investigating it would be through the phenomenon of 'reported speech' in literary texts. The ways that speech is reported in the literature of different eras offer clues to the way the utterance of the 'other' is received and appropriated by the 'self'.

Oriki could be seen as the living embodiment of the dialogic. They are addressed by one person to another and often involve explicit or tacit references to the context of the utterance, the joint 'purview' of speaker and hearer. *Oriki* however are dialogic not just in the sense that all utterance is dialogic, but in a dramatised and heightened form. One could almost say that they are a *representation* of the dialogic. In *oriki* performances, the role of utterance in constituting social being is held up to view. The performer constructs her own persona as a performer in the act of establishing her subject's reputation, that is his, her or its claim to full social existence, to a recognised place in the human world. The mutuality of the process is made vividly evident in the intense dyadic interchange between performer and hearer.

The important role given to 'reported speech' by Vološinov/Bakhtin is highly relevant to *oriki*, for one of most striking things about any *oriki* text is its evasion of a fixed authorial point of view. It is polyvocal in the greatest possible degree. Not only does each unit of a text have the possibility of different origins, a different composer – so that the 'corpus' of *oriki* is literally an assemblage of diverse voices – but also, the prevailing style of *oriki* performance seems deliberately to heighten and emphasise this polyvocality. The 'I' of the chant is in a relationship with the listener that continually varies. It is not just that authorial distance is continually shifting, from moment to moment, but that the conception of authorial voice itself is called into question. At one moment the 'I' is the singer *in propria persona*; the next moment, it could speak from within the *oriki*, in the voice of a member of the group whose praises the performer is singing. It could shift from one representative of that group to another, from male to female, young to old, wife to daughter. The chant modulates continually, as if by reflex, from one voice to another, so that the effect is like an endlessly shifting tissue of quotations without any centre or starting point upon which to anchor them. It is as if the chant were *all* 'reported speech', with no fixed voice to report it. As we shall see, and as a reading of Bakhtin/Vološinov would lead us to expect, these characteristics are related at a deep level with the capacity of *oriki*, more than any other Yoruba genre, to open channels and transcend barriers between beings. That is, their function is to concentrate and enhance the dialogic capacity of all discourse to bring the other into relationship with the self, and in so doing, to constitute social being.

Even when writing of a genre so self-evidently Western and written as the novel, Bakhtin uses language that seems to be made for *oriki*. The novel exhibits 'indeterminacy, a certain semantic open-endedness, a living contact with unfinished, still-evolving contemporary reality' (Bakhtin, 1981, p. 7). It is 'uncompleted', so that 'we cannot foresee all its plastic possibilities' (Bakhtin, 1981, p. 3). Writing of Dostoevsky, whom he judges to be the instigator of a totally new type of novel, Bakhtin says his work is made up of 'a plurality of independent and unmerged voices and consciousnesses, a genuine polyphony of fully valid voices' (Bakhtin, 1984a, p. 6), is '*multi-accented* and contradictory in its values' (Bakhtin, 1984a, p. 15), composed of 'highly heterogeneous materials' which 'are presented not within a single field of vision but within several fields of vision...'(Bakhtin, 1984a, p. 16), with the result that 'each opinion really does become a living thing and is inseparable from an embodied human voice'.

This unexpected congruence raises many questions that will not be addressed here. Among other things, it indicates places where Bakhtin's picture of the historical evolution of European literature develops its own loopholes, places where European literary history could turn round and re-examine itself and recognise its own specificity. But it also suggests that *oriki* are perhaps less foreign to European sensibilities than my account so far has implied. If the student of Dostoevsky and the student of African praise-poetry are recognised as sharing some common ground, a new dialogue becomes possible.

Understanding *oriki*, however, begins not by the application of European theory but from within the *oriki* tradition itself. Careful attention to the texts reveals that *oriki* themselves offer clues on how to 'read' them. The performer not only dramatises and heightens what she is doing in the performance, she also comments on it from within. Her utterance is punctuated with specific observations upon her own performance, general reflections upon the function and importance of *oriki*, comments on protocol, appreciation for the art of her predecessors or self-praise for her own, and explicit commentary on what she has done or is going to do in performing *oriki*. The self-reflexivity of *oriki* is thus a kind of embedded oral critical practice: a practice which, as Ọlabiyi Yai has argued, is unlike European literary criticism in being productive, intimately related to its object and expressed often in the same poetic form as it (Yai, 1989, p. 65). Unlike the Zuni text discussed in Tedlock's seminal paper (Tedlock, 1983, pp. 233–46), there is no sense in *oriki* of an 'original' text in which are embedded later, supplementary, commentaries.[24] In the case of *oriki*, commentary is installed at the heart of every text and is indeed its mode of being. *Oriki* themselves, being inherently self-reflexive, tell us how they could be interpreted.

3

ORIKI IN OKUKU

1. OKUKU TODAY

Okuku is a small northern Yoruba town. It straggles briefly along the main road from Oṣogbo to Ọfa, just before the point where the rich soil of the forest belt gives way to the sandy soil of the semi-savanna. To a traveller on this road, Okuku will appear as the usual blur of brown earth houses with their rusty iron roofs, mixed with imposing two-storey plastered housefronts with 'Brazilian' verandahs, balconies and window-shutters. On the right as you travel northwards (see Map 2) is the market, with its modern concrete stalls laid out in rows under ancient shady trees. Then you pass the great square concrete tower of the Roman Catholic church and the more ornate twin towers of the mosque. On the left the housefronts open out into a wide sandy bumpy irregularly-shaped arena; at the back of it is the Anglican church, and its left margin is the palace wall. The houses continue for another half mile or so up the road, petering out before they reach the Grammar School. The population was put at over 26,000 in the much-derided 1963 census. My rough and ready calculations based on the 1977 electoral register got a figure nearer 18,000. Neither of these numbers is really very informative.

The main road bisects the town. When I first arrived in 1974, it was the only tarred road in Okuku, and in a very bad state of repair. The other big road, Oke Agadangbo, ran at right angles from it through the upper half of the town. It was long, straight, broad and golden from the sandy soil, punctuated by occasional massive leafy trees. Away from these two roads, Okuku was a maze of paths and alleyways opening unpredictably into patches of open ground between buildings. The appearance of the street was deceptive. Housefronts stood shoulder to shoulder in a row, plain concrete blocks or pink and yellow plaster (often it was the plaster that held the mud walls up), with shuttered or louvred windows, and ornate stone railings around their front verandahs, looking very square, self-contained and European. Often, as I made my way up Oke Agadangbo to the house where I stayed on the far edge

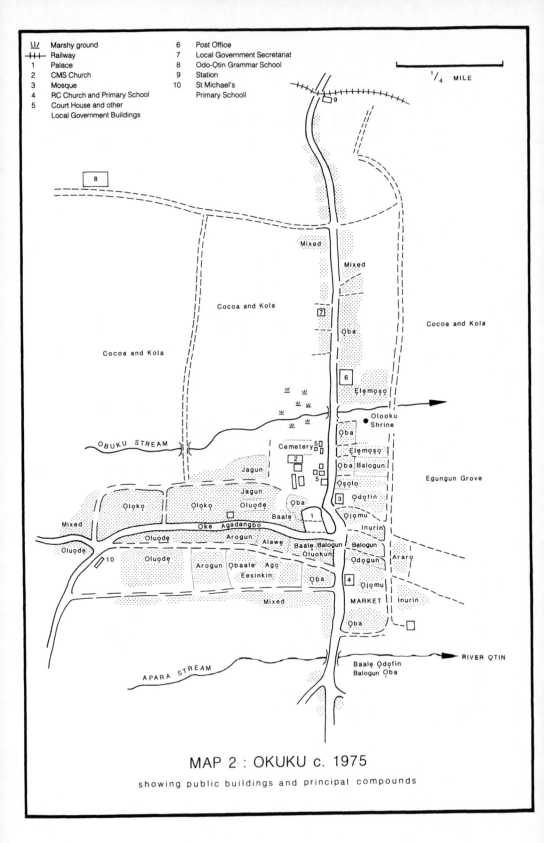

MAP 2 : OKUKU c. 1975

showing public buildings and principal compounds

of the town, I would be called over by an elder taking the breeze in his front porch. I would be ushered ceremoniously into the 'parlour' at the front of the house. Here there would be armchairs and foam-cushioned sofas, coffee tables and picture-rails crowded with posed photographs of members of the family, living and dead. But when the formal part of the visit was over, one of the wives would draw me into the back regions of the house. We would enter a dark corridor with earth walls, huge waterpots in the cool angles of the passages, chickens underfoot, three-stoned hearths smoking near the openings. Through one of these openings we would emerge into the sunshine of a great courtyard, where there would be women plaiting each others' hair, cracking palm nuts, sifting and sorting through heaps of drying melon seeds, or washing clothes in big battered tin basins. I would be led through another doorway into another passageway and walk a long way in the dim light, past the low gated doors of the inner rooms on one side, the archways or openings onto the courtyard on the other, stepping past the stretched-out legs of aged, immobile, lizard-like old ladies, till eventually we would emerge, apparently into quite a different part of town.

It was only when one of the ọba's sisters took me onto the roof of a half-completed building on a little hill to one side of the town that I saw the pattern. From above, the sharp ridges of the russet iron roofs described clearly visible designs of rectangles, squares, L-shapes, T-shapes and straight lines. Their long eaves seemed to jostle and overlap. I saw the outlines of great old compounds with their inner courtyards; but their lines were broken again and again by new, square, two-storeyed houses that rose above them like ships. Here and there parts of the old compound walls had simply been pulled down to make room for the new houses, and the raw ends of the broken structure were left sticking out. The rain of years had reduced other ruins to rounded heaps. Much demolition was going on; many new concrete buildings going up on the old sites. Further out towards the edges of town, all the buildings were new. There were many 'foundations' marking the layout of a future house, waiting for the owner to raise money for the next stage. Some were fresh, but others had become overgrown and looked like ruins before they had been built.

Out here where the town met the bush the evening air was distinctly cooler. Okuku has a definite centre, along the axis of the main road between the palace and the market. At night this part of town generates heat, crowds of strolling people with their lanterns, a perpetual hubbub faintly audible even from the other end of town. As you walk out to the fringes of settlement, the darkness and silence creep up: everyone seems to have shut themselves up inside their houses. Early in the morning men pass that way with their hoes to the local farms; women with baskets on their heads to the markets of neighbouring towns. From dawn, the misty silence is broken by their greetings.

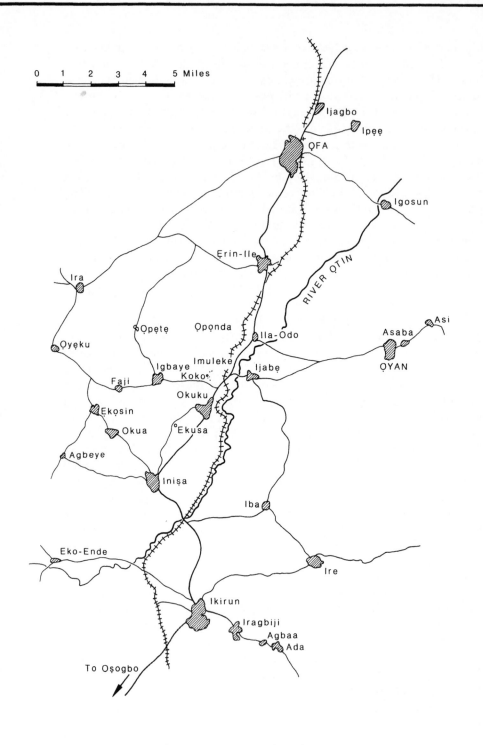

MAP 3: OKUKU AND NEIGHBOURING TOWNS

People build in the bush because they cannot get sufficient land in the centre of town. They do it, often, with a pioneering spirit, and talk proudly of the trees they had to cut down and the undergrowth they had to clear before they could lay their foundations. Their hope and expectation is that in due course more people will follow their example until the outlying areas become part of the town proper. Meanwhile they claim to be suffering, living as they do 'in the forest'. This sense of the encompassing vegetation always being contested at the margins of civilisation underlies the very conception of what a town is.

The creation of a town is a triumph over the bush. The ọba, as the symbolic founder of the town, is responsible for keeping the bush at bay. A successful ọba who maintains and expands his settlement can be commended with this *oriki*:

Sọgbó dilé sọ̀gbẹ́ dìgboro
Ọba asàátàn dọjà.

Turns forest to settlement, turns bush to town
Ọba who turns a rubbish heap into a market.

But the ruins of abandoned houses overgrown with bush, the traces of whole ruined settlements, remain as a warning that at any time the conquest of the bush can be reversed. A town is the prime social unit, the fundamental and enduring source of identity, through which alone full social being can be claimed; yet we are reminded too that a town is a frail construction that can be disbanded, destroyed and overgrown in a matter of years. The history of Okuku, as we shall see, is eloquent testimony to this.

When I first arrived in Okuku in 1974 there was no electricity. A year and a half later electricity was brought. Its effects were gradual. For a long time very few people had the money or the influence actually to get the cables connected up to their houses. Then the habits of a lifetime – rising at dawn, going to bed soon after the evening meal, never leaving the house at night without a lantern, avoiding walking at night altogether if possible, for night is associated with maleficence – all these habits and dispositions meant that the electricity, when acquired, had only a limited role to play. But it did have effects. The last time I visited Okuku I went to see the Ẹlẹmọsọ Awo, the most senior of the surviving Ifa priests, an old man venerated by his colleagues for his quietness and modesty as well as for his great knowledge. He was sitting as usual on the floor in the corner of his parlour, surrounded by his divination instruments and an array of bottles and calabashes used in the preparation of medicines. But on the table at the other side of the room stood a brand-new television.

Another gradual shift was effected by the rebuilding of the main road. It is now a narrow but fast expressway carrying heavy traffic north. It was designed to bypass all the small towns between Oṣogbo and Ọfa. The Olokuku (ọba of Okuku) alone among ọbas had the influence needed to reverse this decision and ensure that the road continued to run right through the centre of his town. Now big towns like Ikirun and Iniṣa are by-passed but all the traffic comes to Okuku.[1] In the last ten years the number of trucks and taxis owned by Okuku people has increased tenfold. The petrol station, owned by another Ifa priest, has done well. At first it was a single yellow tank installed above ground right outside the palace wall. Now it has been moved out to the junction at Kọnta and forms the centre of a new motorpark, stop-off place and provisions market for travellers. A bank has also come to Okuku and the bar and eating place next to it, on the main road, always have customers.

People believe in 'progress', but the slow changes that take place are often, it seems, undertaken in the same spirit that animated the past. The trees on the main road were cut down in the name of progress – Okuku must not appear as a bush, backward town – but the underlying relation of town to forest, of inhabited to uninhabited areas, appears from oral literature to be an ancient one. In the same way, the profile of the palace was drastically altered on the accession of the present ọba, in conformity with a long-standing expectation. When I first came to Okuku, the gateway in the high golden palace wall was surmounted by a pointed gable roofed in corrugated iron. On

Other projects for local improvement appear more sluggish. As long as I was in Okuku, one of the popular places for the youth of Oke Agadangbo to gather was on the waterpipes outside Mrs Akindele's food shop. This great heap of unused pipes became so familiar as a place to sit that people forgot their original purpose. Till today, the only piped water in Okuku comes from a handful of standpipes dotted about the town. In the dry season the water flows intermittently, usually in the evenings, and each standpipe is signalled by the long row of buckets, basins and jerry cans marking their owners' places in the queue for water. Most water is collected from the river; during the construction of the road it could also be bought from the Alhaji who drove the tanker, at 50 kọbọ a drum. There are still no shops in Okuku, apart from one or two tiny apothecary's stores where you can buy aspirin and knitting needles. Buying and selling is done in the big four-day market and in the smaller market held every evening in front of the palace. A few artisans' workshops can be seen. The traditional forge is still operating, and the head of the blacksmith's lineage, Chief Arogun, still salutes passers-by with his anvil from inside the smithy. There is a small printing press; some photographers' studios; a carpenter who displays his marble-topped tables and gilt-ornamented coffins around his front porch; a radio repair man; a cobbler with a dark workshop hung with strips of leather and rubber, shoes in every stage of manufacture and repair; and many women petty traders with small wooden stalls outside their houses, selling soap powder, kerosene, chewing sticks, pepper and onions, and Trebor mints.

either side were raised concrete platforms, six feet deep, also with gabled roofs, supported by pillars. On these shady platforms old women sold condiments, the butcher sold meat, and goats dozed in the heat of the day. It was in this accommodating archway that the ọba would sit enthroned on his beaded chair every other year when the town's *egungun* masquerades came to the ọba's market to dance their respects. But a new ọba is expected to proclaim his intention to uphold the traditional glory of kingship by making expensive improvements to the palace. Oyekunle (1916–34) built the first parlour with glass windows. Oyinlọla (1934–60) built the great stone two-storeyed building in the middle of the palace complex. Oyewusi (1961–80) opened the hall behind the inner courtyard where state occasions are now held. When Oyelẹyẹ ascended the throne in 1981, he improved the front view. The archways, gables and tin roof were pulled down, the platforms removed, and in their place the wall was given a high two-dimensional cement arch, plastered and inscribed with Aafin Olokuku (Olokuku's Palace). The depth, the shade, and the angular promise of induction into a mysterious region within were erased; any passer-by could now see straight into the great open front courtyard of the palace. Intimations of the past were destroyed, but it was done in the spirit of the past.

Okuku is felt by its inhabitants to be of a political and historical importance out of proportion to its size. It is the queen of the Odo-Ọtin district, claiming rights to tribute from seventeen neighbouring villages: rights which were apparently acknowledged by most of these villages, and which were upheld by the colonial authorities when they made Okuku the district capital, responsible for the taxation and chieftaincy affairs of all the towns under it. Some of these towns have now outgrown Okuku, and local politics has revolved for some time around their attempts to shake off their traditional subordination. Most Okuku people take it for granted that their town is more ancient and more royal than the other towns around them. But except at the level of local government committees, inter-town rivalry is of less importance than the many links of trade and kinship that bind the towns of the area together. Many women traders operate full-time in the Odo-Ọtin area, going from one market to another through their interlocking four-day cycles. Many Okuku men marry women from neighbouring towns, and therefore become involved in family and ceremonial obligations there.[2] And conversely, many Okuku women marry men from neighbouring towns and go there to live, bringing back whole teams of co-wives to attend their families' funerals.

The superiority of Okuku is symbolised for the townspeople in the person of the ọba. The Olokuku is classed as a Grade II ọba, of the same rank as many ọbas of much bigger towns. He is the centre of an exceptionally rich and elaborate royal ceremonial complex, and is the inheritor and custodian of the famous collection of ancient beaded crowns (see Beier 1982). The late Olokuku, Oyewusi II, certainly lived up to Okuku's reputation for royal grandeur. He was a charismatic figure, famous for his hospitality and his capacity to impress and attract big people from outside Odo-Otin. At the annual royal and civic festival – the Olooku festival – the great front courtyard of the palace would be solid with Volvos and Mercedes. Within the town, despite the steady erosion of the ọba's actual powers, ọbaship still commands respect bordering on awe. The ọba is the head of the huge royal lineage, whose four branches rotate the title among them. He presides over the three grades of ranked chiefs which constitute the indigenous structure of government. Chieftaincy titles are still the focus of intense interest among those who hold or aspire to hold them, the centre of endlessly ramificating intrigues that have dominated town politics as far back as people can remember. These affairs revolve entirely around the central figure of the ọba. It is he who validates appointments to titles. He can reject candidates or push the interests of those he favours; he can upgrade low-ranking titles, downgrade important ones or even rediscover and reinstate long-abandoned ones. The reigns of some recent ọbas have been characterised by interminable chiefly feuds. Everything turns on who comes to the palace and who does not; who is in the ọba's favour, who boycotts his ceremonies. The loyal chiefs used to come every evening without fail to sit in the ọba's inner courtyard and talk over the events of the day: the rebellious ones' entire existence was coloured by their determination to keep away. The ọba also presides over low-level disputes which the parties concerned do not wish to take to court. His representative sits in the local court itself and reports, every Monday when the sessions are held, on the cases being heard. Those who are summoned by the ọba for some real or fabricated grievance comply instantly and with a fair degree of anxiety. It is dangerous to fall foul of an ọba; the prayer *Ọkọ ọba kò ní í sá ọ lẹ̀sẹ̀*, 'the ọba's hoe will not fall on your foot', still means something to the present-day commoner.

The Olokuku is the nominal head of every religious group in the town. The present Olokuku and his two immediate predecessors have all been Anglicans, but they also preside over all the traditional cults. Every cult must obtain the blessing of the ọba when it fixes the day for its annual festival,[3] and the celebrants must pay an official visit to the palace at the opening and close of the ceremonies. Some festivals give the ọba a much bigger role than this. The Olooku festival, in honour of the town's guardian spirit, is also a cult of royalty. The ancient beaded crowns are brought out for display and ritual attentions, the ọba's head is propitiated and the royal ancestors evoked. The central event of the festival is the ceremonial wrestling match between the ọba and the priest of Olooku.[4] The Ifa festival, the next big event in the ritual calendar, involves the all-night performance of *iyẹrẹ* chants mentioned earlier. This impressive performance is staged at the ọba's doorway where he meets his chiefs on formal occasions and where the shrines to his forefathers and to Ọsanyin, a deity particularly associated with the royal family,[5] are located. The ọba himself is present throughout the vigil, lying in state on his beaded cushion across the doorway, blessing the participants and the town and presiding over the feast that precedes the performance. In the Otin festival in honour of the deity of the principal local river, the central ceremony is a ritual confrontation between the ọba and a young girl representing the 'town', that is, the senior chiefs. The Gbẹdẹgbẹdẹ festival requires the ọba to go in procession to the Ifa meeting house to authorise a ceremonial divination on behalf of the whole town. Finally, the last festival of the ritual year is the Egungun festival, which starts and finishes with a great ceremony at the palace. The ọba is therefore a crucial actor in the principal festivals of the year, the kingpin around which ritual activity revolves. Okuku people are almost all either Christian or Muslim, in proportions of about two to one, and it would be false to claim that there is an unbroken harmony and continuity between 'traditional' and world religions. Many Christians and Muslims are openly hostile to and contemptuous of the remaining 'pagans' and deplore their cult activities. But they are intensely proud of Okuku's greatness, and this greatness is conceived of in traditional and mystical terms and based on a conception of royalty which is indivisible from 'paganism'. Large numbers of people participate fervently in the major festivals whatever their professed faith.

The men of Okuku are almost all farmers, though some combine farming with other occupations including carpentry, barbering, shoe-making, radio repairs, printing, trading in livestock, and produce-buying for the government. Women have traditionally undertaken certain agricultural tasks on their husbands' or fathers' farms, and nowadays those who live full-time on the cocoa farms often do a great deal of work on them, particularly during the harvest in November, when they collect cocoa pods, transport them back to the settlement, and attend to the drying and fermentation processes. Women's principal occupation, however, and the source of their independent income, is still trade and food-processing. On marriage, the husband is obliged to set the woman up with a small amount of trading capital. Some women remain petty traders, selling condiments and small articles from a stall outside their houses by day, and in the ọba's market in the evenings. Others specialise in preparing and selling cooked food such as *akara* (bean-cakes), *mọin-mọin* (steamed bean puddings), or *ẹkọ* (loaves of corn-starch, a cheap staple food). Many women succeed in expanding the sphere of their operations and become full-time traders in larger and more valuable goods – such as cloth, staple grains and flours, dried fish, and yams. Their main outlet for these goods is the big four-day market in Okuku, and on the other days they may go to the four-day markets of neighbouring towns. Many women raise extra money by shelling palm kernels, preparing palm oil in great vats in the farms, and preparing kola for export to the north. Some have succeeded so well that during the busy season they are able to run a business employing many other women. Others specialise in trading in kola, organising its collection and transport to the north.

People's identity within the town derives from their membership of an *ile*, a compound or residential unit based on a core agnatic lineage but usually also including a variety of other groupings. There are between twenty-nine and fifty *ile* in Okuku, depending on how you define them; this indeterminacy is a crucial aspect of the town organisation and one which will be discussed in detail in Chapter 5. Membership of an *ile* assigns an individual to a group which is variably defined in different contexts but which nonetheless exhibits great solidarity. It is the *ile* which holds land in and around Okuku from the ọba and allocates it to individuals or families. The *ile* defines a block of people the individual cannot marry and on whom she or he can call for assistance and support. It provides the individual with an address. It groups people under a *baale* (household head) who organises them for taxation, for communal labour, and for all kinds of ceremonial activities at funerals, marriages and festivals. Membership of an *ile* is the fundamental prerequisite of citizenship.

But perhaps the most important thing to know about Okuku today is that for nine months of each year most of the population is not there. In the 1930s and 1940s Okuku farmland was completely overplanted with cocoa and kola trees. By the late 1940s the soil was becoming exhausted and the cocoa trees were in any case past their best. Starting from 1949, farmers began to go in search of land to rent or buy in the more fertile, thickly forested Ondo and Ijẹsa areas to the south and east. The early days of the *oko iwaju*, frontier farms or 'far farms' as the expression is locally translated, are now recounted as tales of heroism. People talk of the young pioneers' discovery of *igbo dudu* (virgin forest), their approaches to the local owners, the arduous labour of felling the huge trees and uprooting the bush, and the first planting, followed by a seven-year wait for the trees to bear fruit – years during which many of them were too poor to visit home. In one far farm the first group of settlers lived under a rock for two years before they could afford to build the tiny two-roomed mud houses typical of the farm settlements. The first far farm founded by Okuku people was Sunmibare, twelve miles south of Ifẹ. Others are even further afield: Odigbo is three miles north of Ọrẹ, a hundred miles from Okuku. Because of these distances, the farmers took up a more or less permanent existence in the far farms. Other groups from other towns came and joined them, and a formal local organisation was established on the basis of 'quarters' for each town of origin. Now almost the entire able-bodied male population of Okuku has land on one of the fifteen or so far farms colonised by Okuku people; many of the older men have acquired plots in more than one location, and put their younger brothers, sons or wives in charge of some of them while they attend in person to others. Most of these men and their wives – the junior wives if they have more than one – live on the far farms full time. From March till November, Okuku is a town of old men, senior wives, chiefs, ritual specialists and young children.[6]

In November after the main cocoa harvest, the farmers come flocking back with money to spend. In December, January and February houses are built and house-opening festivities are held. Weddings are performed – even now, overwhelmingly in the 'traditional' manner rather than in the church. Every Wednesday (unanimously accepted as the propitious day for the 'bride's outing') parties of richly dressed girls and their retinues of sisters and friends can be seen parading around the town chanting, most affectingly, the 'bride's laments'. Sometimes forty or fifty weddings take place in a single day. This is also the time for funerals, for those who can afford to keep their dead relatives on ice till the high season; or for memorial celebrations and 'turning the dead over' for those who have already done the burial itself. Christmas and the New Year are lavishly celebrated. Families, church groups, and social clubs all bring out their new *ankoo* ('and co.') – the uniform outfit that demonstrates their wealth and solidarity. Then as the rains begin again in March or April, people begin to go back to the far farms for a new agricultural year. They will come back as often as they can afford or are required to: to attend family festivals, funerals and important meetings, and to participate in the Olooku festival and perhaps also in the Ifa, Ọtin or Egungun festivals. Many people also make a point of coming home at Easter and for the August bank holiday, because these are the times when the salaried, educated members of the family who work in Lagos, Ibadan and Kaduna have their holidays. They come for Okuku Welfare Association meetings and other arrangements at these times, and progressive-minded townspeople like to be around when they come.

Except on these occasions, Okuku is a quiet town. Old men sit on their verandahs nodding to passers-by; the ọba sits in his silent palace. Little of the explosive activity that carries trucks and taxis at top speed along the new road penetrates into the life of the town. Women crack palm nuts in a desultory fashion and the *olorị̀sa* (traditional devotees) attend privately to their household shrines. If changes have taken place, they have done so in a sluggish and almost reluctant fashion. The mood in the far farms is quite different. There, people are galvanised by a strenuous work ethic; they are ambitious, enterprising and impatient of anything that impedes 'progress'. In Okuku, by contrast, the prevailing mood is one of something very like nostalgia: a mood informed with memories, animated by an always-present past. Just as the new storey houses rise from among the only partly-demolished old compounds, so the new has not displaced the old in any aspect of life. Traces of the past lie thickly scattered everywhere – in the architecture, in rituals, in jokes, in forms of address, in modes of identification, and in the continual performance of oral texts. The outlines of the past, still showing through the slow accumulations and displacements of modernity, are continually and affectionately retraced. This past inhabits this present above all through the medium of *oriki*.

2. OKUKU HISTORY

There is no written evidence of Okuku's history before the twentieth century. The earliest colonial document directly concerning Okuku is probably the 1911 report on a visit to the area by the Ibadan chiefs and the resident, Captain Elgee, in connection with a boundary dispute between Okuku and the neighbouring town of Iba – a dispute which dragged on into the late 1930s and occasioned much colonial paperwork. From 1933 onwards the A.D.O. for Oṣun North frequently mentioned Okuku and its neighbours in his reports, which dealt mainly with taxation, chieftaincy affairs and land disputes. In 1935 I. F. W. Schofield submitted the first Intelligence Report on Okuku. He estimated the population at 1606 and commented on the 'energetic and adventurous disposition' of the people.[7] For any period before this, however, there is no independent written evidence. But the past is all around the people of Okuku and is preserved and recreated in a variety of ways.

All elders, both men and women, talk about the past, recounting events remembered from their own youth or told them by their parents. Most of these reminiscences revolve around prominent people in the town; but they may also trace the path by which an *oriṣa* or an institution was inherited by a present-day individual, or recall a cult official's predecessors in office. Often they just contrast 'the old days' (*aye atijọ*) with 'the present' (*aye ode oni*). 'In the old days, when people held feasts they would serve pounded yam in troughs, there was so much food'; 'in the old days, there was no money in the town: only three men in Okuku had gowns of *oti* cloth, and anyone else who wanted to wear one had to borrow it from them'.

These stories can evoke a world that it takes an effort of the imagination to reconstruct. Before the first motorable road was built to Okuku in the late 1930s,[8] the town was enclosed by bush, linked only by narrow footpaths to neighbouring settlements. In the nineteenth century it was protected by a town wall enclosing a stretch of *igbo ile*, domestic forest, where people could collect firewood and throw their waste when conditions were too dangerous for them to venture further. Visitors were rare in the town. But parties of traders did arrive with their goods, and were charged a levy at the town gates before they were admitted. There was always a consciousness of a greater power beyond Okuku: first Ọyọ, which exercised overlordship in the semi-mythical era before the fall of Old Ọyọ; then Ilọrin, till the 'Jalumi War' of 1878; and then Ibadan, after its victory in this battle at Ikirun, ten miles from Okuku. Ilọrin and Ibadan made their power felt by posting representatives, *ajẹlẹ*, to Okuku, but few Okuku people had been to Ilọrin or Ibadan.[9] To reach Ibadan was a three-day walk, and not many people knew the paths until the first decades of this century when long marches in search of wage labour became common.

'Everything took time in those days': long periods of initiation into cults; for men, long periods of service as apprentice or bondsman, the long wait for a wife and the longer period of service to their fathers. Women recall that they grew up knowing they had been betrothed from the womb and fearing the power of their future co-wives. The past is remembered as a world where extraordinary spiritual powers were at large, controlled and channelled to their own advantage by those who were strong and lucky. 'We do not have medicine like that any more: the knowledge of it has been lost'. Powerful big men, and a few powerful women – whether well- or ill-disposed – dominated the community in these accounts, attracting and organising all memories of what the past was like.

But *itan*, formal narrative history, is the preserve of old men alone. Both the town itself and the *ile* ('compounds'/'lineages') that make up the town have *itan*. Each *ile* has its own story, concerning its origins, the sequence of events which led to its arrival in Okuku, and the reason for various family customs and taboos. Each *ile* will deny knowledge of the history of other *ile*; histories are part of the repertoire of emblems by which each group demarcates itself from the others.[10] Each tells a partial story which links a particular group to the great events of Okuku's past, but it does not actually tell the story of those events. The only people who tell the story of Okuku as a whole, from the beginning, are the royal elders and the oral performers who serve the ọba. The town's identity is subsumed into that of the ọba, and the town's history is the history of one figure: the 'I' who represents the office successively filled by all the present ọba's predecessors. Even Ajiboye, the son of Ọba Oyekunle (1916–34), though he did not himself become ọba, began his history of Okuku with the words:

> The title devolved on us in Ara. I was the elder brother. The kingmakers said that it was our turn. But Ifa didn't choose the elder brother that our family offered, it chose the younger brother...

All past ọbas[11] are 'I' to their successors. The continuity of the royal line, whose importance is thus stressed, is synonymous with the continuity of the life of the town itself.[12]

The greater weight of history behind the royal lineage can be seen in the way they construct their genealogies. The royal family boasts a king list of up to seventeen names (see Table 1), and the genealogical relations posited between them, though highly variable, particularly in the earlier phases of the story, yield a genealogy with a depth of at least seven generations (see Fig. 1). Commoner lineages, by contrast, trace themselves back to an apical ancestor only three, four or five generations back, even when they claim that he founded the lineage in the remote past (a characteristic of lineages in many if not all Yoruba towns). This foreshortening is accompanied by a tendency to conflate the big watersheds in the town's past: all wars are thought of as the 'Kiriji' war – which actually took place in the years 1879–1886[13] – and the apical ancestor is conflated with distinctly nineteenth-century figures, some of whom can actually be remembered by the oldest living men today.

Representations of the past of the town as an enduring, unified entity, then, lie in the *itan* as told by elders of the royal family. There are many versions, reflecting the position of the elder in one of the four branches of the royal lineage as well as his personal narrative tastes. All the stories, however, have the same narrative and symbolic structure. They move through the same three phases, and in all of them the same relations between *itan* and *oriki* are established. Every version begins with a primordial, semi-mythical era from the origins of the town to the early nineteenth century; there follows a more circumstantially detailed nineteenth-century period, covering the Ilọrin–Ibadan wars which threw the Odo-Ọtin area into turmoil; and then a modern period, from the beginning of this century to the present day. The mythical era is the one where there is most variation in the stories, and where *oriki* play the role of a key mnemonic. From the reign of Adeọba onwards – i.e. probably from around 1830[14] – there is almost complete agreement about the names and order of the ọbas and about what events happened in which reign (a pattern which was also noted by Ulli Beier in his discussion of Okuku history[15]). *Oriki* are more profuse and elaborated, but play a less prominent mnemonic role. From about 1900 onwards, history enters the realm of personal memory, and the story of the town usually tails off into a bald summary of successive ọbas up to the present incumbent. In reminiscences about the period after about 1940, *oriki* are rarely quoted at all.

Whatever the variations, all the versions share the same basic scheme of events in representing Okuku's past. The outline is as follows. The story begins with a chieftaincy dispute in the Ekiti town of Aramọkọ in which a senior brother (Ọladile or Ọladitan) was passed over in favour of a younger brother and therefore left the town – a standard narrative device found in many Yoruba town histories.[16] The senior brother then journeyed into an area of thick forest (with or without an intermediate stop in Imẹsi-Ipole) and founded a new town, Kọọkin. The isolation of this area is stressed in several versions of the story: it is said that the name Kọọkin derives from *ihọ ikin* – thick clumps of palm trees – and that Ifa told the founding prince to settle where the palm-tree forest was thickest. Other story-tellers emphasised that at this period there were no other towns in the area: 'the nearest neighbour to the new settlement was Ẹkọsin, as Ọsogbo, Ikirun and Iragbiji did not yet exist': suggesting a period prior to the late sixteenth century, when Ọsogbo was probably founded.[17] It is agreed by all that the cult of Olooku was brought by the founding prince from Aramọkọ and celebrated in Kọọkin, and that the royal title Alara was retained by the ọbas at Kọọkin. A special relationship was said to have been established with the river Ọtin, though the account of how this came about varies. Ajiboye says that Ọtin displayed her beneficence by sparing all the domestic animals when the river flooded its banks; another

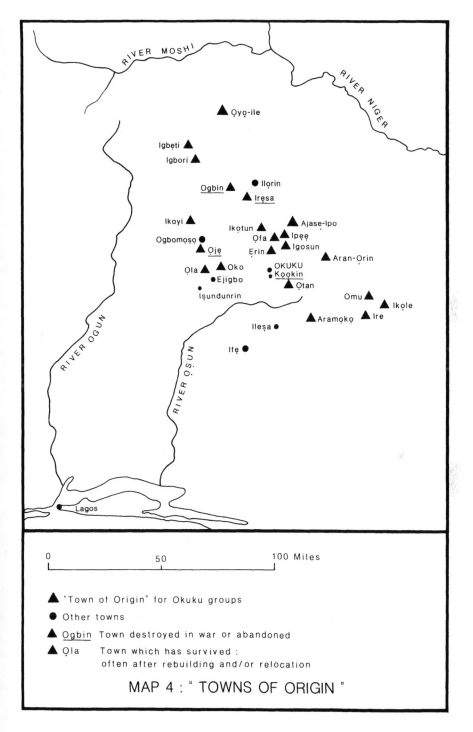

MAP 4 : " TOWNS OF ORIGIN "

Version I (Oyeleye: Oyeleye Branch)

1. Oladitan: left Aramoko over chieftaincy dispute; founded Kookin at a place indicated by the *orisa* Otin. Joined by other groups. Otin predicts that Oladitan will have a son, to be called Otinkanre.

2. Olugbegbe: included in genealogy but not in narrative.

3. Oladile: included in genealogy but not in narrative.

4. Otinkanre: son of Oladitan named by Otin.

Version II (Ajiboye: Oyekanbi Branch)

1. Oladile: left Aramoko over chieftaincy dispute; went to Imesi Ipole, from there proceeded to found Kookin. Joined by other groups. His children were Oluronke Otinkanre, 'the father of us all', a girl Lalubi who married founder of Odofin line, and Olugbohun. Eesa founded Inisa. Araoye, Oladile's 'son' (cf. genealogy) founded Eko-Ende. Arrival of founders of neighbouring towns. Size and prosperity of Kookin. Great flood demonstrates Otin's beneficence. 140 blacksmiths.

2. Olugbohun (?): may have been oba: narrative unclear.

3. Oluronke Otinkanre: 'Had three wives, from whom sprang the three branches of the royal family'. Ijesa Arara war, sack of Kookin.

4. Olugbegbe: not included in genealogy. Magical powers, turns into leopard, eventual overthrow. Only child a daughter.

Version III (official: sources unknown)

1. Prince left Ife and founded Aramoko.

2. Oladile: left Aramoko over chieftaincy dispute; founded Kookin at a place indicated by Ifa. Joined by other groups. Oladile's daughter Lalubi marries founder of Odofin line. Kookin's size and prosperity: iron-work (140 blacksmiths). Foundation of Eko-Ende and Ijabe by sons of Oladile. Foundation of neighbouring towns.

3. Oluronke Alao.

4. Mosin.

5. Oyeledi/Oyededi.

6. Oyedele.

7. Jala Okin: Ijesa Arara war, sack of Kookin. Foundation of Okuku. Disaster of poisoned water in River Obuku. Ruled 13 years before sack of Kookin, for 8 years at Okuku.

5. Alao Oluronke: 21 years on throne. Had 70 *ilari* (messengers) but lost them all in war. Ijẹsa Arara war, sack of Kookin. Alao leads survivors to new site, taking twig of fig tree from old market. Moves river Obuku nearer to new town by magic. Dies 9 years after foundation of Okuku. Rightful successor Oro-oye passed over because of Oro-Oye's mother's fears.	5. Adeọba	8. Olugbegbe.
		9. Ojo Alao.
		10. Ọbadere.
6. Adeọba: recalled from Ilorin to become ọba on refusal of Oro-oye.	6. Oyekanbi..	11. Adeọba. (1830-61)
7. Oyekanbi: 'soon removed from his post'.	7. Ẹdun.	12. Oyekanbi: Ilorin–Ibadan wars. (1861–77)
8. Ẹdun: 'misbehaved', removed by chiefs, Oyekanbi recalled from Ofa.	8. Oyewusi.	13. Ẹdun (1877–8)
9. Oyewusi: on his death, succession of Oyelẹyẹ branch passed over.	9. Oyekunle.	14. Oyewusi: end of Ilorin–Ibadan wars (1878–1916).
10. Oyekunle.	10. Oyinlọla.	15. Oyekunle (1916–34): Native Court, Native Police, D.O.'s Resthouse established. Boundary disputes with neighbouring towns settled.
11. Oyinlọla.	11. Oyewusi II (on throne at time of narrative).	16. Oyinlọla (1934–60): Christianity spread, Primary Schools founded. Chieftaincy Declaration 1956.
12. Oyewusi II (on throne at time of narrative).		17. Oyewusi II (1961–80): Post Office and Police Station up-graded. Electricity introduced. NBN Bank established.

Table 1. Reigns of the Olokuku

Version I (Oyeleye)

Version I (Ajala)

Version II (Ajiboye)

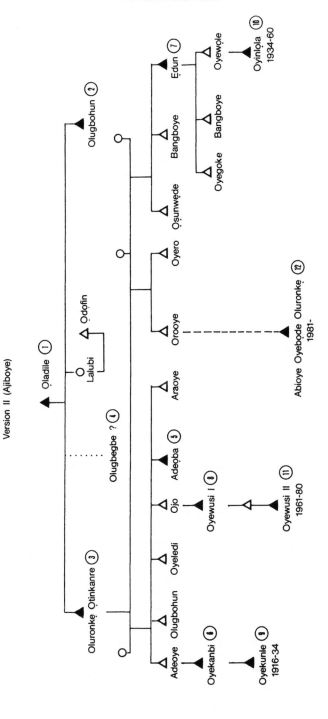

Fig. 1: Genealogies of the Olokuku

royal elder, Oyeleye, says that it was Otin who appeared to them in the thick forest and pointed out the spot where they should settle. Oyeleye also said that Otin ordered or predicted that the founding prince's first son should be called Otinkanre (Otin touches something good) as a sign or acknowledgement of her beneficence.

Everybody agrees that Kookin was a great town. It was swelled by an influx of settlers whose places of origin are often recounted in detail. These settlers are said to have come mainly from further north and west (see Map 4). They are said to have settled not only in Kookin itself, constituting the *ile* of which the town was made up, but also in separate settlements all around the area as tributary towns under Kookin.[18] As in other Yoruba towns, the order in which the constituent *ile* of Kookin arrived was said to determine the rank of the title they held: the first to arrive held the highest title. But this was not the only reason for recording the town's constituent *ile* and their places of origin so painstakingly. In the story of their arrival is embedded a picture of the fundamental nature of the town. Individuals and small groups come from far afield, bringing with them their own customs and emblems associated with their place of origin, and their own chieftaincy titles which would be given a place in the hierarchy of the new town. Their difference is stressed. But each in turn makes a commitment to join in the common project of creating a new place:

> Ladile's eldest son that he brought with him from Ara was Oluronke Otinkanre. Oluronke was the father of us all. After Oluronke, Ladile had a girl, Lalubi. Lalubi married into a family of carvers who came from Oje and said they would stay with us in Kookin. ...The first person to come and settle with us in Kookin was Eesa from Ajase Ipo. Otebolaje the Odofin [the carver from Oje] came next. After that came *ile* Aworo from Apa; *ile* Baale from Aran Orin; *ile* Oloko from Oyo; *ile* Oluode from Ofa. The latter were the people who actually initiated the foundation of Kookin. They were hunters so they were brave enough to go alone through the uninhabited forest. They first left Ofa because of a quarrel about a title – just like us – the younger brother was made oba of Ofa while the elder was by-passed, so he left and went to Imesi where he met Ladile. When they decided to leave, he went ahead to look for a good place. He found a spot in the bush, cleared it and went back and called Ladile to come. His name was Winyomi Araoye, son of Olugbensere of Ofa-Esun. His people sent to him to come back home. He said he wouldn't, he would found a town of his own. (Ajiboye, *ile* Oba)

Ajiboye goes on to list fifteen more *ile*, giving the place of origin for each. By recounting, he was recreating the town in narrative and reaffirming both its inner diversity and its coherence.

Kookin was noted for its iron-work. Several accounts said that there had been 140 blacksmiths at work there; one added that the iron ore was obtained from the mines at Isundunrin near Ejigbo, and that the finished products were

sold as far afield as Ila, Ọyọ, Ilẹsa, Irẹsa and Irẹgba. It was said to have been
'a huge town with three rivers':

> Going right through the town were the rivers Anle and Gọdọgbọ. Going
> along the edge of the town was Pankẹrẹ. Springing from the house where
> they did the dyeing was Agbamudoyin. They lived there a long time.
>
> (Ajiboye, *ile* Ọba)

Little else is said about Kọọkin, and since few historical events are
remembered that can be attributed to the ọbas who ruled there, some of the
narrators telescoped the rise and fall of the great town into only two reigns –
that of the founder who came from Aramọkọ, and that of his son who was said
to be on the throne when Kọọkin was sacked. In some versions, this was Alao
Oluronkẹ, in others Oluronkẹ Ọtinkanre or Jala Ọkin [and in the version given
by Beier's informants (Beier 1982), Olugbegbe].

The sack of Kọọkin is always attributed to the Ijẹsa Arara war. Schofield,
reporting on oral history he collected in 1935, states unequivocally that this
war took place in 1760, but he does not explain how he arrived at this date.
The official history – produced by the ọba's advisers for such purposes as the
publication of a coronation brochure – cites the same date, based on reign
lengths counted back from 1916, a firm date for the death of Oyewusi I: but
as there is no agreement about which ọba was on the throne when Kọọkin was
sacked, this precision seemed questionable (and at that stage, quite possibly
a product of Schofield's report itself, since the ọba had a copy of it and often
referred to it as an authority).[19] What all the historians of Okuku agreed on
was that the Ijẹsa were jealous of Kọọkin's greatness and, some said, particularly
its monopoly of iron manufacture; that Kọọkin was totally unprepared (one
elder added that it was given over to peaceful pursuits, manufactured only
tools and not weapons, and ignored warnings from Ifa that it should arm
itself); and that the destruction was almost total – only the ọba and a handful
of citizens survived (nine adults and a child, it is said). To avoid being found
by the Ijẹsa again, they moved a few miles north of Kọọkin and settled on what
had been the outskirts of its *igbo ile*, or ring of domestic forest. The new town
was called Okuku. Oyelẹyẹ stressed that the ọba who presided over the
resettlement – Alao Oluronkẹ – preserved the continuity of the town by
bringing with him a branch of the fig-tree that stood at the Kọọkin market,
and having it planted in Okuku 'to show where the new market was to be and
to remind people of where they had come from. It was a sign, and it grows
there to this day'.

Around this period there were ọbas whose reigns are remembered in magical
terms. Alao Oluronkẹ himself had magical powers. According to Oyelẹyẹ, he
moved the river closer to the new settlement by creating a supernatural boa
with water spouting from its mouth (cf. Beier 1982:39):

> He said the river was now [i.e. after the move from Kọọkin] too far from
> the town. He bought a boa's head, and told the people to bring him three

loads of *ebolo* vegetable and a bag of salt, and he also bought some
potash. With all these he made a medicine and took it outside the town.
He dug a hole and put the medicine in, and covered it with a big pot.
The medicine changed into a boa, and water spouted from the place.
The boa climbed a palm tree and watched the women coming to the
river. This frightened them, but Alao told them the snake would do
them no harm. The river became Obuku [one of Okuku's principal
rivers]. During the Egungun festival the women would put it in their
chants, saying 'In the year that Alao founded the second Okuku, the
palm tree became a boa, and crawled away'.

The quoted words are an *oriki*, felt by Oyeleye to encapsulate the story he had
just told. Ajiboye's narrative surrounding the same *oriki*, however, was different.
According to him, the Oba Olugbegbe had a younger brother called Ope, who
turned himself into a python that terrified the town. The chiefs drove him out
into the bush 'at *ile* Odofin's farm at Oke Apara' where he became a small
river, which is called Opedere (Ope becomes a python) to this day.

But the most famous of the obas with supernatural powers was Olugbegbe
himself, who was said in some accounts to have reigned before the fall of
Kookin, in others after it. In Ajiboye's version, he used his magical powers to
turn himself into a leopard and wrought havoc in the town every year during
the Olooku festival. The chiefs asked the Alaafin of Oyo to help, but though
the Alaafin summoned Olugbegbe to Oyo he failed to trap him. Eventually
the chiefs found out the secret of Olugbegbe's power from his wife – it was a
lamp he always kept burning, hidden in the forest. They found the lamp and
extinguished it, and Olugbegbe knew then that they would kill him, so he took
chains, called on the earth to open, entered it and was never seen again.

With the reign of Adeoba, the narratives reach the threshold of the
remembered past. At this point the nature of the stories changes as personal
reminiscences only two or three generations old begin to enter the picture. All
Adeoba's successors are confidently named, and reign lengths are sometimes
ascribed to them (see Table 1, which shows the obas named by Ajiboye, Oyeleye
and by one version of 'official' history). The turning point in all these stories
was the 'Fulani war', also referred to as the 'Ofa war' and the 'Ilorin war'. Not
only royal elders, but elders of every *ile* have something to say about what went
on in Okuku during this period of protracted disturbance.

The wars that convulsed Yoruba country from the 1820s almost up to the
end of the nineteenth century had a devastating impact on this area. Afonja's
revolt against Oyo and alliance with the ruling Fulani at Ilorin unleashed a
long series of attacks by the Ilorin forces in a southerly direction. By c.1825
the Ilorins reached Ofa, ten miles north of Okuku, and made it their camp.
From here they launched a succession of raids to the south, overrunning the
whole Odo-Otin area as far as Osogbo, until decisively checked by the Ibadans
in the battle of Osogbo in c.1838 (Law 1970, p. 217). Meanwhile Old Oyo

had been sacked and then abandoned, and refugees were pouring southwards from the whole area around it.[20] Through the 1840s the Ibadans were able to push northwards, finally establishing their own camp at Ikirun, a well-fortified town ten miles south of Okuku. The twenty miles between Ikirun and Ọfa remained a contested area, and Okuku was right in the middle of it. Raids and skirmishes between the Ilọrins and the Ibadans continued inconclusively back and forth between the two camps until 1878, when the Ilọrins joined forces with the newly formed Ekitiparapọ (alliance of Ekiti towns) and prepared to attack Ikirun. It was then that the Okuku people and the populations of all the small neighbouring towns ran for refuge to Ikirun and took up permanent residence 'for seventeen years', as Okuku elders remember, i.e. until the British-engineered peace of 1893. Though the Ibadans won a resounding victory in the 'Jalumi War' of 1878, the Ilọrins continued to raid and harass the area. The Ibadans went to help Ọfa and became involved in a siege that lasted until 1887, when the Ilọrins finally drove them out, sacked the town and massacred the chiefs. Okuku people remember the escape of the ọba of Ọfa, Adegboye, shortly before this, for he was said to have spent several days in Okuku before fleeing further south.

Even after the British-negotiated peace of 1893, the Ilọrins continued to attack the area. Captain Bower and a mainly Hausa garrison were established at the Ọtin River, and the people were encouraged to return to their ruined towns. Many, however, did not feel it was safe to go back until the main Ilọrin army, near Ọtan, had been destroyed by Captain Bower's rockets in 1896. Old men remember the sound of the rockets to this day, and describe with glee what they heard about the fall of Ilọrin the following year. Okuku, in short, lay in a battleground through most of the nineteenth century, from 1825 to 1893. If the earlier period was relatively mild – though involving raids and abandonment of the town on more than one occasion – from 1877-8 onwards the long-term evacuation to Ikirun and the attacks that occurred during the latter phases of the wars are vividly remembered and are described as having been extremely disruptive.[21]

The people of Okuku had no formal military organisation, but bands of fighters were informally set up both to protect the town and to launch raiding parties themselves. During the period of their enforced stay in Ikirun, they farmed on plots lent to them around Ikirun, or went back to their old farms at Okuku by day, returning to Ikirun at night – but this was very dangerous, and they could be captured at any moment by slave-raiding Ilọrins. The buildings in Okuku fell down and were completely overgrown before the people moved back to the town in the 1890s. The dislocations produced by seventy years of warfare were immense. Many lineages were reduced to rumps, many were fragmented and scattered between two or more neighbouring towns, and many parties of refugees hitherto unconnected with Okuku turned up. There is a lot of evidence about the dispersal and regrouping of the population in lineage histories; there is less direct evidence about changes in the power structures of the town, but the stories suggest that the nineteenth century saw the rise of the big man on a scale not seen before. Several chiefs attained towering powers in the town, probably through their successes in slave-raiding and slave-trading. They succeeded not only in deposing two ọbas around the middle of the century – first Oyekanbi and then Ẹdun – but also in reinstating one of them, Oyekanbi, something which in normal times would have been unthinkable.[22] Ambitious individuals seem to have been able to take advantage of the turbulent conditions to exploit the flexibility inherent in the town's political structure to an unprecedented extent.

Pre-twentieth century representations of the past thus seem to fall into two distinct phases: the period up to Adeọba/Oyekanbi, the fall of Ọfa and the battle of Oṣogbo; and the period after that up to the resettlement of Okuku in 1893. The earlier history is recounted only by elders of the royal family; it has a heroic and mythic character, and is extremely variable in sequence and in the correlations between names, reigns and events. There is disagreement even about the names of the founders of Kọọkin (Ọladile or Ọladitan) and of Okuku (Alao Oluronkẹ, Oluronkẹ Ọtinkanre or Jala Ọkin). No two accounts agree on the names or order of the early ọbas, the genealogical connections between them, or about which events should be attributed to which reigns. The stories are consistent, however, in the broad picture they give of the foundation and powers of a great pre-Okuku city state and its destruction by the Ijẹṣa. The later period is one in which there is almost complete agreement about the names and order of the ọbas and about what events should be attributed to each reign; but the description of successive ọbas' deeds is no longer all there is to be said. It is an era about which every lineage has a say. The dislocations in the commoner lineages' narratives – visible in the double form, already noted, where there is a founding ancestor of remote provenance who is also a recognisable nineteenth century figure – may be the result of the social dislocations of the war period. More will be said about this later. The point to be made here is that the nineteenth century wars are part of a common historical experience, and any elder of any lineage feels entitled to talk about what happened then. 'Past time', in ordinary discourse, is seen by these men as nineteenth century time: the 'old days' were the days of evacuations, slave raids, turbulent chiefs, and big men enriching themselves. Each narrator has a different set of references but all are located against this common background. To many commoner elders, Kọọkin is just another name for Okuku, now fallen into disuse, and the past really begins with the fall of Ọfa.

The way the past is recalled in these narratives is better understood by looking at the role *oriki* play in them. In accounts of the quasi-mythical era, what needs to be understood is the nature of their variability, which makes itself felt as a kind of unanchoredness.

Variations between 'testimonies' is of course one of the central concerns of scholars of oral history. The Okuku narratives contain many of the features identified by Vansina (1985). Differences in personal narrative style, for instance, can give rise to two very different accounts. Another obvious factor is the political interests of the narrators and the section of the royal family to which they belong. In some cases, it was clear that variations in the upper reaches of the genealogical tree were brought about when different narrators tried to promote the claims to the throne of their own branch, or to eliminate those of other branches. The tendentiousness of the narrators is sometimes very subtle, and the interests at work are not always immediate or short-term ones. In their accounts of the order in which the founding fathers of the other lineages came to join the first ọba at Kọọkin, both Ajiboye and Oyelẹyẹ *refrain* from making over the story to conform to the present-day rank-order of the chiefs. They preserve discrepancies – a different one in each case – rather than provide a 'charter' for the way things are today. In this way, they remind their listeners that the chieftaincy order was not always as it is now: the ọba has the power to raise and demote, and actually did so in several well-remembered episodes of nineteenth- and early twentieth-century history. They thus keep open the possibility of further adjustments in future.[23]

But creative variation and motivated 'bias' do not fully account for the way episodes, genealogy, and chronology seem to shift and re-form in these stories. Achronicity and inconsistency pervade even a single testimony. Ajiboye for instance insisted that Oluronkẹ Ọtinkanre, according to him the second or perhaps third ọba, and son of the first one, founded the 'three branches of the royal family from which we all came'; but in his narrative he told a long story about Olugbegbe, who could not be fitted anywhere into the three branches as he presented them. Furthermore, Ajiboye's story would loop back in time. His narrative begins predictably enough with the chieftaincy dispute at Aramọkọ, the departure of the elder brother, the foundation of Kọọkin, and the arrival, in order, of all the founders of the *ile* which constitute present-day Okuku. It goes on to tell the stories of how the highest chief in Kọọkin, the Eesa, offended the ọba and was expelled, whereupon he went and founded his own town, Iniṣa (now Okuku's neighbour and its greatest rival); and of how a prince of Kọọkin came to be the ruler of another neigbouring town, Eko-Ende. Ajiboye then describes the greatness of Kọọkin, its sack by the Ijẹsa Arara, and the establishment of the new settlement, Okuku. He tells the story of the leopard-king Olugbegbe. He returns to the Ijẹsa Arara war to add further explanation of the Ijẹsas' motives and additional description of the size of Kọọkin before it was sacked. He goes on to tell the story of the foundation of Iba, another neighbouring town. He reverts to the theme of Kọọkin and its rivers, and the flood which spared the livestock. He then goes right back to the pre-Kọọkin era in Aramọkọ, and explains the origins of the Olooku cult and festival which the people brought with them from Aramọkọ to Kǫǫkin and from Kǫǫkin to Okuku. He jumps forward from there to the reign of Oyekanbi, and then finishes the rest of the story in a few sentences, listing the ǫbas that succeeded Oyekanbi (Ędun, Oyekanbi again, Oyewusi I, Oyekunle, Oyinlǫla, Oyewusi II) up to the present day.

In other words, he tells the story of the foundation and establishment of Kǫǫkin in a straightforward manner, but having done so, he begins to weave back and forth in time, apparently at random. What underlies this is a non-linear, non-sequential mnemonic practice. Almost every episode (including some of those in the 'straightforward' part) is built around or attached to one of four things: the interpretation of a name; location in a still-existing, marked place; explanation of a ritual; or the interpretation of an *oriki*.

An etymological motive sets off several of the episodes in Ajiboye's narrative. The story of the Eesa who was driven from Kǫǫkin for offending the ǫba is built around the name of the town, Inịsa, which is said to mean *Ìnì-Eésà*, the property of the Eesa. The story of how he left Kǫǫkin and went to found his own town is told to 'explain' the name. In some versions, this small keyword opens out into a narrative of great imaginative detail.[24] The whole story is felt to be condensed into the name Inịsa, and the name is the point of the story as well as its trigger. Similarly, the story of the foundation of Okuku itself 'explains' the name Okuku, which is said to mean *Àwǫn òkú tó kú kù*, 'those who are left of the dead'. By thinking of the name, the story is called forth. The story of the foundation of Iba is explained as follows:

> The village of Iba was founded when people came from Apa to Kǫǫkin and asked the ǫba of Kǫǫkin to give them some land. The ǫba did so, and told them to build themselves a farm-hut [*abà*] there to live in. After a while the place became known as Iba because of this.

In the case of the Inịsa and Iba stories, the *motive* is obvious: it is to assert the overlordship of Okuku and the tributary status of the other towns, which are presented as either an offshoot of Kǫǫkin or as late-coming beneficiaries. But the point being made here is the manner in which the story is encapsulated in a durable, permanently accessible mnemonic locus, the name of the town itself.

Other episodes are inscribed in permanent features of the landscape. 'Kǫǫkin was so big that the Igbo-ita forest outside Okuku was at that time the *egungun*'s sacred grove on the outskirts of Kǫǫkin': that is, although the centre of Kǫǫkin was several miles away from the site of Okuku, its outskirts reached to the edge of the present town. The Igbo-ita forest thus becomes a permanent reminder of the size and former glory of Kǫǫkin. There is also a part of the forest called *igbo* Olugbegbe, where I was told I could see the chain that marks the place where Olugbegbe eventually entered the earth and disappeared after terrorising the town with his magical feats for so long ('but only if you're not purposely looking for it'). Other stories are encapsulated within rituals. The wrestling match which is the high point of the Olooku festival is a reminder of a story about the original struggle between the spirit Olooku and the ọba of Aramọkọ, or, in Ajiboye's version, a commoner who became the champion of the the town. The annual enactment of a wrestling match between the priest of Olooku and the ọba is said to have been instituted precisely in order to commemorate the original event; each year, its performance reminds people of the story. Finally, stories about the past are encapsulated in *oriki*, brief and well-known phrases that nonetheless open out into lengthy narratives in the hands of a knowledgeable elder. Ajiboye remembered what he wanted to say about the relation of Kọọkin to the river Ọtin because of the epithet *àyàbùèrò*, 'place where strangers stop and drink':

> One of Kọọkin's *oriki* is *àyàbùèrò*. This is because of a famous flood. The river Ọtin flowed near the town. One year it rained and rained and the river flooded everybody's backyard and all the hen-houses, goat-pens and dove-cotes were carried away. But after about twelve days, when the flood subsided, all the animals were still alive. The river was recognised as a beneficent one and was honoured with the name *à yà bù èrò*, i.e. 'strangers stop to drink its waters'. And that was why Ladile named his first son Ọtinkanre, 'River Ọtin touches something good'.

Oyelẹyẹ likewise concluded his story of the magical boa by quoting an *oriki*: 'And afterwards the women put it into a chant, saying, "In the year that Alao founded the second Okuku, a palm-tree became a boa and crawled away"'.

The whole of Ajiboye's narrative up to Adeọba is based on emblems: the ritual, the geographical location, the name, the *oriki*. Each encapsulates within it or suggests by its associations a story, and the narrative is a collection of such stories. But all these emblems are *simultaneously present* and available to the narrator. They are inscribed in a landscape seen every day (even if it is a mythical landscape containing Olugbegbe's chains); in names heard in every conversation; in rituals performed annually; or in all-pervasive *oriki*. They are all there and available, spread out side by side, as it were, without intimations of chronological succession. The weaving, recapitulating movement in Ajiboye's narrative is the effect of a narrated past which inheres in objects, names and practices contemporaneously surrounding the narrator. *Oriki* not only participate in this mode of recall, they also, characteristically, redouble it. They introduce a kind of second-order emblematisation: for they not only speak of events from the past, they also speak of the other emblems by which these events are remembered. There are *oriki about* the ritual, the landscape, and other durable and visible signs of the past. All these signs are absorbed by *oriki* and given a textual embodiment which makes possible a much greater elaboration. How this is done is discussed in Chapter 5.

In the stories of the post-Adeọba period, *oriki* play a somewhat different role. It is likely that big men became more prominent in the political life of the town in this period, and that the far greater volume and elaboration of personal *oriki* probably testifies to this fact, rather than being merely the result of erosion in oral transmission of earlier personal *oriki*. What is certain is that the big men of the post-Adeọba period are always recalled by their descendants either through extensive personal *oriki* – much fuller and more detailed than the emblematic references of the earlier period – or for the kind of actions and qualities which that style of *oriki* dwells on. But while the personal *oriki* of great men of this age are so much more profuse, their mnemonic role is reduced: they are used to amplify a story whose outlines are known independently. The stories told about this period do not depend as heavily on visible or verbal 'survivals' as those told about the earlier period. And when they quote *oriki*, it is usually to evoke the qualities of a personality rather than to recall events in the history of the town. But even when these stories of the nineteenth century do not mention *oriki* at all, they talk about the *kind* of thing that personal *oriki* were developed to celebrate, and clearly inhabit a specific universe of thought to which *oriki* offer a key.

The twentieth century, for which there is a variety of documentary evidence as well as a wealth of personal memories, is also the period during which the composition of new *oriki* lost its impetus. From the resettlement of Okuku in 1893 till some time in the 1930s prominent individuals were still celebrated and commemorated with lavish personal *oriki*. Ọba Oyekunle (1916-34) acquired a substantial corpus of *oriki* of his own, as did a number of powerful chiefs and medicine men, like Fawande of *ile* Baalẹ, Bankọle of *ile* Aro-Isalẹ, and Toyinbo of *ile* Aworo. Their stories are told in Chapter 6. Ọba Oyinlọla (1934–60) also attracted extensive personal *oriki* celebrating his formidable qualities, but most of his contemporaries did not. After that, the composition of new *oriki* suffered a decline in Okuku. The performance of *oriki* continued unabated and flourishes vigorously even now in a multiplicity of forms. But performers tend to draw on the existing stock of epithets rather than composing new ones specifically attributable to one subject.

The great changes brought by colonialism are spoken of endlessly in personal reminiscence but are directly referred to hardly anywhere in *oriki*. The first Christian convert was made in 1905; Islam was introduced in 1910; the railway from Lagos to Kano reached Okuku in 1904, and transformed the local economy by providing an outlet for surplus production of foodstuffs, especially yams. Farmers and businessmen went in for commercial yam farming in a big way. Substantial amounts of cocoa and kola had also been planted by the early 1930s. As the need for cash grew, to finance the establishment of cocoa and kola farms and for other purposes, a large proportion of the male population took up migrant labour. Most of the older men in Okuku spent several years in Ghana, Lagos or Abẹokuta in the 1920s and 1930s, trading or more often working for the Public Works Department on the railways, roads, plantations, and gold mines.

The reign of Oyinlọla (1934–60) is thought of as the age of stability and growing prosperity deriving from really substantial cash-crop production.

Oyinlọla pioneered the cultivation of a new type of kola (known in the area as *obi Olokuku*) which was extremely popular and made his fortune. Oyinlọla was the first Christian ọba in the town and the first to support education. Having decided that Oyinlọla's predecessor was too weak, the colonial administration proceeded to back up Oyinlọla with police and local court. This was the golden age of the ọba, which his successors have found it hard to live up to. He was able to marry seventeen wives and educate all his fifty-odd children, founding a dynasty which up till today is unquestionably the power behind every civic or communal enterprise.

In the 1950s, the great exodus to the 'far farms' got under way. This shift of focus not only put an end to a number of traditional practices, but also accelerated changes in family structure, notably allowing young men to free themselves of their fathers' control and cultivate their own farms independently or with a full brother at an earlier age. Education also had a transforming effect, though this was partly concealed by the fact that the better-educated sons and daughters of Okuku almost invariably went away to work in bigger towns, only returning at Christmas and Easter. Their presence is made visible, however, by the large and elegant houses that the more prosperous of these people have built around the edges of town, as a monument to their patriotism rather than as a place actually to live.

Little of this, however, is commemorated in the continual performances of *oriki* that take place in Okuku. I will argue in Chapter 6 that the reasons for this arrest in the growth of the tradition of personal *oriki*, following its nineteenth- and early twentieth-century flowering, are associated with changes in the basis of personal power, and with them, changes in the role of *oriki* themselves. What is recreated in *oriki* performances now is an older idiom. But it is an idiom which is not in any sense irrelevant to the present. Indeed, it animates the present and enables people to put a value on it.

3. WHAT *ORIKI* DO

Within this context of Okuku, past and present, we can now return to the question of how *oriki* are constituted as texts. We saw that it is the apparent autonomy of its constituent parts that makes an *oriki* text appear centreless, boundariless, formless and resistant to conventional criticism and conventional historical analysis. To know how the *oriki* text works, I have suggested, we have to know what the performer is *doing*. At the most fundamental level, what she is doing is *naming*. From this starting point flow all the characteristic features of the chant.

It is said that:

A ì í dàgbà ọ̀jẹ̀
Ká má mà lálàjẹ́
Níjọ́ tá a bá gbó
Tá a bá tọ́ ni ọmọ ẹni í ń fi kini.

We never live to a ripe old age
Without acquiring some nicknames
On the day we grow old
In righteous age, our children will use them to
    praise us.

The process of 'acquiring nicknames' – that is, *oriki* – begins with the
naming of a baby seven or eight days after birth. As well as a multiplicity of
other names, the child is given a single *oriki*-name. *Oriki*-names stand out
among the rest, for most of them have the same distinctive structure,[25] and
all of them are used to convey special affection and intimacy by a senior person
to a junior. Like other names, *oriki*-names have meanings. A girl might be
called Àbèní [one whom we supplicate before owning], Àjíké [one whom we
rise to caress], Àdùní [one whom people compete to possess]. A boy might
be called Àjàní [he whom we fight to possess], Àkànbí [the one conceived
without delay] or Àdìgún [one that is tied straight, i.e. proper and decent].

To this name will automatically be attached another one which is associated
with the father's *orilẹ*, i.e. the ancient place of origin by which his extended
patrilineal kin group is defined. The *orilẹ* name is emblematic, and is often
taken from nature (e.g. *Ọkin*, king crane; *Ọwa*, palm leaf stem; *Amọ*, mud),
and less often from human artefacts (e.g. *Aran*, velvet). P. C. Lloyd calls these
'totemic names' (Lloyd, 1955, p. 237), but, as he makes clear, the things they
refer to are not totems in the sense that there is a special relationship between
them and the people named after them: they are strictly emblems by which
large scattered sets of people recognise a relationship amongst themselves.

Thus the week-old baby will already be equipped with an appellation
beginning, for instance, Ajikẹ Ọkin, Ajala Ọwa, or Akanbi Amọ. When people
pronounce these names, the *oriki orilẹ* of the father's lineage follow almost
automatically. These *oriki orilẹ* will be used to salute the child all through its
life. Everybody, therefore, is equipped from the start with *oriki*; women as well
as men, children as well as adults can be saluted whenever the occasion arises.
The *oriki orilẹ*, which are the subject of Chapter 5, remain the most highly
prized social symbols throughout the person's life and the source of their most
profound satisfaction. But as a child grows up and begins to show individual
characteristics, those around it will begin to select, from a common repertoire,
personal *oriki* which are felt to be especially appropriate to it.[26] A child of very
dark complexion could be addressed:

Igbó fi dúdú ṣọlá
Òkèé fi ribiti ṣayọ̀.

The forest makes its darkness a thing of high
    esteem
The hill makes its roundness a thing of joy.

And a tall, good-looking boy could be called:

A-gùn-táṣọ́-lò.

One who is tall and worthy to wear [good] clothes.

As the child grows to adulthood and acquires specific skills and capacities, more specialised *oriki* may be added to his or her corpus. The more outstanding the person, the greater the number of *oriki* that will be added. For this reason, men acquire more than women, and important men acquire more than ordinary men.

An exceptionally knowledgeable *babalawo* might be given this *oriki*, which claims that he has such a deep knowledge of divination that even from outside the house he can tell which of the 256 *odu* (divination figures) another diviner's throw has turned up:

Ó gbọ́ ṣẹ́ṣẹ́ Ifá ó yalé
Ó gbẹ́yìnkùlé mọ iye odù tó hù
'Àìgbọ́fá là á ń wòkè, Ifá kan ò sí ń párá'
Ló tó babaa Fárónkẹ́ ṣe.

He hears the clink of the diviner's chain in someone's
    house and he pauses
From out in the yard, he already knows what *odu* has come
    up
'Not knowing Ifa, we gaze up in consternation, but
    there's no Ifa in the rafters'
This is what father of Faronkẹ is worthy to be called.

A very successful farmer can be saluted with the following *oriki*: it says that he has such a big farm that he actually has separate plots of maize for each kind of dish made from the crop:

Àyìndé alágbàdo-ègbo-lóko
Babaà mi agbìngbàdo èwà lọ́tọ̀
Àyìndé alágbàdo iṣáájú
Baba Ojútọ́mọrí, ní í gbani lọ́wọ́ ebi

Ayinde, one who has maize for pottage in his farm
My father, who plants maize for pudding separately![27]
Ayinde, 'maize that ripens before other people's'
Father of Ojutọmọri, 'is what saves us from hunger'.

These are *oriki* for exceptional men: I found them applied to only two or three people in the whole collection of texts I recorded. They were probably originally composed for a single person, and later borrowed for attribution to other people who achieved similar greatness. Some *oriki* celebrate qualities or attainments that are more universally aspired to – wealth, a large household, many wives, the capacity to resist the attacks of rivals. Other personal *oriki*, on the other hand, commemorate something so particular to one person's life that they remain exclusively his.

The original *oriki* name given to a baby is therefore like a peg onto which a growing string of other attributions is hung – first just the corporately-owned *oriki orilę*, later personal *oriki* that refer to specific qualities or attainments belonging to the individual. But as well as being attached to a name in this manner, *oriki* are also *like* names. Yoruba names all have meanings.[28] Some, called *orukọ amutọrunwa*, are 'brought by the child from heaven': they signify particular circumstances surrounding the birth – a child born feet first is *Ige*, a child born with the caul is called *Ọkę*, and so on. Other names, called *orukọ abisọ*, are 'names given after the child is born', and may reflect the parents' situation or desires or their hopes for the child's future. At its naming ceremony, a child may be given almost as many *abisọ* names as it has well-wishers. Only a few will be kept on for regular use, but many will be remembered for their honorific significance. *Abisọ* names are compressed statements, often in the form of a complete sentence: *Ajeiigbe* means 'Wealth never dries up'; *Morọmọkę* means 'I have got a child to cherish'. Some even contain subordinate clauses: one name for an *abiku*, the child who is born only to die and be reincarnated over and over again, causing a succession of infant deaths in the family, is *Mọlomọ*, which is short for *Ọmọ-ló-mọ-ohun-ti-yóò-şe*, 'It is the child who knows what it's going to do' (i.e. whether to go on dying or to consent this time to stay with its parents). Each name is self-contained, for it has its own meaning which is not continuous or connected with the meaning of the other names belonging to the same person. When addressing someone, there is no reason to say these names in any particular order. Since they are unconnected, there is no necessary sequence. Nor is there any reason, apart from familiarity and habit, to pick one selection rather than another out of the total range the person possesses. A person could be addressed as 'Ogungbile' or 'Babatunde'; as 'Babatunde Ajeiigbe Aderibigbe' or as 'Aderibigbe Babatunde Ayọdele Ogungbile'. The only difference would be that the more names the speaker brings out, the more intimacy he or she would be demonstrating with the family, and the more affection and esteem for the owner of the names. It would be unusual to try to say all of a person's names, but equally unusual to use always and only the same one.

But if the names are in one sense autonomous, each constituting a complete statement with its own field of reference, they are also all connected in the sense that they all belong to, and signify, the same person. They thus become equivalent, and are alternatives to each other.

Names can be used to address people as well as to refer to them, and it is the vocative aspect of naming that *oriki* take up and elaborate. The whole of an *oriki* chant is in the vocative case. The units of *oriki* are also constructed in a name-like way. All the features that have been identified as characteristic of *oriki* are in fact products of the construction of *oriki* as names. Perhaps the most important of these features, noted by Ọlatunde Ọlatunji (1973, 1984), is the high incidence of nominalisation in *oriki*. Phrases and even whole sentences are turned into nouns through the use of prefixes such as *a-* and *ò-* ('one who...'), *à-* ('one who...' in the passive) and *oní-* with its variant realisations a*l-/ol-/el-* ('owner of...'). These nominalising prefixes occur very commonly in ordinary language, in nouns like *apẹja* (*a-pa-ẹja*, one who kills fish, i.e. a fisherman), *òbí* (*ò-bí*, one who gives birth, i.e. a parent), *àjẹkù* (*à-jẹ-kù*, something which is eaten and remains, i.e. left-overs), and *alága* (*oní-àga*, owner of the chair, i.e. the chairperson at a meeting). But in *oriki* they are used much more frequently and are attached to much longer and more complex phrases in inventive ways. This passage from the *oriki* of the *orisa* Loogun-Ẹdẹ, for instance, is constructed almost entirely out of complex sentences nominalised with *a-*, *ò-* and *à-*:

> Pánpá-bí-àṣá, aṣọdẹ-bí-ológbò
> Ò-gbìjà-oníjà-fẹsẹ̀-há-ń-párá
> Ò-tàkìtì-lórí-ìrókò-fẹnu-gbégbá-ẹbọ
> Àbíkẹhìn-yèyé-tíí-yọ-gbogbo-ọmọ-omi-lẹ́nu...

> Swift as a hawk, one who hunts like a cat
> One who takes on other people's quarrels and ends up
>   getting his foot stuck in the rafters
> One who comes somersaulting down from the top of the
>   mahogany tree and seizes the calabash of offerings
>   in his mouth
> Last-born of the Mother [River Ọṣun] who annoys all the
>   children of the water.

Each of these nominalised epithets has been derived from a longer noun-phrase. *Ògbìjà-eníjà-fẹsẹ̀-há-ń-párá*, for instance, is a contraction of the phrase '*Ẹni tó máa ń gba ìjà enìjà, tó sì máa ń fẹsẹ̀ há ní párá*'. The nominalising construction allows the conjunctions, relative pronouns and aspect-markers to be dropped, making possible a condensed, compact noun-like formulation which is nonetheless internally complex. In some cases *oriki* go beyond the rules of ordinary grammar, and attach nominalising prefixes to whole sentences without converting them first into noun-phrases. This happens in the *oriki* of the great farmer already quoted:

> Àyìndé alágbàdo-ègbo-lóko
> Babaà-mi-agbìngbàdo-èwà-lótò
> Àyìndé alágbàdo-iṣáájú
> Baba Ojútọ́mọrí, ní í gbani lọ́wọ́ ebi.

Ayinde, *one who* has maize for pottage in his farm
My father, *one who* plants maize for pudding separately
Ayinde, *owner of* 'maize that ripens before other people's'
Father of Ojutọmọri, 'is what saves one from hunger'.

In the third and fourth lines of this excerpt, *al-* meaning 'owner of' is attached
to the whole sentence *àgbàdo iṣááju ní í gbani lọ́wọ́ ebi*, 'it is early maize that
saves one from hunger'. The effect is to attribute the whole *idea* to Ayinde,
as if it were a favourite saying of his, or a saying particularly associated with
him, and therefore already half-way to becoming an *oriki*. Thus nominalisation
in *oriki* is more flexible and more accommodating than in ordinary speech.
Long complex phrases and even whole sentences can be brought in under
cover of a nominal epithet and made to behave like a noun.

Another structural device in *oriki* for rendering statements into names is
the frequent use of *ọmọ...*, 'child of', which can be put at the head of a line or
even a whole passage of text and has the effect of making everything that
follows into an attribution. In the *oriki* of Ọjọmu's compound, for instance,
we hear:

Ọmọ odó nigi
Ìkòkò lamọ̀
Ọmọ ìyí la yídó
Kẹ́ni má yìí'kòkò
Bẹ́ni bá yíkòkò
Inú alámọ̀ á bàjẹ́.

Child of 'The mortar is made of wood
The pot is made of clay'
Child of 'The mortar can be rolled
Let no-one roll the pot
If anyone rolls the pot
The potter will be distressed'.

'Child of' here means 'descendant of people who own the following
attributions', or 'one of the people who can be called by the following names'.
Ọmọ presents what follows it as an expression which can be applied attributively
to a subject. Even when it introduces a long connected passage, the whole
passage is as it were in quotation marks: it is not a simple statement but a
statement which belongs to someone, or some group, as a name does.

The compression and laconic terseness so characteristic of the style of *oriki*
makes each unit manageable as a name-like formulation. Obscurity and
allusiveness are the result of a deliberate process of packing extensive
meanings into a brief phrase. This gives *oriki* their quality of 'heaviness': they
are dense with an implicit significance which is known to be there even when
people do not know what it is. To work as names, they must be compact and

condensed, encapsulating meanings rather than displaying them, and indicating that there are narratives to be told rather than narrating them. Just as given names can be abbreviated or expanded, so can *oriki*: they are quotable and attributable items. But they go beyond mere names, and become signatures: names imprinted with the distinctive personality of their bearers, from which much more can be read than is at first put on view. It is *oriki* that the drummers play to announce a visitor's arrival at the palace, for the *oriki* is heavier, more memorable, more identifiable from its form alone, and more significant than the visitor's ordinary names.

The performer of *oriki* continually reminds the hearers that what she is doing is naming her subject. She can do this by interjecting the subject's given names – his *abiso* – again and again into the *oriki* text. This is a way of calling the subject's attention to what is being said to him, of insisting that he give his total and undivided attention to the performance, and of underlining the fact that the whole performance is in the vocative case. The incessant interjection of personal names is one of the most recognisable features of *oriki* style. The personal names are an interruption into the *oriki* text; but they are also clearly *in apposition* to the *oriki*, reminding us that the *oriki* too are being used attributively in relation to a given subject. We have already seen a number of examples of this; let me quote again the *oriki* of Ayinde, the great farmer:

> Ayinde, one who has maize for pottage on his farm
> My father, one who plants maize for pudding separately
> Ayinde, owner of 'maize that ripens before other people's'
> Father of Ojutọmọri, 'is what saves one from hunger'.

When the singer interrupts herself to call 'My father!' she seems to be addressing the subject directly. 'Father of Ojutọmọri' is even more of an interruption, breaking as it does right through a nominalised sentence ('maize that ripens before other people's is what saves one from hunger'), and seems obviously to be addressed to the listening subject. 'Ayinde', interjected twice, occupies a position that could be both vocative and nominative: 'Ayinde is a person who has maize...', or 'Ayinde, listen to me, you are a person who has maize...' In either case, the name 'Ayinde' is parallel to the *oriki* that follows it. The performer may also quite explicitly inform us, after a long passage of *oriki*, 'That is what they call so-and-so', or '... is worthy to be attributed to so-and-so'. At the end of the passage honouring the great *babalawo*, quoted above, the performer tells us 'This is what father of Faronkẹ is worthy to be called'.

In the Enigboori excerpt quoted and analysed in detail in the second chapter, the performer uses both these ways of making attribution explicit. In the space of only seven lines, she addresses Babalọla directly four times and ends up '...*ni wọn ń ki baba Bánlẹ́bu*', '...is how they salute the father known as Banlẹbu':

<u>Ewu child of Alao</u>, the first steps of the child delight its mother
<u>Babalola</u>, the child opens its arms, the child delights its father
The way my father walks delights the Iyalode
<u>Eniigbori, child of the father named Banlebu</u>
If people don't find me in the place where they boil *ijokun* dye
They'll meet me where we go early to pound indigo
<u>Eniigbori, that's how they salute the father known as Banlebu.</u>

Thus we are never allowed to forget that when the performer utters *oriki*, what she is doing is bestowing on the subject a plethora of elaborations of, and alternatives and equivalents to, his own names. Even quite long passages of *oriki orilẹ*, often patterned and with a certain amount of narrative development, can be rounded up and presented to the subject as an attribution by the use of devices such as these.

The autonomy of *oriki*, then, is like the autonomy of names; and *oriki* are therefore equivalent to each other and interchangeable in the manner of names. At one level, each unit of *oriki* is quite separate, inhabiting its own universe of reference; but at another level, it is equivalent to all the other units belonging to the same subject. They are interchangeable in the sense that they are all alternative ways of addressing the same subject. A unit can be substituted for, or added to, others without altering the nature of what is being done. Like names, the units can be performed in any order, and any selection from the total can be made. It is this that makes the text radically unlike the texts that common sense European criticism defines as 'poems'. The name-like quality of *oriki* units makes it possible for a performer to vary the order from one performance to the next; to perform a different selection from the corpus each time; and to repeat units at will, returning to them again and again if she wishes. This means that the 'text' can be highly unstable. Each performance of a given subject's *oriki* will be different from all others. Habit and a kind of thematic drift does lead, in some performers' productions, to a 'silting-up' effect, where certain units tend to appear in the same order each time. This is particularly true of *oriki orilẹ*, the most widely-known and often-recited of *oriki*. But in principle there is nothing to prevent the performer from breaking up these clusters. Indeed, there is an aesthetic preference for variation and surprise in performance, the most skilled performers producing the most fluid and variable texts, as we shall see in the next chapter.

It is because the constituent units of a chant are not only autonomous but also equivalent to each other that the form of a chant is not produced out of its determinate internal relationships, and there is no 'sense of an ending'. Since any unit could equally well occupy any position in the performance, and any unit that has been left out could equally well replace any one that has been included, there can be no boundaries to the chant that could be said to have been determined by its inner structure. More units could be added indefinitely without altering the 'form' of the chant. To close it, the performer needs signposts, clear formulas that will signal to the audience that she intends to stop.

The 'naming' that *oriki* do is of a specific effectuality. When a performer utters *oriki*, she addresses herself intensely and exclusively to the subject, whether he or she is living or dead, human or spiritual being. In a festive gathering she will address many subjects, often interrupting her chant to turn to an important newcomer or moving from person to person in a circle of auditors. But as long as she is addressing one person, she concentrates entirely on him. If the subject is a living human, present at the performance, she can be seen leaning towards him, bestowing her words on him, almost visibly creating and maintaining a powerful dyadic bond. And the subject is visibly affected. He appears locked into the relationship, galvanised by what he is hearing; he seems to expand, to take on afflatus, and to be profoundly moved. Much of what the performer does can be seen in terms of strategies of insistence. She asks the recipient again and again 'Are you listening to me?', 'Are you attending to what I am doing?', 'These are your *oriki*'. By calling him, interjecting his names into the chant and by continually reminding him that *oriki* are equivalents and alternatives to these names, she engages him in an intense dialogue in which, though silent, he is constitutive of her discourse. The vocative is also evocative. *Oriki* call a subject's qualities to life, and allow them to expand.

Uttering a subject's *oriki* is thus a process of empowerment. The subject's latent qualities are activated and enhanced. This is true of all subjects. A living human being addressed by *oriki* will experience an intense gratification. He or she has associated *oriki* since earliest childhood with affection, approval and a sense of belonging to a group. At the same time that your *oriki* offer you the security of group membership, they confer on you alone – as long as the performance goes on being addressed to you – the marks of distinction. The recipient of an *oriki* performance is deeply moved and elated. Many recipients respond by giving the performer more money than they can afford. To describe the experience, people say *Orí mi wú*, 'My head swelled' – an expression used to describe the thrill and shock of an encounter with the supernatural, for instance if you meet a spirit on a lonely forest path. *Oriki* arouse the dormant qualities in people and bring them to their fullest realisation. The ọba is most fully an ọba, most securely located in his glory, when he is enhanced by the royal *oriki*. Warriors in the nineteenth century would be raised to the pitch of courage needed to go to battle by the stirring utterance of *oriki*. *Oriki* performers often seem to be screaming, so urgent and intense is the process of empowerment.

The dead, addressed by their *oriki*, can be recalled to the world of the living. It is in and through an *oriki* chant that the performer empowers and encourages the ancestor to return to the living household of his descendants. Offerings are made at the *oju oori*, the grave shrine inside the house, and kola is thrown in a simple form of divination to ascertain that the ancestor has accepted them. Now all that remains is for him actually to get up and come. But to do this, he needs to be empowered with the surge of energy that makes possible such transitions. This can only be provided by 'making his head swell' through the galvanising and enhancing properties of *oriki*. The ancestor's journey is pictured as an arduous one. The *oriki* singer may exhort him to spring up and make his way quickly over the great distance that separates the world of the living from that of the dead, but to stop and rest if it is too tiring:

> Babaà mi gbobì, yóò womọ
> Babaà mi rọ̀ wáyé o
> Pàrọ̀rọ̀ wá, o wáá jèéwó
> Babaà mi rọ̀ wáyé ọ wáá jiyọ̀ wáá jepo
> Babaà mi ń mutí àdáàgbẹ ẹ ṣe baba lọ́fẹ
> Babaà mi ọfẹrẹ gégẹ́ o
> Babaà mi ọ̀fẹ̀rẹ̀ gẹ̀gẹ̀
> Ọfẹrẹ fààfaa lẹtùú fò
> Porogodo làkókó sọgi
> Baba, òkè ì í láwèrè láyà
> Baba, bó bá mọ̀ lé ọ láyà ọ yà sinmi.[29]

> My father has accepted the kola, he will watch over our children
> Father, transmigrate back to earth
> Transmigrate, come back and eat *èéwó*[30]
> Father, transmigrate back to earth, come and eat salt, come and
>   eat palm-oil
> My father drinks from a never-drying fount of wine, tell father to
>   be sprightly
> My father, spring to your feet
> My father, spring to your feet
> The guinea fowl flies up as free as the air
> The woodpecker taps the tree with a rattling sound
> Father, heights never make the monkey lose his breath
> But father, if it's tiring you, stop and rest.

Thus *oriki* make possible the crossing from the world of the dead to the world of the living, making the past present again.

Orịṣa and other spiritual beings are treated in the same way: *oriki* uttered to them both empower them, and localise them in the human community whether through possession or more simply by securing their presence at a shrine. Every fourth day, an *orịṣa*'s devotees perform an early-morning ceremony at its household shrine. Food or just kola is offered; the *orịṣa*'s acceptance is solicited; prayers and incantations are uttered; and one of the women chants the *oriki* of the *orisa*. Without the *oriki*, the presence of the *orisa* could not be secured. On bigger occasions the performance is of course more spectacular. At the Sango festival, the most important ceremony is the public possession of the head priest in the oba's market place. The devotees and the public gather; the devotees form a circle and begin to dance round in single file, singing cult songs. Then three women, each with a few supporters, separate themselves from the circle and take up positions outside it. These women begin to call on Sango with his *oriki*. The *bata* drummers back them. The women start their chant in an orderly fashion, taking it in turns to chant the *oriki* and allowing their supporters time to repeat the chorus after each line. But they steadily become more impassioned. They step up the pace, interrupting each other more and more until they are all shrieking at the tops of their voices. As the sound reaches its greatest intensity, the priest, who has been waiting at the side of the arena, suddenly leaps up and with a great answering cry of 'Hooo!' rushes into the centre, rapidly stripping off his outer garments, leaving only a pair of purple velvet shorts. Bare-chested and staring-eyed, he rushes into the centre of the circle, scattering the dancers. The *oriki* chanters follow him, singing his praises ecstatically, while the crowd flees. He then begins a series of stunts and feats that convince the onlookers he is indeed possessed: Sango has been called down from his place '*lágbede méjì ayé òun òrun*' ('half-way between heaven and earth') by the frenzied chanting of his *oriki*, and has entered and transfigured the human devotee.

Equally dramatic effects are achieved when *egungun* – ancestral masquerades – are saluted with their *oriki*. Each family takes great competitive pride in its own *egungun*'s ferocity, especially the families that possess *eegun alagbo*, the masquerades that carry medicines and parade round the town, overturning market stalls and terrifying innocent by-standers.[31] But the power of *egungun* depends on human action to maintain and restore it. After being kept in store for two years (the festival is biennial) the *egungun* has become limp and feeble; its powers have to be deliberately restored by human action. This takes the form of making a sacrifice to its head – dripping the blood of a decapitated chicken over the mask – and at the same time, chanting its *oriki*. Human attention can also have longer term effects on the *egungun*. The royal *egungun* Paje used to be much more savage 'in the old days' than it is now. Its priest told me: 'This *egungun* was more ferocious in the old days, we tamed him. If we want him to become ferocious again we'll make sacrifice to his head and we'll salute him with his *oriki* over and over again. If we keep on like that saluting and saluting him, he'll get up, he'll begin to rush around, he'll threaten people. Everyone will run away!'. When an *egungun*'s powers have been diminished over a long period they can only be restored by intensive and prolonged utterance of *oriki*. It is not the *oriki* by themselves but the process of attributing them, the action of uttering them and directing them at the subject, that is effectual. The longer you go on, the more effectual it will be:

À á kì í, kì í, kì í – 'we'll salute and salute and salute him'.

Oriki performance then is not just a matter of piling up prestigious and reputation-enhancing encomia. It actually effects changes of state. The subject is translated. The living human is translated into his own fullest existence: *oriki* awake his potential powers and expand the social space he occupies. The spiritual world is translated into the human world, brought in and localised; but this implies not domestication so much as an intensification of the powers of the spiritual beings. It is by being invoked, called upon, that the *orisa* or *egungun* attains its most concentrated being. The past is translated into the present: great men and women of the past are called on to be present in the affairs of their descendants and to lend them some transmitted glory. *Oriki* can do this because they are felt to encapsulate, in compressed and concentrated form, the very essence of their subjects' natures. They hold the 'secret' of the subject – the principles of its being – and their utterance releases its true powers. *Oriki* must be addressed to the subject, whether present or absent, living or dead; and it is the intense one-to-one bond between utterer and recipient that allows the utterance to be effectual. *Oriki*, that is, open channels between beings through which powers can pass and potentials emerge.

The centre of the chant, then, is the subject himself or herself. He or she is the living instance and occasion for it: not just the 'hearer' or the 'audience', but the heart of the performance and the very principle of its constitution. Each unit of the text is directed to him or her. Whatever their origins, separate and often untraceable as they are, all of the units of a corpus in performance converge at this point. Seen as a finished artefact, the 'text' may seem to disintegrate into a jumble of fragments; heard in action, the principle of its coherence becomes apparent. As so often, this principle is continually referred to by the performer herself, in the act of performance. She frequently reminds both the subject and other listeners that in uttering *oriki* she is bestowing on him the greatest of gifts, a heightened state of being.

The effectuality of *oriki* lies in the intensity and length of the process of salutation. The more epithets a performer bestows on her subject's head, the more effectual the process. If a chant seems to have no sense of an ending, no closure, this is precisely the impression the performer wants to create: she wants you to think that she could go on forever. In *rara iyawo* the bride can boast:

> Máa wí máa wí ní í sodó iyán
> Máa rò máa rò ní í sorógùn okà
> Bé e ní n wí mo lè wí dòla
> Isé mi ni, òwò mi ni
> Éè í sú mi
> Éè í rè mí...[32]

'Speak on, speak on', that's the way of the pestle

'Keep talking, keep talking', that's the way of the stirring-stick
If you want me to speak, I could speak until tomorrow
It's my work, it's my trade
I never weary of it
I don't get bored with it...

Profusion is highly valued. Cleanth Brooks, doyen of American New
Critics, urged that criticism 'reject the obese poem, the overstuffed poem'
(Brooks, 1947, p. 221). But the fatter and more fully-furnished an *oriki* chant,
the more gratifying to the recipient.

The impulse to profusion is what underlies the incorporativeness of *oriki*
– an incorporativeness so far-reaching that it has created doubts about
whether to define *oriki* as a genre or as a material. *Oriki* chants seem to be a
category which swallows everything and leaks into everything, exhibiting a
boundarilessness which goes well beyond the constitution of individual
performances. The performer, in addressing a subject, will seize on materials
from whatever source is available: not only from other *oriki* corpuses, but from
other literary genres too. With a skilled sleight of hand she will convert these
diverse materials to attributions for her subject.

Borrowing personal *oriki* from other individuals is so common that there
is a permanently-available stock of unanchored attributions, applicable to
whoever qualifies – the skilled *babalawo*, the great hunter or medicine man,
the successful farmer. The great majority of epithets thought of as 'belonging'
to a particular person in Okuku turn out, on further investigation, to have
entered the corpus of at least one other person. People often take over *oriki*
from a particular person of their acquaintance, sometimes on quite tenuous
grounds. Enquiring about an obscure epithet I heard in a performance in
honour of the Oluọdẹ (the Head of the Hunters) of Okuku, I was told that it
was a personal *oriki* acquired by the Oluọdẹ of Igbaye, a neighbouring town.
Since they were both Heads of Hunters, the Oluọdẹ of Okuku felt he was
entitled to share the *oriki*, even though this particular epithet made no reference
to hunting. Specialist performers frequently bestow on their subjects *oriki* that
they have learnt elsewhere. The *oriki* of *orisa* – contrary to the assumptions of
many scholars of Yoruba religion – also float and are borrowed by devotees
seeking material with which to enhance the reputation of their own divinity
(see Barber, 1981b and 1990b). Even *oriki orile*, which are often described as
the most stable and clearly demarcated of *oriki* – defining, as they do, large and
enduring social units – seem to tolerate a considerable degree of overlap.[33] It
is therefore impossible to conceive of *oriki* as belonging to clearly defined
corpuses each of which belongs exclusively to one subject. Despite the fact
that *oriki* are felt to encapsulate the essential character of each subject – its
difference and distinctiveness – it is in practice impossible to draw a definitive
line around any subject's corpus, even at the abstract level of the total

potential units any performer could know.

Oriki are like a material rather than a genre in the sense that they can be performed in numerous different modes. Certain performances are referred to simply as '*oriki*': for example, the recitation, in a speaking voice, of *oriki orile*, as a morning greeting or to congratulate or honour someone. But, as we have seen, there are other performances which have their own names: like *ijala*, the hunters' chant, *iwi*, the chant of the *egungun* performers, *rara* the royal bards' chant, *rara iyawo* (in standard Yoruba, *ẹkun iyawo*) the bride's lament, and countless localised performance modes such as *olele* (in Ijẹsa), *alamọ* (in Ekiti) and so on. These chants are distinguishable by their vocal qualities and their musical contours (see Vidal, 1977, Olukoju, 1978), but all of them are constructed from the same basic material: *oriki* of various kinds. Each chant concentrates on the *oriki* appropriate to the context for which it is being performed: in *ijala*, the *oriki* of animals and those of Ogun, the hunters' god, are prominent; in *iwi* the *oriki* of Ologbojo, the legendary founder of the *egungun* cult, are usually included. Some chants also include a good deal of supplementary material relating to their function. The performer of *iwi* is an entertainer, and will include jokes, advice and topical comments with the *oriki*. The performer of *rara iyawo* is a bride, leaving her family in solemn circumstances, and she has a large repertory of laments, expressions of gratitude and farewell to her people, and reflections upon her impending change of status. But in their core content, and in their form, all these chants are the same; their features derive from the possibilities inherent in the form of *oriki*. This dual existence, as a genre ('*oriki*') and as a building block of other genres (such as '*ijala*', '*iwi*', '*rara*' and '*ẹkun iyawo*') has led Ọlatunde Ọlatunji to devise a two-pronged classificatory system which distinguishes 'feature types', recognisable by internal formal features (e.g. *oriki, ẹsẹ Ifa*, proverbs, incantations) and 'chanting modes', recognisable by the manner of vocal realisation (e.g. *ijala, iwi, ẹkun iyawo*). He explains that not only are chanting modes built up out of materials provided by the feature types, but also one feature type may incorporate another – *oriki* may use a proverb, *ẹsẹ Ifa* may contain *oriki*, and so on (Ọlatunji, 1973, 1984).

This is a helpful approach which avoids many of the problems encountered by any attempt to impose a single system of classification of genres on Yoruba oral literature. But its very success as a scheme means that it does not correspond to local practice. In Okuku at least, there is no exhaustive and systematic classification of genres of oral literature. *Oriki* as a basic and irreducible source from which many performances are derived is always acknowledged; any question about the meaning of an item abstracted from an *oriki*-based chant is likely to draw the response, '*Oriki ni*', 'It's *oriki*', as if this were all that needed to be said. But not all performances – in fact, very few of the total range – have a name that corresponds to Ọlatunji's idea of the 'chanting mode'. In Okuku, the only named chanting modes based on *oriki* are *ijala*, *iwi* and *rara iyawo*. Each of these is specialised in some way. *Ijala* belong exclusively to the guild of hunters, *iwi* to the association of *egungun* entertainers, while *rara iyawo*, though learnt by all girls, are performed only once, in very special circumstances, in each girl's life. These modes are therefore marked out from the broad many-stranded stream of daily household performance, which is not named. If you ask 'What kind of performance is that? What is it called?', people are likely to reply '*Ó ń ki ènìyàn ni*' (She's saluting people) or, if the subject is a water divinity, '*Ó ń pàgbo ni*' (She's saluting the medicinal infusion [made from the sacred water]), and if the occasion is a funeral and the subject is the deceased person, '*Ó ń pòkú ni*', (She's calling the dead). In other words, the performance is conceived not as a classifiable object – a genre – but as an activity defined in terms of the circumstances which occasion it.

But the indefiniteness that surrounds the concept '*oriki* chant' is not only the result of local lack of interest in genre classification. It arises, more fundamentally, from the porous and disjunctive form of *oriki*, which permits performances to be extremely incorporative. An *oriki* chant makes use of all kinds of materials. Proverbs, for instance, are always ready to hand, and a skilled performer may use strings of them. Often they are used not as a straight commentary on life from the persona of the performer, but attributively, as a piece of wisdom associated in some way with the subject:

> Ọmọ Abógunrìn, ọmọ Àdìó eléte ò pa lójú ẹni
> Baba mi, ẹhìn ẹni là á gbìmọ̀ràn ìkà
> Àdìó bọ́ ọ gbọ́ bọ́ ọ lọ́ ò gbọ́
> Abógunrìn baba mi o lémi ní ń ṣe fúnni?
> Ọmọ ìṣẹ́ lẹ̀kọ-àjọmu tó bí mi
> Baba mi, ìyà ni ṣòkòtò àkitibọ̀
> Bí ò fún wọn lẹ́sẹ̀ á mú wọn doókún
> Akíntáyọ̀ baba mi ó ní ohun ẹni ní í mọni lára.

> Child of Abogunrin, child of Adio, 'the plotter doesn't plot before
>   your eyes'
> My father, 'It's behind your back they make their evil schemes'
> Adio, 'If you hear about it and say you didn't hear',
> Abogunrin my father said, 'what harm can it do you?'
> Child of 'Sharing the hot gruel's an inconvenience' who bore me
> My father, 'Sharing a pair of trousers is a pain'
> 'If they're not too tight in the legs, they'll be cramped at the knees'
> Akintayo my father, he said, 'Having one's own things is really
>   more convenient'.

All these sayings are well-known reflections on human society, identifiable as *owe* (proverbs) and with an independent existence outside the context of the *oriki* performance. At the same time, they are chosen because they express views which fit very well with the philosophical ambiance of personal *oriki*, belonging as they do to the ruthless struggle between competing big men. The world is deceptive; people who appear well disposed may be scheming against you behind your back; it is undesirable to be dependent on other people – having to share one's breakfast or one's trousers with someone else leads to problems, and, by implication, so does any other over-close association with another person. It is good to be detached, independent, indifferent to the machinations of one's fellows. All these sayings are quoted as the characteristic utterances of the subject, Abogunrin: 'Abogunrin my father said...', 'Akintayọ my father, he said...', suggesting perhaps that he was in the habit of making philosophical remarks of this kind. But the association of the subject with the proverbs goes further than this. The implication is that Abogunrin's behaviour exemplified the lesson taught by the proverbs: he himself was a living proverb, remaining aloof and undeceived by his fellow-citizens. Whether he actually said these things or not is irrelevant; he deserves to have the proverbs associated with his name for a better reason. Thus the proverb itself becomes an *oriki*, an alternative to a name, and the subject can be addressed as 'Child of "Sharing the hot gruel's an inconvenience" who bore me'. 'Sharing-the-hot-gruel's-an-inconvenience' here clearly stands in the place of a name, turned into one by the familiar and simple technique of prefacing the expression with *ọmọ...*, child of, like so many other *oriki*.

But much more substantial texts than proverbs or series of proverbs can be equally easily incorporated into an *oriki* chant. In a salutation of members of *ile* Aro-Isalẹ, Ṣangowẹmi at one point launched into the following excursion:

> Àkàndé ọmọ 'Ṣòfẹ́ ṣèlérí', ọmọ 'ọrọ̀ nísàn'
> Ìgbà ẹ̀ẹ̀kíní tí mo mẹ́gbàá jó
> Ìgbà ẹ̀ẹ̀kèjì tí mo tún mẹ́gbàá lù
> Ìgbà ó wáá dẹ̀ẹ̀kẹta àtàtà
> Àkàndé, mo wáá kúkú mẹ́gbàáà mi wálé
> Mo wá i kó kéré ó dinú oko o
> Mo wáá délé
> Ìwọ lọmọ 'Bóǹgbó ò gbó
> Emi loǹgbìn ó gbìn?
> Bóngbìn ò gbìn,
> Emi loǹhù ó hù?
> Bóǹhù ò hù
> Emi loǹdàgbà ó dàgbà?
> Bóǹdàgbà ò dàgbà
> Emi loǹtanná ó tanná?
> Bóǹtanná ò tanná
> Emi loǹso ó so?

Bóṅso ò so, Ayọ̀délé,
Emi loṅlà ó là?
Bóṅlà ò là
Àkàndé, emi loṅyọ ó yọ?
Bónyọ ò yọ
Emi loṅjá ó jàá, Bánkọ́lé Ayọ̀délé Gbọtifáyọ̀?
Bóṅjá ò já, ọmọ Abẹ́gun-légbẹrẹ,
Emi loṅtà ó tà?
Bóṅta ò tà
Emi lóṅdá ó dàá?
Bóṅdá ò dá ńlée wọn
Emi lóṅká ó kàá?
Bóṅká ò ká,
Emi lóṅtà ó tà?
Gbà oṅtà wáá tà tán, Ṣọ̀fẹ́-ṣelérí,
Em'oṅpÀsàndé ó pÀsàndé?
Bí Aláràn-án ò rán, emi leégún fi ṣé
Ọmọ Abẹ́gun-légbẹrẹ, ògògó mo i pajàá Mòjè.

Akande child of 'Get gifts and promises', child of 'Wealth at Isan'
The first time that I took sixpence to the dance
The second time that I gave sixpence to the drummers
When it came round to the third time
Akande, I just brought my sixpence home
I used it to buy cotton seed, I took it into the farm
I came home
You are the child of 'If the winnowers don't winnow
What will the planter plant?
If the planter doesn't plant
How will the sprouter sprout?
If the sprouter doesn't sprout
How will the grower grow?
If the grower doesn't grow
How will the bloomer bloom?
If the bloomer doesn't bloom,
How will the fruiter fruit?
If the fruiter doesn't fruit, Ayodele,
How will the splitter split?
If the splitter doesn't split,
Akande, how will the comer-out come out?
If the comer-out doesn't come out,
How will the picker pick, Bankọle Ayọdele Gbọtifayọ?
If the picker doesn't pick, child of Abẹgun-lẹgbẹrẹ

What will the spinner spin?
If the spinner doesn't spin,
What will the buyer buy?
If the buyer doesn't buy in their lineage,
What will the folder fold?
If the folder doesn't fold
What will the seller sell?'
When the seller has finished selling, 'Get gifts and promises',
With what will the praiser of Asande praise Asande?
If the people of Aran don't sew clothes, how will the masquerade
    dress to come out?

What we have here, starting from '*Bóngbìn ò gbìn*' ('If the planter doesn't plant') and going right up to '*Bóntà ti tà tán*' ('When the seller has finished selling'), is an extended sequential poem, known as *arọ*, which used to be recited by children in the old days as part of moonlight story-telling sessions.[34] It traces the stages of cotton cultivation – the planting, growth, harvest, processing – culminating in the production and sale of cloth. Mastery of a long poem of this type would have been an exercise of memory for the child, getting it right a *tour de force*, and the riddle-like formulations (*ongbìn, onhù, ondàgbà* and so on – the planter, sprouter, grower – are, as in English, odd-sounding nonce-words made up to intrigue) a source of great amusement. Ṣangowẹmi too includes the passage as a *tour de force*, but in her performance there is an extra skill involved – the skill of attaching this long, independent and apparently irrelevant text to the *oriki* of her subject. She does so with ease, casually and almost inconsequentially. The opportunity to introduce it arises as she repeats some of the *oriki orilẹ* of *ile* Aro-Isalẹ, her subject's compound, related to *ile* Baalẹ and sharing with them the distinction of being associated traditionally with the *egungun* entertainment masquerade. The *oriki orilẹ* revolve around the theme of professional entertainment, the lineage members' skills as performers, and the rewards they get from the public ('Get gifts and promises', 'Child of Wealth at Isan'). The young people of the lineage are supposed to be irresistibly drawn to drumming and dancing, and to attending the performances of strolling players. A young man who has sixpence will spend it on drummers rather than serious things. But if the drummers do not play, he will bring the sixpence home and spend it on seed for his farm instead. The seed sprouts, grows, flowers, bears fruit, splits its pod, and produces cotton which is spun, woven and sold. At the end, Ṣangowẹmi turns the whole lengthy *jeu d'esprit*, by a kind of sleight of hand, into an elaborate salute to her subject:

When the seller has finished selling, 'Get gifts and promises'
With what will the praiser of Asande praise Asande?

The entire sequence is thus made to look as if it led up to this conclusion: every stage of the cotton cycle is seen, after the event, as a metaphor for the process of praising. If the farmer does not plant the seeds, cotton will not grow; if the praise-singer does not have materials, she will not be able to praise her subjects. As so often, the performer is doing her job and reflecting upon it at the same time. Her conclusion to this passage reveals the importance, to the performer, of laying her hands on textual materials with which to fill out her chant. She has just demonstrated, in the use of the *arọ*, what good use she can make of these borrowed texts. Finally, for good measure, she ties in the passage not just with Asande as an individual ('With what will the praiser of Asande praise Asande?'), but also with the *oriki orilẹ* of his lineage, with which she began. The cotton cycle results in cloth; cloth is the principal prop and symbol of the masqueraders:

> If the people of Aran don't sew clothes, how will the masquerade
>   dress to come out?

Thus we are brought back to where we began. And all of this display, the performer makes clear, is done in Asande's honour and attributed to him.

If other genres provide ready-made materials which can effortlessly be incorporated into *oriki* chants, then the stock of materials on which the chanter can draw to produce any given realisation of her competence becomes incalculably wide. 'Oral tradition' appears less like a hierarchy of classified and boundaried genres and more like a vast pool of textual resources into which the performer can dip at will.[35] An *oriki* chant, then, is *essentially* incorporative; its centreless and boundariless form makes it endlessly accommodating. Its mode is to subsist by swallowing other texts.

Clearly, the appropriate starting point in approaching such a performance is not a concept of a definable, demarcated genre, but an apprehension of process. The way *oriki* are constructed, out of a multiplicity of quasi-autonomous, equivalent and interchangeable fragments, in a fluid, incorporative and agglomerative mode, suits their purpose perfectly. If *oriki* simultaneously bring to realisation the potential of unique individuals, and remove categorial barriers that hinder the flow of power from one being to another, it is their apparent formlessness that enables them to do so.

The performer exploits the possibilities inherent in this form to achieve remarkable effects. What has been discussed so far is the fundamental character of *oriki* in general. All *oriki* performances are a process of naming, all are composed of textual items that are name-like in structure and function, and all involve a transcendence or transformation of state, whether mild or dramatically powerful. But, like the word itself in Vološinov's account [Vološinov (Bakhtin) 1973a] this protean and polysemic form is always only potentially meaningful until it enters into a specific context whose parameters define and pin down the utterance. *Oriki* are performed in a multiplicity of contexts and with a multiplicity of intents. These factors enter into the chant and are perceptible in both their form and their content. Some performances are more fluid than others, some are more patterned, connected and stable. Some contain a great variety of different kinds of materials, others are relatively homogeneous. Some are private utterances, some are public set-pieces. Only by looking at concrete performances in particular circumstances can the potentialities of the form be apprehended.

4

CONTEXTS OF PERFORMANCE

1. THE VARIETY OF STYLES

The same *oriki* can be performed in strikingly different styles – not usually identifiable as discrete genres, but occupying a continuum from the relatively fixed to the relatively fluid, the relatively coherent to the relatively fragmented, the relatively homogenous to the relatively heterogeneous. I begin this chapter by comparing two passages which both contain the same *oriki orilẹ*, those of the Ale-Ọyun people, represented in Okuku by *ilé* Ọlọkọ. The first is from a performance of *rara iyawo* (bride's lament) by a young girl practising with her friends before her wedding day. The second is from a performance by Ṣangowẹmi on the occasion of the Ogun festival; it is addressed primarily to the Oluọdẹ, the Head of the Hunters, who was a prominent elder in *ilé* Ọlọkọ. The two passages are at opposite ends of the stylistic continuum.

Rara iyawo is the first performance style a girl learns, in her childhood and adolescence. The style is simple and easily mastered. It is also the least characteristic of *oriki* chants, in the sense that the features discussed in the last chapter – the intense vocative mode, the interjections, the insertion of personal names, and so on – are at their least developed. Ṣangowẹmi's chant, by contrast, displays these features in their most full-blown form, taking them almost to extremes.

This difference is partly to be understood in terms of the stages of the learning-process. Women master chanting styles gradually, starting with *rara iyawo* and moving on, as they gain maturity and experience, to more complex and fluid styles. This shows that the fragmentedness and apparent shapelessness of the mature woman's chant is not an accident, nor the mere outcome of 'orality': it is a hard-won, gradually attained skill, the product of long habituation and experience. The more experienced and artful the performer, the more fluid her performance. This chapter goes on, after the initial comparison of styles, to trace the development of women's mastery of them.

But variations in style also arise from the different purposes to which performances are put. The utterance of *oriki* always creates and maintains relationships: but the intensity, proximity, intimacy and indeed the point of these relationships depends on whom the performer is addressing and in what circumstances. The 'context' of performance can be seen as the whole web of social and spiritual links which, in any *oriki* chant, the performer draws on and recreates. Context in this sense is implicated in the innermost constitution of the chant. The focus and intent of a *rara iyawo* chant are unique in the whole repertoire of orientations available to a performer, and this is the main reason for the unusual stylistic features of the chant which enable it to be recognised as a distinct genre with its own name. After her marriage, the maturing woman is called upon to participate not just in one but in a whole range of expressive acts using *oriki*. Each performance shares the same fundamental properties, but each is also shaped by a specific intent and orientation. The occasions range from diurnal domestic greetings to formal, massed chants at a compound ceremony. In the last two sections of the chapter, I examine first the marriage ceremony and then a funeral to demonstrate the significance of 'context' in the formation of the specific textual properties of the chant. The example of the funeral demonstrates the range of styles that a complex social drama can call up, and the flexibility of the *oriki* chant as it is turned from one purpose to another.

(a) Rárà ìyàwó:

> Nígbà tí mò ń bọ̀ wáyé
> Màmáà mi, mo kóbì egbèje
> Nígbà tí mò ń bọ̀ wáyé
> Màmáà mi, mo kóbì ẹgbẹ̀fà
> Nítorí ikú kọ́, nítorí àrùn kọ́
> Nítorí orogún ayé
>
> Èyí tí í ṣe elénìní ọrun
> Orogún tí mo bá wù ó ní
> Ọmọ ará Òkín, n ni yóò ṣèyáà mi
> Ire lónìí oríì mi àfire.
>
> Iléè mi ni mo jókòó sí
> Òdẹ̀dẹ̀ mi ni mo tiẹ̀ wà
> Eléyín ní í jogún èrín
> Òun náà ló ní n wáá ṣikèjì òun
> Ire lónìí oríì mi àfire.
>
> Màmáà mi ṣe yayì tó wèmi
> Kò jé n tọrọ aṣọ lọ́wọ́ abúni
> Kò jé n tọrọ èwù lọ́wọ́ àwọn sègànsègàn
> Aṣọ èyí tó wù mí ni mò ń ró
> Kò jẹ̀ kí n ró kíjìpá làgboro
> Ire lónìí oríì mi àfire.

Lójó òní mo fẹ́ kìlú àwa
Àgbà ló jẹ́ 'mọ ará Ọ̀yọ́
Ọmọ ará Ọ̀yọ́ mo fẹ́ kìlú àwa o
Níbo ló jọlé?
Níbo ló sì wáá jọlé babaà mi?
Ọ̀yọ́ ló jọlé
Ọ̀yọ́ ló mọ̀ wáá jọlé babaà mi.
Àparò mélòó péré
N náà ló ń bẹ ní Ọ̀yọ́ àwa?
Àparò mẹ́ta péré
N náà ní ń bẹ ní Ọ̀yọ́ àwa.
Ọ̀kan ń ṣe ká ba ká ba
Ọ̀kan ń ṣe ká fò ká fò
Ọ̀kan ń ṣe ká fò piri ká relé Alé-Ọ̀yun.
Nígbà tó di lẹ́ẹ̀kìíní
Mo dáko súrú
Súúrú sùùrù súúrú sí Anlé-Ọ̀yun
Eṣú ṣe bí eré
Eṣú mú mi lóko jẹ
Nígbà tó dilẹ́ẹ̀kèjì ẹ̀wẹ̀
Mo tún dáko súrú
Súúrú sùùrù súúrú sÁnlé-Ọ̀yun
Eṣú ṣe bí eré
Eṣú mú mi lóko jẹ
Mo kéjóọ̀ mi ó dilé Alé-Ọ̀yun
Alé-Ọ̀yun ti ní tèmi ẹ̀bi ni.
Mo ní torí kí ni?
Ó ní ìgbà tí eṣú ò lóko tí ò lódò nkọ́,
Emi lọọ ní kéṣú ó mọọ jẹ?

...

Owó ọmọ ni mo ní ó bá mi ká lọ
Àní bíbẹ̀ un ò jọ̀nà, bíbẹ̀ un ò jọlé
Màá yáa tètè bókoòbò'mîin lọ
Mo gbágbè mo rỌ̀yọ́-ilé
Ọmọ Ọlóyòọ́'lé ti gbágbè lóríì mi
Mo ní baba, kí o pé, torí kí ni?
Ó ní torí Ògégerẹ́ ni mí
 Èmi tó rọ́rùn kó sègi
Ire lóníì oríì mi àfire.[1]

When I was coming to the world
My mother, I brought 1400 cowries' worth of kola
When I was coming to the world

My mother, I brought 1200 cowries' worth of kola
Not because of death, not because of disease
Because of the co-wives of this world,
The ones that bring their enmity from heaven.
Whatever co-wife I may chance to have,
Child of the Okin people, may she be a mother to me,
May good luck attend me today.

I was sitting quietly at home
I was staying quietly in my house
'The owner of good teeth inherits laughter'
It was he who said I should come and be his partner.
May good luck attend me today.

My mother did me proud, to my great satisfaction
She didn't let me go begging for cloth from abusive people
She didn't let me go begging for gowns from the scurrilous
I'm wearing this cloth that I like very much
She didn't let me go through the town dressed in *kijipa* [coarse
    cotton cloth]
May good luck attend me today.

Today I want to salute our town
He is a senior man, offspring of Oyo
Offspring of Oyo people, I want to salute our town.
Where might our home be?
And where might the home of my father be?
Oyo is our home
Oyo is the home of my father.
How many bushfowl
Are there in our Oyo?
There are only three bushfowl
In our Oyo.
One said 'Let's sit, let's sit'
One said 'Let's fly, let's fly',
One said, 'Let's whirr off and go to Ale-Oyun'.
The first time round
I made a little farm
A little tiny farm at Ale-Oyun
Locusts came as if in jest
Locusts ate my farm up.
The second time around
I made another little farm
A little tiny farm at Ale-Oyun

Locusts came as if in jest
Locusts ate my farm up.
I took my case to the palace of Ale-Ọyun.
Ale-Ọyun said I was in the wrong.
I said why?
He said, 'When the locusts have no farm and no river,
What do you expect the locusts to eat?'
...
Money and children, I say they should go with me
I say if that is not the way, if that is not the house
I'll quickly turn and go another way.
I took my calabash and went to Ọyọ town
The prince of Ọyọ took the calabash from off my head.
I said, Sir, excuse me, why did you do that?
He said it's because I am a slender beauty
I have a neck worthy to wear blue *ṣegi* beads
May good luck attend me today.

This excerpt is made up of five distinct sections, each of which is internally coherent. The end of each section is marked by an unvarying closing formula, '*Ire lónìí orìi mi àfire*' (May good luck attend me today) which could be said to be the hallmark of *rara iyawo* in Okuku: every performance uses it. Each section has a different theme. The first is a reflection on the prevalence of hostile co-wives and a prayer that in her new home she will meet only kindly ones. The second says that she, the bride, was quite happy at home until the bridegroom sought her out and persuaded her to become his wife. The third praises her mother for looking after her, providing her with suitable finery and thereby saving her from humiliation at the hands of malevolent gossips. The fourth and longest section is part of the *oriki orile* of *ile* Ọlọkọ. The last section – which occurs after other sequences of *oriki orile*, omitted in this quotation for reasons of space – also sounds like a quotation from the *oriki orile* of *ile* Ọlọkọ, this time connecting them with Ọyọ rather than Ale-Ọyun. But it is deftly turned into a comment on the bride herself, suggesting that her beauty makes her worthy of the bridal finery in which the performer would actually be dressed when she performs the chant in public on her wedding day.

The bride's chant therefore incorporates a variety of material in addition to *oriki orile*. These sequences, reflecting on her impending change of state, expressing her gratitude to her parents, her grief at having to leave or – as here – her pride in her husband-to-be, make up a large part of most performances of *rara iyawo*. They are not linked to each other nor performed in any set order: each sequence is self-contained, its closure clearly signalled by '*Ire lónìí orìi mi àfire*', and can be regarded as a single unit. Different brides will know a different range of units, and each will perform them in her own order, probably repeating several times those she knows or likes best. To this extent, a performance of *rara iyawo* is flexible.

But each sequence is invariably repeated almost word for word the same way. Each sequence is always completed before the bride moves on to another. And each owes its inner coherence to a high degree of patterning, based on structural parallelism and repetition. The performer moves through these sequences steadily and methodically, omitting nothing. In the section of *oriki orile*, for instance, the forward movement is initially slowed down by a pattern of question and answer, involving almost exact repetition: 'Where is home?/Where is the home of my father?/ Ọyọ is home/ Ọyọ is the home of my father'. The *oriki* per-taining to Ọyọ are then introduced through an elaborate figure of the three bushfowl, again presented through a repetitive question-and-answer sequence: 'How many bushfowl/Are there in our Ọyọ?/There are only three bushfowl/In our Ọyọ'. Each bushfowl in turn does an action which leads towards the key name, Ale-Ọyun, where the story of the locusts is set. This story – the heart of this particular *oriki* – is again set out step by step: 'The first time round....The second time around...' with full repetition at each stage. The result is a style that sounds stately and quaintly formal. Even though the bride is often nervous and tearful, and utters the lines at high speed, the measured, leisurely and methodical unfolding of each theme still makes itself felt. Lines are of even length, well marked with breath pauses and almost always end-stopped. There is almost no deviation from the theme, interpolation of other matters, or even interjection of vocatives apart from the standardised 'My mother...' (and, in other texts, 'My father', 'My brother', or 'My companions...'). There is heavy use of a few standard formulas, most notably 'May good luck attend me today', always used to close a section; but also 'Today I want to salute our town', a stock opening, and 'If that is not the way/ If that is not the house...', a way of announcing either closure of a section of *oriki orile* or the intention to embark on another one. *Rara iyawo*, then, are more predictable than other modes of *oriki* chanting: easy to remember and easy to follow. The style is transparent; though the inner meaning of the *oriki orile* is not at all self-evident, they are set out with an appearance of conscious lucidity.

(b) Ṣangowẹmi's chant:

> Akótipópó ọ kú ọdún o
> Ọdún ọdún ni ọdún ayọ̀ ni yóò ṣe
> Akótipópó ọmọ Ògúntónlówò
> N ò roko Ògúntónlówò n ò yẹ̀nà
> Ògòngògongọ làrán ọkọ Ṣaóyè
> Ajílóngbégbé ló wáá tó ọkọọ Jéjé ṣe, Àyìndé wáá ṣojú olóbò
>   bó ṣòkòtò
> Gbà tí olóbò ò gbà mọ́ baba gbé kàgbáa rẹ bọtan, ọmọ ẹkẹ́ re
>   ní Mọjà

Ìwànú ọmọ Òrándùn
Pẹ́ẹ́ ni wọn óò re jẹ̀gbẹ la múkú wá ń mú erin, olórí ọdẹ
  ajólù Ẹyọ̀
Àjẹ-fẹ̀hìntì ni mo jògbodò níwálẹ̀ òʼgà
Tọ́ ọ bá lè súnmú lásùnúnjù idà ẹlẹsuku ẹja ni wọn ń fi
  lani lẹ́nu
N óò yáa bẹ́ṣú relé Alé-Òyun, 'mọ bẹbẹ aṣọ, Ìwànú ọmọ
  Òrándùn
Ìwànú ni ìyá Òpó jẹ́, ó dìgbà ẹ̀ẹ̀kíiní mo dáko lÁlèé-Òyun
  nlé olórí-ọdẹ
Ẹṣú wáá jẹ mí lóko
Mo wáá kéjọ́ òhún rÒyọ́, Ọlóyọ̀ọ́ ti wí, ó léjọ́ọ̀ mi, ẹ̀bi ni
Èmi Àbèní ń pè ọ́, olórí ọdẹ, ajólù Ẹyọ̀
Ó wáá dìgbà kèjì èwè, mo kó ẹjọ́ọ̀ mi rÒyọ́, mo ní ẹṣú ń jẹ ń
  lóko
Ó ní ńgbà tí ẹṣú ò lóko tí ò lódò
Ó lémi ni ẹ ní késú ó mọ́ọ jẹ, ó ní omi ń bẹ lÁnlé-Òyun, ó
  ní ẹ mú fọṣọ
Ògẹ̀dẹ̀ tí ń bẹ lÁnlé-Òyun, ó lọ́mọdé ò gbọdọ̀ sa á jẹ...

Akotipopo greetings for the festival
This year's festival will be a festival of joy
Akotipopo son of Oguntonlowo
I don't hoe the farm, Oguntonlowo, I don't clear the path
'Jutting velvet', husband of Saoye
Ajilongbegbe is worthy to be the husband of Jeje, Ayinde
  went and took his trousers off in front of a female
When the female refused him, the father just stuck his
  legs back in his breeches again! – son of 'A good
  forked stick at Moja'
Iwanu child of Orandun
Suddenly, they'll go and eat yam pottage, 'Bring death and
  I'll bring an elephant', Head of the Hunters, one who
  dances to the sound of the Ẹyọ drum
I ate *ogbodo* yam till I couldn't stand up at Iwalẹ Ọga
If you wrinkle your nose too much they'll slit your mouth
  with a blade made of fish-fins
I shall go with the locust to the home of Ale-Oyun, child
  of voluminous cloth, Iwanu child of Orandun
Iwanu is the mother of the Opo people, the first time
  round
I made a farm at Ale-Oyun at the house of the head of the
  hunters

The locusts came and ate my farm
So I took my case to Ọyọ, the lord of Ọyọ said I was in
    the wrong
It is I, Abẹni, calling you, Head of the Hunters, one
    who dances to the sound of the Ẹyọ drum
Then the second time around, I took my case to Ọyọ, I said
    the locusts are eating my farm up
He said when the locusts have no farm and no river
He said what do you expect the locusts to eat, he said
    there's water at Ale-Ọyun, he said use it to wash
    clothes
The bananas that are at Ale-Ọyun, he said the children
    must not cut and eat them, it's dirty children
    that immerse their clothes in water, Iwanu child
    of Ọrandun....

This is Ṣangowẹmi at her most turbulent. Her delivery was like a rapid, jumbled cry, with sudden infrequent pauses of uneven length and a continual tumbling forward movement – so that whenever an utterance seemed to have reached its grammatical end she would tack something else on. Her breath-units were far longer than in *rara iyawo*: indeed it seemed to be part of her virtuoso technique to prolong them to the utmost.

Like the performers of *rara iyawo*, Ṣangowẹmi incorporates a variety of materials into her chant. But here it is not nearly as easy to see where one type of material ends and another begins. The chant does not fall into clearly marked segments, each treating a particular theme, as in the excerpt from *rara iyawo*. Instead it is an eclectic mixture of fragments hurled promiscuously on top of each other. It opens with greetings and good wishes appropriate to the occasion, the feast being held by Ogungbile the Head of the Hunters. Throughout the performance Ṣangowẹmi calls upon Ogungbile with a variety of names and appellations, insisting on his attention: 'Akotipopo', 'child of Oguntonlowo', 'Ajilongbegbe', 'Ayinde', 'Iwanu child of Ọrandun', 'Head of the Hunters'; some of these belong to Ogungbile in person, others to his father Oguntonlowo, or to more remote ancestors. All enhance his presence at the feast and all are bestowed on him by Ṣangowẹmi with this intent.

The *oriki* which she addresses to him before she reaches the theme of the locusts are fragmentary in the extreme, and often almost impenetrably obscure. ' "Jutting velvet", husband of Saoye' comes from the personal *oriki* of the 19th century ọba Adeọba, and was included because Jẹjẹ, the mother of Ogungbile and the wife of Oguntonlowo, was a direct descendant of this ọba. 'Ayinde took off his trousers in front of a female...' is a personal *oriki* belonging to Oguntonlowo, who was renowned for his exploits as a hunter and as a womaniser. This passage is a fragment of a longer and more explicit *oriki*, which according to Ṣangowẹmi was composed by Oguntonlowo's fellow-hunters to tease him. An elder of a neighbouring compound[2] explained that during the nineteenth century wars Oguntonlowo was carried as far as the Ijẹṣa town of Imẹsi, where he began laying siege to the local girls. Sometimes he was successful and sometimes not: if not, he would just tie up his trousers and move on to the next:

Ògúntónlówò n ò roko
Ògúntónlówò n ò yẹnà
Ó dóJẹ̀sà ó bá wọn dó 'Yìn-mí-nù'
Ògúntónlówò babaà mi ó dó ẹrú Ọwá kunkun bí ẹni ń lagi
Àyìndé wá ṣojú olóbò bọ́ ṣòkòtò
Gbà olóbò ò gbà mọ́, baba gbé kàgbáa rẹ bọtan

Oguntonlowo I don't hoe the farm
Oguntonlowo I don't clear the path
He fucked the Ijẹṣa, he fucked 'Leave-me-alone' [in Ijẹṣa
      dialect]
Oguntonlowo my father he fucked the subjects of the Ọwa
      [ọba of Ilẹṣa] like someone splitting logs
Ayinde went and took off his trousers in front of a
      female
When the female refused him, the father just stuck his
      legs back in his breeches again!

Other phrases are fragments of *oriki orilẹ* whose meaning and provenance I was unable to establish.

Ṣangowẹmi's exposition of the well-known locust story is similarly elliptical and broken up. No sooner has she announced the theme ('I will go with the locusts to Ale-Ọyun') than she takes off at a tangent with the interpolation 'Child of voluminous cloth, Iwanu child of Ọrandun', even adding 'Iwanu is the mother of the Opo people' before getting back to the story. The interjections continue: after the first phrase she adds 'in the house of the head of the hunters', after the second 'It is I Abẹni calling you, head of the hunters, one who dances to the sound of the Ẹyọ drum'. The story itself, instead of being methodically unfolded step by step as in the *rara iyawo*, proceeds apparently erratically in fits and starts. The narrator goes to Ọyọ to complain about the locusts straight away (not after the second occasion as in the *rara iyawo*) and is found guilty; but the reason for this is not given until the second visit, when the Lord of Ọyọ tells him/her 'What do you expect the locusts to eat?' This is the climax of the story, but Ṣangowẹmi proceeds instantly and without any indication of closure to another theme (the water, bananas and dirty cloth) which she links on with the greatest of ease. On paper her performance looks fragmented, but in performance, the dominant impression is of a sinuous and confident – some would say over-confident – fluidity, demonstrated by an almost reckless disposal of themes.

Two chants based on the same *oriki orilẹ*, therefore, can be realised in such different styles that the relationship between them is hardly recognisable. Here we have two texts each at an extreme pole of the fluidity-fixity continuum. The *rara iyawo* is made up of relatively long internally-coherent passages, each clearly demarcated and ostentatiously patterned. These passages are repeated with little variation in wording. Little attempt is made to introduce embellishments or to link one to the next except by a few well established formulas. Two kinds of materials are used in the chant – *oriki orilẹ* and special passages specific to the bride's status and condition. (Occasionally well-developed passages of personal *oriki* may also be included, but this is not common.) The two are kept distinct in the performance; after performing her laments and thanks to her parents, the bride may announce her intention to start on the *oriki orilẹ* by some such formula as 'Today I want to greet our town'. She may perform as many as four different *oriki orilẹ* (one for each of her grandparental lineages); but each is likely to be represented by only one or perhaps two themes (of which the locust story is an example) which will be given a full and extended treatment, expanded by repetition and patterned introductory structures. Ṣangowẹmi's performance on the other hand was characterised by great fluidity: no two performances in this style would ever be the same. Rather than elaborate a single theme at length, her procedure was to leap rapidly from theme to theme, breaking off abruptly, often saying only a brief phrase of an *oriki* before switching to something else, and interrupting any semblance of narrative continuity with persistent vocative interjections. These two performances differ therefore in regard to the degree of fragmentation or coherence; the degree of fluidity or fixity; and the degree of variety or homogeneity in the materials used. Other performances fall somewhere between these two extremes.

These differences are not determined by any recognised conventions or rules of genre. There are infinite degrees of variation along each of the axes described. Two broad factors, as I have suggested, shape the configuration of any performance: the experience and status of the performer; and the nature of the occasion and of the relationships being established in the performance.

2. THE MASTERY OF *ORIKI* PERFORMANCE

Although everybody who lives in Okuku acquires at least a latent knowledge of some of their own lineage's *oriki orilẹ* while still very young, it is only little girls who are expected to take part in performances of *oriki*-based chants. The few young boys who master oral poetic performance are those born into a family where there is a male specialist of some kind: a *babalawo*, who teaches his apprentices to chant the verses of the great Ifa corpus of divination poetry; a hunter expert in *ijala*; or, before its disbandment, the group of entertainment masqueraders in *ile* Baalẹ. Other boys are not expected to perform chants; at most, they will learn to join in the processional songs which accompany numerous 'outings' around the town – such as funeral parades or the biennial forays of the family *egungun* into the market, palace and public streets.

Young girls, however, begin to play a role in the public performance of all kinds of songs and chants from quite an early age. All through their childhood they accompany their mothers and older sisters on festival and funeral parades; they participate in the oral performance that underpins family rituals within the house; and they have their own songs that go with the games they play amongst themselves. By the time they are adolescent they are able to hold their own in the performance of the genre that is the special preserve of young women, *rara iyawo*. On the 'bride's day', the day before she goes to her husband's house, each bride is escorted by a party of younger girls from her compound. As the bride chants her laments and farewells, they provide a sympathetic chorus. Their role can be quite substantial; sometimes the performance develops into a dialogue where the chorus has almost as much to say as the bride:

Lílé:	Dúdúyẹmí abójò-ṣú o
	Lójọ́ òní mo rí mọ̀mọ́ọ̀ mi
	Ire lónìí orìí mi àfire.
Ègbè:	Lójọ́ òní elégbè gbóhùn rẹ o
	Elègbè gbóhùn rẹ ròkè o
	Elègbè ló lójọ́ òní o
	Ojọ́ òní elégbè gbóhùn rẹ o
	Ire lónìí orìí mi àfire.
	Lójọ́ òní ẹ má gbàgbé àwa o
	Ekèjì mi olùfẹ́
	Ekèjì mi ọ má gbàgbé àwa o
	Ire lónìí orìí mi àfire.
Lílé:	Kí ni n óò gbàgbé èyin ṣe o?
	Èmi èyin ò sọ̀rọ̀
	Sọ̀rọ̀ nínú onígbàgbé o
	Ekèjì mi kí ni n óò gbàgbé èyin ṣe o?
	Ire lónìí orìí mi àfire.
Ègbè:	A pe egúngún orí ò yá egúngún
	A pòrìṣà ṣe orí ò yórìṣà
	Nígbà tí àwa ń pè ọ́ o
	Ekèjì mi orí ò yá iwọ o
	Ire lónìí orìí mi àfire.[3]
Solo:	Duduyẹmi [Blackness-Suits-Me], dark as the
	threatening rain
	On this day I see my mother –

<blockquote>

            May good luck attend me today.

Chorus: On this day the chorus supports you resoundingly
            The chorus raises up your song on high
            It's the chorus that holds sway today
            This day the chorus supports you resoundingly
            May good luck attend me today.

            On this day, do not forget us
            My dear playmate
            My dear playmate, don't forget us
            May good luck attend me today.

Solo: How could I forget you?
            What you and I said to each other
            Was not said to be forgotten
            My companion, how could I forget you?
            May good luck attend me today.

Chorus: We call the *egungun*, the *egungun* doesn't listen
            We call the *oriṣa*, the *oriṣa* pays no attention,
            When we are calling you
            My playmate, you don't respond.
            May good luck attend me today.

</blockquote>

These lovely verses are chanted by the chorus of young girls in unison. In language, structure, style and manner of delivery they are indistinguishable from the solo part. The girls are therefore familiarised with the performance of bridal laments long before their own wedding days. They also pick up the *oriki orilẹ* that make up a large part of these chants, by listening to other brides performing and by repeating the verses amongst themselves in play. Quite young girls – about nine or ten years old – often volunteered to '*sun rárà*' for me, and would usually produce a short and standardised version of their lineage *oriki orilẹ* with one or two verses of gratitude, lamentation and self-contemplation thrown in. But two or three months before the date of their wedding, young women would go into intensive training. They would go to an older woman in the compound – often there was an acknowledged expert all the girls in that house would consult – and ask to be taught the 'real thing': *oriki orilẹ* of greater length and complexity than they had formerly known, and those of other lineages, for instance their maternal grandparents'; and elaborate and copious laments, reflections on marriage, thanks to their relatives and so on. They would do this learning privately, with a view to surprising everybody on the day. Because of the shortage of time, they tended to learn by word-for-word repetition, a process made easier by the highly patterned and repetitive style of *rara iyawo*.

Some girls showed greater aptitude and interest in the chant than others. During the festive period every year when dozens of brides would be celebrating their 'outing' on the same day, the differences were quite noticeable. Some girls would repeat the same handful of verses over and over again to each group of listeners; others would attract a crowd as they held forth, elaborately and at length, their repertoire of material seemingly inexhaustible. But this one day is the only opportunity for even the most gifted of girls to give a public performance of *rara iyawo*. After marriage, it would not be proper to chant this genre publicly. A woman who liked the poetry could sing to herself when alone, but she would never again have an audience and a chorus.

This early mastery of a genre was not lost, however. In learning to perform *rara iyawo*, young women mastered extensive passages of *oriki orile* and sometimes also of personal *oriki*. These materials would be recycled in other performances in her married life. Not only the *oriki* themselves, but the verbal materials out of which the *rara* text is constructed – stock formulas, standard pairs and triads of lexical items, poetic idioms to be discussed in later chapters – would form the basis of other styles of performance, styles depending less on set patterns and long coherent sequences than *rara*, but sharing some of the basic ingredients of this chant nonetheless. The young wife would attend funerals and family rituals both in her parents' house and in her husband's. All of these involved chants, made up chiefly of *oriki orile* and the personal *oriki* of famous ancestors. Often, in a solemn ceremony, an experienced older woman of the household would take the lead, as soloist, and the rest of the women would repeat each line after her in chorus. The younger women would thus gradually get used to the style and language of this type of chant through participation in communal performances. Eventually, if the need arose, she would be able to lead the performance herself. Other occasions offered opportunities to those who were especially gifted. Funeral ceremonies provided a forum for impassioned solo performances by the bereaved: but these performances were not compulsory. A woman with special talent would begin to find herself called upon whenever one of her relatives (more or less distant) was involved in a public ceremony.

Some women became expert at chanting through their dedication to a particular *orisa*. *Oriki* is the central channel of communication between devotee and god, and a woman who found herself among the dwindling band of devotees would be given endless opportunity and incentive to become expert at *orisa pipe* (*oriki* chants to the *orisa*): opportunities at every four-day devotional session, at the monthly cult meeting, and at every feast during the long drawn out ceremonies of the annual festival; incentive in the form of a supportive and encouraging audience of fellow cult members, who would exert considerable pressure to get a young devotee to play her part. When the cults were still well attended, it was the duty of the younger women to perform *orisa pipe*, while the elderly women presided over the performance without actually taking part. Nowadays, there are not many young women still learning the *oriki* of the *orisa*, and their elders often have to shoulder the responsibility themselves. But one can still get glimpses of the extraordinary, electric ambiance evoked by their performance, in which performers would be visibly galvanised into surpassing themselves and each other in fluency and intensity of expression.

There were thus a number of spheres in which women could excel in *oriki* performance. Some women became recognised experts within their compounds; they would be called on to take the lead at every family ceremony, and approached by younger women to impart to them their skills. After the more or less obligatory performance of *rara iyawo* on her wedding day, however, a woman was never constrained by custom to do more than join the chorus in group performances. The extent of her mastery of the art depended on her own interest and talent. There was a quiet reward in the esteem her mastery brought her. To outsiders these women's gifts would generally remain hidden. *Obinrin ile*, the wives of the household, did not regard themselves as entertainers or as specialists, however gifted they were. When I asked to record their performances, they showed a dignified awareness of their own powers, but they never asked for acknowledgement in the form of money, as professionals did. But they and their own people were proud of their knowledge and talent.

Their sense of self-worth sometimes took the form of a protective shyness which differentiated them markedly from specialist performers like Ṣangowẹmi. Sometimes this attitude seemed connected with a religious prejudice. One elderly woman performed a marvellous dirge during the funeral of her co-wife; she was gratified that I recorded it and asked me to come back on another day, when she would have time and peace of mind to give me an even better performance. But on the appointed day she told me that she could not do it; excessive chanting was associated with paganism, and her Aladura church would not like it. There seemed to be nothing in the words of her first performance that a Christian would particularly object to, and other women in the household laughed and tried to persuade her to perform for me again; but she never did. Reluctance to put on a performance for an audience, however, is not always associated with Christian conviction; it seems to be an intrinsic aspect of the women's definition of their own role as performers. Specialists who perform for a living have to overcome this kind of modesty: *egungun* entertainers boast that they prepare their children for their future profession by washing their faces with a special soap that takes away all shame. (And it is characteristic of the culture that those who are different should make this into a matter of pride.) Ordinary townswomen, however, only perform for a public larger than their own compound on rare occasions: at the high point of a festival or at certain points during a funeral. These occasions are always ones of high intensity and seriousness, in which the communication the chant establishes with the dead or with the *orisa* is paramount and the function of the performance as entertainment has receded to the background.

A specialist like Ṣangowẹmi, who derives most of her income from performance, is by contrast an entertainer. She thrives on large mixed crowds and her great experience enables her to adapt her style to almost any situation. Her performances were always more breathlessly varied, eclectic and fluid than those of ordinary *obinrin ile*. They also contained a large dash of showmanship and self-display. The *obinrin ile* established their own role in the interchange effected by the utterance of *oriki*, and commented on its significance in the act of performing. But Ṣangowẹmi went further; she always presented herself as performer, at the same time that she addressed her subject. She more often included her own *oriki*; boasted of the artistic feats she had accomplished or was going to accomplish; and drew attention not only to her own skill but to the gratification that this produced in the hearer. Unlike the *obinrin ile*, whose performance was bound up with their own compound and domestic life, Ṣangowẹmi was to be seen at every social gathering, amongst crowds of rowdy men, at big meetings at the palace, and at all the public events in neighbouring towns.

This difference was reflected in the quality and texture of their chants. *Obinrin ile*, despite their modesty, were well aware that their capabilities in some respects exceeded those of a professional. Ṣangowẹmi knew a bit of every *oriki* in Okuku and beyond. Indeed, her knowledge of lineages and attached lineages, of genealogical relations and individual nicknames in every family, was astonishing; and she also knew *oriki* of all the *oriṣa* and all the *egungun*. She was present at every public event, and had something to say to everybody present. During the early days of my research I found my recordings monopolised by Ṣangowẹmi: she was always there, always twice as vociferous as everyone else. But then a kind advisor, a *babalawo*, told me 'There's too much Ṣangowẹmi in your recordings. She is fluent but she is superficial. She doesn't know as much about any compound as the people of the compound itself.' I began to notice that there were domestic ceremonies, private family functions, where Ṣangowẹmi did not come, and where the floor was taken by quiet elderly women of the compound: women who once they got going produced chants of unparalleled beauty, more subtle and less ostentatious than Ṣangowẹmi's sometimes tediously dazzling displays. The difference was always explained in terms of depth: *obinrin ile* knew, perhaps, only a few lineages' *oriki orile* and a few people's personal *oriki*. But those that they knew were acknowledged by their owners to be *ijinle ọrọ*, deep words. They were fuller than Ṣangowẹmi's renderings of the same *oriki*, and contained idiosyncrasies and details that hers did not. They contained less showmanship but more substance.[4]

The sister of the *babalawo* who warned me of this difference was called Faderera. She was an *obinrin ile*, but had become more attached to the *ile* of her father and brother than that of her husband after her second husband from this lineage died. She was one of the most movingly expressive performers I ever heard. She seemed to have total command of the idiom of *oriki*. She used it to utter seemingly private thoughts as well as conventionally appropriate public ideas. During the Egungun festival she would lead the chant in honour of the ancestors of her lineage. The other daughters of the family would repeat each line after her. But on one occasion, after this formal public performance was over and the participants had dispersed, Faderera came back alone. She knelt down again at the grave-shrine, and addressed the ancestor again, this time on a note of private anguish. She was seeking relief for a painful problem in her life, and her words were both personal and poignant:

> Baba, ọ ọ̀ ríkọ́ bó ti móhùn mi pè yaya
> Ipẹayédá o!
> Babaà mi sọ mí níyè
> Babaà mi fún mi lọ́kàn balẹ̀ nílé ayé o
> Mọ̀ mọ̀ jẹ́ n rójú kí n ráyè gbọ́ tìẹ
> Ẹ̀dùndùn ọ̀ràn kan ń mọ̀ ń dùn mí, Mobómiléjọ́
> Babaà mi, bá n gbọ́hun tí ń dùn mí lọ́kàn mi...

> Father, don't you hear the cough that has shattered my voice?
> Ipẹayeda! [father's name]
> Father, restore my memory
> Father, give me peace of mind in this world
> Give me the means and opportunity to attend to your call
> One thing is causing me great pain, Mobomilẹjọ
> Father, help me to deal with what is causing such pain to my heart...

No other woman that I heard ever used precisely these formulations, with their eloquent suggestions of urgency and intimacy. Faderera was one of the Okuku women who was a master of the art of *oriki*, but who used her great talent only within the compound.

In one performance she paraphrased just what her brother the *babalawo* had told me: she claims the insider's unchallengeably superior knowledge of her own lineage *oriki*.

> Ta ni ó mọlé jù mí o
> Ọmọ Awóyẹmí, ta ní í mọlé ẹni juni í lọ?
> Àní n óò kìlúù mi
> Ọyágbénjó Fadérera
> Mo kini kini
> Mo kìnyàn kìnyàn
> N ò rẹ́ni tí yóò kì mí mọ́
> Fọláwé Wúràọ́lá ọmọ óò kì mí gbèsan.

> Who knows my house more than I do?

Child of Awoyẹmi, who knows anyone's house more than the
    person herself?
I say I'll salute my town
Oyagbenjo Faderera
I saluted and saluted people
I saluted everybody
There was no-one to salute me in return any more
Fọlawe Wuraọla, my children will repay me in salutations.

However, what is also revealed in this passage is the permeability of the
border between the professional and the *obinrin ile*. There is no absolute
distinction. Faderera's range may be more limited than Ṣangowẹmi's, but her
skill is as great, and she knows it. The fact that she boasts of her skill in the
very act of exercising it testifies to this, for as we have seen, self-comment and
self-advertisement are the hallmarks of the entertainer.

The development of a performer and the degree to which she gravitates to
Ṣangowẹmi's end of the scale depends partly on her background. Both
Ṣangowẹmi and Faderera had exceptional parents which help to account for
their outstanding skills as performers. Faderera was the daughter of the great
babalawo Awoyẹmi, Ọba Oyinlọla's personal diviner and senior title-holder
in the cult of Ifa. Her mother was a devotee of Ọya. Faderera said:

When my father celebrated his *egungun* feast, after he'd cast the kola and
it had come out propitiously, he would begin to call on his father with
all kinds of appellations. He would call his father, his father's father. We
would gaze at his mouth as he spoke, we would gaze and pick up the
words ourselves. We'd repeat it after him, all of us children, and support
him with a chorus. That's how I came to have the gift for it. I would learn
it all. Of course, while a person's father is still alive we don't take
something over before his eyes. But when he died, I took over and began
to chant as he used to do – I replaced him. My mother also used to salute
herself, and salute her father. She would perform during the Egungun
festival and she might do it on ordinary days just for pleasure, or
whenever her parents came into her mind. I would retain it all.

But if Faderera's father was unusual in excelling in the domestic *oriki*
performances that are normally the province of women (Faderera stressed
that they were quite separate from his professional expertise in chanting Ifa
verses), Ṣangowẹmi's mother was even more extraordinary, for she was a
fully-qualified practising *babalawo*, the only female one Okuku remembers.
This woman, about whom more will be said in Chapter 7, took part in all the
meetings and activities of the otherwise male Ifa cult association, and also
travelled for long periods performing divination for clients and adding to her
knowledge of Ifa. Ṣangowẹmi travelled with her, and acquired the habit of
performance. However, it was not Ifa that she learnt, but *Ṣango pipe*, for her

mother was also a notable Ṣango priestess. Ṣangowẹmi's career was then
boosted by a colonial intervention:

> During the *egungun* festival I would take part in the vigil, singing the *oriki*
> of the *egungun* priests, and one time Ọba Oyinlọla picked me out as the
> best performer. The European arrived – Adunni [Susanne Wenger]
> from Oṣogbo – and called us all to the 'Barracks' [the D.O.'s Residence
> on the outskirts of Okuku] where she asked us to come forward one by
> one – there was Adekunbi, the mother of Michael Oyekọla, Erewẹnu,
> Kọlaade, Omironkẹ of *ile* Ọjọmu, Ẹrẹ-Ọsun of *ile* Ẹlẹmọṣọ. She wanted
> to select the best vocalist. She selected me, and told the ọba that I was
> the one chosen. Then I was taken to Gbọngan for the competition for
> the best vocalist in Ọsun Division. Then in the time of politics – 1952
> – we began to perform the *oriki* of all the politicians, Akintọla, Awolọwọ,
> all the Action Group leaders. I went to many towns, and many of them
> were known to me because I had accompanied my mother there on her
> travels.

What these accounts show is that Ṣangowẹmi was one among many brilliant
performers, and in the early stages of her life did not necessarily see herself
as different in status from her peers. But her exceptional youthful experience
made her stand out among them; she won the competition, and from then on
became more and more of a professional, travelling far afield to attend big
events, and making her appearance at every social occasion in Okuku where
money was being spent. Her former companions stayed at home and
remained within the domestic tradition. But some of them – like Faderera –
had unusual backgrounds and exceptional gifts too, and knew themselves to
be extraordinary performers. Ṣangowẹmi, therefore, remains as one end of a
continuum, not as a discrete and isolated category of performer.

Learning methods also occupy a continuum, with something like rote-
learning at one end and something like Parry and Lord's notion of 'composition
in performance' at the other. The young girl getting ready for her wedding day
memorises long sequences of *rara iyawo* and then repeats them with little
variation. At the other pole, a young apprentice – like Ṣangowẹmi in her youth
– would learn by following her mistress to public performances and trying to
join in wherever she could. She would learn by doing: continual exposure to
the sounds and techniques of performance and repeated attempts to imitate
them would gradually lead to mastery. As she became more experienced and
more confident, she would begin to use her materials more freely. The more
expert a performer, the more she would introduce variations, surprises,
interruptions and idiosyncratic passages of her own. Throughout her
professional life she would go on picking up new materials and new ways of
presenting old ones. The fragmentedness, eclecticism and fluidity of
Ṣangowẹmi's chant represented an extreme of professional competence and
confidence, the outcome of a lifetime of experience. Again, however, the

difference in learning methods, though clearly a real one which correlates with different degrees of fixity and coherence in the performances, is a difference in degree rather than in kind. As we have seen, the young bride is *not* in fact merely memorising ready-made chunks of material: she has become accustomed to the style, form and content of *rara iyawo* through many years of participation in other girls' ceremonies before she settles down to prepare intensively for her own wedding day. Professional performers learn by doing: but they also fix passages of *oriki* and other materials in their memories – passages of varying length, some of them many lines long – and produce them in more or less unvarying form each time they use them. Mature *obinrin ile,* who fall somewhere in the middle of the continuum, learn new material by formal repetition in public or domestic ceremonies. They may also go to a senior woman and ask to be taught especially important *oriki* word for word.

The distinction, in fact, between memorisation and improvisation, though it has been much relied upon by theorists of oral literature, is not a very useful one. While Lord was clearly wrong to suggest that *all* oral performance is produced by precisely the same process of 'composition in performance', the whole continuum as I have described it is actually occupied by varying versions of this, some leaning more towards repetition of fixed passages, others more towards free creative variation within the parameters of the given performance style. What is central to all variants is habituation: that is, that performance is picked up through practice rather than produced through the operation of consciously mastered rules. This notion, elaborated by Pierre Bourdieu (1977), is important to the understanding of what an *oriki* performer is doing in and by performing *oriki*, and I will return to it in the last chapter.

3. THE BRIDE'S ENJOYMENT

The distinctive style of *rara iyawo* is, as I have shown, well adapted to the youth and inexperience of the performer. The exceptionally coherent, highly patterned, and formulaic character of this genre, with its simple repetitive structures, makes it easy for a beginner to master. Unlike the mature woman, the bride has no chance to improve her public performance by gradual and repeated exposure, because she performs *rara iyawo* publicly only on a single occasion: an occasion, moreover, when she has many other things on her mind besides poetry. *Rara iyawo* therefore has to be in a style which can be quickly grasped and produced more or less mechanically.

However, the unusual style of this chant – with its absence of the interpolations, ejaculations, rapid allusions and unfinished quotations characteristic of other *oriki* chants – is also produced by the structure of the occasion on which it is performed. *Rara iyawo* thus make a revealing test case. By comparing the occasion of their performance with other occasions on which more common styles of *oriki* are performed, the essential and fundamental fit between the form of a chant and its intent, purpose, or point will become clearer. The way that the chant's organisation and texture are shaped by what the performer is doing in her performance will become apparent.

The day on which the bride performs *rara* is known as *faaji iyawo*, 'the bride's enjoyment'. It is the day before she actually goes for the first time to take up residence in her husband's house. Since Thursday, in Okuku, is the auspicious day for marriage, *faaji iyawo* is always on a Wednesday. From January to March every year, Wednesdays are the days when brides are to be seen on parade. On the morning of her *faaji* day, the bride stays at home receiving visitors. Her hair is elaborately plaited and she is adorned with gold earrings, bangles and necklaces. She changes from one sumptuous outfit to another every fifteen minutes or so, in order to show off the extent of her trousseau. Her family stay with her and her younger sisters and companions gather. In the afternoon she begins her outing. Accompanied by her escort of young girls, she goes first to her own parents within the compound and kneels ceremoniously in front of them. She chants verses expressing her gratitude to them for all they have done; her regret at leaving; her respect and affection for them. Tears sometimes stream down the bride's face as she does this. She will add the *oriki* of her father's and mother's lineages. Her parents give her their blessing and she moves on to other senior members of the compound, repeating the performance for each in turn. There are verses to address to each of her principal relatives. She then sets off on a tour of the town, escorted by her chorus. She goes to each compound where she has relatives, performs for them and receives blessings and small gifts of money from each. Her outing lasts all afternoon and into the early evening. Before dawn the following morning she is escorted by the women of her compound to the husband's house and her married life begins.

The day of the bride's enjoyment is exactly at the turning point of the protracted process by which a woman born into one lineage is incorporated as wife into another. The process involves a double movement: first the man is introduced to the girl's lineage and must ingratiate himself with them; then the girl is introduced into the husband's lineage and must adapt herself to living among them.[5]

Even today, marriage is a matter between two lineages, not just two individuals; and in the past, it could be conducted without reference to the wishes of the girl and man concerned. A girl could be promised to a friend of her father's before she was born. When they were young, men who are still only in their fifties now expected their fathers to 'marry a wife for them'; and this meant that they left not only the financial negotiations but even the selection of a suitable bride to the father and his advisors. Arrangements between the two parties were carried out mainly through formal visits by delegations representing each lineage. The use of go-betweens to conduct courtship meant that sometimes the girl did not even know who her husband was to be until her wedding day. An old man, particularly if he was of repellent appearance, could send his handsome younger brother to do the courting, and stories are told of desperate last-minute struggles on the sleeping mat when the unfortunate girl discovered who her husband really was.

The first movement, then, was the introduction of the man's people to the woman's. The man had to establish himself in her family's esteem. Once the question of a marriage had been mooted and its prospects investigated by an Ifa priest, the elders of the man's family would pay the woman's family a formal visit to thank them and show their respect. The visiting party would be ceremoniously shown round the compound and all its outlying buildings, so that they would recognise the full extent of the lineage to which they were planning to ally themselves. They would also be shown which houses the other daughters of the family had married into, so that they would be able to recognise a female affine wherever they met one. After that, the man or his senior relatives were expected to offer a series of tokens of respect to the woman's family. Once a year the man would perform ọwẹ, voluntary labour, for his prospective father-in-law. This would involve bringing a large party of young men from his own *ile* to work for a full day on the father-in-law's farm. He would also be expected to present him with a load of yams and a chicken every year on the day the father-in-law celebrated the festival of his *orịṣa*.

If the girl was betrothed while still a child, these annual dues would be paid for years. When the girl was old enough to be married, the *ịṣihun* ceremony for 'opening discussions' and the *parapọ* ceremony for 'uniting people' would be performed. On both these occasions the man's people sent gifts of kola, strong drinks and money to the woman's people. The woman's family divided them meticulously so that every member of the compound received a share and was thus symbolically implicated in the new relationship. After this the bride price would be paid. The money was raised by the man's father, but sent formally by the *baale* (head man) of one compound to the *baale* of the other. Then the date of the wedding could be fixed, after consultation with a *babalawo*. The man's father would then indicate his gratitude by sending the woman's father a cock, known as *adiẹ idajọ*, 'the fowl of the date-fixing'.

Up to this point, therefore, every stage of the proceedings represented respectful approaches by the man's family to the woman's. The man and his people had to show that they were serious about the marriage; that they recognised the importance of the family they wanted to ally with; that they knew every member of this family, however extensive; and that they were grateful for being allowed to marry one of its daughters. The girl, ensconced in the heart of her people, was the prize for which the man's family had come to beg.

This attitude of extreme respect lasts throughout the husband's life. To belittle or mistreat one's in-laws is the worst possible breach of manners. The man must remain forever grateful for being given the woman. Immediately before the wedding day, however, the woman herself begins the second movement of the process, a complementary inversion of the first movement.

The night before her *faaji iyawo*, the girl and her *egbe*, an informal group of age-mates, perform a ceremony symbolically marking her severance from her former status and her natal lineage. A calabash is ceremoniously broken; seven songs are sung; and kola divination is done to see if her marriage will prosper.

The *faaji iyawo* itself is thus a moment when the girl has been detached from her former status but not yet inducted into her new one. Early in the morning after her day of enjoyment, the bride is escorted to her husband's house. At the threshold, she is stripped and washed by the husband's female relatives, wrapped in a new cloth and taken to the compound shrine before being conducted to her room.[6] She stays there for three days, hardly speaking, her head covered in a cloth; and when she needs to go out to the bathroom she is escorted by one or two little girls of her own compound, who have stayed with her. The clothes she came in are taken back to her own compound. There then begins a series of symbolic acts demonstrating her willingness to contribute her labour and her property to her husband's people. On the sixth day after her arrival they show her where all the married daughters of the compound live – the counterpart to the groom's earlier introduction to the married daughters of the bride's family – and she ceremoniously sweeps their yards for them. After that she has to draw water and grind pepper for each of the women of her husband's compound in turn. On the ninth or the fifteenth day, her people bring her dowry of household equipment – plates, cooking pots and utensils – that she has been collecting for years. It is put on display, and then divided amongst all the members of the husband's family. Even small children receive something: for every person already there before she arrived is considered to be senior to her, and every one of them is implicated in the process of acquiring her services. She is required to treat even the smallest boys with respect, calling them by avoidance names, for they are all her husbands.[7] This division of her property is a sign that the transfer of the bride to her new home is complete. After about three months she will take up all the duties of a compound wife.

The 'bride's enjoyment', then, falls at the point at which the contractual process inverts itself: the man, as suppliant, has been introduced to the woman's family; now the woman, as subordinate, is introduced into the man's family. It also falls between two ceremonies which mark the bride's transition from belonging to her father's lineage to belonging to her husband's. The girls' evening game symbolises, with the breaking of the calabash, her break with her own lineage. The early morning ceremony at the husband's doorway, when she is stripped of her former clothes, washed, and wrapped in a new cloth, symbolises her incorporation as a new person into the husband's lineage.

For a man, getting married for the first time is an unqualified improvement in status. As a young unmarried man he was no more than a subordinate in his father's household, working for his father on the farm but having no control over the household income. A wife made him the nucleus of a new household. She was the foundation stone of his future existence as an independent social being. Even though he might remain technically under his father's control until the old man's death, he would be recognised by other people as a social being in his own right. For the man, then, the bride was a prize of unparalleled value. The long process of paying respect, giving gifts and working for his future in-laws expressed, in ceremonial form, the importance of the man's own achievement in getting a wife. And after that, each succeeding wife he married would be another improvement in status, a new indication of the man's importance and success.

But for the woman, the situation was much more ambiguous. On the one hand, marriage or rather the motherhood that was expected to follow it meant attainment of full adult status. A woman without children would be a more unhappy being even than a man without a wife; she would have no voice, no influence and no respect. Moreover, it was the husband who was responsible for setting a woman up in business. Without marriage, she would have less chance of becoming well established as a trader or food-seller. On the other hand, marriage for a woman meant leaving her natal compound and the people she could count on for support and affection, to go and live among strangers. These strangers were thought of as essentially hostile, and co-wives especially were assumed to be implacably opposed to each other. It would be only after many years and many children that she would attain a position of security and authority within her husband's household. Despite the symbolic separation from her own people, a woman would remain closer to them, in some ways, than to her husband's home. If her husband lived in the same town as her parents, she would attend the monthly family meeting, the *farajo*, of her compound. She would take part in any ceremony involving the *omo-osu*, the daughters of the family. Eventually, if she disagreed too seriously with her husband, or if he died and she refused to be inherited by one of his relatives, she could return to her father's household. Some women even maintained a working arrangement with their husbands, where they continued to have children for him but lived at home with their parents. But in spite of this continued background support from her family, the woman was still in a less happy position than her brothers, who stayed with their own people all their lives and suffered no division of interests and loyalties. The woman's situation as mediator between two lineages could sometimes be manipulated to her advantage; but it also contained inherent disabilities. She could play husband off against parents only up to a certain point, as this ironical comment, from a woman's chant in honour of the *orisa* Erinle makes clear:

'N óò lọ, n óò lọ'
N lobìnrin fi í dẹrù bọkùnrin
'Bọ́ ọ bá lè lọ ọ mọ́ọ yáa lọ'
N ni bàbáà mi fi kọ́lé ẹrù sára ìyáà mi.[8]

'I'm going, I'm going'
That's how women frighten men
'If you want to go, then hurry up and be gone'
That was how my father built mansions of fear in my
      mother's heart.

If the ceremonies of the marriage process seem to undergo a double movement, turning on the pivotal point of the 'bride's enjoyment', this reflects the ambiguity of the woman's actual change of status. Marriage is indeed a glorious attainment for her; but it is also a revelation of the fundamental weakness of her position compared with a man's, and the beginning of a long subordination to another family's interests. This ambiguity is reflected subtly but with great clarity in the content of *rara iyawo*. Indeed, it could be said to be their principal subject matter.[9]

The transformation of the woman's status is celebrated in verses that make it clear what she hopes for in marriage:

Èmi mọ̀ ń reléè mi nù-un
Èmi ń reléè mi rèé lówó
Èmi mọ̀ ń reléè mi nù-un
Èmi ń reléè mi rèé bímọ
Bẹ́ ẹ bá lóríi yín ó sìn mí
Á sìn mí á bá mi dé yàráà mi
Ire lónìí oríi mi àfire.[10]

I'm going to my new home now
I'm going to my home to have money
I'm going to my new home now
I'm going to my home to bear children
If you say your good luck will escort me
It will escort me right to my room
May good luck attend me today.

Her change of status brings with it increased dignity:

Èmí ti kúrò ní 'Bó bá di lálẹ́ ọ wá'
Mo kúrò ní 'Bó bá di lábọ̀ ọ mọ̀mọ̀ yà'
Èmí mọ̀mọ̀ wáá dẹgbẹ́ aláàròbo
Aláàròbo tí wọn ń pè lọ́kùnrin
Ire lónìí oríi mi àfire.[11]

I've left the stage of 'Come in the evening'
I've left the stage of 'Drop in on your way back'
I've joined the club of mothers of new-born babies
Mother of a new-born baby that is a boy
May good luck attend me today.

She is no longer a young girl who can be teased and flirted with; she will now
have the greater responsibility and greater prestige of being the mother of a
new baby – preferably, of course, a baby boy.

But this enhancement of status also involves a loss. The bride must give up
her playmates and her carefree life, a life of dressing up, going out and showing
off:

Aré eléwe wọn ò sú mi í ṣe
Gèlè ẹrù kan ò tó mi í rù rejà
Ọpá aṣọ póùn kan kò tó mi í wérí
Èmi mọ̀mọ̀ wáá ti kúrò níwòyí
Eyín-èrín mo jọlá babaà mi
Ire lónìí orìi mi àfire.[12]

I am not yet tired of young girls' games
A towering head-tie is not big enough for me to wear to market
Cloth of a pound a yard is not enough to wind round my head
But now I've left that time behind
'Laughing teeth', thanks to my father's standing
May good luck attend me today.

More poignant than this is the sense of her loss of the security she enjoyed in
the midst of her family. If she had been a man, she could have stayed with
them forever:

Ọdẹ ń wù mí mo ní n ò lápó
Àgbèdẹ ń wù mí mo ní èmi ò lẹ́wìrì
Nígbà tí ilé baba ń wù mí í gbé
Èmi Àbíkẹ́ Ọmọ́tánbàjé
Ọmọ ará Ọ̀kín mo ní n ò ya ọkùnrin
Ire lónìí orìi mi àfire.[13]

I would have liked to be a hunter, but I have no quiver
I would have liked to be a blacksmith, but I have no bellows
When I would have liked to go on living in my father's house
I, Abikẹ Ọmọtanbajẹ
Child of the Ọkin people, I did not turn into a man
May good luck attend me today.

As a woman, she is helpless. The contract which transfers her to another

man's house is made without consulting her: she has as much say in it as a
sheep being put up for sale:

> À ń pète àgbò
> Àgbò ń jẹ lẹ́hìnkùlé
> Nígbà tí èmi ò sí ńlé
> Eyín-ẹ̀rín ni wọn ń pèteè mi
> Ni wọn ń pète pèrò
> Pète pèrò ni wọn gbowó ìdájọ́
> Gbowó ìdájọ́, ó dọwọ́ èmi nìkan o
> Ire lóníì oríì mi àfire.[14]

> They're making arrangements about the ram
> The ram is grazing in the yard
> When I was not in the house
> 'Laughing-teeth', they made arrangements about me
> They plotted and planned
> Plotted and planned till they got the date-fixing fee
> Got the date-fixing fee, but the rest is left to me alone
> May good luck attend me today.

They make the decisions, she says, but it is she alone who has to live with the
consequences. And the consequences she envisages can be dire: hostile in-
laws, jealous co-wives, petty meanness and unfairness of all kinds. The
following verse complains that while her brother is swelling the ranks of her
own lineage, she is serving the interests of another lineage: and one that does
not even treat her well:

> Ṣe bí bá-n-kúnlé lọkùnrin
> Ṣe bí bá-n-túlé lobìnrin
> Ṣe bí ilé onílé lọmọ rèé kún
> Ta ni óò bá n tóyèe babaà mi ṣe?
> Ńbi onílé gbé búni tá ò gbọdọ̀ bú
> Tólódèdè gbé búni tá à gbọdọ̀ fèsì
> Bọ́ ọ gúnyán wọn á ló ní kókó
> Bọ́ ọ rokà tó mọ̀ rí lẹbẹlẹbẹ
> Àlàkẹ́, wọn á leeta da si
> Kàkà wọn ó pè ọ́ kọrọ kí wọn bá ọ wí
> Wọn á pèyáà káà, wọn á pèyá ń pópó
> Wọn á pe bàálé ilé abẹnu-gbọ̀ọ̀rọ̀
> Wọn óò tún peni tí ò ní í wòran mi...[15]

> For a man is someone who swells the household
> While a woman is someone who depletes it
> For a daughter goes to swell someone else's household

Who then will improve my father's status?
Where the householder abuses you and you mustn't answer back
Where the owner of the premises abuses you and you mustn't reply
If you pound yam they'll say it's lumpy
If you prepare yam pudding that is fine and light
Alakẹ, they'll say it's not well mixed
Instead of calling you to one side to tell you off
They'll call the most senior woman of the compound,
     they'll call in a senior woman from outside
They'll call the head of the house with his big mouth
And they'll call in the people who have no sympathy for me.

The bride's position on the day of her 'enjoyment' is a double one in a further sense. The 'bride's enjoyment' is the only day when the bride herself is incontestably the sole actor, the centre of attention. Her family, relations and age-mates become a sympathetic chorus and audience; it is she who, as conspicuous in her finery as an *egungun*, leads the way and conducts the performance. This day provides her with the only forum for the expression – through the deflecting medium of *rara iyawo* – of her feelings about the long-drawn out process by which she is transferred to her new status. But while it is her day of action and expression, it is also the day when she is most an object on display. The bride is the prize the man has long striven for. She is shown to the world to demonstrate just what her parents are bestowing on him. The performance of *rara iyawo* is part of the display. Her competence as a performer is an accomplishment that demonstrates her intelligence, her diligence, her maturity and presence of mind. But more than this, her expressed sentiments are themselves part of the display: a proper filial gratitude, a becoming reluctance to enter the married state, combined with a modest pride in her impending fulfilment as a woman, are all attitudes which embellish her and enhance her value in the public eye.

This duality of the bride, as both actor and object, is imprinted on both the form and the content of *rara iyawo*, and is the fundamental source of this genre's unusual features. Everything the bride says in *rara iyawo* is intended to direct attention back to herself. The genre, in fact, is a long reflection on, and dramatisation of, the bride's change of status. It asks the audience to look at her, observe her glory, recognise the transition she is undertaking. The verses, that is, are not detached philosophical reflections on marriage in general but invitations to the onlooker to acknowledge that this particular girl is at this moment embarking on married life. Her very act of *going* is dramatised (in Yoruba, the verb 'to marry', for a woman, is 'to go to the husband's house'). She asks the public to recognise that her departure is permanent and involves a profound change for her:

Mọ̀mọ́ọ̀ mi n ó ò sì mọ́ọ lọ nù-un

N ò lọlọ ẹja tó lọ tí ò mọ́ débú
N ò lọlọ ìkòrò tó lọ tí ò dódò wẹ̀
Èmi ò lọlọ légbéǹlègbé
Légbéǹlègbé tó lọ tí ò délẹ̀ omi.[16]

Mother, I'm ready to go now
I'm not going in the way of a fish, that goes without
    reaching the deep pools
I'm not going in the way of an *ikoro* fish, that goes
    without reaching the river to swim in
I'm not going in the way of a tadpole
A tadpole that goes without getting to the bottom of the
    water.

In other verses she calls attention to her own beauty, not as an individual's boast but as the essential attribute of a phase in her life, when she is poised on the very threshold of adulthood. She celebrates the perfections of unspoilt youth at the very moment of departing from it. The verse asks the audience to acknowledge this moment:

Odò kan òdò kan
Tí ń bẹ láàrin ìgbẹ́
Ará iwájú ò gbọdọ̀ débẹ
Èrò ẹ̀hìn ò gbọdọ̀ débẹ
Èmi débẹ mo bù bójú
Ojúù mi wáá dojú oge
Ìdíì mi wáá dìdí ìlẹ̀kẹ̀
Ìlẹ̀kẹ̀ tá a bá kà tí ò bá pé
Àní ẹ mọ́ọ túṣọ̀ọ̀ mi lọ.[17]

A certain river, a certain river
In the middle of the forest
People at the front must not go there
People at the rear must not go there
But I went there and splashed my face
My face became the face of lovely youth
My waist became a waist adorned with beads
Beads which if you count them and they're not complete
I say you should strip me and take my clothes away.

These lines suggest a magical quality to a young girl's perfection. Her beads are complete – she is a virgin, and therefore deserves her beauty and the finery that adorns it. The implication seems to be that as soon as she marries, the moment of perfect radiance is past. The audience should bear witness to this moment that will soon be forever lost.

Her performance is thus self-reflexive, a dramatisation of the actual moment at which she is the centre of attention. It is true that her utterances are apparently directed outwards, addressed to an audience, and often to specific, named listeners: her mother, father, brothers and sisters. It is also true that to do honour to her parents and grandparents, she repeats the *oriki orilẹ* of their lineages. In any other *oriki* chant, this would at once open a channel for intense communication, and most of the communicative energy would flow away from the performer towards the recipient of the *oriki*. It is the recipient's head that would 'swell'. But in *rara iyawo*, it is as if this process were immobilised. The *oriki* circles back to the bride and becomes a reflection on *her* state. When she goes out on her parade, she carries in her hand an emblem of her *ile*: a miniature gun if she belongs to *ile* Ọlọkọ, the compound associated with hunters; a miniature drumstick for *ile* Alubata, the *bata* drummers' compound, and so on. The *oriki orilẹ* that she performs, although ostensibly addressed to members of her family, assert her own membership of the group.

Sometimes this is made explicit in the words of the *oriki* themselves. In the long excerpt from a *rara iyawo* version of the *oriki* of *ile* Ọlọkọ quoted at the beginning of this chapter, the performer gave the narrative a final twist which turned it, retroactively, into a comment on her own beauty. The story tells of an 'I' who went twice to Ọyọ to complain of the locusts who ate his crops; but it is finished by an account of a third visit, by an 'I' who is now the bride herself, in which the lord of Ọyọ tells her she is worthy of rich adornments. A similar thing happens in the following rendering of the well-known *oriki orilẹ* of the Ọlọjọnwọn people (here, *ile* Ọdọfin):

Njọ́ tí Làgbàí ń toko ọnàá bọ̀
Gbogbo igi n sá gílogílo
Ìrókò wọn á mì lẹ̀ngbẹ̀
Èmi ò mọbi Làgbàí óò sọlẹ̀ sí, ọmọ Kújẹ́nrá
Ẹ ní ó sọlẹ̀ẹ́'lẹ́ẹ̀ mi kí n lówó n bímọ
Kí n sòwò kí n mọ̀ tìẹ̀ jèrè
Èrè tí ò bá sì ní í pé
Kó sì wáá parí dà lẹ́hìn mi.[18]

On the day that Lagbai was coming from the wood where he did
    his carving
All the trees were running hither and thither
The mahogany trees were shuddering
I don't know which one Lagbai will land on, child of Kujẹnra
Tell him to land on my house, so that I get rich and have children
So that I trade and make a profit
And trade which is not profitable
Let it turn back and depart from me.

The usual treatment of this theme, in *oriki* chants other than *rara iyawo*, builds it up into a celebration of the lineage occupation of wood-carving. The line 'I don't know which [tree] Lagbai will land on' would be followed by a passage developing the idea that the trees are all afraid of Lagbai, the founding ancestor of the Ọlọjọnwọn, because of his incredible prowess as a carver. He can bring a dead piece of wood to life by giving it human features unparalleled by any other carver for detail and completeness. Only true Ọlọjọnwọn people can do this: their slaves and servants cannot copy their inborn skills, which mark them out as a lineage...[19] But in the *rara iyawo* version, the theme veers from a lineage occupation to the bride's own future. 'Landing on' a tree to carve it is converted to 'landing on' a household to bless it, and by what amounts to a verbal sleight of hand the performer launches herself into a prayer for her own prosperity in marriage.

Even when she does not do this kind of explicit conversion, the performer of *rara iyawo* still seems to be directing the *oriki orilẹ* to herself rather than to another subject. This is brought about partly by the textual framework of comments on marriage in which the *oriki* appear, which has already set the direction of attention towards the bride, and partly by the absence of vocative interjections. The bride, unlike other performers of *oriki*, does not insert the names of her addressee in apposition to the *oriki*; she does not call on him to pay attention or insist that 'that is how So-and-so is to be saluted'. The few interjections that appear are almost always to herself, part of the process of directing the listener's attention back to the speaker. The features most characteristic of other *oriki* chants are absent here. The chant proceeds steadily and methodically through its well-marked repetitive sequences as if the presence of the listener did not affect it.

The structural role of *rara iyawo* in the marriage process therefore gives *rara iyawo* its distinctive characteristics as a chant. On the one hand, it is a set piece, performed on the day when the bride is shown off to the world as the prize her future husband has won. Its function is to display her, not to make other people's heads swell. It continually circles back on itself, producing an effect curiously formal and static in comparison with the forward thrust of most *oriki* chants. But on the other hand, it is the bride's one moment of action and expression. In its simplicity of diction, its clarity of structure, and its luminous, lucid imagery, it achieves a poignancy that no other chant does.

In all her subsequent performances of *oriki*, the woman directs her attention not to herself as she steps out onto the stage of adult activity, but to other actors on this stage: above all, to the important male centres of social and political power in her compound and town; to the influential dead and other spiritual beings; and to the collectivities that constitute her father's and her husband's *ile*, past and present.

4. DEATH AND OTHER WORLDS

The events leading up to and following a wedding are a long and elaborate series, but the context of the performance of *rara iyawo* is straightforward. There is one clearly defined key performer in each ceremony, and a co-ordinated and equally well demarcated group of supporting performers; the performance takes place on a single occasion at a specified time; and the texts themselves, despite the internal ambivalence of their themes, are structurally exceptionally coherent and transparent.

But after her wedding, all the occasions where a woman will subsequently participate in the performance of *oriki* will offer a much broader and more variegated canvas of expression. The most important ceremonial complexes are funerals and festivals. In both, there is a wide range of participants who perform different kinds of chant. There is not just one focus and one drama, but a variety of them, involving different but overlapping sets of participants, and sometimes overlapping in time too.

The example I examine here is a funeral. Of all ceremonials, funerals are the most frequently held and the most inescapable: everyone will sooner or later have to be one of the central performers in his or her parents' funerals, but before and after that all women will be continually required to participate in a lesser capacity in other funerals. If the deceased was an old person, a very large number of women are mobilised to contribute to the celebrations. First there are the *ọmọ olooku*, the children of the deceased, who organise the whole event and are at the centre of all the principal scenes. Then, if the deceased belonged to a traditional cult, there are the fellow cult members, who may have strong claims on the deceased and who perform – sometimes in opposition to the wishes of the *ọmọ olooku* – special ceremonies over the body. Then there are sets of women, related to each other either as *ọmọ-ọsu* (daughters of the same lineage) or as *orogun* (wives of the same lineage). If the deceased was elderly and had many children, the sets of *orogun* may run into dozens, for each daughter and granddaughter may be married into a different compound and will have her own set of 'co-wives'. These sets are mobilised at different moments and to perform different roles throughout the proceedings. Certain family ceremonies designed to affirm the solidarity of the deceased's lineage, for instance, involve all the daughters of that lineage. Other ceremonies involve all the wives of the deceased's lineage. And from the second day of the funeral onwards, young women related to the deceased by birth – usually granddaughters, through the daughters as well as the sons of the deceased – will come to the funeral ceremony bringing with them a party of their 'co-wives', all dressed alike, to go in procession round the town singing funeral songs and collecting money. Finally, both men and women, but especially women, who are related in any way to the deceased may attend the funeral as individuals and contribute performances or join in the songs and chants of others if they wish.

Not only this, but a funeral ceremony moves rather rapidly, in seven days, through a number of dramatic stages signifying first the shock of loss, and the sense of the absence of the deceased; then the progressive separation and departure of the deceased's spirit; and then the reconciliation of the survivors to their loss through affirmations of continuity. These dramatic moments are enacted principally through *oriki* chants. The *oriki* therefore express a range of contrasting moods, suggested by different styles of chanting. Some are slow and solemn, involving a large collectivity of women, led by a soloist and backed up by a massed chorus. Others are highly individual and personal, the wild lament of a bereaved daughter or wife. They also express different philosophies, offering, at different moments, different views of what the dead are and where they go. But these moments are not clearly ordered as a series; there are eddies of feeling, an ebb and flow and an overlapping of phases within the general progression described. Furthermore, there is a shifting and indeterminacy in the subject to whom the *oriki* are addressed. There are in fact several overlapping subjects, and the principal subject, the deceased, takes on several shapes and relationships to the performers. It is only the powerful channel of *oriki* that can establish a link with the rapidly receding person who has died. But at some moments the deceased is addressed as a person who has just gone out – a living absence; at other times, he or she is addressed as a corpse, an object of fear and mystical danger; other utterances are addressed not to the deceased as an individual but to him or her as part of a collectivity of ancestors. Furthermore, the dead bring with them a web of connections. Some of the *oriki* are addressed to the *ọmọ olooku* they have left behind; some to the relatives who have preceded them to the other world and who are pictured as waiting there to receive them; others again to an abstract entity, as much place as person, which represents the past and its inhabitants in a generalised way. A funeral, therefore, is a highly complex event inviting a much wider and more subtle range of expressive acts than a marriage. What is the same is the centrality of *oriki* performances. Without *oriki*, a funeral could hardly take place.

Funerals vary according to the customs of the lineage and the cult group of the deceased. What follows is a composite and schematised description taking examples from a number of different funerals I actually observed. The aim is to suggest the way in which the 'same' material – *oriki* – takes manifold forms and accomplishes a variety of expressive purposes depending on the performer, her relationship to the deceased, and the moment in the complex event that she is celebrating.

From the moment that a death is known, the closest women relatives may raise a lament announcing it. Once, in the dead of night, I heard this cry from a neighbouring house, rising with tragic and unearthly effect into black empty air:

Ará Òkukù ẹ wáá wo wàhálà mi
Ọkọọ wa dọmọọlẹ̀ ó ti lọ
Ọkọọ wa dọmọọlẹ̀ ó dará òrun
Ará Òkukù ẹ wáá wo wàhálà mi.

People of Okuku, come and see my plight
Our husband has become a child of the Earth, he has gone
Our husband has become a child of the Earth, he has become
    a denizen of heaven
People of Okuku, come and see my plight.

If the person who died was old enough to have grown-up children and grandchildren, the death is made public by *itufọ*: that is, a formal announcement to the ọba, together with the gift of 'five shillings' (originally, 20,000 cowries; nowadays, fifty *kọbọ*). After this, the chanting of *oriki* as lamentation begins in real earnest, and continues for seven days more or less continuously.

As soon as the death has been announced, the wives and daughters of the immediate family send for the rest of the *ọmọ-ọsu*, the married and unmarried daughters of the lineage. When they have assembled, they set off in a procession round the town, collecting more *ọmọ-ọsu* on the way. As they go, one or two women noted for their ability will chant the *oriki orílẹ* and personal *oriki* of the deceased. This chanting is a way of announcing the death to the world at large. On their return the women will keep up the chanting by the side of the corpse where it lies in state. The following is a description of the first morning of the funeral ceremony of one Ẹfuntohun Arinkẹ, an elderly woman married into *ile* Baalẹ, but belonging by birth to an Ikoyi lineage from Ikirun. She was a Ṣango priestess and she died on the last evening of the Olooku festival. The announcement of the death had to be delayed, for otherwise the bereaved would have been fined by the ọba for 'spoiling' the festival, the opening one in the yearly cycle. But the Ṣango cult as well as the immediate family knew about it and began their preparations in secret. The next morning the death was announced to the ọba and around the town. On their return to the house where Ẹfuntohun had been laid out, the chant was raised by the elderly *ọmọ-ọsu* of *ile* Baalẹ – that is, the daughters of the lineage of the deceased's husband, who had himself died some years previously. They gathered on the front porch and kept up a flow of *oriki* and lamentations, at first as individual solo performances, then after some time as a collective performance, one very old woman singing the lead and the rest repeating each line after her. (The younger women were somewhere else in the house, singing group songs with clapping and dancing, without any co-ordination with the elders' performance; and this was typical: later, in the funeral procession itself, the same overlapping and clashing of performances could be seen, as some groups sang songs and others simultaneously, and immediately adjacent to them in the street, chanted *oriki*.) The elderly *ọmọ-ọsu* of *ile* Baalẹ, on this occasion, kept up their chant until the Ṣango cult members arrived to do their ritual on the corpse. The first performer, Iwẹ, a daughter of Ẹfuntohun, began by speaking of a sense of loss, and of the discomforting absence of someone they had been living with till then:

> N ò rí ìyàá mi mọ́ o
> Béwúrẹ́ bá jẹ yún jẹ wá o
> Àrìnkẹ́, yóò máa fẹ̀gbẹ́ nùgiri
> Ọ ọ̀ rágùntàn kan bọ̀lọ̀jọ̀
> Bó bá jẹ yún jẹ wá
> Ìyàá mi Àrìnkẹ́, yóò máa fẹ̀gbẹ́ nùgiri
> N ò rẹ́ni mẹ́gbẹ̀ẹ́ nù
> N ò rẹ́ni mẹ́gbẹ̀ẹ́ nù mọ́ o.

> I cannot see my mother any more
> If a goat goes grazing and comes home
> Arinkẹ, it will rub its sides on the wall
> And look at the big black sheep
> If it goes grazing and comes home
> My mother Arinkẹ, it will rub its sides on the wall
> I have no-one to rub sides with
> I have no-one to rub sides with any more.

She then went on to the *oriki orilẹ* of Ẹfuntohun's own people from Ikirun, who were Onikoyi, celebrated for their prowess in war:[20]

> Ẹ̀sọ́ Ìkòyí o
> Ẹ̀sọ́ Ìkòyí n ló ti múKòyí ròde
> Ká a wáá jí ńjoojúmọ́ ká a dira ogun...

> War captains of Ikoyi
> The war captains of Ikoyi have summoned the child of Ikoyi
> 'Let's rise every morning and arm ourselves for battle...'

The Ikoyi warriors, that is, have called Ẹfuntohun up; she is to rise and go when they summon her. But Iwẹ soon abandoned the Ikoyi *oriki*, probably because she did not know it well. Ikirun, Ẹfuntohun's town, is not an immediate neighbour of Okuku; and in Okuku, the only compound with the same *oriki orilẹ* was a small one with which she may not have had much contact. After five more lines, she turned to a much more familiar theme: the personal *oriki* of Ẹfuntohun's late husband, who was Iwẹ's father. This was introduced by a device very common in the funeral chants in honour of women whose husbands have predeceased them:

> Ọmọ Jọ́ṣelọlá ó gbaya ẹ̀ lọ́wọ́ọ̀ mi, ọmọ Àdìgún ẹléwàa bùjé
> Ojọ́ṣelọlá a-mú-dúdú-wumọ́ọ́-ṣe...

Son of Jọsẹlọla has taken back his wife from me, son of
   Adigun, one with the beauty of blue-black dye
Ojọsẹlọla, one who makes his blackness the envy of others...

She develops this theme, adding the *oriki orilẹ* of the husband's lineage, which is also the performer's own lineage, at some length, occasionally directing it to the deceased by repeating and varying the introductory device, for example:

Ó gbaya ẹ̀ lónìí o, ojú dá o.

He took his wife back today, it has left us desolate.

But she also includes comments on the woman herself, commending her fastidious manners and her kindness to her children:

N ò rí ìyáà mi mọ́ o
Iyáà mi kú, iyeè mi bỌ́lọ́un lọ, bọ̀ọ̀kìíní ìyá ọ̀gá
Abiyamọ tí í jẹmọọ rẹ lẹ́nu bí iṣu
Afínjú, bí wọ́n rejà wọn ó mọ́ọ rìn gerere, iyeè mi,
Ọbùn rejà pa ṣìàṣìà
Ọbùn ràìràì ni yóò rẹrù afínjú wọlé o.

I don't see my mother any more
My mother is dead, my mother has gone to God, wealthy,
   dainty mother
Mother of children, who talks constantly about them with
   anxiety and affection
Fastidious people, if they go to market they walk there
   smartly, mother,
A slob going to market shuffles along
The filthy sloven will carry the dainty one's burden home.

At this point Ọmọtunwa, another elderly daughter of *ilé* Baalẹ took over from Iwẹ, with a salute addressed to the assembled mourners:

Ìyáà mi kú, iyeè mi bỌ́lọ́un lọ
Ọ kúùdèlé ẹni tó ròrun
Àpèkẹ́ ọ kúùdèlé ẹni tí ò sáyé
Ọ kúùdèlé ẹni ó bóóde
O wáá fà té bí ẹni tí ò sí
Ẹfúntóhún ṣe bí ẹni ó bóóde.

My mother's dead, my mother's gone to God
Condolences on being left behind in the house of one who went
   to heaven
Apekẹ, condolences on being left behind in the house of one who

is no more
Condolences on being left behind in the house of one who just
   slipped out
She went to sit aloof like someone who is no more
Ẹfuntohun went as if she were just slipping out for a while.

Then another senior *ọmọ-ọsu* took up the chant from Ọmọtunwa, and this
time the rather haphazard interplay between different performers gave way to
a pattern óf leader and chorus. They lamented the shocking fact of death
itself: Ẹfuntohun was a corpse, unable to get up. But this horror was
immediately offset by the reflection that death which comes in old age and is
properly celebrated is a fitting one. They then went on to associate her with
all the male elders of the compound, for since she was 'wife' to all of them,
her death was a collective loss:

Àrìnkẹ́ ò leè ǹde, éè leè ǹde
Ká a kú lọ́mọdé, Ẹfúntóhún
Ká a fẹsin ṣèrẹ́lẹ̀ ẹni
Àdàgbà àìládìẹ ìrànà
Ẹ ẹ̀ mọ̀ pékú tó báni lẹ́mọ̀ṣọ́ ò ṣini pa
Àrìnkẹ́ ò leè ǹde, aya Omítúndé o
Àrìnkẹ́ ò leè ǹde, ayaa Bàbáyẹjú o
Àrìnkẹ́ ò leè ǹde, éè leè ǹde
Aya Ikúbọlájẹ́ ò leè ǹde
Aya Òkúsìndé kí ló ṣe tọ́ ọ̀ leè ǹde?
Aya 'Igbó fi dúdú ṣọlá' ò leè ǹde
Babaà mi 'Òkè fi rìbìtì ṣayọ̀'....

Arinkẹ cannot get up, she can't get up
It's better to die in one's youth, Ẹfuntohun
And have a horse killed in one's honour
Than to grow old without even a chicken for the burial rite
But don't you know that death when it strikes down an aged
   person has done no wrong
Arinkẹ cannot get up, the wife of Omitunde
Arinkẹ cannot get up, wife of Babayẹju
Arinkẹ cannot get up, she cannot get up
Wife of Ikubolajẹ cannot get up
Wife of Okusinde why can't you get up?
Wife of 'The forest's darkness is its pride' cannot get up
My father, 'The hill's roundness is its joy'....

From this point, the leading singer elaborates the personal *oriki* of the man
known as Igbo-fi-dudu-ṣọla, 'The forest's darkness is its pride', a big man of
ile Baalẹ, and this goes on until the Ṣango cult members arrive.

The ọmọ-ọṣu of *ile* Baalẹ, then, have dwelt much on the deceased's role within the compound, as a 'wife' to all the lineage's senior men and as mother to the younger members. They acknowledge, as fully as they can, the lineage from which she came, even though they do not know much of that lineage's *oriki*. They are preoccupied with the immediate impact of her death: lifelessness ('Why can't you get up?') and the sudden absence of a familiar figure, which still seems unreal ('She's gone to sit aloof like someone who is no more/Ẹfuntohun is like someone who just slipped out for a while'). They are addressing the corpse as if it were still a person, from whom the life had only temporarily absented itself. In so far as the other world is mentioned at all, it is simply 'heaven' or the unspecified place to which her dead husband is summoning her. Most of the performance, in fact, is made up of the *oriki* of her husband, his fellow elders and his lineage in general. Even in death the ambivalence of a woman's position, born into one lineage and married into another, is not resolved. At the beginning of the chant Ẹfuntohun has been 'summoned' by the Enikoyi, her own lineage ancestors, to rejoin them; but throughout the rest of the chant she is pictured as being reclaimed by her dead husband, and as belonging still to the collective male elders of his lineage.

The Ṣango cult members expressed a different range of interests and a different mood in their chant, which began the moment they arrived on the scene. Ẹfuntohun was an *adoṣu,* a cult initiate of the inner circle. Before she could be buried, a secret ritual had to be performed to remove the *oṣu,* the power-giving ritual substance that had been implanted in her scalp on her initiation half a century before. This was what the Ṣango cult had come to do. When they first arrived with the *bata* drummers, a wave of excitement went through the compound. The ọmọ-ọṣu fell silent and their laments were replaced by the characteristic sounds of the Oniṣango's own chant. Only the other *adoṣu,* led by the male head of the cult, the Baalẹ Ṣango, could go into the room where the corpse lay. The ritual, which was protracted, was performed behind closed doors.[21] Meanwhile, the rest of the cult members, all women, stayed outside and kept up the chant throughout the ceremony. The chant was led by a soloist, who would deliver a number of lines of *oriki* and other matter. Then the chorus would respond with a refrain which was different from the soloist's lines and which varied slightly from one repetition to the next, but always unanimously, an effect characteristic of *Ṣango pipe* in other contexts too.[22] While the soloist's delivery was rapid and stirring, the chorus half-sang their lines, slowly and with a solemn, indeed menacing, effect. In this chant, Ẹfuntohun's husband's personal and lineage *oriki* are not uttered, and neither are her own lineage *oriki*. What is stressed is her personal character; her role in the cult; her relationship with other cult members already dead, whose *oriki* are added; and above all the terrifying nature of a cult death and the rituals associated with it. The singers warn the by-standers:

Solo: Ẹfúntóhún ọjọ̀ òní ṣòro
         Ègbèrì ì í wojú òkú, Ẹfúntóhún o
         Ṣàngótọ́lá, 'ẹni ó mọ́ bòórò lọ
         Àrìnkẹ́ 'ẹni ó mọ́ bòórò lọ
         A-wẹ́-bí-abẹ́rẹ́ Àrìnkẹ́
Chorus: A ì í wò ó
         A ì í wọ̀rọ̀
         A ì í wo Òìṣà Mọgbà
         Bọ́ ọ wò ó fírí ọ kú fírí
         Bọ́ ọ wò ó bàrà ọ kú bàrà
         A ì í wo Òìṣà Mọgbà
Solo: Mo ló wáá dojú òkókó, babaa Tóówojú
Chorus: Eépà, eépà, eépà
         A ì í wò ó
         A ì í wọ̀rọ̀
Solo: Àrìnkẹ́ wáá daìíwòó, a-wẹ́-bí-abẹ́rẹ́
         Ẹni bá wojú orò í bórò lọ ni
Chorus: A ì í wo Òìṣà Mọgbà.

Solo: Ẹfuntohun, today is dangerous
         The uninitiated must never look a corpse in the face,
             Ẹfuntohun
         Ṣangotọla, lest they go away with the rite [to heaven]
         Arinkẹ, lest they go away with the rite
         Slender-as-a-needle Arinkẹ
Chorus: We never look at Oriṣa Mọgba [a version of Ṣango]
         If you look swiftly, you'll die swiftly
         If you look long, you'll die long
         We never look at the Oriṣa Mọgba
Solo: I say the height of the hot season has arrived, father of
             Toowoju
Chorus: Eepa, eepa, eepa [indicates presence of supernatural]
         We never look at it
         We never look at the sacred
Solo: Arinkẹ has become a forbidden sight, slender-as-a-
             needle
         Anyone who looks at the forbidden will go with the
             forbidden
Chorus: We never look at the Oriṣa Mọgba.

This frightening warning dramatises the actual moment of the performance, the moment when the ritual is being carried out on the other side of the closed door. As the soloist says at one point, 'The height of the hot season has arrived', meaning that the ceremony has reached the moment of its most intense danger. The earlier performance by the ọmọ-oṣu seemed like a kind of holding operation: to keep each other company in the presence of death and in the absence of the dead woman – almost, in fact, to keep that absence itself company – while awaiting the next stage of events that mark the severance of the dead from the living. But the Onisango performance, in marked contrast, was to push events forward. Not only the performance of the ritual itself, which effected another stage of the procedure, but the way the dead woman was addressed showed this. The ọmọ-oṣu were lamenting 'Arinke cannot get up, she cannot get up', when the Onisango burst in; and their first words were

Àrinkẹ ǹde ǹde ǹde e e e
Ǹde ǹde là á ṣolú, Ẹfúntóhún ǹde
Sàngótọ́lá olóriṣà Àrìnpé
Ǹde ǹde là á ṣawọ̀
Ǹde ǹde là á ṣèyàwó ọjọ́ òòjọ́ tí ò gbọdọ̀ pọkọ ẹ̀ lóókọ ...

Arinkẹ get up get up get up
We say 'Get up get up' to the lord, get up Ẹfuntohun
Ṣangotọla the oriṣa-worshipper, Arinpe,
We say 'Get up get up' to the awọ̀ [meaning obscure]
We say 'Get up get up' to the bride married today who is not
    allowed to call her husband by name...

The Onisango are there to activate the dead, to move her on to the next stage of her journey away from the world of the living. She is compared with a new bride who, like a corpse, would be covered from head to foot with a new cloth and who would keep apart and silent, huddled motionless in a private room for the first days of her married life. The dead woman, like the bride, it is implied, is undergoing a transition; like the bride, she must be urged to take the step forward that moves her into a new state of being. Her oriki are being used to inspire her, to give her the courage and the will to go on. Throughout this chant, Ẹfuntohun's death is referred to as a journey, always an arduous one, but pictured in different ways. At one point she is said to have gone into the ground, bearing a heavy burden:

Àrìnkẹ́ wáá wọlẹ̀ẹ́lẹ̀ lọ, ọ kú ẹrù tá ò ranni
A-wẹ́-bí-abẹ́rẹ́ ọ kú ẹrù tá ò ranni
Bórí bá ń tani a mọ́ọ gbérí o
Àrìnkẹ́ bọ́rùn bá ń wọni àá sọ̀
Onísàngó Àrìnkẹ́ ọ kú ẹrù tá ò ranni.

Arinkẹ has gone into the Earth, greetings for your load that no-one
    can help you to carry
Slender-as-a-needle, greetings for your load that no-one can help
    you to carry

If your head hurts you lift up the load to relieve it
Arinkẹ, if it's breaking your neck you'll lift your load down onto
  the ground
Oniṣango Arinkẹ greetings for the load which no-one can help you
  to carry.

At another moment, the journey is to 'heaven'; this time the burden is
specified as the ritual calabash of Ṣango, and again the idea is that no living
human can help the dead to carry this burden to the next world:

Awo ò wò ó, ọgbẹ̀rì ò wò ó, ta ni óò rugbá Ṣàngó dọ́run?

The initiated don't look at it, the uninitiated don't look at it, who
  will carry Ṣango's calabash to heaven for her?

Finally she is pictured as being carried away in a river, in an image that is
characteristically polysemous:

Báṣẹ́ bá mumi á tán nínúu rẹ, ìgèrè tó bá mumi á jòólẹ̀
Onísàngó Àrìnkẹ́, mọ́ọ bómi lọ èmi óò mọ́ọ ṣofẹ.

If the sieve drinks water, the water will soon drain out, if a fish-
  trap drinks water it will all leak away
Oniṣango Arinkẹ, go with the water, I will stay behind and cheer
  you on.

This image begins with the notion of life as water in a sieve or wicker basket-
trap, draining away and being lost. But the dead woman is then imagined as
being carried away by that water as by a great river; the living cannot
accompany her on this journey, but can only encourage her from their vantage
point in this world.[23] She is also pictured as arriving at the other end, to be met
by a large reception committee. All her fellow cult members, now dead, are
listed:

Kì í ṣe kékeré Enísàngó
Ọ bá Òkéyẹ̀bi ṣe
Ọ bá Kúdomi jẹ
Ọ bÓyèníran ṣe
ÀtÒkèyíọlá Ẹfúnjọkẹ́
ÀtÌyálásẹ̀ Ṣàngó
Àtọmọ Ọyágelú ọmọ ọlọ́kọ́ idẹ
ÀtÒgúndàpọ̀ babaà mi
Ó jalápatà lówó, ọmọ agelúgelúmbí
ÀtÒgúnwọlé Ògúnfọnná Mákanjúọlá
Gbogbo wọn ni óò mẹsin wá kòyáà mi, ọmọ alọ́tí-lẹ́mu

She was not an untried member of the Ṣango cult

She was there at the time of Okeyẹbi
She was there together with Kudomi
She was there with Oyeniran
And Okeyiọla Ẹfunjọkẹ
And the Iyalase Ṣango [a senior female title in the cult]
And the child of Ọyagelu, child of the one who has a hoe of brass
And Ogundapọ my father
He owed the butcher money, son of one who pounded indigo in
    huge quantities
And Ogunwọle Ogunfọnna Makanjuọla
All of them will bring horses to meet our mother, child of one who
    has both beer and palm-wine

Like the ọmọ-oṣu, the Oniṣango group use naming and oriki to provide a continued context in which the dead woman will be enmeshed even in the other world. The other world itself is in both cases conceived of in the vaguest possible terms; what is concrete is the networks of relationships with other people which are projected into it. But the ọmọ-oṣu seem to see Ẹfuntohun being claimed either by her husband's lineage (which is also theirs) or by her own; the Oniṣango, on the other hand, disregard both these groups (and their oriki), and propose to reunite Ẹfuntohun with her former colleagues in the cult. It is their oriki that are extensively heard in this performance.

Once the ritual had been completed, the cult members of the outer circle and all the members of the family were asked to come and look at the corpse prepared for burial. Although most of the family were Christian and normally rather contemptuous of Ṣango rituals, they seemed very proud of the totem-like figure of the old lady, completely swathed in cloths and with patches of blood marking her eyes. Photographs of her were taken and later distributed to friends of the family. When the corpse had been sufficiently viewed, the cult members went in procession to the banks of a local stream, Awẹrẹ. Two of the most senior male title-holders in the cult, the Baalẹ Ṣango and Ẹlẹmọṣọ Ṣango, went ahead to bury a calabash containing the dead woman's oṣu, cut from her scalp, together with other ritual substances.(Perhaps the image of Ẹfuntohun 'going with the water' was suggested by this riverbank ceremony.) As the cult members returned in procession they sang cult songs interspersed with snatches of the oriki of Ẹfuntohun.

Other cults had similar rituals of separation for a cult member before burial. The worshippers of Ọya and Eṣu, like the Oniṣango, initiate and empower inner circle members by applying oṣu, which is removed on death. The ritual, as Peter Morton-Williams has persuasively argued (Morton-Williams, 1960b), arises from the this-worldly orientation of the cults. The powers held by the living are retained by them; the dead are stripped of all the appurtenances of the cult before they can be buried. Other cults like Orisa Oko and Ogboni, according to Morton-Williams, have complex and highly secret pre-burial rituals, concerned not so much with the detachment of the dead from their living associations as with a reaffirmation of the interdependence and continuity of the living and the dead. Clearly, however, the difference between the two kinds of cults is a matter of emphasis rather than an absolute distinction. As the *oriki* chants show, the Oniṣango assert continuity of association amongst their dead and living members even in the very act of performing the ritual of separation.

If the death took place in the evening, the burial will be postponed until the following day. In that case, a wake will be held throughout the night during which the women of the household and other relatives keep up a continual performance of songs and chanting, several groups often performing independently and simultaneously.

Burial takes place about four in the afternoon, after a big procession in which the empty coffin, often accompanied by a large photograph of the deceased, is carried all around the town, followed by drummers and groups of singing and chanting women. On their return, certain ceremonies are carried out in the compound before the corpse is put into the coffin. The most important of these is the formal interrogation of various groups that the deceased was associated with. The compound elders, seated beside the coffin, which is laid across two upturned mortars, ask each group in turn if the deceased left his or her affairs in order, if there is any matter left unsettled, or if there are any debts to be paid. Only when all have answered no can the corpse be put in the coffin and buried inside the compound building.

The night after the burial there is a private family ceremony symbolising the departure of the deceased's spirit. Around eleven at night, the elders will gather at the freshly heaped grave and the rest of the family will assemble nearby. A calabash is placed on the grave mound. The most senior man takes up a big stick and calls on the deceased by name in a loud voice. The third time he calls, a distant voice will answer 'Hooo!' The lanterns are put out and a white-garbed figure rushes out through the compound and into the street. At the same moment the senior man smashes the calabash with the stick, seizes the chicken someone is holding ready, and pulls off its head, dripping the blood onto the broken calabash. The egress of the white figure is the signal for all the women to burst into lamentation and *oriki* chanting. The drummers at the same moment begin to play very loudly.

The women stay inside chanting while the men follow the white figure at a safe distance as it dances slowly down the street to the smithy. There it washes its face in water from the blacksmith's trough which is believed to have magical properties. After that it goes to heaven.[24]

The third day from the burial is reserved for *oro ile* – family ceremonies, performed for the deceased, whether male or female, by the members of his or her own (i.e. father's) *ile*. Each lineage has a ceremony of its own, and its function is largely emblematic, marking the unique identity of the lineage. As we shall see in the next chapter, the signs of identity put on display in *oro ile* are the same as those celebrated in the principal themes of *oriki orilẹ*. Thus Ẹfuntohun, the first day of whose funeral has just been described, had an *oro ile* performed for her that enacted the twin themes of warfare and thievery, themes that also figure prominently in the *oriki orilẹ* of Ikoyi.

But the enactment of *oro ile* is not just a dramatic or symbolic equivalent to the performance of *oriki orilẹ*; it may in some cases also contain a performance of *oriki orilẹ*. This was so in the *oro ile* of *ile* Ọlọkọ, who claimed origins in Iwata, and whose emblem was *opo*, a housepost. There is a short post in the centre of *ile* Ọlọkọ which is used only for this ritual. It is dressed up in fine cloths for the seven days of the funeral. The cloth symbolises the traditional occupation of the Opo people, who were a lineage of weavers, but it also recalls the story of an Alaafin, their ancestor, who is said to have had two hundred doorposts carved with the face of his mother and dressed in velvet.[25] When the post has been dressed up, the *obinrin ile* (compound wives) gather near it and say prayers that the deceased may have a good end. Kola is thrown in a form of divination at the foot of the post until a favourable outcome is obtained. Then the women move outside to an open but shady space near the compound. All the male elders of the compound assemble, the most senior being seated on a row of chairs. The women kneel down facing them. One woman recognised for her ability begins solemnly to chant the *oriki orilẹ* of the Opomulero line. The rest of the women repeat it after her line by line. Their words express profound respect for their 'husband', that is, for the collective membership, female as well as male, of the lineage, into which these women have married:[26]

Ọmọ Ẹrúbàmí mo kúnlẹ̀ fólówóò mi...
... Mo mọ̀ mọ̀ foríbalẹ̀ fólówóò mi
Ọmọ Ẹrúbàmí mo foríbalẹ̀ fólówóò mi
Ọmọ Ẹrúbàmí Aláàfin Ọ̀yọ́
Mo mọ̀ mọ̀ foríbalẹ̀ fólórí, ọmọ Abímbówó
Ọmọ Ẹrúbàmí mo kúnlẹ̀ n ò ṣaṣa.

Child of Ẹrubami I kneel for my husband...
... I bow down indeed for my lord
Child of Ẹrubami I bow down for my lord
Child of Ẹrubami the Alaafin of Ọyọ
I bow down indeed for my lord, child of Abimbowo
Child of Ẹrubami I kneel, I show no disrespect.

The *oriki orilẹ* of the Opomulero people are the heart of this performance. The singer concentrates on those parts of the *oriki* that elaborate the theme of the post and the cloth. As we saw in the discussion of *rara iyawo* earlier, the Opomulero *oriki* contain another substantial and extensively-developed theme based on the story of the locusts, the farm in Ale-Ọyun, and the Alaafin's

verdict. But in this performance, that part of the *oriki* is ignored. The ceremony
revolves around the emblematic post whose physical presence is before them.
The first *oriki orilę* the women quote, therefore, are these:

> Ará ilú Ọyun, ara ń gbó mi láṣọ
> Kẹkẹ ta dúndùn, aṣọ ledidi ènìyàn
> N óò bọ́ ọ rèlúù rẹ, ọmọ kálukú ló láṣọọ rẹ
> Egbínrín ńkọ́? Aṣọ òpó ẹyin ni.
> Egbìnrìn ńkọ́? Aṣọ òpó ẹyin ni.
> Kẹlẹkúlú laṣọ àró-pẹkun òpó
> Eńńlẹyò ilée yín ni wọn ń tí í rógi láṣọ

> Native of Ọyun town, I'm wearing my clothes out
> The spinning wheel spins merrily, cloth is the covering of people
> I'll go with you to your town, child of 'Everyone has their own
>   cloth'
> What about *egbínrín* cloth? It's your post's cloth.
> What about *egbìnrìn* cloth? It's your post's cloth.
> *Kẹlẹkulu* is the very best of all the post's cloths.
> Ilẹyọ people, it's in your family they dress up a post in cloth.

The identity of the group is conceived of in terms of a place of origin. The
assembled members of *ile* Ọlọkọ are identified, first and foremost, as *ara ilu
Ọyun* (natives of Ọyun town), and to introduce the *oriki orilę* the performer
says 'I'll go with you to your town'. The utterance of the *oriki* is itself a kind
of 'going', for in performance she takes the owners of the *oriki* back to their
source, recalling them to a sense of their common origin in a named location.
This sense of place provides a metaphor for death:

> Ìyáa wa relé Ọyọ́, ọmọ Akẹnjẹkùn Sàbi
> Iyee wa relé, ọmọ akankan eyín erin...
> ... Àṣá gbé kowéè, ó gbé ọmọ Abímbówó o
> Yọòyè relé Ọyọ́ rèé ṣọmọ-ọba

> Our mother has gone to Ọyọ, child of Akẹnjẹkun Sabi
> Our mother has gone home, child of one as tough as the elephant's
>   tusk
> ... The hawk carried off the *kowee* bird, it carried off the child of
>   Abimbowo
> Yọoye has gone to Ọyọ to be a princess.

Yọoye, a daughter of the lineage, has gone back, in death, to her place of
origin. Her 'wives' – the women married into her natal compound – do her
honour by performing a ceremony that recognises her most essential identity.
They assert that her bonds with the Opomulero people can never be broken.
'Ọyọ' – not the present-day city but the ancient city of origin – becomes

another way of thinking of the afterlife.

And – as in the *rara iyawo* and the Ṣango chant already discussed – the performers are conscious of their own role. The performance includes commentary on itself and on the proceedings of which it is a part. The performance is to do public and collective honour to Yọoye. In the act of doing this, the women congratulate those present for the part they are playing:

Ó lẹ́ ẹ kúù bá n dárò o, ẹ kúù bá n dárò iyeè mi
Sèyìn dòkú, sèyìn dòkú
Ẹ̀yin tẹ́ ẹ bá sèyìn dòkú, ọmọ ni yóò tẹ́yìn gbogboo yín ṣe

Thank you for your sympathy and support over the death of my
    mother
Performing a fitting funeral for the dead
You who are helping to perform a fitting funeral for the dead, you
    will have children to give you a good burial too.

After the *oro ile*, there are three days in which all the daughters and granddaughters of the deceased take it in turns to bring parties of their compound co-wives (*orogun*) to go round the town in procession, singing funeral songs. Sometimes those among them who are close relatives of the deceased overlay this singing with solo chanting of laments and the deceased's *oriki*. On the night of the sixth day, a farewell vigil is held by the Ṣango or Ogboni cult if the deceased was a member. The devotees go round the town in procession all night singing cult songs. The Orisa Oko cult has secret rituals that it performs during the sixth night.

On the seventh day is the *inawo*, the spending of money, when the heirs have to provide food, drink and drumming on as grand a scale as they can manage. Lavish expenditure is considered a mark of respect to the dead, as well, of course, as being a demonstration of the wealth and status of his or her heirs. This is the kind of occasion that specialist and professional performers would come to from neighbouring towns, and Ṣangowẹmi would be there from start to finish. Her performance on these occasions demonstrated the beginning of a process of domestication of the death. At the funeral of Ọyawale, an elderly Ọya devotee and very senior man in *ile* Nla, the deceased was lamented, and still addressed as a beloved companion only just embarking on his lonely journey to an unknown world, as he had been in the earlier stages of the funeral. Puzzlement and reproach were notes still to be heard in Ṣangowẹmi's chant. But at the same time much more of the chant was concerned with putting the death into the context of the social experience of the living. Much of it was addressed not to the deceased but to the survivors. The death of one person seemed to open the doors of memory on the deaths of many others, and her chant became a survey, that concluded with the sad but philosophical comment:

Olóìṣà ìṣẹ̀n báyé wáá lọ gbáà

The *oriṣa*-worshippers of the old days have all gone beyond recall

Oyawale's death was thus seen as part of a general process of decline. And his solitary journey in unknown realms was now pictured in contrast to the good time the celebrants were having on earth, at his funeral: they would have liked to send him a part of the feast, but rather humorously doubt whether human food would be acceptable to a denizen of the other world:

Bá a bá wáá mohun tí òkú jẹ ní Wáìsà
Àbá wáá rọtí-ọkà fÁyàndá

If we knew what the dead eat in the Unknown Land
We'd buy guinea-corn beer for Ayanda

and she warns him to watch what he eats when he is underground:

Mọ́ jọkùn kí ọ mọ́ jẹkòló
Oyáwálé ohun tí gbogbo ẹgbẹ́ Ọlóya ń bá ń jẹ ni kí ọ mọ́ọ jẹ

Don't eat millipedes, don't eat worms
Oyawale you'd better eat what the rest of your fellow-devotees of
    Oya eat

And those who spend money and effort on Oyawale's funeral today will be recompensed in future, when their own children do the same for them. His death is now seen not only as part of a wider process, but as part of an endless cycle of investment and profit, of moral and material expenditure and reward, over the generations, and crossing between human and spiritual worlds:

Ọmọ Oyáwálé, gbogboo yín ni óò rérè ọmọ jẹ
Ọmọ Oyáwálé baba Ọlóya, Òkín ọmọ Àyèéjìn
Ọmọ́kéhìndé ò ó rérè ọmọ jẹ o
Ọmọ́ṣèjìwáyé, ò ó rérè ọmọ jẹ, ọmọ Oyáwálé baba Ọlóya
Orí óò jẹ́ ọ tó ìyá ọhún gbé...
Oya ni óò fi púpọ̀ san
Ọmọ Oyáwálé, Olóndà ń wá ń darí ọkòọ́ bọ̀
Owó igbá tí ẹ ná fún Oyáwálé
Òìṣà Òkè ni óò fi púpọ̀ san
Oya óò darí agbọ̀n sílé èyin...
Bá a ń bá ń bẹ láyé, Oyáwálé, ká a mọ́ọ ṣe rere
Bá a bá ṣe rere sílé ayé, ọmọ a-bérè-jí ará Ìsokùn
Bá à bá sí mọ́, ọmọọ wa óò mọ́ọ jèrè oore lọ ni
Oyáwálé orí óò jẹ́ kọ́mọọ̀ rẹ ó jèrè oore...

Children of Oyawale, all of you will reap the benefit of
    your own children

Children of Ọyawale the Ọya-devotee, Ọkin people of Ayejin
Ọmọkẹhinde, you will reap the benefit of your own children
Ọmọsejiwaye, you will reap the benefit of your own
    children, son of Ọyawale the Ọya-devotee
Your destiny will let you give your mother a grand burial...
Ọya will repay you abundantly
Child of Ọyawale, the Returner of Blessings is bringing his vehicle
    this way
The money you brought out from your calabash to spend on
    Ọyawale
Orisa Oke[27] will repay abundantly
Ọya will direct the basket [of wealth] to your house...
While we're on earth, Ọyawale, let us do good
If we do good to the world, child of One-who-rises-with-the-
    python, native of Isokun
When we are no longer on earth, our children will carry on reaping
    the benefits of our actions
Ọyawale, your Destiny will allow your children to reap the benefits
    of your good deeds...

In this passage Ṣangowẹmi addresses first Ọyawale's twin sons
('Ọmọkẹhinde' and 'Ọmọsejiwa'), who are among the principal celebrants at
the funeral feast, and then the deceased, Ọyawale himself ('While we're on
earth, Ọyawale, let us do good'), in a transition that involves no change of
register or tone. There is a perfect continuity suggested in this chant between
the living and the dead, between Ọyawale and his children, and between them
and their own children of the future. None of these texts has shown any
interest in what the 'other world' is like. They stress, rather, the impossibility
of knowing. But in the very act of bidding farewell to the one crossing into that
world irretrievably, the chants re-establish a continuity and completeness of
communication which is almost sociable in tone, so assured and comfortable
is it.

If the deceased was a man, there is a final ceremony to complete his
severance from the world of the living. On the morning of the seventh day a
masquerade representing his spirit (an *egungun rere*),[28] will come out and take
his leave of the family. This is another occasion for the impassioned solo
chanting of *oriki* and laments. The widows, dressed in rags, will be escorted
by drummers, *egungun* priests and a crowd of family members and well-
wishers out of the town towards the path to the dead man's farm. As they are
going, the widows will chant snatches of *oriki*, competing with the drums and
each other, while the rest of the women sing funeral songs. At the beginning
of the farm path the crowd will be told to stop. The *egungun* priests will lead
the widows forward up the path to a place, prepared by the *egungun* cult in

advance, where there is a yam heap dug for each widow and one extra one representing *ofo*: emptiness. The *egungun* priest called Ẹlẹmọsọ Agan calls the name of the deceased. He calls again; and on the third call there is an answering 'Hooo!' and the *egungun* emerges from the bush. Drumming begins. Each widow then pulls up her own yam from beneath the *egungun*'s foot, which he places on each heap in turn. Each widow then presents the *egungun* with symbolic gifts: an egg, money, and a ball of thread representing the wick of a lamp and signifying that she will never light a lamp for him again.[29] The *egungun* blesses them by placing his foot on their upturned palms. Then the crowd escorts him back to the town. Once again the widows chant wild and tearful laments on the way. At home, each widow cooks and pounds the yam she was given, and the *egungun* emerges again that evening to come and eat the food. Then, seated in the compound, he calls the widows, children and younger relatives to come and kneel by him. He prays for them, blesses them and departs for ever.

After this, the dead man's spirit, up till then still close to the human world, has gone to its own realm. The departed can now only be present among the living by returning at prescribed times as an *egungun*, or through ritual invocations at his grave. But *oriki* remain as a vital link between the living and the dead. Throughout the funeral, the deceased has been continually and intensely addressed, with exhortations, farewells, regrets, reproaches and warnings. After the funeral is over, communication becomes less concentrated, but it continues, and the idiom hardly changes. He or she is still addressed in *oriki* in the same tone, the same terms, as living subjects. The dead remain, in *oriki*, perpetually and potentially present.

Plate 1.　　His Highness James Ọlọsẹbikan Oyclousi II

Plate 2.　　Ṣangowẹmi

Plate 3.   Ṣangowẹmi

Plate 4.   A bride

Plate 5.   A royal bride

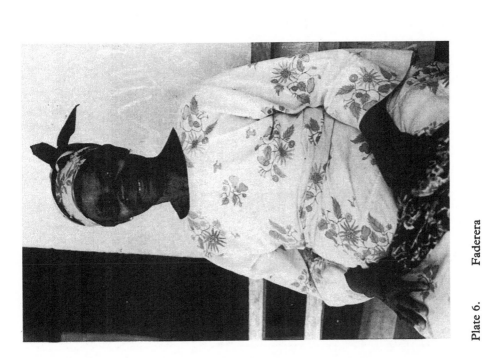

Plate 6.   Faderera

5

THE *ORIKI* OF ORIGIN

1. INTRODUCTION

Oriki orilẹ are the *oriki* of a place of origin, a homeland. What people say is that their people originally came from an ancient town, whose name they remember even when the town has long been defunct. They picture masses of people scattering from these original towns to other places all over Yorubaland. People from the same place of origin – the same *orilẹ* – say 'We are one'. When they meet in the course of trade or other travel they recognise an obligation to help each other, and observe a prohibition on intermarriage. They have a number of things in common. They may share certain food taboos, special funeral customs, a particular *oriṣa* or a specialised occupation such as carving, blacksmithing or *egungun* entertainment masquerading, all of which are traced back to the town of origin. But the most important thing they have in common is the *oriki orilẹ* themselves. These *oriki* are all about the place of origin, and affirm the distinctive attributes of the place and its people. It is mainly through their shared *oriki orilẹ* that these scattered groups recognise a relationship. They cannot trace the links between themselves, beyond saying that, because they share the same *orilẹ*, they know they are 'one'.

When they left the town of origin, the stories say, these small groups settled somewhere else: either they founded a new town, and waited for other groups to join them, or they inserted themselves into an existing one. Within the town where they settled, their *oriki orilẹ* took on a new importance. Each incoming group took up residence as a unit conceived as a kin group: a patrilineage. A simplified version of local theory would say that each of these localised patrilineages constituted a separate *ile*, a 'house', or compound, and that these *ile* were the fundamental social and political units in the town. Historical narratives, already described in Chapter 3, represented the town as a collection of *ile*, each coming from a different place of origin and each having its own traditions; and these separate units were pictured as being held together by their common allegiance to the ọba, who was descended from the founder of the town. Each *ile,* in this picture, would stress its own inner unity and separateness from other equivalent groups. It would know its own history and deny knowledge of others'. It would identify itself, and could be recognised by others, by its distinctive *oriki orilẹ*. Sometimes it happened that two groups from the same town of origin would arrive separately in a new town and each would establish its own *ile*. In that case, they would recognise their relationship through ceremonial actions and would be forbidden to intermarry, but otherwise would behave as two separate political and social units. This did not happen often enough, however, to undermine the function of *oriki orilẹ* as symbols of the separate identity of *ile*.

Townspeople often identify others by reference to the *orilẹ* of the group they belong to: '*Àwọn Ọlófà wọnyẹn tó wà nísàlẹ̀ Òkukù*' – 'Those people of Ọfa origin who live at the bottom end of Okuku'. They continually identify themselves and their children as members of their own group by citing the *oriki* of origin: so a mother might murmur to her newborn child '*Ọmọ Ọlófà ni ó, Mọjà-Àlekàn...*' – 'You are a child of the Ọfa people, people who are called "Mọja-Alekan"...' It is *oriki orilẹ* that people most often recite as a form of greeting, to congratulate someone or show them affection and approbation. *Oriki orilẹ* tell each individual where he or she belongs in the town: they establish the person on the social map, and give him or her a background without which he or she would scarcely exist as a social being. *Oriki orilẹ* thus have a dual claim on people's emotional loyalties: they relate them to their source and through that to large numbers of people all over Yoruba country, in a shadowy but nonetheless deeply felt unity; and they place them in an immediate, concrete social context within their own town, assigning them a social place and a body of people to whom they belong, and who belong to them.

Of all *oriki*, they evoke people's deepest responses. They are not only rooted in people's earliest memories, bound up with their deepest sense of their own place in the world, but they are also associated with the emotional gratification of others' affection and esteem. They hold pride of place in almost all Yoruba chants. They form the basic building blocks in the eclectic and flexible performances which draw also on personal *oriki*, prayers, blessings, witticisms and topical comments. As we saw in the last chapter, they can appear in extended sequences, formally elaborated, as in *rara iyawo*, or broken up into allusive fragments, which those who know them will mentally complete. They can be heard deeply entangled with the personal, individual *oriki* of big men from the past, whose names and reputations are cherished by their descendants. *Oriki orilẹ* gradually absorb certain personal *oriki* in this way, becoming, among other things, the collective memorial to great men of the past. When the personal *oriki* of a great man are remembered as his own, distinct from the *oriki orilẹ* of the whole group, they can still be intimately mixed with *oriki orilẹ* in performance. Origin is the foundation of identity; the individual, whose personal *oriki* commemorate his or her personal achievements, distinctions and idiosyncrasies, cannot be conceived of except as a member of the larger group that claims common origins. Just as the group's identity is fed and renewed by the fame of individual members, so the individual members derive glory from the inherited, collective fame of the *orilẹ* to which they belong. The dialectical process by which individual and group reputations feed, and feed on, each other, is thus visible in the very form of *oriki* chants: in which personal *oriki* are absorbed into *oriki orilẹ* and *oriki orilẹ* are addressed intensively to individuals.

Because of their deep roots in people's self-conception, *oriki orilẹ* are cherished in transmission. They are more stable than other *oriki*. In a performance of *oriki orilẹ*, as in other *oriki* performances, there is fluidity, fragmentation and variation in wording. But *oriki orilẹ* have a core set of images and references which are considered to be unchanging. If a performer gets it wrong – if she attributes the wrong *oriki orilẹ* to her subject, or if she confuses two different ones – the recipient of the performance will be alienated and even insulted.[1] There is felt to be more at stake with *oriki orilẹ* than with personal *oriki*, where borrowing and blending is the order of the day. With *oriki orilẹ* it is important to get it right. *Oriki* themselves comment on this:

> Bí ò sí orílẹ̀ a ò mẹwẹ
> Bí ò sí orílẹ̀ a ò mòwè.

> If there were no *orilẹ* we should not know itching-beans
> If there were no *orilẹ* we should not know bean-sprouts.

That is, we should not know one thing from another, and the distinctions of the social order would be blurred.

There is no doubt that *oriki orilẹ* are still, today, highly valued by Yoruba people even when they no longer live in a traditional compound. Collections of them are published by academic and popular presses alike; they appear regularly in newspaper obituaries; they are quoted as slogans on the backs of lorries. But their very pervasiveness has stood in the way of analysis.

A preliminary question that needs to be asked is what is the nature of 'origin', as represented in these *oriki*, and what kind of bonds are envisaged amongst the people who share them? A second question, which leads into the very heart of the problem of how to describe Yoruba social structure, is what groups actually do claim 'common origin' in any given town. When *oriki orilẹ* are mapped out over a whole community, showing all the groups that identify themselves by a separate 'origin', and the relations between them, it becomes clear that the simplified picture of social structure I have just described is not adequate. Indeed, it is only used in certain contexts, notably in the formal and as it were abstract recital of town and family histories. When the stories go into greater detail, or are told for a specific purpose, a rather different picture emerges: one which is corroborated by daily processes of interaction and by living memories of relations between groups. Instead of the regular pattern of residential patrilineages postulated by the simplified picture, it reveals groupings constituted according to a variety of principles and joining forces for a variety of purposes. Since the most influential descriptions of Yoruba social structure available in anthropology have used the segmentary lineage model, which is in a sense an edited, amplified and rigorously presented version of the simplified indigenous picture, the investigation of *oriki orilę* in action may contribute much to our understanding of how social cohesiveness and division, alliance and dissociation, actually work in one Yoruba town.

Oriki orilę then can be used like a 'trace element', in the sense intended by Terence Ranger[2], to show up the constitution of social groups in the town. It then becomes clear that in the rather mixed picture that emerges, *oriki orilę* play an active and constitutive role. If the town were indeed made up of autonomous residential patrilineal kin groups, united for all purposes and separate from all equivalent groups, *oriki orilę* would be almost redundant; at best, they could be seen as a reflection or endorsement of an established system whose boundaries were already maintained by every social action and relationship. But in a situation where *ile* are less clearly defined than this, and where different groupings can be called forth by different situations, *oriki orilę* play a part in the actual definition and constitution of groups. They are a way of laying claim to identity, rather than just a way of acknowledging membership of an already fully constituted corporate group. Depending on how they use them, people may loudly proclaim their membership of a group, or assert their independence. They may also use them to negotiate the many ambivalent and borderline relationships. It is only by locating *oriki orilę* in this context of social action that their true importance emerges; and at the same time, it is only then that the true subtlety of Yoruba social structural principles is revealed.

2. THE IDEA OF ORIGIN

Origin, in *oriki orilę*, is always construed in terms of place, whether a town (Ọyọ-ile, Ọla, Ikoyi) or, less commonly, a cultural area focused around a town (Ijẹsa). Many *oriki orilę* fill out this 'sense of place' by dwelling on the characteristic natural features and resources of the town of origin. The *oriki orilę* of Irẹsa have as their central theme the thick palm forests surrounding the two towns, Irẹsaadu and Irẹsa pupa ('black' and 'red' Irẹsa). In Igbẹti, further north, it is shea trees that are celebrated. Many *oriki orilę* dwell on the abundance of water sources, naming all the rivers that are said to flow past or through the town. But landscape and geographical features are treated not as *natural* but as *cultural* resources. The trees and rivers are part of civilisation, domesticated and imbued with human significance, as both sources and signs of wealth to a people. The palm trees of Irẹsa are given such prominence because they provide the raw materials for the production of palm oil. Palm oil is the basis of trade, and is also, like salt, a fundamental ingredient of civilised life. Abundance of salt and palm oil together indicate social wellbeing:

Epo bá n ká relé
Mo mẹ̀bẹ́ mèrò
Mo mòdì epoò mi gìrì latà
Mo ṣubú yẹ́gẹ́ mo fẹnu gúngbá epo
Mo fàgbọ̀n ìsàlẹ̀ mo i bọyọ̀ lÀlọ̀
Mo yíìká bọwágún
Mo dọ̀dọ̀bálẹ̀ bọwàmọ̀.

Palm-oil come home with me
I know how to sell it and calculate the price
I sealed my palm-oil tightly into a big pot
I tumbled down, I hit my mouth on a calabash of palm-oil
I plunged my jaw into salt at Alọ
I bent my shoulder to the ground to worship the young palm tree
I prostrated to worship the dried palm spines.

Rivers, similarly, provide the water which is the basis of the wellbeing of a human community. They are often associated with the ọba or the royal family, who, as we have seen, are the custodians of the whole town's identity, so that abundant water indicates abundant blessings and honour for the town:

Ará odò Ọrọ̀
Ará Kọọkin
Àyà-bu-èrò
Aásin re ò gbẹ
Gọ̀dọ̀gbọ̀ ò dé n lẹ́ran'sẹ̀
Obukú ń ṣẹ́ sí mi lẹ́nu.

Native of the River Ọrọ
Native of Kọọkin
Place where travellers stop to drink
The River Aasin doesn't dry up
The River Gọdọgbọ doesn't reach as high as the edge of my sole
The River Obuku flows into my mouth.[3]

Oriki orilẹ, then, are about places in interaction with people: places that have been made by people out of the available natural resources; places which bless their inhabitants with prosperity and wellbeing.

Much of the oriki of these primordial towns is devoted to the people who belong to them: their occupations, the orìṣa they worship, their customs and taboos. And here the idiom of the oriki seems to hint at a preoccupation with origin in a sense that goes deeper than that of a mere geographical starting point. The oriki orilẹ of Iremogun, for example, are built around the theme of the Iremogun people's distinctive occupation of blacksmith. They boast that without blacksmiths, no tools would be made and no work done; there would be no farming, no wealth, and no civilisation:

> Àgbẹ̀dẹẹ̀ mi rìbìtì nÍrè
> Àìsí Enírè a ò roko
> Àìsí Enírè a ò yẹnà
> Ìbá má sìí Enírè a ò ti gbẹ́dẹ́ ẹrú ṣáájú.

> My smithy is round in Ire
> Without the Ire people we wouldn't be able to hoe our farms
> Without the Ire people we wouldn't be able to clear the paths
> If there were no Ire people we wouldn't be able to herd slaves
>   along in front of us [to work on the farm].

In a similar vein, the Opomulero people of Iwata claim that without the cloth they weave, people would have to go naked, revealing the deformities of nature:

> Bí ò sí aṣọ
> Mo ní à bá ṣìṣe
> Bí ò sí aṣọ
> À bá ṣìwà hù
> Bíi kókó
> Bí oówo
> Bí ìkù
> Bí àgbáàrín...

> If there were no cloth
> We would surely be at fault
> If there were no cloth
> Our blemishes would be exposed
> Like lumps
> Like boils
> Like swollen hips
> Like grape-sized swellings...

The origin celebrated by *oriki orilẹ* has overtones of the origin of civilisation. Not only are all the arts by which nature is converted to culture put at the centre of *oriki orilẹ*, but also, that this contrast is made quite explicit. It is the art of the blacksmith which enables the human community to transform itself and remove itself from the animal existence of the forest: metal tools create for the first time the possibility of clearing the bush, and of setting 'farm' and 'town' in opposition to 'forest' – an opposition which, as we have seen, is fundamental to the Yoruba conception of civilisation.[4] Cloth and clothes refine these distinctions further. Semi-nakedness is all very well on the farm, but no-one in his or her right mind would go into the town like that. As the proverb says, '*Àìfęni peni, àìfènìyàn pènìyàn, ní í mú ará oko san bàntę wǫlú*': 'Only the "bush-man" [lit. farm person] who has no respect for public opinion would come into town in his shorts'. Clothes set humans apart from animals; decent clothes transform the sweating farmer, who struggles with nature at close quarters, into a civilised man of means and leisure. In the *oriki orilę* of Ǫję, the idea of transformation is even more vividly represented. The Ǫję people are carvers. Shapeless blocks of wood are turned, under their skilled hands, to images of human life. The natural tree, transformed into a carved figure, becomes part of human culture:[5]

> Ǫmǫ òpagidà sǫgi dènìyàn
> Gbígbę lę́ę́ gbę́, ǫmǫ Ajíbógundé o
> Ńjó ijó kííní ńkǫ́? Ǫmǫ Ajíbógundé
> Ó wá gbé ńgboro ó ń lǫ sínúugbó o
> Igi ń sá lu apá, ìrókò ń sá lura wǫn
> A à mǫbi tí Làgbàì ó sǫlę̀ sí
> Ó gbę́gi ń kǫrǫbǫtǫ ní kǫrǫbǫtǫ
> Igi ò lójú igi ò lę́nu
> Igi ò látànpàkò ęsę̀ méjèèjì
> Ó tún wá dęlę́ę̀kęta èwèwę̀
> Ǫmǫ bíbí Ǫlójèę́ ńkǫ́? Ó wá gbé ńgboro ń lǫ sínúugbó
> Ó wá gbę́gi náà dénú ayé
> Igi lápá igi lę́nu ó wá látànpàkò ęsę̀ méjèèjì
> Ó bu pélé sígi lę́ę̀ké òtún
> Ó bùbàjà sígi lę́ę̀kę́ òsì
> Ǫmǫ 'Kújęnrá ó wá gbę́gi náà dé Ọ̀yǫ́-ilé.

> Child of 'One who transforms a piece of wood, turns it into a
>   person'
> Carving is your metier, child of Ajibogunde
> What happened on the very first day? The child of Ajibogunde
> He lived in the town, he went into the forest
> The mahogany bean trees knocked against each other, the
>   *iroko* trees ran into each other in their fright[6]
> Nobody knows which one Lagbai will pick on.
> He carved a piece of wood and made it smooth and round
> The wood had no eyes, the wood had no mouth
> The wood had no big toe on either of its feet
> But the third time round [sic]
> What did the true-born son of Ǫję do? He lived in the town, he
>   went into the forest
> He went and carved a piece of wood and brought it out on view
> The wood had arms, the wood had a mouth, and it had a big toe

on each of its feet
He cut *pele* marks on the wood's right cheek
He cut *abaja* marks on the wood's left cheek[7]
Child of Ikujẹnra, his carving took him as far as Ọyọ-ile.

Lagbai, the carver, is part of the civilised world: he lives in the town, and only goes into the forest to collect the raw materials of his craft. He converts the raw material into a human artefact, and as a result of his skill he achieves fame and success in the human community. 'His carving took him as far as Ọyọ-ile' conveys the ultimate achievement: success in the eyes of the capital of the Ọyọ Empire and, by implication, in the eyes of its ruler the Alaafin. The opening line, 'On the very first day', is a standard formula introducing a tripartite narrative structure (note that the performer takes this structure so much for granted that she skips the second day) but it also hints at the primordial. Arts such as carving are the foundations of human culture.

But right at the origin of human culture is installed, in *oriki orilẹ*, the idea of social difference. The carver, like the weaver and the blacksmith, creates culture for the whole community, not just for his own people. But note the finishing touches to the carving. What makes the image really lifelike is the incision of facial marks: 'He cut *pele* marks on the wood's right cheek/He cut *abaja* marks on the wood's left cheek'. Facial marks are emblems of social difference: they belong to the repertoire of signs by which groups distinguish themselves. To be fully part of human culture, it is necessary to be socially differentiated. The carved image of course belongs to no social group, but it is humanised by the *generalised* representation of social differentiation: the marks of one group on the left cheek, and of another on the right. In the same way, carving itself is made into an emblem of difference: only certain groups are carvers, just as certain groups are weavers or blacksmiths. Difference is what the *oriki* celebrate.

The kind of divisions that arise from occupational specialisation are horizontal, between social groupings of comparable status and function. Each group proclaims its own specialisation to distinguish itself from other similar groups. But *oriki orilẹ* also assert that from the moment of origin, society is characterised by vertical divisions. Citizens are not all equal; and the status of the privileged is defined by its difference from that of the deprived. These distinctions are built into the very structure of *oriki orilẹ*. A fundamental and continually recurrent figure is the triadic set '*ẹrú, iwọ̀fà, ọmọ bibí inú*': slave, bondsman, free member of a house. It is invariably used to emphasise the superiority of the free member over the slave and bondsman. Slave and bondsman are attached to the free person's group, but can never really share that group's attributes. One version of the Ọjẹ *oriki* says that the slave carved an image but it had neither eyes nor nose, nor toes on either of its feet; the bondsman carved an image, with the same result; then the true-born son of the house carved one, and 'The wood had arms, the wood had a mouth, and it had a big toe on each of its feet'. The superior skill of the 'true-born son' is reflected in the higher rewards he gets for his work. As a *rara ìyàwo* version of the *oriki* says:

Òwòn pagidà sọgi dènìyàn
Ẹrú Ọjẹ́ ti gbẹ́nà pegbèje
Ìwòfà Ọjẹ́ ti gbẹ́nà pẹgbèfà
Ọmọ bíbí inú Ọjẹ́ ti gbẹ́nà pẹgbẹ̀ẹ́dógún.

Owọn who transforms a piece of wood and turns it into a person
The slave of Ojẹ made a carving that sold for 1400 cowries
The bondsman of Ojẹ made a carving that sold for 1200 cowries[8]
The true-born son of Ojẹ made a carving that sold for 7500 cowries.

The slave and bondsman are represented as being excluded from the cherished ceremonials of the group that owns them. The royal descent group 'owns' the cult of the Ọtin, the principal local river. The Ọtin festival is celebrated with the emergence of a stunning array of images, heavy carved headpieces carried by the devotees, representing male and female figures. Pride in this display can be expressed, in the *oriki*, as the yearning to take part in it:

Ǹ bá là, ma dère
Ǹ bá là, ma dÒtònpòrò
Ǹ bá là, ma ti gbẹ́dẹ́ ẹrú ṣáájú.

If I were rich, I would become an image
If I were rich, I would become Otonporo [the most important of the images]
It I were rich, I would herd slaves along the farm path ahead of me.

But it can also be expressed as the specific exclusion of the royal family's slaves and bondsmen from the privilege; only 'ibilẹ Iṣẹṣu' (the 'native' Iṣẹṣu people, i.e. the 'true-born sons') are allowed to carry the images:

Ẹrú ilée wá gbọ́n
E è ìi dère
Ìwòfàa wa ò gbọdọ̀ dÒtònpòrò
Ìbílẹ̀ Ìṣẹ̀ṣú n óò gbÁpà léri.

The slaves of our house are wise
They never become images
Our bondsmen are not allowed to become Otonporo
Native Iṣẹṣu, I will carry Apa [another Ọtin image] on my head.

The presence of slaves and bondsmen heightens the standing of the 'true-born son' not only by the sheer contrast of their positions – privilege against deprivation, inclusion against exclusion, skill against lack of skill, true belonging against attached status – but also because the slaves and bondsmen are themselves part of the 'true born son's' possessions. It is a sign of wealth and wellbeing to be able to 'herd slaves along the path' to the farm, and to have a household where slaves labour in the workshop or smithy for the benefit of the master. In the *oriki orilę* of Ọla, an ancient city 'on the road to Ogbomọṣọ',[9] these two ideas are conjoined. The slaves and bondsmen, who trade in low-value goods, are contrasted with the 'true-born sons' who deal in the most valuable commodity of all, human beings. That is, the true-born sons use the profits from their servants' work to buy further servants:

> Ẹrú Ọlọ́là wọn á tèẹ́gún
> Ìwọ̀fà Ọlọ́là wọn á tògbùngbùn
> Ọmọ bíbí Ọlọ́là wọn á ràkókó ẹrú wálé.

> The Ọla people's slaves will sell silk-cotton shoots
> The Ọla people's bondsmen will sell silk-cotton sprouts
> The true-born children of Ọla will buy well-formed slaves and
>   bring them home.

Conceptions of social differentiation and specialisation are thus indivisible from conceptions of social hierarchy. The celebration of difference in occupation, religious practice, and customs is in the first instance a marker of boundaries between equivalent, free social groupings from different towns of origin but with equal social status. However, the characteristics attributed to each of these groups are brought into focus by the contrast not only with each other but also with the unfree categories that are attached to each group. The contrast is here between attributes possessed as of right, by virtue of membership of the group, and the same attributes imperfectly possessed, or not possessed at all, by a penumbra of people associated with the group but not belonging to it. In this way the attributes in question are given the value of intrinsic, authentic, quasi-natural characteristics, desired but never fully obtainable by outsiders. The power of the attributes as identifiers is thus enhanced. In the act of learning to distinguish themselves as members of a social unit within a town, people also learn that the members of the town are not all equal.

Everything in *oriki orilę* functions as a mark of identity, a means of social differentiation. Often, *oriki orilę* take as their theme the very symbols by which groups demarcate themselves. Facial marks usually identify people as coming from a particular area;[10] they are cited with much elaboration in *oriki*:

> Òkòò mi rèri àbàjà
> Àbàjà pókí n wọn ń bù nÍrèsé
> Ẹni kọ pélé yalé iyá lọ ni.

My Oko people cut broad *abaja* marks
At Irese they make thin *abaja* marks
Anyone who cuts *pele* marks has deviated
    into his mother's line.

Special taboos and observances which distinguish a group are treated in the same way. The *oriki* of the people of Aran-Orin origin make much of the fact that newly delivered mothers in their group are forbidden to eat palm oil, salt or pepper in their food for seven days after the birth. The *oriki* of *ile* Oba state that 'My Ara people never eat *ewe* beans/ I will have nothing to do with bean-shoots at Otin/ I must not trifle with the *olodooyo* plant as long as I live'. *Oriki orile* can thus become a kind of meta-identifier. They not only repeat, in the medium of words, signs of identity already existing in the form of visible symbols and practices; they are also able to elaborate and comment upon the value and meaning of these signs. They have a double capacity to emblematise social difference.

It is only as elaborated emblems that *oriki orile* can be understood; read as narratives, or as the praises of past heroes, they remain opaque and yield little of their meaning. *Oriki orile* revolve around a small number of highly distinctive signs, revealing that their essential point or purpose is to distinguish groups of people and assign them marks of identity. It will be shown later in this chapter that their form, structure and use of language are all animated by the intent to emblematise.

Place, horizontal social differentiation, and hierarchy are thus bound up together in the notion of origin; and this origin is the beginning of civilisation. This complex of ideas is concentrated into what is essentially a collection of unitary images: emblematic representations that function like signs. The constitution of living, evolving social identities is construed in terms of a remote past. This 'past' is therefore inscribed in every social alignment formed in the present. However, it is not essentially a historical past (though notions of historical change do occasionally enter *oriki orile*). The core emblems are located in a timeless, originary moment, the beginning of human society itself.

One of the key ambiguities at the centre of social identity will by now have become fully visible. *Oriki orile* are one of the principal means by which groups of people who regard themselves as *kin* recognise each other and assert their unity. But they do so in terms of a common *town* of origin, and not, in the first instance, in terms of ancestry. The key emblems in *oriki orile* are always associated with the names of places. *Oriki orile* do include allusions to illustrious men and women among the ancestors of the group, but these allusions are attached to the notion of the town of origin. *Oriki orile* do not trace genealogies, nor do they revolve around the notion of a lineage founder. The members of a group assert that they are 'one' because they all came from the same place of origin, and distinguish themselves from people coming from other places. Narrative accounts of town history do the same thing. When Ajiboye described the formation of Okuku, for instance, he said that the people of *ile* Qloko came from Qyq, not that they were descended from Tela; and the elders of *ile* Baale remembered that their people came from Aran-Qrin but said they did not know who brought them. This suggests that kinship cannot be seen as the only principle by which people structure their social world. At the very roots of identity, it seems, kinship and residence are intertwined and mutually defining. Neither is prior to, nor determinant of, the other. To suggest how this might have come about, some speculative history is required.

3. IDENTIFICATION THROUGH TOWN MEMBERSHIP

Why does the ancient town of origin have such a grip on the imagination of people long since settled elsewhere? Why do the emblematic references of *oriki orile* command such profound emotional allegiance and universal respect? The answer to these questions must lie in the history of Yoruba town formation and dissolution. Though our knowledge of this history is partial and fragmented, there is enough evidence in oral narratives to suggest at least an outline of a historical explanation.

In pre-colonial northern Yorubaland the town was the principal political unit. Johnson and other sources show that it was towns – together with their political hinterlands – that formed alliances, waged war and made peace with each other. Subordinate towns, placed in that position either through conquest or, as in the case of those that surrounded Kqokin, by accepting land from an already-established settlement, could expand and outgrow the overlord town. They might then enter into a struggle for independence, recasting history in the process. The unitary identity of a town was made visible in the wall that enclosed it, marking it off from the surrounding bush and protecting it from outsiders. A strong town would become the focal point for a wide area in times of war, as neighbouring settlements looked to it for refuge.

In this context of inter-urban rivalry and warfare, each town or state would assert its own identity, making much of any claim to fame it might possess. *Oriki orile* must have come into existence when towns began to define themselves in relation to their neighbours. Sometimes the *oriki* are explicitly addressed to outsiders, defying them to belittle the town:

> Wón lÉníkòtún ò lódò
> Bé e bá se tán e bá mi sébi dandan lérí olúware
> Ta ń ní dà yà bí omi Ìpákùn?
> Ta ń lÁfélélé omi ayaba tí í jí í pon ón mu?
> Ta ń lèyí tí í wínmo lóngbe tòjò tèèrùn?
> Ta ń lèyí tí í wínmo lóngbe tòdá kóókó?[11]

> They say the Ikotun people have no river
> When you're ready, come and curse that person heartily for me

Who has water that gushes like the river of Ipakun?
Who has Afẹlẹlẹ the royal wives' river, that they rise to drink from?
Who has the one that quenches people's thirst wet season and dry?
Who has the one that quenches people's thirst during absolute
     drought?

Some *oriki orilẹ* have passages that seem actually to have been inspired by the outsider's point of view.[12] They point out characteristics or habits which an outsider might be struck by, but which one would expect the townspeople themselves to take for granted. Dialect, for example, is not usually something that speakers are conscious of unless an outsider comments on it:

Wọn ì í pé wọn ó wẹ nÍkọlé
Wọn á ní wọ́n ó tami 'ára
Kí wọ́n ó tami 'ára, Mòsí-Òjóọ́rọ́.

They never say they're going to wash in Ikọle
They'll say they're going to 'splash water on their bodies'
That they're going to 'splash water on their bodies',
     Mosi-Ojọọrọ.[13]

Preferences in food, similarly, would seem peculiar only to outsiders. The *oriki orilẹ* of Omu make that very peculiarity one of their central themes:

Ewúuyán, wọ́n dÓmù, wọ́n á dòtun
Níbi wọ́n gbé bí mi lọ́mọ
Òtun á sì dÓmù, áá dìkàsì
Ìjà ewúuyán ni wọn ń jà lÓmù
Iléè mí wù mí
Àwọn tí ò gbọ́n tí ò dà
Wọ́n ní wọ́n gúnra wọn lódó, wọ́n lọra wọn lọ́lọ
Ìjà ewúuyán ni wọn ń jà lÓmù
Iléè mí wù mí
Wọ́n fúnra wọn lówó wọ́n fúnra wọn lọ́mọ
Wọ́n fúnra wọn lọ́mọ, Mòsí-Òjóọ́rọ́...[14]

Yesterday's pounded yam, when it reaches Omu, is like yam
     freshly pounded
In the town where I was born
And freshly-pounded yam, when it reaches Omu, will be stale!
They were fighting over stale pounded yam at Omu.
I like my house.
Those who have no sense or reason
Say that they're pounding one another with pestles, that they're
     grinding one another with grinding-stones
It was stale pounded yam they were fighting about at Omu.

I like my house
They give each other money, they give each other children
They give each other children, Mosi-Ọjọọrọ...

This passage presents the Omu people's taste for *ewuuyan* (rewarmed pounded yam) as an oddity, in contrast to the normal preference for fresh pounded yam. It says that if you took fresh pounded yam to Omu, it would be despised as much as *ewuuyan* is despised in other places. But the observation, if it originated with outsiders, has clearly been taken on board by the insiders: it is cited with pride, as one of the townspeople's distinguishing features. There is even a characteristic note of defiance – only ignorant fools will fail to understand that in Omu the only thing worth fighting over is stale pounded yam – and an equally characteristic linkage with the themes of prosperity and fertility: as well as 'pounding each other' and 'grinding each other', they 'give each other money' and 'give each other children'.

In a more general sense, this play of perspectives between insider and outsider is built into all *oriki orile*, because all of them seize on those features which *differentiate* their town from others. It is with other towns in mind that *oriki orile* make their definitions.

One can speculate that in the hypothetical 'primordial towns of origin', individual townspeople, when dealing with the outside world, would define themselves by the identity which was known to outsiders: that is, the identity of their town. Inside the town, going about their daily business, they probably did not have much need of *oriki orile* which were common to everyone there. If the early northern Yoruba towns contained, like modern ones, a collection of notional patrilineal kin groups, one can picture each of these distinguishing itself within the town by a body of lineage *oriki*, most likely the accumulated personal *oriki* of lineage ancestors.[15] But outsiders would only recognise the *oriki* that defined the town as a whole to the outside world. These would include not only the *oriki* pertaining to the characteristics of the town and townspeople at large, but also the *oriki* of the ọba's lineage. Since the ọba incorporated the identity of the whole town, and since it was through him that dealings with other towns were conducted, the royal *oriki* were a recognisable sign of identity to outsiders. Many *oriki orile* contain references to the royal lineage of the town and to past ọbas and many, as we have seen, associate the town's natural features with the ọba. These *oriki* would become paramount when conditions were such that there was a strong need for townspeople to identify themselves to outsiders.

This speculation is supported by the fact that a similar process of identification through town membership is going on today. The 'far farms' founded by Okuku men on rented cocoa land many miles to the east and south of Okuku were gradually swelled by the arrival of other groups from other towns. In Sunmibare, the first Okuku-founded far farm, dating from 1949, there are groups from Ikirun, Ibadan, Ifẹ, Ilobu, Aran-Ọrin, Ọtan and Oṣogbo. Each set of townspeople occupies its own quarter in the new town. The political organisation of Sunmibare is based on these divisions, each set of townspeople having its own representative on the town council. The representatives participate in policy decisions and transmit them to their own group. Individuals are identified in terms of where they come from. If one asks who lives in a certain house, one will get an answer like '*Ará Ọtan ni*' (It's an Ọtan person) and people might even be saluted with a few phrases from the royal *oriki* of their home town. These groups of fellow-townsmen are not necessarily internally related by kinship. In their home towns, they may belong to different compounds and regard themselves as quite distinct. But in the farm town they have to define themselves to outsiders who know nothing of these internal relationships. To outsiders the primary identification is through membership of a common town of origin.

Conditions in pre-colonial Yorubaland were probably such that there was a constant and widespread need for people to be able to identify themselves to outsiders. Even before the outbreak of the nineteenth century wars, the evidence suggests that there was a high incidence of population movement. People who were dissatisfied with their town of origin for one reason or another would leave. A section of a compound, or an individual with a few kinsmen and friends, would set off to join another town or found their own. Every lineage in Okuku told a story beginning with some such departure from their original home. Among the commonest reasons given were defeat in a chieftaincy dispute, the recurrent deaths of children or persistent barrenness in women, and the search for better farmland. The advantages of belonging to an established town were often outweighed by the possibilities offered by a new place. A group that founded a new town would become the ruling house there, owning and distributing the land to newcomers. A group that joined an established town could expect favourable treatment, for every town was trying to expand by recruiting new people. In the era of Kọọkin, in the seventeenth and eighteenth centuries, movements of groups and individuals seem to have added up to a local population drift south and west. The histories of fifty 'lineages' and 'attached lineages'[16] in Okuku indicate that people often travelled great distances after leaving their town of origin, and that it was not uncommon for a group to uproot itself a second and even a third and fourth time and move on if their earlier choices proved unsatisfactory. As P. C. Lloyd observes, 'these migrations seem to have been deliberately undertaken by men bent on conquest or gain, or else fleeing from destruction, not the slow drift of men seeking new farmland nor yet a small-scale movement caused by incompatibility of temperament within groups of kinsmen' (Lloyd, 1955, p.240). Often part of a group would leave and part would stay behind, so that lineages would become more and more widely scattered throughout the towns of the area.

As the quotation from Lloyd indicates, another cause of population movement was warfare. Though the period before the nineteenth century wars was relatively stable, localised warfare was nonetheless very common, and in the course of these wars whole towns could be scattered. Several of the towns of origin claimed by Okuku *ile* are said to have been founded in the aftermath of the Tapa invasion of Ọyọ, perhaps in the sixteenth century.[17] One of them, Ikoyi, the Ọyọ military outpost, became a permanent military settlement, and it appears that other towns did too. The *oriki orilẹ* of Ẹrin-ile near Ọfa, like those of Ikoyi, deal extensively with the town's success and expertise in warmaking. The Ijẹsa Arara war, as we have seen, is said to have wiped Kọọkin out in 1760, leaving only ten survivors. Johnson (1921) describes towns routinely declaring war on their neighbours for the sake of prestige as well as for more substantial economic and political reasons. Several Okuku groups claim to have left their towns of origin because of war.

The fear that a town would dwindle or disband completely seems to have been taken seriously. In *iwure* (good-luck chants) addressed to ọbas, there are prayers that this will not happen; and successful ọbas are often praised for holding the town together. An Ifa verse, very probably dating from before the nineteenth century, gives us a vivid image of a town's sudden dissolution. Ọbara was destitute, wandering in the bush and on the point of hanging himself, when he looked up and saw thousands of people swarming towards him. He asked them what they were doing in the bush, and they replied that their town had disbanded and that they had been wandering about for days. Now that they had found Ọbara, however, they would make themselves his subjects and form a new town with him as ọba.[18]

In the nineteenth century, disturbances caused by war became chronic and endemic. The rate of population movement increased enormously. War scattered hitherto united lineages and sent them as refugees into different towns. Some towns were obliterated; others expanded and were strengthened when they took in large refugee populations. In the Odo-Ọtin area, the disruptive effects of the wars have already been described. Many local towns were wiped out: Akunyun, for instance, once a town only a mile or two southeast of Okuku, was destroyed completely and its population scattered, part of it to Okuku. Okuku, after being abandoned for many years, was then reconstructed out of the rumps of its former *ile* together with many new groups who came as refugees. At least twenty-four of the fifty 'lineages' and 'attached lineages' listed in the Appendix arrived as refugees from the wars, and most of them when they arrived were composed of only a handful of people. By the end of the nineteenth century, almost all the old lineages were fragmented and mixed with segments of many stranger lineages. In the early twentieth century the influx of strangers continued. The ọbas Oyewusi (d.1916) and Oyekunle (1916-34) encouraged immigrants and gave them land in order to rebuild Okuku's population.

Warfare between towns simultaneously intensified a town's identity as a political unit, and scattered its population. Since *oriki orilę* both affirm a town's identity and through it establish the identity of townspeople among strangers, one could expect a period of intensified warfare to increase the use and importance of *oriki orilę*. Many of the longest and best-known *oriki orilę* now extant are those of northern towns which were destroyed (Old Ǫyǫ, Ikoyi, Oje, Ogbin, Irẹsa) or heavily attacked (Igbẹti, Ola, Oko, Igbori, Ẹrin-ile) in the early nineteenth century[19]. It is possible that the refugees, scattered all over Yorubaland, kept their grip on their identity in the face of chaos by elaborating the *oriki* of their home town until it became an extended, full-blown expression of their loss and yearning. *Oriki orilę*, with their strong emotional charge, are associated with lamentation. Chants based on *oriki* are 'wept' (*sun*), 'cried' (*ke*) or 'called out' (*pe*).

Still, *oriki orilę* in some form clearly antedated this period (many of them refer to much earlier events), and the evidence of pre-nineteenth century inter-town relationships and population movement suggests that identification through town membership would have been brought into play from an early date. Whenever a group left its 'town of origin' and went to settle somewhere else, it needed to have an identity which its new fellow-citizens would recognise.

As the fragments of *orilę*-groups scattered, their versions of the *oriki orilę* gradually altered. This seems to have happened in several ways.

People could incorporate into the *oriki orilę* the *oriki* of their own lineage. Two different lineages from the same town of origin would then have *oriki orilę* which shared some of the same basic themes but also included material that was different. When the town of origin was fairly close by and the departure from it fairly recent, memories of lineage difference *within* the town of origin could remain strong.

After leaving the town of origin, different groups had different experiences, stayed in different towns and sometimes took on new customs or began to worship new *orisa*. There is the example of the Ijẹsa group from Ẹfǫn who went to Ǫyǫ and settled there as herbalists to the Alaafin, quoted in Chapter 2. After recounting this episode, the *oriki orilę* go on to declare that for this reason the group now cuts Ǫyǫ facial marks rather than Ijẹsa ones. *Ile* Ǫjǫmu, one of the lineages from Ǫfa, must have passed through a town where Ori Oke was an important *orisa* at some point in their history. Their *oriki orilę* begin with the lines:

> Ǫmǫ a-rókè-mú-gùn
> Ǫmǫ a-rǫ́ba-tún-yan
> Ǫmǫ a-rówǫ́-dunyè-tí-ò-jẹ
> Ẹni a ní kó jǪlǫ́fà tó kǫ̀...

> Child of one who has a Hill to climb

Child of one that has an ǫba to swagger about
Child of one who had money to contest a title, but did not do so
Someone they wanted to make ǫba of Ǫfa and who refused...

The 'Hill' is Ori Oke. The first two lines are absent from the *oriki* of *ile* Ǫsǫlǫ,
which is descended from the *same branch* of the same royal family of Ǫfa and
whose *oriki orilę* are otherwise the same. *Ile* Ǫlǫyan, of Ikǫtun origin, however,
also adopted Ori Oke as their principal *orișa*. Their own *oriki orilę* are quite
different from the Ǫfa ones, but they open with the same two lines as those
of *ile* Ǫjǫmu:

Ǫmǫ a-rókè-mú-gùn
Ǫmǫ a-rǫ́ba-tún-yan
Ìkòtún 'mǫ a-rókè ǫmǫ Èná
Òkè là á bǫ́baá rè nÍkòtún.

Child of one who has a Hill to climb
Child of one who has an ǫba to swagger about
Ikǫtun, child of one who has a Hill, child of Ęna
We go with the ǫba to the Hill in Ikǫtun.

Even after settling in Kǫǫkin or Okuku, lineages would add new bits to
their *oriki orilę*, reflecting their position in the town. *Ile* Balogun and *ile* Baalę
both came from Aran-Ǫrin in the Kǫǫkin era. Some elders said they actually
came as one lineage and only split into two after arrival. Others said that the
Baalę people came separately and were already settled in their own village
near to Ijabę when Kǫǫkin was destroyed and Okuku founded. The new site
encroached on the *ile* Baalę people and they became absorbed into Okuku
(the name Baalę fits with this story, for a Baalę is a village head). Whichever
story is accepted, both agree that the two lineages were originally 'the same'.
Their *oriki orilę* are substantially the same, but a comparison of the standardised
opening lines of each shows that the people of *ile* Baalę have incorporated
references to one of their chiefs and to the quarter of Okuku where their
compound is situated. The *ile* Balogun *oriki* begin:

Ǫmǫ Aláràn-án
Ǫmǫ Așòsùn
Ǫmǫ adǫ́kǫ-níbi-owó-gbé-so
Ilá Àrán ń sunkún póun ò lépo
Ǫ̀sùn Àrán n sunkún póun ò níyǫ̀
Ę já a relé rèé bàtę'lá...

Child of the Aran line
Child of Asǫsun
Child of one who makes men-friends where the money is plenty
The okro of Aran is complaining that it has no palm oil

The *ọsun*-plant of Aran is complaining that it has no salt
Let's go home and eat unflavoured food...

Those of *ile* Baalẹ begin:

Ọmọ Baálẹ̀
Baálẹ̀ a-dàwọnwọn-sẹ́sin-lẹ́nu
Ọmọ ọlọ́dán méje Àgádángbó
Ọmọ a-dọ́kọ-níbi-owó-gbé-so
Ilá Àrán ń sunkún póun ò lépo
Ọ̀sùn Àrán ń sunkún póun ò níyọ̀
Ẹ bá já a relé rèé bàtẹ́'lá.

Child of the Baalẹ
Baalẹ, one who fastens jingling harness to the horse's mouth
Child of one who has seven fig trees in Agandangbo quarter
The okro of Aran is complaining that it has no palm-oil
The *ọsun*-plant of Aran is complaining that it has no salt
Let's go home and eat unflavoured food...

The Baalẹ is the principal title of *ile* Baalẹ, and Agadangbo is the quarter where *ile* Baalẹ is located (now a street). The second line of this passage is the personal *oriki* of an earlier chief Baalẹ, referring, typically, to his ownership of a horse. Here we have an example of the incorporation into *oriki orilẹ* of the personal *oriki* of ancestors of the lineage, a gradual and continual process which little by little differentiates the *oriki orilẹ* of all lineages that nonetheless continue to claim to be 'one'.

So despite the high value placed on the supposed antiquity and unchangingness of *oriki orilẹ*, they do gradually diversify with the different history of each group that claims them. In this way they make finer discriminations than mere membership of the wide and shadowy set of people claiming common origins in an ancient town.

4. *ILE* IN OKUKU

When a group of newcomers decided to settle in a town, it did not always conform to the simplified model and establish a new *ile* of its own: sometimes, instead, it would join an already-existing one. One way or another, however, it had to belong to an *ile*, for this was the most important organisational unit in the town. It was the social unit which gave people their claims to membership of the town. Only outsiders temporarily resident in Okuku – like schoolteachers and civil servants appointed to local government posts – live in rented rooms and do not belong to any Okuku *ile*. Such outsiders, even today, are very few in number. The first question that is asked when people are trying to place a member of the community is '*Ọmọ ilé wo ni?*' – What *ile* does s/he belong to? – and it would be impossible to have even a slight acquaintance with someone in town without locating them by reference to an *ile*.

The question 'What *ile* does s/he belong to?' would receive an answer such as '*Ọmọ ilé Ọ̀jọmu ni*' or '*Ọmọ ilé Nlá ni*' – S/he is a member of Ọjọmu's compound, or a member of Great Compound. *Ile* are all named: but not, as Schwab (1955) claims is the case in Oṣogbo, after a 'founding ancestor'. Many *ile* are named after a town title held by their members (e.g. *ile* Ọjọmu, *ilé* Ọdọfin, *ile* Baalẹ) or, less commonly, a religious title (e.g. *ile* Aworo Ọtin, the priest of Ọtin, and *ile* Oluawo, the head of the herbalists). Some have a descriptive name: *ile* Nla (large *ile*), *ile* Araromi (comfortable *ile*: so called because it was built on the edge of town and enjoyed extra space and peace), and *ile* Ago (temporary camp: because it was the most recent *ile* to be established in Okuku, its founders arriving around 1915). Some are known by the nickname of an illustrious forebear – but *not* the 'founding ancestor' – for instance *ile* Ọlọkọ (*ile* of 'Canoe-owner', a nickname for the nineteenth century warrior Gbangbade), and some by the traditional occupation of its members, for instance *ile* Alubata (*ile* of the *bata* drummers). Some *ile* have two alternative names: *ile* Ọlọkọ can also be called *ile* Ṣaiwo, after the town title held by this *ile; ile* Aworo Ọtin can likewise also be called *ile* Balogun; and *ile* Oluawo, *ile* Arogun. In some cases an *ile* continues to be named after a title that it no longer possesses. *Ile* Oluọdẹ was named after the great Winyọmi, who was the Oluọdẹ or Head of the Hunters, probably in the early nineteenth century (see Chapter 6). After his death, the title passed to a member of *ile* Ọlọkọ, and has remained there ever since, but *ile* Oluọdẹ has not changed its name.

Ile are physical entities, places where people live together. Yorubas who speak English always translate *ile* as 'compound', and some *ile* actually still are single residential units: the large, four-sided buildings with a spacious open yard in the middle, well described by Lloyd (1955) and Fadipẹ (1970). Others have broken up into clusters of separate buildings, usually a mixture of new *petẹẹsi* ('upstairs', or two-storey houses), *ileelẹ* ('bungalows' or one-storey houses) and portions of the old compound building that remain standing. Large *ile* have also acquired scattered outposts on the edges of the town, where more space is available for building, and *ile* Ọba, the royal *ile*, has blocks of land in several parts of the town. But the *ile* that old men and women recall from their youth were large, communal buildings; they faced inward rather than out, and most of the life of the compound was conducted within their walls, invisible to the outside world. Long corridors enclosed an open square or rectangular space. Within this space, most domestic tasks and household crafts were done: weaving, dyeing, basket-making, and shelling palm-nuts and melon seeds. Domestic animals were penned here when the narrow entrances to the compound were barred at night. Here, too, evening storytelling took place. Family meetings were held within the courtyard, and the family dead were buried there.

But the word *ile* means not just a building, but the people within it. Even when a compound has spread into many buildings, it is still considered a single *ile*, with one internal organisation and one head to represent it. Only if a compound became very large indeed would it split into two separate organisational blocks. This has only happened in one case within living memory, during the period of the flight to Ikirun.

Internally, the compound was organised into four sections: the young men, led by a *Balogun* chosen by themselves; the younger and more active wives, led by the *Iya Ipeere* who 'is the *Balogun* for the married women in the compound'; the elderly women, led by the *Iyaalele*, the most senior of all the wives in terms of the order in which they arrived at the compound; and the *Baale*, the leader of the senior men and the head of the whole compound, chosen by the senior men from amongst themselves. When any activity involving the compound members as a whole was called for, the *Baale* and the *Iyaalele* would supervise it, but the actual work would be done by the younger men and women led by their respective Baloguns. The *Baale* represents the compound to the ǫba and council and transmits decisions back to the compound members. He supervises the settlement of internal disputes, the proper conduct of family festivals and ceremonies, the division of inheritances among the heirs, and the allocation of the corporately held compound land, if any remains undistributed.

Ile are the social units through which individuals get access to land. Membership of an *ile* gives you a body of people who can sometimes be called on to supply free labour (for instance, when a man 'serves' his future in-laws with annual *ǫwę* (voluntary labour), it is the members of his *ile* who come and do the work). The *ile*, until recently, undertook – in theory at least – to provide the bride price when one of its male members married. Up till today, the *ile* makes sure its members are properly buried. Fellow members of one's *ile* are duty bound to support with their presence any celebration or ceremony that one holds: marriage, child-naming, housewarming or religious festival. They are one's 'people', and without a solid background of people one is socially non-existent. The *ile*, as defined by the people of Okuku to the government, is also the main administrative unit. Taxes are collected compound by compound, and the individual's relations with modern local government are always mediated through representatives of his or her *ile*. ('Wards', though they exist in local government records, are of little importance in actual practice and people rarely mention them.)

Ile are associated with the ownership of corporate property, mainly titles and land. This does not mean that everyone resident in the compound has a right to this property, but it does mean that the property is definitely associated with a named compound. All the land surrounding Okuku is divided into blocks whose borders are well known and the major blocks are readily identified with particular compounds. Most of the senior town titles are likewise recognised as belonging to specific *ile* – and, as we have seen, many *ile* are known by the name of the title they hold. The distribution of titles and the status associated with them is not a tidy one. Some compounds hold more than one title (*ile* Balogun has four); some do not hold any; some share a title with another compound. Some compounds have access only to junior *aladaa* (cutlass-carrying) titles, which can be moved much more freely from one compound to another. As we have seen, the rank of the title claimed by a compound is associated with the order of arrival of the founders of the compounds – the compounds owning the highest titles claim to have arrived first – but the compounds themselves are not ranked accordingly. Nor is the *Baale*, the head of the compound, necessarily the holder of the compound's principal title or of any title. Nonetheless it is quite true that each *ile* holds on to whatever property it possesses with great vigour. Ownership of titles is one of the objects of intense and protracted struggle between the ọba and leading townspeople. In a number of cases it is remembered that the ọba succeeded in transferring a title from one compound to another. Struggles over title reach far back into the nineteenth century; in the twentieth century land also began to be a bone of contention, which the ọba could sometimes take from one compound and give to another, always in the teeth of furious resistance. Land and title, then, are talked of as the corporate property of compounds, and though not inalienable, this property is the object of intensely proprietorial struggles.

At first sight, then, the *ile* seems a strongly unified and easily recognisable social unit. This impression is reinforced by the literature on northern Yoruba social structure. Two views have been presented of the constitution of the *ile*. Lloyd (1954, 1955, 1960, 1965, 1968, 1971, 1974), Schwab (1955) and others have represented the fundamental social unit as a localised agnatic descent group, unified because it is in fact or in fiction a single body of patrilineal kin. Fadipẹ (1970), Sudarkasa (1973) and Eades (1980), on the other hand, offer an alternative model where the significant social unit is the compound, defined primarily by the common residence rather than by the kinship of its members. They point out that a single compound may contain two or more separate descent groups, living together on an equal or unequal footing. The functioning unit, in this picture, is the residential group – the compound, whether containing one lineage or many – rather than the descent group as such.

This second model accommodates the variability and adaptability of Okuku social organisation much better than the segmentary lineage model. It does imply, however, that whatever the internal composition of the compound, its external boundaries are always clearly defined. In other words, both models suggest, with different degrees of emphasis, that there is a clearly recognisable social unit, with well-marked boundaries, which functions as the principal building block of social structure in all contexts. The disagreement is about the criteria according to which this unit is defined.

The segmentary lineage model, of which Lloyd is the most lucid and influential exponent, postulates a vast grid of kinship relationships as the basis of Yoruba society. The scattered groups recognising unity through possession of a common *orilę* are described as 'patrilineal clans', descended from a putative common ancestor, though unable to trace their genealogical relationships. The compound is described as the residential manifestation of a segment of one of these clans, that is, as a localised patrilineage. 'Thus all the inhabitants of a compound trace their descent from a common ancestor' (Lloyd, 1955, p.237). These localised patrilineages are described as strongly corporate, their membership uniting for all significant purposes – land-holding, title-holding, political representation, communal labour, marriage – and excluding members of other groups. Modifications to this picture are introduced, however. Lloyd shows very clearly that in practice most compounds include other people as well as the members of the patrilineage who founded it. There are 'stranger segments' of other clans who attach themselves to a resident patrilineage as guests. There are also groups descended through a daughter rather than a son of the patrilineage – and who therefore should belong to the woman's husband's lineage – who become full members of the woman's natal lineage and may even, in the interesting cases observed by Lloyd, take titles in it (Lloyd, 1955, p.245). However, the implication of this account is that since the localised patrilineage has a strong corporate ideology and well-defined boundaries, attached segments must be either thoroughly incorporated, so that within three or four generations they have been absorbed virtually without a trace, or they must leave to found their own separate *ile*. They must be either in or out. 'No man will ... admit that he is a lineage member by adoption' (Lloyd,1955, p.241). In Okuku, however, as well as groups that were absorbed or detached in this manner, there were groups that remained poised on the boundaries, neither in nor out, for very long periods without showing any sign of moving either way – and without making any attempt to conceal their dual or ambiguous status.

Eades on the other hand suggests that it is the compound and not the lineage which has strong boundaries, for it is the compound which constitutes an exogamous unit, and which functions as the principal organisational structure in the town. This suggests that if more than one lineage inhabits a compound, their identity as compound members overrides their identity as members of lineages. People 'think of themselves as members of compounds rather than descent groups' (Eades, 1980, p.49), and the clear line of demarcation is around the group that belong together in one compound.

Eades's lively and refreshing contribution, brief as it is, succeeds in coming to terms with actual usage in northern Yoruba towns. As he points out, people rarely talk of '*idile*', the term chosen by the segmentary lineage theorists to translate 'lineage'. They talk of *ile*, which as we have seen is usually translated as 'compound'. His approach also has the merit of raising further questions which segmentary lineage theory did not have to address: in particular, questions about identity. In the segmentary lineage model, identity as a descent group is represented as dominant, and the boundaries of the residential group coincide with those of the descent group. This leads to the unfounded assumption that all the markers of identity used by an *ile* define a single, unified localised patrilineage and are couched in the language of kinship relations. *Oriki* are represented by Schwab as a kind of poetic genealogical charter.[20] But if, as in Eades's model, compounds are not coterminous with lineages, then two different principles are at work. If a compound contains two or more kin groups, then the question arises as to how compound identity is affirmed, and how and in what circumstances the kin groups are recognised. If, as Eades suggests, the residential principle is paramount, then one must ask to what extent the compound is able to define itself as a solid, homogeneous unit when it is so internally diverse, and whether the 'lineages' within the compound maintain separate identities which are significant for certain purposes.

In Okuku, it was not possible, in the end, to propose either the 'compound' or the 'lineage' as the fundamental social unit. Rather, the principle of descent and the principle of residence were entwined and interpenetrated at every level, down to the foundations of social identity. And this identity was continually re-defined according to the circumstances, giving rise to different 'groups', differently recruited in different situations, so that no single definition of a primary social unit was in the end possible. One term – *ile* – was used for almost all significant groups: but it turned out to refer to different kinds of units in different circumstances. The word *ile* has overtones of kinship as well as residence: it is a 'house' in the sense of a dynasty (as in the 'house of Lancaster') as well as a 'house' in which people live. Which connotation came to the fore depended on the circumstances. The term *ile* could also be used inclusively or exclusively. It seemed to shift its boundaries whenever you looked at it.

When I first arrived in Okuku I was told authoritatively that there were seventeen compounds in the town. I naturally set out to interview the *baale* of each compound and learn the history and genealogy of its members. But as I proceeded, more *ile* appeared. I realised that seventeen was simply a traditional number, and that my informant had overlooked a number of small or new ones. The number went up to twenty-four. Then as time went on I kept hearing – not when I made formal enquiries, but only in casual conversation – about still more '*ile*' that I hadn't known existed. There were *ile* within *ile;* *ile* attached to *ile;* *ile* that were sometimes recognised as such, and sometimes not. Some, I realised, could be accounted for simply as sections of larger , as described by segmentary lineage theory: if four branches of one all build their own houses, each house can be referred to by the name segment's founder without calling into question the unity of the larger *ile*. But other cases were less straightforward. There were *ile* that were sometimes described as being part of another compound and sometimes as independent units. There were *ile* which were lumped together as one organisational unit, and which shared a *baale*, but which nevertheless claimed equal and independent status, and had their own names and buildings. There were *ile* which claimed to be separate but which lived under one roof. And there were all kinds of permanent and significant relationships *between ile* that the picture of unitary, separate, bounded groups had not prepared me for. By the time I left Okuku three years later I had arrived at a list of twenty-nine *ile* which seemed to be generally accepted, for most purposes, as independent compounds, and a further twenty-one units which though attached to 'host' compounds nevertheless had varying degrees of autonomy. These *ile* and attached groups are shown in the Appendix, with information about their *oriki orile*, stories of origin, rules of exogamy and relationships to other groups. But since definitions of *ile* were relative and depended on the functional context, any list such as the one I constructed is not only provisional – if I had stayed longer, new situations would have revealed further groupings – but also misleading if it is taken as a description of solid and permanent social units. It should be read, rather, as an indication of the range of possibilities open to social groupings as they adjusted their boundaries according to context.

The lability and complexity of the social structure was to be understood in the following terms: instead of having a determinate number of solidary, bounded units each of which operated as a corporate group for all purposes, somewhat different groups were recruited for different purposes. The boundaries of any *ile* depended on what it was being invoked for. Title- and land-holding; co-residence; co-operation in communal work, whether for the oba or for other members of the *ile;* internal administration and social control; town administration and taxation; exogamy: each of these functions might call upon a different range of 'members'.

In Okuku, each *ile*, as in Lloyd's account, was constructed around a single, notionally agnatic, descent group. Each *ile*, that is, was recognised as having a core of real or fictional kin, a 'lineage' represented as three to five generations in depth and descended from a named male ancestor. These genealogies, as was seen in Chapter 3, are greatly foreshortened and there is considerable – not obviously motivated – variation in the version given even by two very closely related members. But if lineage elders disagree about the interrelationships of people named in the genealogy, they do almost always agree about who is included and who is not. This core group is invoked for one crucial purpose: access to title. If the compound owns a title – and especially if it is a senior olopaa (staff-carrying) one – it is only those people who are recognised as belonging to the core group of agnates that will be allowed to compete for it. In Okuku, 'children of females' – i.e. descended through a daughter rather than a son – are almost always excluded when it comes to title. In some compounds the core group is large; there are compounds, indeed, which are almost entirely composed of one agnatic kin group, conforming to the classic segmentary lineage model.

But most compounds contain a number of other groups, also describing themselves as patrilineal kin groups, that are not agnatically related to the core lineage. In some compounds the core group is actually outnumbered by this kind of 'attached lineage'. Such sections come into existence, as we have seen, when a man or a party of men arrive as strangers in the town and are offered hospitality by an already-established compound. In many cases there is a matrilateral link to promote this attachment. The newcomers are housed in the compound and land is usually made available for them to cultivate food crops. After about two generations the land will be acknowledged as theirs, to be inherited by their children.[21] They can then be described as *ǫrẹdẹbi* – friends become family. In the course of normal expansion and dispersal into separate houses these groups will sooner or later build their own. Sometimes two or more sets of strangers build together, but they continue to be regarded as part of the compound of the host lineage.

These sections are not on an equal footing with the core lineage, for they are excluded from access to the title. But what is remarkable about them is the sheer variety of relationships which they can enter into with the 'host' lineage and with other groups in the town.

Some attached lineages do conform to the segmentary lineage model in that they are almost completely amalgamated with the host lineage. They are always called by the host lineage's name, they own lineage land, and they participate in all compound activities. Only when a title falls vacant is their separate origin referred to: otherwise, both host and guest lineages are shy of suggesting that there is any difference between them. But there are also sections that are less completely absorbed into the host lineage. Although they use the name of the host lineage for identification at all times, they do not deny or conceal their separate origins. They do not relinquish their family *orisa*, special funeral observances or the recognition of other groups sharing the same *orilẹ*. They combine with the host lineage for all purposes except title-holding, but their different origin is still, after a hundred years or more, openly acknowledged by both sides and there seems no prospect therefore of their being absorbed into the host lineage without a trace.

But the most interesting cases are those attached lineages which are sufficiently independent of the host lineage to maintain a kind of permanent dual identity. For some purposes they regard themselves as part of the host lineage and call themselves by its name. For other purposes they are autonomous. Faderera's family, *ile* Awoyẹmi, *(*1b in Appendix*)* is an example. It was founded by Bọlakanmi, son of Olunlade, a member of the royal lineage of Ọla, an 'ancient town', sometime before the nineteenth century. Bọlakanmi left Ọla with a large body of kinsmen and supporters ('two hundred people') after a succession dispute, and travelled to Oyan. The party of immigrants was welcomed and given the title Eesa, in second position after the oba himself. They settled there for some time, after which 'some of them remained there, and some scattered'. In the reign of Edun of Okuku, in the middle of the nineteenth century, a group of them, led by Bolakanmi's son, moved on. Bolakanmi's mother was Edun's elder sister by the same mother, so his group took up residence in Okuku as guests of *ile* Oba. They are debarred from the obaship but for all other purposes can today be counted as members of *ile* Oba, Edun branch. They share the royal family's exemption from communal work and the right to dress their daughters in the oba's regalia on their wedding-days. They are the custodians of Paje, the oba's *egungun*. Alternately with another attached segment of *ile* Oba, they fill the post of Araba, the oba's own Ifa priest. They attend the monthly family meeting or *farajo* of *ile* Oba, and play a significant part in it – one of their family is currently the secretary of the meeting and another, Faderera's brother the Ifa priest, has a prominent role in the settlement of disputes.

However, they also exist as *ile* Awoyemi in their own right. They have a separate *farajo* of their own to which the descendants of their ancestor Awoyemi Akanbi come. Sometimes, also, descendants of the group that remained in Oyan will come if they are in the neighbourhood. This *farajo* is held on the same day as all other *farajo* – the last Friday of the month – but earlier in the morning, so that they can finish it in time to attend the *ile* Oba meeting. At festivals the head of the household participates in the oba's sacrifice and feast, like all other members of *ile* Oba, but unlike the rest he also holds a big sacrifice and feast of his own. On this occasion his ancestors are saluted and their origins recalled. Faderera performs the Ola *oriki orile*, never the Kookin *oriki* belonging to *ile* Oba. The ancestors of the royal lineage proper are not mentioned. All the members of *ile* Awoyemi are called *Abe*, their own 'totemic name', not *Okin*, that of *ile* Oba.

There are several attached lineages in Okuku that have this kind of relationship to their hosts. Often, their exclusion from the title held by the core agnatic group is compensated for by their exclusive access to a religious title. Araba, Oluawo Onifa and Alapinni are all traditional cult titles that belong exclusively to one or two semi-autonomous attached lineages.

There is no sign, in any of these cases, of incipient erosion of the attached lineage's identity. Nor, on the other hand, is there any sign of impending separation into an autonomous lineage. At least two of these attached lineages – *ile* Awoyemi described above, and *ile* Elemoso Awo (19b in Appendix) – appear to have maintained a relationship with a host lineage on the same footing of dual identity since the middle of the nineteenth century.

The composition of a compound, then, is variable. There is always a core agnatic lineage. This lineage has exclusive access to the principal title if the compound has one. But title-holding is usually the only function for which the core lineage members alone are recruited. Attached lineages live in the compound, share in all compound activities, usually hold compound land and in varying degrees partake in a compound identity. These attached groups can remain autonomous for some purposes and identify with the core lineage for others; and this dual status can endure for long periods. How the various *ile* are identified depends on the context, and on the interests at stake. For example: if they are looking for building plots, members of the segment 1b in the Appendix will say they are members of *ile* Ọba (*ile* Ọba is the only compound that still possesses unused land); but when the Ifa cult title Araba is being discussed, they say that they, as members of *ile* Awoyẹmi, will be entitled to it when it next falls vacant.

For some purposes and in some situations, people could be recruited on an even broader basis. The history of residence patterns this century, for instance, does not conform at all to the model of exclusive, solidary residential units. Two independent *ile* with their own names, their own *baale*, and their own corporate property (land and titles) could actually live in the same building for long periods. After the return from Ikirun in 1893, only eight buildings were at first erected to house the whole population. After some time, a number of *ile* built together in pairs. Each pair would share all compound activities but would retain their separate names, authority structures and identities. The Appendix shows four such pairs. One of them, *ile* Oluawo (7) with *ile* Oluokun (20), stayed together until 1954; the others split up a few years earlier. It was also possible for one *section* of an independent *ile* to leave that compound and live with other people without relinquishing its original identification. For example, *ile* Aworo Ọtin (8a) built a compound of its own after the return from Ikirun, but one section of the main agnatic lineage went to live in *ile* Jagun and did not return to *ile* Aworo Ọtin until 1953. This happened because a wife of *ile* Aworo Ọtin was from Ada, where the mother of Chief Jagun also came from. She felt safer with a fellow townswoman after all the disturbances of the last evacuation of Okuku, so she took her sons with her to live in Chief Jagun's household. [Note that this link, as described by the people concerned, was, in the first place, between two *women,* and in the second place, not based on kinship but on common (recent) membership of another town.] All the sons grew up in *ile* Jagun and lived there all their lives, but they were still members of *ile* Aworo Ọtin in their own eyes and everybody else's.

Two groups, each recognised as an *ile* in its own right, could therefore live together for long periods within one compound. If co-residence in a single compound did not always mean that people belonged to the same *ile*, neither did the fact that they combined together to do communal work. Work which was allocated to a compound as a whole included labour on the *baale*'s *ajoyeba* land (land belonging to the title, for the use of successive incumbents), labour on the royal farms or on town projects, *ọwẹ* on behalf of any man of the compound who required it, and the important work of preparing for ceremonies such as funerals, marriages, child-naming and house-opening. The internal organisation of the compound made it easy to mobilise all its members to participate in these functions. Those mobilised always included all the people actually living in the compound. When two independent *ile* lived under one roof, they would always combine to do communal work (in some cases one would claim that the other 'served' it, but this would be denied by the latter). But the grouping for communal labour could also include people who did *not* live in the same compound. *Ile* Jagun (14), though it had its own compound soon after the resettlement of 1893, did communal labour with *ile* Oluawo (7) and *ile* Oluokun (20), who were living together in another compound. Whenever communal labour was required these three *ile* would be called on as a unit and would work together. Similarly *ile* Odogun (10), *ile* Osolo (13) and *ile* Araro (12) formed a single unit for communal labour. Sometimes an early, brief period of cohabitation was followed by a much longer period of co-operation. *Ile* Oloyan (16) went on combining with *ile* Odogun (10) for communal work long after they had ceased to share a compound, and the same was true of *ile* Alawe (15) and *ile* Baale (4). Sometimes complicated arrangements about co-operation reflected the multifarious and indeterminate relations between two groups. *Ile* Elegbede (23) was one of the groups that arrived from Otan early this century. They associated themselves on arrival with *ile* Oluawo (7) to whom they were related by marriage, rather than to the other Otan groups. They lived for some time in the Oluawo compound, and when they built their own, it was on land made available for them by *ile* Oluawo. They are sometimes classed as part of *ile* Oluawo, sometimes as a separate compound belonging to the Otan group. When communal work is called for, the men of *ile* Elegbede always unite with the men of *ile* Oluawo, sharing the same *Balogun*. But the women do not unite for communal work. The wives and daughters of *ile* Elegbede have their own separate organisation with their own *Iya Ipeere*.

Equally variable and overlapping discriminations are made by the rule of exogamy. According to Lloyd, exogamy is distinctive of a 'clan', and, at the local level, of the clan segments localised as residential agnatic descent groups. The boundary drawn around the descent group as an exogamic unit thus coincides with all other practices that define the lineage as a corporate group. According to Eades, it is not the lineage but the compound which is an exogamic unit, reinforcing his claim that it is the compound and not the descent group that constitutes the basic building block of Yoruba social structure. But in Okuku, exogamic units overlapped and intersected, because they were constructed *both* according to residential *and* according to kinship principles. People living in the same compound cannot intermarry, even if they belong to separate groups unrelated by kinship. People recognised as a kin group cannot intermarry, whether they live in the same compound or not. People who claim a common town of origin are considered to be 'one' and do not marry each other. This blurs rather than strengthens the boundaries of groups. For if a compound contains an attached lineage of different origins, this lineage, but *not* the rest of the compound, will be forbidden to marry into other *ile* with which it shares the same *orile*. For example, *ile* Oguntayọ (5b), though very closely associated with its host lineage *ile* Ọlọkọ (5a) – indeed, for most purposes indistinguishable from it – observes different marriage prohibitions. The main lineage of *ile* Ọlọkọ (5a) are free to marry into *ile* Alubata (22) and *ile* Oluawo Onifa (2d), but Oguntayọ's segment (5b) is not, because it shares Ikoyi origins with them and is therefore regarded as related to them by kinship. Thus the rule of exogamy may actually divide a compound rather than mark its boundaries. At the same time, however, the rule asserts the importance of groups created by co-residence. It covers all groups who once lived in the same compound, even if they are genealogically unrelated and even if they subsequently moved into separate compounds. Thus all the pairs of lineages that were co-residential in the past are forbidden to intermarry. If one nuclear family within a compound goes to a 'far farm' and there shares a house in its early pioneering days with another family from a different compound – something which often happened – all the descendants of these two men would be forbidden to intermarry even if the period of house-sharing was short. Even a strong bond of friendship between two men is sufficient grounds for them to set up a prohibition on marriage between their descendants if they so wish.

In Okuku, then, constituencies whose boundaries were drawn not only by kinship and by common residence, but also by common organisation and co-operation, sometimes coincided, but sometimes cut across each other. All groups entered into a variety of relationships with other groups, according to expediency. The strains of the nineteenth century wars and the consequent depletion and fragmentation of the population meant that strategies had to be adopted to reconstruct workable units in the town. It is quite possible that before the nineteenth century, there was less diversity in the *ile* and in the relationships between them, fewer 'stranger' groups and weaker bonds between and across compounds. Perhaps *ile* were more unitary and more strongly bounded. On the other hand, both Lloyd and Eades have suggested that the descent group has become more strongly corporate in relatively recent times. Okuku oral history offers no evidence either way. What is noteworthy, however, is the readiness with which twentieth century *ile* have amalgamated, the variety of forms which their amalgamation took, and the length of time that some of their arrangements lasted. Bearing in mind the probable high degree of population mobility *before* the nineteenth century, one may suspect that flexibility of group boundaries, and the possibility of invoking a variety of principles of recruitment, was already present in the social system then, to be drawn on in different ways and with increasing intensity as the need increased. Perhaps, in this case, the strongly-bounded unitary corporate group was never more than one of several available models, towards which actuality tended, more or less approximately according to the historical circumstances.

5. THE DEMARCATION OF *ILE* BY *ORIKI ORILE*

If the town is made up, not of well-defined, strongly corporate groups, but of a variety of bodies of people recruited for different purposes and entering into variable relationships with each other, then the question arises: which of these bodies of people are demarcated by *oriki orile*? Each party of newcomers brings with it, as we have seen, the *oriki orile* by which it is recognised. But it subsequently enters into a variety of relationships with other groups: with a core lineage and other attached lineages if it joins an established compound; sometimes with other compounds for co-residence or communal work; with other lineages sharing the same *orile* within other compounds.

Oriki orile are in fact the last thing that any group will relinquish. An attached lineage may live in the host's compound, be called by its name, receive land from it and participate fully in its internal government and all its activities, but it will still preserve a memory – even if only in private – of its own *oriki orile*. As long as it does this, it will be excluded from access to the principal compound title. And it will retain a relationship, marked by exogamy and ritual obligations, with other core and attached lineages in other compounds if they share the same *orile*. If it abandons its *oriki orile*, this is a sign that the last barrier has been crossed and that the attached lineage has now become fully amalgamated with the core lineage in its compound, even for the purpose of title-holding. For obvious reasons it is impossible to know how often this happens.

However, occasionally there is evidence that a merging has occurred: for instance when the pace of an attached lineage's incorporation is forced, so that even after it has been absorbed by the core lineage there are still people who remember the time when it was a separate segment. This happened in *ile* Oluode. A daughter of the main agnatic line went to marry a husband in Ira. When he died she returned to her father's compound, not only with her own children but with those of her co-wives who were quite unrelated to *ile* Oluode. All of them took up permanent residence in *ile* Oluode. All the children were at first saluted by the *oriki orile* of their father, the Ira man. But one of these sons, Odelade, was so successful a big man that he overshadowed all the men in the main lineage and eventually took a title. In the following generation this title, to which his son succeeded, was made the principal one, and its holder became the *baale* of the whole compound. This meant that he must be of the core lineage. So because of Odelade's pushiness, a stranger lineage had been incorporated *de facto* after only two generations. Although these events are too recent to have been forgotten yet, the Ira *oriki orile* have been abandoned. Members of Odelade's branch of the compound are saluted only by the *oriki orilẹ* of the main agnatic lineage.

It may also happen that when one lineage incorporates another, evidence is left in the *oriki* themselves, for sometimes instead of the attached lineage's *oriki* being completely abandoned, they may become combined with those of the main lineage. This seems to have happened in the remote history of *ile* Ọlọkọ. *Ile* Ọlọkọ claims descent from the royal lineage of Ọyọ, and uses the '*Erin*' (Elephant) emblem in their *oriki orilẹ*. But, as we have seen, they also use the '*Opo*' (Housepost) *orilẹ* from a town of origin called Iwata. According to Babalọla (1966b), one branch of the Ọyọ royal family was of Opomulero descent; but it was a different descent group from the Erin line. Both these sets of *oriki* are attributed to the main agnatic line of descent of the founder of *ile* Ọlọkọ. When questioned about the presence in one lineage of two *orilẹ* – with two different emblems, *Opo* (Housepost) and *Erin* (Elephant) – elders said '*Ọkan nàá ni*' ('It's all one') and seemed uninterested in the question of whether in fact two different lineages were merged to constitute that 'one'. All the members of the lineage that claims this mixed *orilẹ* have access to the principal town title belonging to the compound. If merging did take place, the only evidence is in the combined *oriki orilẹ*: and to the lineage members themselves, the two *orilẹ* have become one.

But if we do not know how common it is for attached lineages to abandon their *oriki orilẹ* in the process of becoming incorporated into the core lineage of their compound, we do know that a great many attached lineages remain unincorporated and demonstrate this status by preserving their own *oriki orilẹ*. Each of the twenty-one *ile* listed in the Appendix as being attached, more or less closely, to a main lineage in a compound, is demarcated by its own *oriki orilẹ* and maintains a relationship with other groups in the town which have the same *orilẹ*. All the main lineages, the cores of compounds, of course preserve their own *oriki orilẹ* and can appeal to them in chieftaincy contests when they want to eliminate a female or stranger branch. Within the compounds, the distinctions that *oriki orilẹ* make show which people can claim to be real agnates.

However, the *oriki orilẹ* were not always used in the same way. How they were used depended on the precise relationship between host and guest lineages. For example, an attached lineage that had no independent existence and which was the same as the host lineage for all purposes except title-holding would keep rather quiet about its separate *oriki orilẹ*. They would probably only be performed on occasions when no other members of the compound were present – for instance, as early morning greetings in their own part of the compound. Ṣangowẹmi, who knows the origins of every lineage segment in Okuku, would salute members of such attached lineages with their own *oriki orilẹ* if she went to greet them in their own house on a private visit. But on a public occasion, she would salute them with the *oriki* of the core lineage – though she would sometimes bring in a few lines of their own *oriki* as well. The more independent the attached lineage, the more publicly it would proclaim its *oriki orilę*. Those that occupy an apparently permanent semi-attached status always use their own *oriki orilę*. As these lineages usually own an important cult title, they play a prominent part in many ritual or ceremonial events, and for this reason have conspicuous opportunities to make their *oriki* known. Each of the three most important 'semi-attached' lineages in Okuku happens to have an exceptionally talented performer. Faderera, as a daughter of the important semi-autonomous lineage *ile* Awoyęmi, always plays a prominent part in ceremonies there; Ęrę-Ọṣun is married into *ile* Ęlęmọṣọ Awo, which is attached to *ile* Ęlęmọṣọ but which is distinguished, as its name suggests, by the fact that the head of the household is the Ęlęmọṣọ Awo in the Ifa cult; and Ṣangowęmi herself was married into *ile* Oluawo Onifa, a lineage attached to *ile* Ọjọmu and again distinguished by having as its head the most senior of all the Ifa priests.

Thus *oriki orilę* are consciously used by performers to assert lineage boundaries and relationships. As a general rule, an outsider always uses the *oriki* that make the broadest discriminations, while the insider hangs on to those which differentiate his/her group most finely. But the more independent an attached lineage is, the more aware the outsider will be of the *oriki* that distinguish it from other groups.

*

Oriki orilę taken as emblems of identification have presented us with two apparent contradictions. They demarcate units in the town which are conceived as descent groups, but they do it in terms of a common town of origin. And instead of reinforcing the boundaries of important organisational units – the compounds – they maintain internal divisions, demarcating the many fissures within each compound, and perpetuating them. Though their animating intent is to affirm group solidarity and pride, their effect is to insist on the diversity of people's origins, and their separate past experience, however small the fragments become.

The groups that *oriki orilę* demarcate are not coterminous with most of the social units that actually function in the life of the town. Within any given *ile*, the people claiming unity through *oriki orilę* often do not function as a discrete and exclusive group for any purpose but one: that of title-holding, and then only in the case of the core lineage. The core lineage will try to preserve its own boundaries so that it retains exclusive access to the compound title; other attached groups, whether they like it or not, will thus be kept separate. But apart from this function, each group recognising unity through *orilę* will operate almost all the time in amalgamation with a variety of other groups: land-holding, residence, communal labour, town administration and the regulation of compound affairs all call forth groups in which the 'lineage' demarcated by *oriki orilę* acts in combination with other lineages or parts of other lineages.

Although *oriki orile* are so much cherished, the perpetual negotiability of these relationships rubs off onto them. *Oriki* that appear to be different are declared 'the same'; *oriki* that appear single then unravel into separate strands. Continually merging and diversifying, matted and intertwined, their aspect changes according to the perspective of the user.

6. *ORIKI ORILE* OF THE MOTHER

There is a further reason for the dense imbrication of references in *oriki orile*. Identity in terms of an agnatic descent group is always shot through by identifications through the mother. One of the crucial openings in the wall erected around a group by *oriki orile* is the '*ile iya*': the mother's house. It is not normal to attribute to a subject only the *oriki orile* of his own – that is, his father's – patrilineage. He must also be saluted '*ní ìdí ìyá*': on the mother's side, by the *oriki orile* of his mother's patrilineage. Many *oriki* texts make this requirement explicit, proclaiming, for instance:

> Ìpàkọ́ wọ́n jọlé ìyá, Awóyẹmí, iwájú tọ́ ọ rí n ló jọlé baba
> A à lèràrìnjù, Àkàndé, ká a sọlé ìyá nù
> Mobómiléjọ́, ká a gbélé baba ká i léjú gẹgẹẹgẹ
> Imí ìdájí oo, Akínsòwọ́n
> Ara ìyáà rẹ ni
> Ìtọ̀ ìdájí, ara ìyáà rẹ ni.
> Ìyá ló ní wíwẹ̀ kúnkùn
> Mobómiléjọ́, baba tọ́ ọ rí n ló ní jíjẹ múmu
> 'Jọ́ kan dùgbẹ̀
> Àkàndé, ijọ́ kan dùgbẹ́
> Ọmọ ì í fi í sọlá dá ìyá ẹ̀ tán[22]

> The back of the head is like the mother's house, Awoyẹmi, the forehead is like the father's
> However far you go, you can never throw away your mother's house
> Mobomilẹjọ, and, living in your father's house, treasure that above all
> Early-morning shit, Akinsọwọn
> It's your mother who is dirtied with it
> Early morning piss, it's your mother who is dirtied with it
> The mother's job is washing and powdering the child
> Mobomilẹjọ, the father's job is providing food and drink.
> Because of the days when she was heavy
> Akande, because of the days when she was pregnant
> The child never uses its position to mistreat its mother completely.

The mother's house and the father's are inseparably locked together in

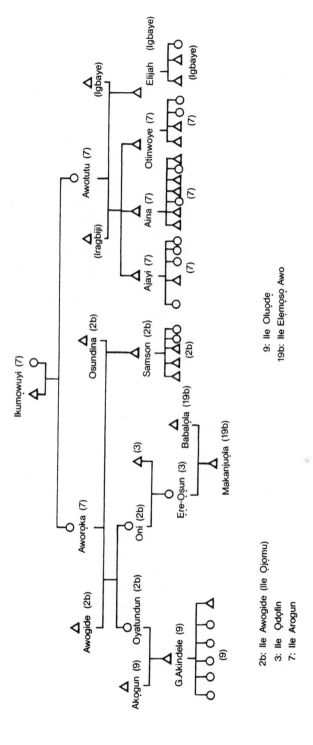

Fig. 2: Descendants of Awotutu and Aworọka

every individual's identity, just as the forehead and the crown of the head are inseparable aspects of a single entity. Introducing the *ile iya* into a performance of *oriki orilẹ* does two things. It defines the subject more precisely, for mothers are the source of difference within a lineage. Full brothers (*ọmọ iya*: children of the mother) are socially virtually indistinguishable, but brothers with one father but different mothers (*ọmọọ baba*: children of the father) are socially distinct. Inheritance is divided according to the number of wives the dead man had, and each group of *ọmọ iya*, however large or small, will share one equal portion. The segmentation of the lineage, likewise, is reckoned according to branches springing from each of the co-wives of the apical ancestor.[23] Each wife, therefore, is the source of a separate sub-segment within the lineage. While the *oriki orilẹ* of the father affirm the solidarity of the whole group, the *oriki orilẹ* of an individual's mother assert that this man has his own position within the group. Secondly, the woman is the source of contacts, assets, and alliances *outside* the lineage. She brings with her, on marriage, a thread which can be used to draw in great bodies of affines who may supply support, land, shelter, and even in some cases a permanent home to her descendants. The apparently solid patrilineality of the Okuku social system conceals far-reaching and long-maintained relationships 'on the mother's side'.[24]

An example of this is the story of the sisters Aworọka and Awotutu, daughters by the same wife of Ikumọwuyi of *ile* Arogun, a great nineteenth century medicine man and the earliest remembered holder of the title Oluawo Oniṣeegun (Head of the Herbalists). Aworọka married Awogide, the head of a lineage attached to *ile* Ojọmu. She had two daughters by him, Ọyatundun and Oni. On his death she was inherited by Awogide's son by another wife, Ọṣundina, and had several sons by him including Samson Adebisi (whose life story is told in Chapter 6). Awotutu married a man in Iragbiji and had three sons for him. When he died, she married another man in Igbaye, taking with her the youngest of her sons. She had another son for the Igbaye man, and this son, Elijah Fọlayan, is now the oldest of the surviving children of the two sisters. Once a year a meeting is held at his house in Igbaye to 'discuss family business', settle problems, and contribute money to a fund intended to promote the interests of the members. The meeting is attended by all the children, grandchildren and greatgrandchildren of the two sisters, whether descended through males or through females. It thus involves, among others, Samson Adebisi (*ile* Ojọmu), Ẹrẹ-Ọṣun (*ile* Ọdọfin, married into *ile* Ẹlẹmọṣọ Awo) and G.A. Akindele (*ile* Oluọdẹ). It involves the families of the sons born to the Iragbiji and Igbaye men, and all the descendants of Aworọka's children by both her husbands in *ile* Ojọmu. It does not include any one else from any of these compounds not descended from Aworọka or Awotutu. The children of Awogide and Ọṣundina by other wives, for instance, are excluded. Although the annual meeting and the savings fund represents a relatively small investment of time and money, it shows how relationships through women can be kept active over long periods and how they can bring together people who, in terms of patrilineage, are widely separated. Women can be mobile. Awotutu moved from Okuku to Iragbiji to Igbaye, and as she moved she took a son with her, thus establishing close links between two groups of men who belonged not only to different patrilineages but also to different towns.

Links through women take many forms and are ubiquitous in the networks of relations between fragments of lineages. Many attached lineages were actually brought to the town by a woman who had relatives in the 'host' lineage. Some groups were the 'sons of females' mentioned by Lloyd. *Ile* Awoyemi, one of the 'semi-attached' groups described above, was an example, being descended from a daughter of *ile* Oba, Edun's sister. In *ile* Ojomu – one of the *ile* with a very large number of attached groups – Awogide's section was attached because his mother was a daughter of *ile* Ojomu; but there were other kinds of links as well. Akoda's section came when Akoda's mother brought her children to stay with her sister, who was married into *ile* Ojomu. We have seen how a wife of *ile* Aworo took all her children to live in *ile* Jagun because she was from the same town as Jagun's mother. Connections through women could draw in new parties of people to swell the compound, through ties that could be based on kinship, marriage, friendship or common town membership.

The value of these connections is affirmed in *oriki* performances. In the passage just quoted, to forget one's mother is represented as unforgivable because a mother's bond with her child is the most fundamental relationship of all. The mother suffered to bring the child into the world and to see it through its infancy, and for this reason, however important a child may become in the world, he can never cast his mother off altogether. Passages like this, asserting the importance of the *ile iya*, are used to signal an intention to switch theme, from the father's to the mother's *oriki orile*. Almost all performances of *oriki orile* contain such switches, and usually, as the signalling device shows, the transition is clear and the distinction between the two sets of *oriki* is maintained. But sometimes the transition is not marked in any way. Intrusive passages or even mere phrases of one *oriki orile* may suddenly appear in the midst of the performance of another. Those in the know will be able to explain that the intrusive element derives from the *ile iya*. But the frequency and ease of their juxtaposition makes it more likely that some of the *oriki* of the *ile iya* will sometimes get absorbed into the *oriki* of the *ile baba*. Structural relations between groups provide conditions highly conducive to such merging.

Oriki orile emerge as dense mats of references: but the concentration of traces which an *oriki* chant contains do not explain their own history. They do not tell you why a performance within one compound should call up several different *oriki orile*, or how this situation arose. Disentangling the references made by *oriki orile* often requires formidable inside knowledge of the history and interrelationships of innumerable small groups in Okuku: a knowledge to which most inhabitants of the town have incomplete access, and from which I as a newcomer and outsider was often completely excluded. Middle-aged and elderly people, especially those who took an interest in the intricacies of social networks, often had an enormous field of discriminations at their command. They could track down links between *ile* and segments of *ile* apparently inexhaustibly. Nonetheless, no-one knew it all. Each *oriki* chanter made her distinctions from the standpoint of her own field of knowledge, which did not completely overlap with anyone else's. Not only this, but the performers themselves often could not fully explain why they made certain identifications or how certain links had arisen. Sometimes there was a parallel tradition of *itan ile* which shed light on these questions, but the fields of reference they covered only partly overlapped with the field evoked by *oriki* performers. Each performance, it seems certain, is surrounded by differential layers of interpretation, determined by the knowledge, interests, age and position in the community of the hearers.

Oriki orile are like talismans, potent symbols through which lines of demarcation are drawn or covered over according to the needs and interests of the users. In a society subject to continual population movement, the ancient core of emblems surrounding each town of origin provides each wandering group with a strong and unmistakable label. But the endless accretion and diversification of *oriki orile* enable those groups to make more detailed discriminations within the towns where they settle. What they emphasise and what they conceal; how loudly they proclaim their origins and affiliations, and in what company; how the insiders' version differs from the outsiders'; what subsidiary *oriki orile* they incorporate (for instance, from a mother's lineage): all these are clues to what exactly someone is asserting when he or she performs *oriki orile* or has them performed on his or her behalf.

7. EMBLEMATIC LANGUAGE

At the funerals of old men and women in Okuku there is sometimes a drama put on by the members of their lineage. This drama is called *oro ile* (family ceremony, ritual belonging to the *ile*), and its purpose is emblematic. It exhibits in spectacular fashion one of the themes associated with the deceased's *orile*. Because these themes are also at the centre of the *oriki orile*, the *oro ile* points out, by analogy, the emblematic quality of the *oriki*. Here is an example. It occurred during the funeral of Ẹfuntohun Arinkẹ described in Chapter 4. Ẹfuntohun came from another town, Ikirun, but married into *ile* Baalẹ and stayed there so long that she lost touch with her own people in Ikirun. It was known, however, that her lineage claimed origins in Ikoyi, so her husband's family asked *ile* Alubata (22) and *ile* Oluawo Onifa (2d) to help by doing their *oro ile* at her funeral. Both of these *ile* claim origins in Ikoyi, though they arrived separately in Okuku and attached themselves to different, unrelated host lineages.

On the third day of the funeral the daughters of the two lineages armed themselves with switches and danced to the *dundun* drums, singing:

> Wọ́n mọ̀ mọ̀ ní ẹ wá ṣọrò nílé
> Gbogbo Ìkòyí ẹ doríkodò, ọmọ ogun
> Wọ́n mọ̀ mọ̀ ní ẹ wá ṣọrò nílé

> They're calling you to come and do a family ceremony
> All you Ikoyi people gather round, children of war [or
>   'warriors']
> They're calling you to come and do a family ceremony.

Meanwhile a young boy of the lineage was dressed up as a woman and armed with a bow and arrow, while a girl was dressed up as a man and armed with a long sword. The twin themes to be enacted were the two legendary occupations of the Ikoyi people: warfare and robbery.

The two actors set off on an expedition around the town, pausing every so often to stage a scene in which the girl-dressed-as-a-man pursued the boy-dressed-as-a-woman, brandishing her long sword at him while he cowered, dodged and sought refuge behind the band of singing women. Occasionally the boy-dressed-as-a-woman retaliated by aiming his bow and arrow at the other and feigning a shot. Then they confronted each other and took it in turns to sing tauntingly, while the women provided the chorus:

Solo 1: Ojú olè rèé!	Chorus: Olè!
Solo 2: Owó olówó!	Chorus: Olè!
Solo 1: Aṣọ aláṣọ!	Chorus: Olè!
Solo 2: Ẹ̀wù ẹléwù!	Chorus: Olè!
Solo 1: Fìlà onífìlà!	Chorus: Olè!
Solo 2: Gèlè onígèlè!	Chorus: Olè!
Solo 1: Ọmọ ọlọ́mọ!	Chorus: Olè!
Solo 2: Ojú olè rèé!	Chorus: Olè!

Solo 1: There stands a thief!	Chorus: Thief!
Solo 2: Someone else's money!	Chorus: Thief!
Solo 1: Someone else's clothes!	Chorus: Thief!
Solo 2: Someone else's gown!	Chorus: Thief!
Solo 1: Someone else's cap!	Chorus: Thief!
Solo 2: Someone else's head-tie!	Chorus: Thief!
Solo 1: Someone else's child!	Chorus: Thief!
Solo 2: There stands a thief!	Chorus: Thief!

After they had toured the town performing this scene, they returned to the graveside where they had started. There the two actors mounted overturned mortars and confronted each other, threatening each other with their weapons. Each had a party of women behind to restrain them. Then the girl-dressed-

as-a-man was given a hen, the boy-dressed-as-a-woman a cock, and they
proceeded to flail each other with these while the women sang:

Solo: Ọmọ Eníkòyí, èyin dà?
Chorus: Àwa rèé, lóòró gangan!

Solo: Children of Ikoyi, where are you?
Chorus: Here we are, standing tall!

The ceremony was finished by an offering of palm oil, cotton fibre and
water at the foot of each mortar, and divination was done at each with kola
nuts which were then thrown onto the grave mound.

This drama unites the two themes of fighting and stealing into a single
image: the two actors, each of which has 'stolen' the other's clothes, attacking
each other with weapons. That these themes are emblems for the Ikoyi people
is underlined by the women's songs summoning the '*ọmọ Enikoyi*' and
demanding their participation.

Thievery and warfare are also the two most prominent themes in the Ikoyi
oriki orilẹ̀. One version presents them like this:

Èṣọ́ Ikòyí o!
Ká wáá jí ńjọọjúmọ́ ká díra ogun
N ló mú Yánbílolú túgun
Eníkòyí olórí olè tí í dábùro
Àgbàlagbà olè abifìlà gòngò
Wọ́n lÓníkòyí ó mọ́ jalè mọ́ o
Wọ́n wáá sẹ́ẹ́gún, Eníkòyí ń fẹ̀sẹ̀ gbóbẹ!
Oníkòyí olórí olè tí í gbáàgà aṣọ.[25]

War-captains of Ikoyi o!
'Let's rise every morning and arm ourselves for battle'
That's how Yanbilolu scattered the enemy
Ikoyi man, head of the thieves, who wears a cap of felt
Master-thief who wears a cap turned down at one side
They told the Ikoyi people not to steal any more
They brought out the masquerades, the Ikoyi man swiped a knife
     with his feet!
Ikoyi man, head of the thieves, who made off with a hamper of
     clothes.

The analogy of the *oro ile* suggests that what might look like references to
real people and real incidents in the past are included in the *oriki* for their
emblematic value. The Ikoyi man who was so adept at stealing that he could
even do it with his feet, in the midst of a public entertainment, may indeed
really have existed, but in the *oriki* he represents all Ikoyi people. He is the

epitome of the qualities that have been chosen to characterise them and distinguish them from descendants of other *orilẹ*.

Other *oro ile* are emblematic in the same way. The Oko people are famous for the jealousy of the women, and much of the Oko *oriki orilẹ* is on this theme. For their *oro ile* they stage a furious confrontation between 'husband' and 'wife' (again, both parts are played by the wrong sex) in which the 'wife' accuses the husband of mistreating her and favouring her co-wife. One of the Ọfa emblems is the wrestling match which is performed in the annual new yam festival. In the *oro ile*, little boys are organised to wrestle in pairs at the graveside. *Oro ile* show that the principal themes associated with an *orilẹ* can be summed up in a single dramatic image: two people fighting and stealing; two boys wrestling; a jealous wife berating her polygamous husband. Although so much more elaborate, *oriki orilẹ* are doing something equivalent. They circle around a theme, embellishing it in artful ways, but the *point* of them is to put on display a motif which could be summed up in a word or an image. The 'totem' of the Opomulero people from Iwata is Opo, a housepost. The story of the ancient ọba of Iwata who was a master carver of houseposts has already been mentioned. In some magical way the posts, or the logs from which they were carved, were associated with the fertility of the ọba's wives and the continuation of his lineage. At a later date, when the Iwata line had become incorporated into the Ọyọ royal lineage, there was an Alaafin who had two hundred houseposts carved in commemoration of his mother. In funeral ceremonies for their members, the Opomulero people, as we have seen, set up a miniature post inside the compound and wrap it in cloth, in commemoration of this Alaafin's action, to assert the identity that they share with the deceased. The *oriki orilẹ* make much of the theme of the house-post, and particularly of the house-post wrapped in cloth. A *rara iyawo* version goes:

Èmi lọmọ òpó kọrọbítí kọrọbítí
Èmi lọmọ òpó kọrọbìtì kọrọbìtì
Èmi lọmọ òpó róṣọ òpó gbàjá
Ilé wa ni wọ́n tí í rógi láṣọ, Alé-Ọyun.

I am the child of the round round post
I am the child of the round round post
I am the child of the post that wears a wrapper, the post that ties
    a sash
It's in our house they dress a post in cloth, Ale-Oyun.

In this version the word *opo* is embellished with the phonaesthetic adjectival expression *kọrọbítí kọrọbítí* and its tonal variant *kọrọbìtì kọrọbìtì*. Reference is made to the custom of dressing a post in cloth, and the last line affirms that this is a practice that distinguishes the Opomulero people. There is no hint of why the post is dressed in cloth, of what the post itself represents or of the history behind it. The point of the passage is to place before the hearer the emblem itself, in a pleasing setting. In the funeral chant version quoted in Chapter 4, even more elaboration occurs, this time around the word *aṣọ*, the cloth in which the post is said to be wrapped. Three names of cloth are mentioned; two of them, *egbínrín* and *egbìnrìn*, are again tonal variants of the same word, included for decorative purposes. Only in the last line is a historical connection hinted at in the reference to the Alaafin of Ọyọ.

In circling around the theme of the post dressed in cloth, the *oriki* are making an emblematic presentation of what is already an emblem in real life. Opomu-lero people wrap a post in cloth and set it up as their family emblem; the *oriki* wrap the cloth-wrapped post in a decorative integument of words to display it.

The language of *oriki orílè* continually embellishes key motifs, and devises decorative settings to present them in. A position where the motif can be displayed is often elaborately prepared. In the following passage from the *oriki orílè* of the Omu line, the key words are *omitoro ẹsin*, broth made from horse, a special dish that distinguished the Omu people. But these words do not appear until the last two lines of the passage. All that goes before prepares a setting in which they are finally presented:

> Béwúrẹ́
> Bó bá sọnù lÓmù
> Kẹ́ ẹ má mu lọ̀ mí
> Ta ní í sẹgbẹ́ẹ gbéran-gbéran?
> Àgùntàn kan bọ̀lòjọ̀
> Bó bá sọnù lÓmù
> Kẹ́ ẹ má mu lọ̀ mí
> Ta ní í sẹgbẹ́ẹ gbéran-gbéran?
> Adìẹ òkòkó
> Arágbàdo-yọ̀
> Bó bá sọnù lÓmù
> Ẹ má mu lọ̀ mí
> Ta ní í sẹgbẹ́ẹ gbéyẹ-gbéyẹ?
> Ẹsi ògòdòngbó
> Agbámù-rodò
> Bó bá sọnù lÓmù
> Ẹ wáà mú un lọ̀ mí
> Ọpọ́n ńlá n mo i jomitoro ẹsi
> Mo i jomitoro ẹsi, Mòsí-Ọ̀jọ́ọ́rọ.[26]

> If a goat
> Gets lost at Omu
> Don't come to me about it
> Who are you calling a member of the goat-thieves' gang?
> If a big black sheep

Gets lost at Omu
Don't come to me about it
Who are you calling a member of the sheep-thieves' gang?
A mother hen
Who rejoices at the sight of maize
If it gets lost at Omu
Don't come to me about it
Who are you calling a member of the poultry-thieves' gang?
A massive horse
That carries its great pot-belly to the river
If it gets lost at Omu
Why then, do come to me about it!
I drink horse-broth from a huge dish
I drink horse-broth from it, Mosi-Ojooro.

The first four lines establish a syntactic structure which is then reinforced
by two more repetitions. It has the form:

If a ———
Gets lost at Omu
Don't come to me about it
Who are you calling a member of the ——— gang?

Occupying the first slot are the names of three domestic animals, goat, sheep
and hen, the first a bare noun, the second qualified by adjectives, the third by
a nominalised construction (literally translatable as 'One-who-rejoices...').
The second slot is occupied by the name of the kind of thief who would steal
the domestic animal named in the first slot (gberan-gberan: stealer of domestic
sheep and goats; gbeye-gbeye: stealer of fowl).

But in the fourth occurrence of this structure the 'massive horse' is
presented – qualified, again, by a nominalised construction – and the sense
of the message is reversed. If a horse is missing, do come to me about it. The
final line of the established structure is dropped, and replaced with the key
sentence which proclaims the reason for the missing horse: the Omu habit of
eating horse-broth. The first three occurrences of the structure are
preliminaries, establishing a pattern into which the reference to horse and
horse-broth can be fitted. They prepare a place for the key motif. The
reference to goat, sheep and hen have no intrinsic significance; they point
away from themselves towards the appearance of the key word, which is
signalled by the reversal of sense in the last repetition of the pattern.
Nevertheless they have a kind of gravity, and take up time, as each one is more
elaborately qualified than the last. The language of oriki orile seems to stand
still, as, instead of making a statement, it prepares a space into which a small
phrase can be inserted.

The framework in which the motif of the horse-broth is displayed is appropriate. Goat, sheep and hen belong to the same semantic universe as the horse. All four are domestic animals which, in Omu at least, can be eaten. But horse and horse-broth are not the only motif that can be displayed in this structure. The Ọlọjẹ *oriki orilẹ* use precisely the same sequence to present the motif of *aja dudu*, black dog, which is one of *their* family emblems and which fits the slot just as well. (Dogs too are ritually eaten.) The structure does not *give rise* to its conclusion, the presentation of the emblem; it prepares a space for an emblem which is already formed. The emblem can also be displayed in other frameworks, and the framework can be used to display other emblems.

Underpinning this kind of structure are lexical sets of two or three related items. These sets are so well known that as soon as the first item in a set is mentioned, the hearer will expect the others. On these sets are built up structures, usually tripartite, through which the *orilẹ* emblems are presented. It is common for two such sets to be operated together:

> Ọmọ omi ṣe mẹ́ta wọ́n á ṣèṣe
> Omi ṣe mẹ́ta wọ́n á hanrọ̀ lÓfà
> Òkan ní ẹ pẹnlá sí òun
> Kóun ó dòkun
> Òkan lóba ó ní ẹ pàgbò sí òun
> Kóun ó dọ̀sà
> Òkan lóba ó ní ẹ pàkùkọ gàngà sí òun
> Kóun ó dAgúnbẹ́lẹ́njẹ́ ọmọ là kÓfà ó kún tété
> Èyí a pẹnlá sí, èé lè dòkun nínú ilé ọkọ
> Èyí tá a pàgbò sí ò lè dọ̀sà
> Èyí tí a pàkùkọ gàngà sí, ó dAgúnbẹ́lẹ́njẹ́, ọmọ dàálẹ̀ ká a ríbi tógún
>   pín.[27]

Child of 'There were three rivers that misbehaved'
There were three rivers that ran wild at Ọfa
One said they should kill an *ẹnla* cow [a humpless breed] for it
So that it could become an ocean
One said the ọba should kill a ram for it
So that it could become a lagoon
One said the ọba should kill a big cock for it
So that it could become the river Agunbẹlẹnjẹ, child of 'Get rich
    so that Ọfa will teem with people'
The one we killed an *ẹnla* cow for couldn't become an ocean in my
    husband's house
The one we killed a ram for couldn't become a lagoon
The one we killed a big cock for, it became Agunbẹlẹnjẹ, child of
    'Restore all that you have inherited so that we can redivide it'.

The river Agunbẹlẹnjẹ[28] is the emblem that this passage is bringing out. It is one of the major rivers running past Ọfa, associated with the Ọfa royal family and a source of pride to the whole town. To present it, the *oriki* makes it one of three bodies of water, each requiring a sacrifice in order to become the kind of water it wishes. The first time the basic formula is used it takes the form:

One said they should kill a —— for it
So that it could become a ——.

In the first slot is a set of domestic animals, in decreasing order of size and costliness, that are commonly offered as sacrifices. In the second slot is the well known lexical pair *okun* (ocean) and *ọsa* (lagoon) and then the key word of the passage, the name of the river, embellished with a phrase of Ọfa *oriki*. In the second series of repeated structures, the same two sets of lexical items are linked again:

The one we killed a —— for couldn't become a ——.

On the third repetition there is, as in the Omu example, a reversal which signals the arrival of the key phrase:

The one we killed a —— for *did* become a ——.

The two bodies of water that asked for the most costly sacrifices could not achieve what they wanted, but the third one, who only asked for a fowl to be sacrificed, succeeded in becoming the precious and highly-regarded Agunbẹlẹnjẹ river.

The set of animals – *ẹnla* cow, ram and cock – are appropriate because they constitute a series of sacrificeable domestic animals of different sizes and values, but there is nothing inevitable about this selection; the composer could equally well have chosen other animals as long as they fitted the series: *ewurẹ* (goat) or *aguntan* (sheep) instead of *agbo* (ram), for instance; *adiẹ* (chicken) instead of *akukọ* (cock). This is not true of the pair *okun* (ocean) and *ọsa* (lagoon). Once *okun* has been mentioned, there is no choice but to complete the pair with *ọsa*. This is one of the fixed lexical sets that underpin the structures not only of *oriki orilẹ* but of many other genres of Yoruba oral poetry.

These lexical sets include *ẹru, iwọfa* and *ọmọ bibi inu* (slave, bondsman and true-born child); *ila* and *ikan* (okro and garden egg); *igun* and *akalamagbo* (vulture and hornbill); *epo* and *iyọ* (palm oil and salt); *osun* and *aro* (camwood and indigo). Some sets of three have two fixed members and a variable third one: *aluko* and *agbe* (*aluko* bird and blue touraco) always go together, but can be followed either by *odidẹrẹ* (parrot) or by *lekeleke* (cattle egret). When the third member is *lekeleke*, this set is often matched with another one, *osun, aro* and *ẹfun* (camwood, indigo and chalk) because the red of camwood, the blue of indigo and white of chalk match the colours of the three birds.

These lexical sets appear in songs, proverbs, Ifa verses, *oriṣa pipe* (invocation of *oriṣa*) and *iwure* (poetic prayers) as well as in *oriki orilẹ*. They are always used to set up a structure of repetition, but the meaning attached to them varies according to context. They can play many different roles, ranging from full-blown characters in a story to the most limited and neutral tokens in a figure of speech. The same sets of words can appear in one context with an ambiance of symbolic meaning, and in another context devoid of any significance beyond sheer habitual association together. In Ifa verses, for instance, vulture and hornbill may play a symbolic role as the consumers of sacrifices and corpses; in *oriki orilẹ* the same pair can appear as structural pegs wholly devoid of symbolic significance.

In one Ifa verse,[29] Ọrunmila is searching for his enemy Eko and receives directions on the way from *ila* (okro), *ikan* (garden egg) and *eniyaya* (a vegetable with pinnate leaves added to the standard pair *ila/ikan* to make up a trio). Having defeated Eko, Ọrunmila then rewards his three helpers; *ila* henceforward bears twenty fruits, *ikan* becomes blood-red, and *eniyaya* bears fifty fruits. This story – like many Ifa stories – celebrates Ifa's triumph over hostile powers. But it also has an etiological theme, explaining how the three vegetables came to have the characteristics by which we know them. The trio are not only important characters in the story but are also partly what the story is about. Attention is focused on them and their intrinsic qualities: their fruitfulness and the changes they undergo in growing to maturity. Ọrunmila's beneficent power is demonstrated by his capacity to bestow on these three 'characters' their essential properties.

In *oriki* the same pair, okro and garden egg, are represented with the same properties, bearing fruits and growing to maturity. But here they are used as structural devices to direct attention towards something else. They can be set up in different ways to introduce different things. Here are three examples:

(1)
Ilá so, ó gbàgbé, ilá kó
Ikàn so, ó gbàgbé, ó wèwù èjè
Ìyá mi mọ́ pe mo gbàgbéè rẹ

Okro fruited and forgot, okro went to seed
Garden egg fruited and forgot, it put on a garment of blood
My mother, don't ever say that I have forgotten you.

In this passage the key word is *gbagbe*, to forget, and the statement for which the performer is paving the way is the assurance that she has not forgotten her mother (the passage is part of the preliminary homage in which performers acknowledge their predecessors and teachers). The okro's going to seed, and the garden egg's red hue, are signs that they have been left too long, the result of forgetfulness. Okro and garden egg are forgetful, she is not.

(2)

Bílá bá foríbalẹ̀ ilá wọ́n á máa kó
Bíkàn tó bá foríbalẹ̀ áá wẹ̀wù ẹ̀jẹ̀
Agbánréré tó bá foríbalẹ̀ yóò làwo fỌlọ́finra

If okro bows down, okro will go to seed
If garden egg bows down, it will put on a garment of blood
If the antelope bows down, its horns will grow for the Ọlọfinra

Here the key word is *foribalẹ*, to bow down or pay homage. The performer, in the course of paying her respects to the powers that be, is asserting that it is through homage that people gain the blessing of long life. So this time the okro is said to fruit and go to seed, the garden egg to go red, as a result of having paid homage. Going to seed and becoming blood-red are here taken as a sign that the fruits have lived to a ripe old age unmolested: a desirable fate. A third item is added to spin out the theme still further: by paying homage the antelope lives long enough to grow its horns to their full size. In this passage the statement to which all this is directed is left implicit: 'And I, so that I may have a long and prosperous life, am also paying homage'.

(3)

Ilá tó sojú ìyá ẹ̀ so, Ọyáwálé baba Ọlọ́ya
Ikàn tó sojú ìyá ẹ̀ wẹ̀jẹ̀
Oílàkí tó rAájì tí ò há lójú Ọyáwálé baba Ọlọ́ya

The okro that goes to seed before its mother's eyes, Ọyawale the
    devotee of Ọya
The garden egg that put on a garment of blood before its mother's
    eyes
Oilaki who went to Mecca and got back safely before the eyes of
    Ọyawale the devotee of Ọya

This time the key word is *soju*, before the eyes of, during the lifetime of. The statement being foregrounded is that Ọyawale's twin sons (Oilaki is the *oriki* of twins) went to Mecca and returned unscathed during his lifetime, for which the credit goes to him. The okro's fruiting and the garden egg's ripening are therefore said to have happened in the presence of the parent plants (true enough, as the seeds drop from the ripe fruit onto the ground beneath).

These examples show quite clearly that the sets of images are not included for any permanent symbolic value of their own. They can be made to serve whatever meaning the performer wishes to direct attention to. In one case the ripening and fruiting of okro and garden egg are held to be the results of carelessness and forgetfulness; in another they are held up as a desirable end, the reward for humility. The only constant feature is the pairing of *ila* and *ikan*, and the matching of this set with *so/ko* (bear fruit/go to seed) and *wẹwu ẹjẹ* (put on a blood-red garment). Structures are built up around these sets to prepare a conspicuous place for the key word of whatever theme is being treated.

In these ways ready-made lexical sets are drawn from the current literary tradition and used to build the structures typical of *oriki orile*. The lexical sets become pegs on which to hang a framework whose purpose is to present a single motif. These frameworks are endlessly varied but always in a sense static, woven around a single point and directed away from themselves towards that point. The motif itself is irreducible: it is elaborated but not explained. Sequences of *oriki orile* may be extended and elaborated and even take on a quasi-narrative form. But the whole structure is erected in order to fill a space, to prepare a slot into which a small, indivisible sign is placed: often a single concept, like 'abundant palm oil', 'blacksmith' or 'Ori Oke'. In *rara iyawo*, the simplest of the women's chants, the performers often confine themselves to the artful elaboration of only two or three such signs for each *orile*. In the more flexible performances of mature women, greater profusion of signs may be achieved, and with an elaboration that is less orderly and more dynamic. However, whatever chanting mode is being used, *oriki orile* remain essentially emblematic. It is this that makes them emotionally so highly charged. They condense into memorable and repeatable signs people's sense of the accumulated wealth of their own group's past: a past concentrated above all in the moment of origin when everything became what it now is. Precisely because it is embalmed in condensed, inscrutable yet endlessly decorated images, this wealth appears to be imperishable.

6

THE *ORIKI* OF BIG MEN

1. BIG MEN, REPUTATION AND *ORIKI*

Okuku, like other Yoruba towns, is hierarchical. As we have seen, it was part of a larger system of authority, nominally subordinate in turn to Ọyọ, Ilọrin and Ibadan, and also claiming overlordship over a number of neighbouring towns in the Odo-Ọtin area. Internally too, Okuku was and is hierarchically structured. The immense privilege and mystically-conceived authority of the Olokuku made him 'second to the gods'. Beneath him, the chiefs constitute a hierarchy that is elaborately ranked and graded, and the holders of titles regard these distinctions of status as being of supreme importance. Within the community at large, steep differences of status are permanently maintained. As the last chapter showed, each compound is internally stratified; and outside the compound too, everybody has to know who is senior and junior to them in order simply to be able to address them correctly. Consciousness of relative seniority is acute, in some situations even overriding gender distinctions. 'You are a small boy to me', 'I had given birth even before you married', 'I was walking before you were born' are comments that are heard continually as the hierarchy of seniority is reproduced in daily life.

In the past this hierarchy was animated by a dynamic, competitive struggle for self-aggrandisement which permeated the society from top to bottom. There was scope for people to create a place for themselves and expand it by their own efforts. Like the 'Big Men' of New Guinea, they did it through the recruitment of supporters. A Yoruba proverb, often written up as a motto on parlour walls and the sides of lorries, says *'Mo lówó, mo lénìyàn, kí ló tún kù tí mi ò tíì ní?'*: 'I have money, I have people, what else is there that I have not got?' Money was one of the principal ways of gaining public acknowledgement as a big man; but 'having people' constituted that acknowledgement itself. Wives and children, visiting matrilateral relatives, attached 'stranger' segments in long-term residence, bondsmen, labourers, visitors, friends and adherents of all kinds, from the most permanent to the most casual – all were the 'people' on whose acknowledgement the ambitious man's standing depended. If their recognition were withdrawn – if they left, or transferred their loyalty to another patron, or chose another house to drop in on for gossip and advice – the man would lose his public standing. His position depended on public recognition: and recognition of course bred more recognition, for a man with a great reputation would attract great numbers of adherents whose regard would in turn boost his reputation still further.

In this process of self-aggrandisement, *oriki* played a crucial part. They were the main instrument through which reputation was publicly acknowledged and enhanced. In an *oriki* performance before a large audience the big man was put on display. The more extensive and intensive the repertoire ascribed to him, the more illustrious his name would be. *Oriki* singers were sensitive barometers of relative status. In a public gathering they would take care to address those they perceived as the most important first and at greatest length. If a still more important person walked in, they would break off their chant and turn their attention to the newcomer. The most conspicuously successful men would have the largest corpus of *oriki*, for drummers, specialist singers and the townspeople in general would be more likely to compose epithets for the qualities and actions of outstanding, highly visible men. In public performance, their accumulated epithets would be held up for all to recognise. The constitutive role of *oriki* in a big man's rise is commented on in the texts themselves. They often speak of the performance as a gift from singer to addressee, calling attention to the profusion of epithets the singer has heaped upon him: 'I have given you an *atin-in* mat, now I'll add an *ore* mat to my gift';[1] 'We always call someone by three names, but I'll add more'; 'This is what I have bestowed on you, take it with you when you go'. The performer, fixing the subject with her concentrated and unwavering attention for as long as she addresses him, dramatises the role of supporter to a big man. If recognition and acknowledgement are what make his claims to status valid, then the praise-singer offers him this relationship in an ideal form. She enacts a concentrated regard and acknowledgement, calling attention to the relationship between herself as admirer and him as object of admiration; and he visibly swells and takes on status under the treatment.

Not only the act of performance, however, but also the words of the texts bestow on the big man the regard of 'people'. The use of other people's names in these *oriki* reveal most clearly their role in the creation of big men. *Oriki* are full of allusions to genealogical relationships. But these are never records of family trees; they do not preserve the details of kinship links or make precise distinctions among them.[2] Instead, *oriki* raid the genealogy in order to heap on the chosen subject a wealth of attributions. The actual relationships between all the people whose names are brought into play may be known to some members of the audience independently of the *oriki*: but it is certainly not through the *oriki* tradition that this knowledge is transmitted. The impression *oriki* performances give is rather one of a great profusion of relationships, ordered by only one principle: their common connection to the central subject of the *oriki*. The intention which animates these *oriki* is to build up one figure through, and often almost at the expense of, others. Fixing a man accurately on the genealogical grid puts him in his place; *oriki*, on the other hand, create the impression that the big man is at the centre of everything, and, indeed, that the other members of the family tree exist only by virtue of their relationship to him.

Here, for instance, is part of a performance in honour of an important man of *ile* Ọlọkọ whose mother was from *ile* Oluawo. Ṣangowẹmi, the performer, first saluted him with reference to his father's lineage, and then turned to *ile* Oluawo: in this passage, she concentrates on connecting the subject with one illustrious ancestor, Ajayi, the great herbalist of that compound:

Ọlọ́ṣundé Aílẹ́wọ́lá Ògídí-Olú Àkànó
Jáayinfá babaa Bílẹ́wumọ, Àjàyí ògbórí-ẹfọ̀n nÍbàdàn
Bí ò sí Aílẹ́wọ́lá, ogun ìbá kólé Adó
Àìsí Àjàyí, ogun jà ó jà Òkìtì
Ìsí Ọlọ́ṣundé, ogun rè kóBòkun
Àkùkọ kọ ọ̀lẹ pòsé, babaa Tóhún wáá mọ́kọ́ gbẹrẹ bí ẹni ń lẹ
Ó wáá dáná ọkọ́ mọ́ gbòngbò lẹ́hìn
Ó ní bọ́ ọ bá lẹ́gbàá kìṣì, babaà mi, Àrẹmú,
Ó ní á mú un relé rèé gbéyàwó
Ọlọ́ṣundé Ògídí-Olú, Jàámódù, babaà mi, ó ní bá a bá kú,
     ó lọ́mọọ̀ rẹ ní í peni ní baba
Ọmọ Alọlá, ọmọ Ògúnkẹ́yẹ, ọmọ Àtàndá Awúrèré gbọ̀ṣọ́...

Ọlọṣunde Arilewọla Ogidi-Olu Akano
Jaayinfa father of Bilewumọ, Ajayi 'One who bore off the head of
     a buffalo' at Ibadan
If it were not for Arilewọla, Ado would have been captured in
     battle
With Ajayi absent, war raged and overthrew Ekiti
Without Ọlọṣunde, war brought down Ibokun
The cock crows, the lazy man sighs, father of Tohun picked up his
     hoe like a man who is lazy
Then he went and blazed his way through the roots with his hoe,
     hurling them behind
He said if you have sixpence in cash, my father, Arẹmu,
He said you'd better take it home and get yourself a wife
Ọlọṣunde Ogidi-Olu, Jaamodu, my father, he said if we die, he
     said at least we'll have children to call us their father
Child of Alọla, child of Ogunkẹyẹ, child of Atanda
     Awurere the finely-dressed...

The subject of the chant is being saluted through Ajayi, his mother's father, and Ajayi himself is magnified with a whole range of names attached in different ways. Ọlọṣunde was one of Ajayi's given names, Arilewọla an honorific nickname ('One who has a house to trail honour in'), Jaayinfa and Jaamodu both Ifa names deriving from the fact that Ajayi's father's family were noted *babalawo*. 'If it were not for Arilewọla, Ado would have been captured in battle': this and the two following lines belonged originally to the famous Ajayi Ogbori-ẹfọn, Balogun of Ibadan, whose name was well remembered in Okuku, since it was he who marched to lift the siege of Ikirun, where the Okuku population had taken refuge, in 1878[3]. Ajayi of *ile* Oluawo was not a warrior and had no connection with the Ibadan leader; he was given the *oriki* simply on the strength of sharing the *oruko amutọrunwa*, Ajayi. But the name of Ajayi of *ile* Oluawo is also amplified by associating it with his own ancestors and descendants. He is the 'father of Bilewumọ' and the 'father of Tohun'. He is also the 'child of Alọla', 'child of Ogunkẹyẹ', 'child of Atanda Awurere the finely-dressed'. No indication is given of the relationships between these people. Since the proliferation of personal names and nicknames is regarded as desirable, it is quite possible that Alọla, Ogunkẹyẹ and Atanda Awurere are all alternative names for the same person – who could be Ajayi's father, his mother's father, his father's father, his father's brother, his great-grandfather, or some other relative of an ascendant generation. It is equally possible that the names refer to three separate people – each of whom could stand in any of these relationships to the subject. Furthermore, it is not at all self-evident from the text alone that the person being addressed as 'child of Alọla', etc., is still Ajayi; the performer could equally well have finished with Ajayi, and be addressing these cognomina directly to the living subject of her performance. Only a person with intimate knowledge of the subject and his compound would grasp how many people were actually being referred to and how they were related to the addressee of the chant. The performer moves through layer upon layer of association, bringing in names from all directions. The only fixed point in this sliding profusion is the addressee himself, on whom the performer fastens her gaze. Masses of other people's names are brought in, but not to establish and clarify a genealogy: on the contrary, they are brought in to establish that – for the moment – the addressee is the centre of this social universe, and that he 'has people' in abundance.

Oriki, then, are at the centre of a crucial political process. It is a process conducted largely by men. Women as well as men may have ambitions and may build up a position for themselves in the town. A number of such 'big women' are remembered, and some exist today. But they could not follow the route taken by the big men, for women were part of a man's household rather than the head of their own. They could not recruit 'people' in the same way, and reputation does not play the same crucial and constitutive role in their careers as in men's. Women remain, by and large, the agents rather than the objects of the process of aggrandisement through the performance of *oriki*.

2. HIERARCHY AND THE DYNAMICS OF SELF-AGGRANDISEMENT

The ọba was endowed with both mystical and material attributes that set him definitively apart from the rest of the population. Beneath him were three grades of male chiefs and one of female chiefs. Of the male chiefs, the *ọlọpaa* or staff-carrying ones were the most senior. Their mark of office was the bamboo staff, and they alone among the chiefs were allowed to wear coral beads. They were internally ranked, and the top six were recognised [at least since the reign of Oyinlọla (1934–60)] as the *iwẹfa mẹfa* or kingmakers. These chiefs constituted the ọba's council, which normally met every day to discuss the affairs of the town. They participated in the judicial process and took a share of the fines and fees that accrued from it. The *aladaa* or cutlass-carrying chiefs were junior to the *ọlọpaa* chiefs, and were said to have been their 'followers' in an earlier era. Schofield (1935) reported that each *ọlọpaa* chief had a 'line' of *aladaa* chiefs who would follow him to the palace and wait outside while he conducted his business there, later helping to inform the town of whatever decisions the council had decided to make public. Nowadays the *aladaa* chiefs sit in the palace with the ọba and senior chiefs, but there is still strong consciousness of their lower status. Finally, the palace chiefs make up a separate and less important group. They do not constitute part of the council, but are regarded as being especially close to the ọba and much involved in the regulation of his household affairs. Today only three palace titles are occupied – the Ṣọbaloju, the Ọbaale and the Ẹlẹmọna (see Table 2).

The women chiefs are headed by the Iyalode, a title which alternates between wives of *ile* Oluọdẹ and wives of *ile* Balogun. The Iyalode is considered the head of all the women of the town, with special responsibilities in the market. She settles disputes over weights and measures and deals with cases of cheating in the market. She used to have a string of subordinate chiefs, among them the Ọtun Iyalode, the Ileju Iyalode, the Eesa Iyalode, and the Ọdọfin. According to one woman, 'Every *ile* would choose two women, one would hold a title and the other would be her follower, when they went to meetings in the Iyalode's house'. Only the Iyalode, however, is prominent in town affairs. She joins the six kingmakers in the selection of a new ọba and is always present at important ceremonial and deliberative meetings at the palace. The other women chiefs are so inconspicuous that most people – women as well as men – do not know who they are, or even that they exist. Whether they were formerly more prominent, and suffered from the characteristic blind eye of the colonial adminstration, which codified the local political structures with an overwhelming bias towards the male institutions – or whether the women's offices were always a shadow institution without the power and prestige enjoyed by the male chiefs, is not known.

In the nineteenth century, the rest of the town's population were either ordinary free citizens, *iwọfa,* or slaves. Ordinary citizens were not ranked, but members of the very large royal lineage enjoyed certain privileges that

Senior Town Chiefs (*ìlú ọlópàá*)		Junior Town Chiefs (*ìlú aládàá*)	
Title	Owned by	Title	Current holders
Òjọmu	*Ilé* Òjọmu	Jagun	*Ilé* Jagun
Òdòfin	*Ilé* Òdòfin	Ẹlémọ́ṣọ́ọ́	
	(*Ilé* Àwòrò Òtìn)[a]	Akọgun	
Baálẹ̀	*Ilé* Baálẹ̀	Ológemọ	*Ilé* Jagun
Inúrín	*Ilé* Nlá	Eésinkin[b]	
Ṣáìwò	*Ilé* Ọlọ́kọ̀	Ọbálá	*Ilé* Àwòrò Olóókù
Arógun	*Ilé* Olúawo	Òtún Baálẹ̀[b]	
Alálà	*Ilé* Àwòrò Òtìn	Òtún Ológemọ[b]	
Ọlọ́mi[b]	*Ilé* Olúọdẹ	Eléjù[b]	
Aláwẹ̀	*Ilé* Aláwẹ̀	Alápèẹ́[b]	
Ọlóyàn	*Ilé* Ọlóyàn		
Olówóèyìn	*Ilé* Olúọde		
Ọṣólọ̀[c]	*Ilé* Ọṣólọ̀/Ìníṣà		
	branch of lineage		
Balógun	*Ilé* Àwòrò Òtìn		
Olúòkun[b]	*Ilé* Olúòkun		
Àró[c]	*Ilé* Àró-Òkè		
	Ilé Àró-Ìsàlẹ̀		
Òdọgun[d]	*Ilé* Òdọgun		
Olúkòtún[d]	*Ilé* Olúọde		
Sábà[d]	*Ilé* Olúọdẹ		
Oṣólú[d]	*Ilé* Àwòrò Òtìn		

Palace Chiefs

Title	Current holders
Ṣóbalójú	*Ilé* Àwòrò Òtìn
Ọbaálé	*Ilé* Ọbaálé
Ẹlémọ̀nà	*Ilé* Ẹlémọ̀nà
Mógájì[b]	
Máyégún[b]	
Àrẹ Ìkọ́lábà[b]	
Àrèmọ[b]	

a. The title was held by this compound once only.
b. Title currently vacant
c. Title alternates between two compounds.
d. Recently promoted from junior grade.

Table 2: Chiefs in Okuku (1975)

members of other lineages did not. They were exempted from communal labour on the town walls and roads; their daughters brought in a higher bride-price than ordinary girls; and they had access to much larger reserves of uncultivated land than members of other compounds – a consideration that became increasingly important from the beginning of this century onwards. Members of other large compounds or compounds holding important titles also enjoyed a certain prestige of a more informal kind.

Iwofa were a large, fluctuating but semi-permanent category of men who served as bonded labourers in other compounds as a form of interest on a loan. Some, also known as *asingba,* entered into this arrangement voluntarily, for a loan they took out themselves. They usually served only one day out of four or eight, and were free to work on their own farms the rest of the time. Many *iwofa*, however, were lent out by other people, usually a senior relative, and were sent to live full time in the creditor's house until the loan was repaid. Many of them had to stay there for years, and there were stories in Okuku of *iwofa* who had simply run away when they eventually realised that the debt for which they were bonded would never be paid off. Theoretically it was always possible, however, for an *iwofa* to redeem himself by raising the money to pay back the original loan; though they were usually treated less well than free members of the household, there was always the expectation that their status could change.

This was apparently not true of slaves, though little information was available about them. Men and women could be either born into slavery or captured in war. The stigma lasted as long as slavery was remembered, making it difficult for people to talk about specific cases. It was clear, however, that the grand office-holding, property-owning slaves characteristic of bigger cities were not known in Okuku. Slavery was never mentioned except as a degraded and shameful status. Oral texts emphasised the disadvantages of slaves in comparison to *iwofa* and free people. No mention was made, in Okuku people's reminiscences, of slaves being able to redeem themselves by payments to their master. On the contrary, all stories stressed that the only hope for a slave, and especially a war-captive, was to run away. It was said that most of them sooner or later did so, making slave owning unprofitable. Female slaves, however, were often married by the captor and gradually became absorbed into the family.[4]

The oral texts suggest, however, that there may have been a more stable period before the nineteenth century when slaves were an established feature of the local hierarchy. The most common social division referred to in *oriki* is the tripartite one discussed in the last chapter, *eru/iwofa/omo bibi inu*: slaves, bondsmen, true-born children of the lineage – as if these were at one time the fundamental social categories.[5] The categories have now become hardly more than a poetic idiom, used, like other lexical sets, as a structuring device. It is impossible, of course, to be sure that it was ever more than this; but it seems highly likely that such a pervasive and unchanging ideational structure should have been motivated by real social divisions, if only obliquely. At the very least, the prevalence of the idiom suggests that society was assumed to be hierarchical – whether or not the poetic categories corresponded to the real major social divisions at any period. *Iwọfa,* unlike slaves, persisted well into the present century, the last one being remembered to have obtained his freedom in 1939. A modified form of *asingba,* or voluntary servitude, is still practised today 'in a polite way', as one senior man put it: someone in need of a loan may agree to 'thank' the lender by doing some work on his farm. The large households with six or ten permanent *iwọfa* in residence, however, do not seem to have lasted beyond about 1930.

These hierarchical relationships correlate with differential control of labour and consequently land. Until the second or third decade of this century, as will be shown later in this chapter, though lineage land was a jealously guarded patrimony, actually getting access to land for farming purposes was never a problem. What determined an individual's wealth was his or her control over labour, with which to make and work the farm. In Okuku, the ọba had command over the labour of others that no-one else even approached. His household was large, because he had almost unlimited access to new wives, there being a custom that the Olokuku could 'pick a girl' from amongst the townspeople every year during the Olooku festival. In addition to the labour of his many children, younger relatives, and especially maternal relatives sent to profit from his high status, the ọba had at his disposal a large number of slaves. It is said that during the nineteenth century wars, after each slave-raid, every compound whose men had been involved was obliged to hand over one of its captives to the ọba.[6] Elders' reminiscences of the late nineteenth century suggest that, unlike the heads of other households, the ọba was able to retain these slaves in large numbers, either because their prospects and treatment were better there, or because of the presence of royal officials to oversee them. But the ọba also commanded the labour of the ordinary free townspeople for specific services. Until the reign of Oyinlọla (1934–60) each ọba, on installation, claimed one man from each compound to serve as his messenger. These men had their heads half-shaven as a sign of their function which gave them the name *ilari* (divided head), and they lived in the palace and were entirely at the ọba's disposal. The royal farms, which were extensive, were worked on not only by the ọba's slaves but also by the townspeople as a whole. Each compound was responsible for one plot and would periodically send groups of its younger members to clear, plant and harvest that area. Maintenance of the town walls and the palace buildings was also done by communal labour. The ọba also commanded the fruits of other people's labour in the form of tribute. During the annual Olooku festival each compound was required to present him with gifts of money and farm produce. The representatives of the seventeen subordinate towns also came to pay their tribute of yams, money and livestock. This custom is still maintained in token form, and the payment of *isakọlẹ* for the use of royal land by other compounds and *owo ile* whenever a new house is built are customs that have continued undiminished.

In some compounds, the *baale* (often also a senior chief in the town hierarchy) was entitled to similar services from his own compound members, though on a much smaller scale. Some compounds had *ilẹ ajoyeba*, chieftaincy land, for the exclusive use of the *baale*. Once a year – or more often – he could call on all the younger men of the compound to do *ọwẹ*, communal labour, on this land. In *ile* Oluawo the *baale* controlled a large tract of palm trees. The women of the compound were obliged to collect the palm nuts and manufacture palm oil from them on his behalf. One member of this compound recalled a *baale* in the 1920s who 'kept all the oil in his room and all the proceeds when he sold it' but added that 'most of it was for when he celebrated his festival'. In general, the *baale* of a compound was said to have had little direct advantage from his position in terms of actual command of labour, though of course heading a large compound brought other benefits, the most important being the potential support of a large number of people in social and political affairs.

The ordinary free male compound member would at first owe all his labour to his father or senior brother, or whoever was head of the household to which he belonged. As he grew up he would be allowed to make a small farm plot of his own, and the rest of his career would be determined by his success in first establishing his own independent household, with or without his father's consent, and then expanding it by recruiting further household members. He controlled his own labour and that of his children, until they in turn managed to assert their independence. If he prospered, he might also come to command the labour of matrilateral relatives and *iwọfa* and, in the nineteenth century, sometimes slaves as well.

A boy or young man sent out as a full-time *iwọfa* by an older relative had no control over his own labour, let alone anyone else's. Denied the opportunity to start his own farm, he would be held back in the competitive struggle to establish himself until the relative paid back the loan. Those *iwọfa* who served the creditor only once every four or eight days could start a farm, but the labour they lost on the days of service not only reduced the size and productivity of their own farms, but also expanded those of the creditor, and thus the differential advantages tended to become entrenched. Finally, a slave apparently had no control at all over his own labour. All his work enhanced his owner's status and perpetuated his own. Even his own children belonged to the master and worked for him, preventing the slave from ever establishing his own household. An *oriki* remarks:

Ẹrú kì í bímọ kó mú 'á, ohun tó bá bí olówó rẹ ló ní ni.

No slave has a child and keeps it, any child a slave has belongs to
the master.

A person's position in the hierarchy therefore meant real differences in
productive capacity.

With the exception of slavery and membership of the royal lineage,
however, no status carrying privilege or disadvantage was ascribed: all were,
to a greater or lesser extent, achieved. The ọbaship itself was open, each time
it fell vacant, to a large number of eligible candidates. It was said that 'in the
old days, whenever the throne was vacant, the strongest ọmọba (prince) simply
threw the others down'. A loose system of rotation between segments of the
royal family emerged some time in the nineteenth century, but it was not
rigidly followed until after the Chieftaincy Declaration of 1956 – and even
this, as we shall see, was initially treated as an opportunity to manipulate the
succession rather than to stabilise it. Both before and after the Chieftaincy
Declaration, several contestants could emerge in a single segment, and would
compete with each other for the support of the family, the chiefs and the town
at large. In the past as now, much money would be spent on this, both in direct
gifts and in generalised displays of conspicuous consumption.[7] Eventually,
the leading town chiefs, in consultation with Ifa, would make the decision.
Few installations met the approval of everybody. Most Olokuku had to
endure feuds, faction fighting and dissident chiefs or rivals who claimed that
the ọba was wrongly chosen. Olugbegbe, in the pre-nineteenth century era,
and Oyekanbi and Ẹdun in the middle of the nineteenth century, were all
deposed by their chiefs. The position of ọba, then, was achieved, often after
a great struggle, and maintained only by a continuation of that struggle.

Installing an ọba makes him into a person of a different sort from the rest
of humanity. Elaborate and protracted rituals of transition precede his actual
assumption of office.[8] During this period he is stripped of his former status
and invested with royal attributes. He is instructed in the history of the royal
family and in the esoteric ritual duties pertaining to his position. He used to
spend three months (now reduced to three days) living anonymously without
family or friends in the house of the chief Ọdọfin, one of the most senior town
chiefs, during this period of instruction. The investiture endows him with
mystical attributes. Taboos against eating in public, leaving the palace except
on ritual missions, stumbling as he walks, prostrating even to his own father,
all set him apart, thenceforth, as a sacred being. By becoming ọba he steps into
a stream that is conceived as having flowed continuously since the days of the
founder of his dynasty: there has only ever been one Olokuku, and on his
installation he becomes the single 'I' that has remained unbroken since the
foundation of Kọọkin. But this process, by which the new ọba is set apart from
other people and absorbed into a continuous, mystical and historical identity,
does not in any way preclude continued competitive struggle to maintain and

enhance his position. The ọba is both the 'second to the gods', a being of a different order from his chiefs, and at the same time another big man in a town full of them. He too has to struggle to attract people to him: both new residents to the town, and loyal supporters from among the existing population. Control over people which is sometimes represented as a 'right' turns out to be an achievement on the ọba's part. Not every ọba, for instance, would have *ilari* offering to serve him on his accession. Oyekanbi, who reigned in the middle of the nineteenth century, was remembered for the *ilàrì méfà tó là lóòjọ́*, the six *ilari* that he made on a single day, and the explanation given for this *oriki* was that 'not every ọba would get such a willing response – six people coming to offer themselves as *ilari* in one day! Some ọbas might get only one or two, because people might not want to be made his *ilari*'.[9]

But the representation of the ọba as both a mystically endowed spiritual being and as a big man is in no way a contradiction, for, as I have argued elsewhere (Barber 1981b), spiritual beings themselves are like big men. Both *orisa* and big men are endowed with their powers by the attentions of followers; if the regard of their followers slackens, their powers wane. The ọba's powers, though inherited, are also continually recreated, and sometimes expanded, by his active recruitment of support and his struggle to put down any big man who dares to challenge him. In Okuku, as in the towns examined by Lloyd (1960, 1968, 1971), he does not enjoy harmonious and consensual rule, either as a figurehead or as an autocrat: on the contrary, he is involved in a struggle which engrosses political action at every level in the society.

Like the ọbaship, the town and palace titles are achieved through competition and the recruitment of supporters. Each title may be contested by several people within the lineage, and though age automatically confers seniority, other attributes such as wealth, influence and leadership qualities may outweigh age. It is true that some people start with advantages and some have access to higher posts within the formal hierarchy than others. Most of the senior *ọlọpaa* titles are the patrimony of only one lineage, or at most of two lineages who alternate or compete for it. So only someone born into *ile* Ojọmu has the chance of eventually becoming Ojọmu, the *igbakeji ọba*, second to the ọba, and someone born into *ile* Alawẹ is most unlikely to attain a title higher than Alawẹ, half-way down the list of *ọlọpaa* titles (see Table 2). But even within the formal hierarchy of titles, enterprising and successful men found scope for manoeuvre. The grade, rank and accessibility of these titles was not immutable. Indeed, much of the political struggle that went on in Okuku throughout the nineteenth and twentieth centuries revolved precisely around efforts by chiefs and oba to rewrite the order or resist such rewriting.

The ọba could raise or lower the position of titles in the rank order. The top town chief was Ọdọfin until the time of Olongbe (mid-nineteenth century) who was a good friend of Oyekanbi and was rewarded by having his *egungun* title, Ojọmu, converted into a town title and given first place. At one time

Baalẹ (now in third position) was first. Similarly, titles could be promoted from one grade to another. An example of this occurred in the reign of Oyewusi II (1961–80) who, in the course of a long feud with many of the ọlọpaa chiefs, promoted four of the junior *aladaa* chiefs – Saba, Olukọtun, Ọdogun and Oṣolu – to ọlọpaa status. And titles which had become accepted as the property of one lineage could be offered to another lineage if the ọba was strong enough and the recipients brave enough to risk the wrath of the slighted lineage. Oyinlọla took the title Ọdọfin from the lineage which claimed to have held it since the foundation of Kọọkin, and gave it to his favourite messenger Aaṣa of *ile* Balogun. On Aaṣa's death it was restored to the original owners; but the new Ọdọfin was one of the leaders of the feud against Oyewusi II. Eventually he died in the thick of intrigue, and the title was passed back again to *ile* Balogun, who currently hold it. These alterations were always the result of the ọba and chiefs pitting their wills against each other.

Itan are always produced to legitimate such claims. But no such manoeuvre could succeed if the parties trying to alter the status quo did not have clout: the clout derived from supporters, wealth and reputation, rather than from office. This was as true of the ọba as of the chiefs and would-be chiefs.[10] Accession to office, and especially to high office such as the most senior of the town titles, added to a powerful man's power. It gave him a recognised position, his for life; a place in the visible formal structures of government; access to certain material advantages such as fees and fines; and the expectation that, by virtue of his position, he would have influence – an expectation that would in turn attract supporters to his side and thus endow him with influence. Title was also a highly prized end in itself. Struggles to attain titles, and subsequently to get them upgraded or to defend them from downgrading, were conducted with a passion and intensity that often engrossed the chiefs almost to the exclusion of all else. They certainly did not operate merely as 'representatives' of their lineages; they were individual ambitious men fighting for their own advantage with a grim determination that suggests that title was bound up with personal ambition rather than with the honour of the lineage as a whole. Indeed, the ordinary members of the lineages concerned seemed, throughout the feuds that split Okuku while I was there, to be quite uninterested in the whole business. Title, then, was a goal of ambitious men, which gratified not only by adding more to his power but simply in itself as an acquisition. But no one could attain such an office if he were not already well on the way to becoming a big man.

What is more significant, but less often discussed in other work on Yoruba towns, is the fact that there was considerable scope for ambitious individuals to build up a position for themselves *outside* the hierarchy of titles. A man whose standing was acknowledged by numerous adherents was an important man by virtue of that recognition. His status might eventually be acknowledged by the formal conferment of a title, but this was a result rather than a cause of his importance in the town. A man with no title, or a small or low-ranking title, could still be recognised as a very big man, and could wield considerable political influence as a result.

The hierarchy of Okuku was kept in place by constant vigorous pressure from both sides, as one party attempted to redraw the lines that demarcated statuses and another tried to prevent this happening. This pressure was supplied by the continually self-renewing drive by individuals to self-aggrandisement. The political events in the town were fuelled by this drive.

Until recently the underlying factors in a big man's rise remained constant. A man always needed 'people'. Recruitment of people proceeded through a variety of channels, but was most commonly based on the establishment of a large household and the production of wealth. It was always directly or indirectly at someone else's expense. Directly, when a warrior captured a slave; or when a would-be big man needed to raise money to marry a new wife or hold a big feast, and lent out his younger brother or son as interest on a loan; or when a man married in order to use a woman's labour and procreative power to swell his household. Indirectly, when a man's power became magnetic enough to attract supporters away from other big men. In this system, nothing succeeds like success; one man's success breeds another man's failure; and almost anything is possible even for those born without advantages. It is therefore a highly dynamic, highly competitive, individualistic and fluid society, and the culture which it has produced reveals this.

Oriki, which helped to create big men, and *itan*, which gave narrative form to memories of them, illuminate better than any other source the centrality of this dynamic to the life of the town. They also reveal that the definition of a big man and the methods he adopted to attain greatness underwent historical changes between the early nineteenth and the late twentieth century. They show, too, that at any given moment, there were a number of different routes available to the would-be big man and a variety of qualities or attributes that were regarded as a sufficient claim to greatness. Big men found their own ways to recruit supporters and gain reputation, adapting to the historical circumstances and to their own immediate opportunities. *Oriki* and *itan* thus present us with a rich, overcrowded array of personalities, all evoked in highly charged imagery, and all distinctive. It is impossible to do justice to the sheer proliferation and abundance of memories, stories and epithets. But the range and variety of big men's careers, and the way they changed over time, can at least be selectively illustrated.

3. BIG MEN IN THE EARLY NINETEENTH CENTURY

Stories of big men before the fall of Ọfa in c. 1825 are rare. Whether this is because of the failure of memory, or whether the turbulence unleashed by the nineteenth-century wars threw up figures more remarkable than those who preceded them – and so more likely to generate narratives – is impossible to tell. It is certainly true that from around the middle of the nineteenth century there are detailed stories about a lot of big men, who are definitely associated with the wars and even with specific episodes in them. But for the period before that, what remains is a few examples of *oriki*, sometimes quite full-blown, attached to figures whose historical period is uncertain and about whom little other information is forthcoming. The *oriki* themselves are far from being firm evidence, because of the fluidity of their mode of transmission, but they offer the only glimpse of what this period might have been like.

One of these early big men was Winyọmi of *ile* Oluọdẹ, remembered as the first Head of the Hunters in Okuku. Characteristically, he is represented both as a legendary founding ancestor of remote provenance, and as a real personality on the threshold of living memory.[11] Genealogies offered by elders of the *ile*, however much they varied in other respects, always put Winyọmi in the position of apical ancestor, and the *itan* of *ile* Oluọdẹ always began with the statement that Winyọmi 'brought them from Ọfa' (their *orilẹ*) to join the first ọba at Kọọkin. One elder, Chief Akọgun, went further than this, claiming that Winyọmi, a great hunter and experienced in exploring the forest, was actually the one to discover the site where Kọọkin was to be founded. Here Winyọmi seems a being in the remote past with no definite characteristics except those essential for the myth of origin: his courage and his powers as a hunter. But Winyọmi's *oriki* encapsulate other stories, which are told with more narrative detail. Johnson Onifade, one of the present generation of elders of *ile* Oluọdẹ, quoted these *oriki* in the course of his narrative:

> Dínà mọ́ yà
> A-dóminú-kojo
> Ó pàgbọ̀nrín ó pa túùpú
> Ó pa èyí tí ń dá wọn nígi lọ́nà oko.

> 'Blocks the road and doesn't budge'
> 'One who fills the coward with apprehension'
> He kills antelope, he kills the bush-hog
> He killed the thing that was terrifying them on the farm path.

This was the story that arose from the *oriki*:
> When they were at Kọọkin, Winyọmi had a friend in Ọtan. His friend's son used to carry an *egungun* masquerade during the festival, and one year he got into a fight. He was a sword-carrying *egungun* and he sliced his opponent in half. The man died, and the friend's son ran to Kọọkin to seek refuge with Winyọmi. In due course the people of the dead man gathered their forces and came *en masse*, heavily armed, to get vengeance. Winyọmi was informed of their arrival and went out into the road. He saw them coming in the distance. When they got nearer they saw him standing there blocking the whole road. They asked him if he was

harbouring the murderer. Winyọmi said yes. Then he added, 'I am going to close my eyes, and when I open them you will have disappeared'. He closed his eyes and when he opened them he saw everybody running for their lives. They knew he was a great medicine man and they feared him, that is why they ran. This is why he is called 'Blocks the road and doesn't budge', and 'One who fills the coward with apprehension'.

Other stories suggest a period distinctly later than the foundation of Kọọkin. One describes Winyọmi confronting the Ọtan people 'with medicine and with his gun', suggesting a period after c.1820.[12] The vagueness of the historical placing of Winyọmi, and the scope for conflation of several figures, seem to be enormous. However, hardly any of the stories linked Winyọmi with the 'Ilọrin war'. It was Ọlọmi, Winyọmi's 'son' (i.e. someone of a later generation – possibly many generations later) who was said to have 'taken them to Ikirun' when Okuku was evacuated in 1877-8, and another 'son', Ogunṣọla, was recalled as a famous fighting man in the Ilọrin-Ibadan wars.

The few notions associated with Winyọmi's name in *itan* suggest a big man of a certain kind, and even indicate the bases of his position: 'He was consulted whenever anything happened. He had many children. He was rich from farming and from selling meat. He had medicine, and he was courageous. He was the Head of the Hunters. He founded the *egungun* Arọbatẹ'. 'He was a hunter. He had many children. He killed elephants. He was the first Oluodẹ in Okuku'. But it is in his personal *oriki*, transmitted at their fullest by the women of *ile* Oluodẹ and not by the men who tell *itan*, that we find a detailed representation of the nature of his position. On the surface of the unspecific image of the wealthy, successful and prolific hunter, the *oriki* imprint details that give a better idea of the concept of personal greatness:

Wínyọmí Enípèẹdé Olórí-ọdẹ
Àrèmú dínà mọ́ yà, Enípèẹdé a dóminú kojo
Lákùọ̀ òjò kẹni mọ́ fébùrẹ́
Ẹni ó kánláa Wínyọmí olúwaẹ ní ń wáaápọn
Dáalé mọ́ dàá òde, baba ọkọọ̀ mi
Àìdá òràn ló dùn
Àlàmú ní bọ́ ọ dáràn ẹgbàá
Ó ní baba tọ́ ọ ní á jẹun lórí ẹ
Aṣọ Òìbó ò lálòpẹ́
Wínyọmí ní 'Fífẹgẹ ló ṣe é fẹgẹ'
Apàgbọnrín pa túùpú, olórí ọdẹ
Ó pèyí tí ń dá wọn nígì ń Gọ̀dọ̀gbọ̀
A pa fún wọn kébòlò [dànù]
Àlàmú ni wọn ń polórí ọdẹ
Baba ọkọọ̀ mi pàyí tó ń dá wọn nígì lÁnlé.[13]

Winyǫmi Enipęęde Head of the Hunters
Arẹmu, blocks the road and doesn't budge, Enipęęde, one who
    fills the coward with apprehension
In the time of early planting, let no-one pluck the *ebure* plant
Anyone who plucks Winyǫmi's okro is looking for trouble
'Get into trouble at home, don't get into trouble outside', my
    husband's father
'Not getting into trouble at all is best',
Alamu said 'If you get into trouble to the tune of two thousand
    cowries'
He said, 'Your own father will take his cut of the settlement'
European cloth doesn't wear well
Winyǫmi said 'What it's good for is showing off'
One who killed antelope, killed wild boar, Head of the Hunters
He killed the one that was terrifying them at Gǫdǫgbǫ
He killed so much meat for them they threw away their vegetable
It's Alamu they call 'Head of the Hunters'
My husband's father killed the one that was terrifying them at Anle.

This Winyǫmi cannot be a figure from the remote past. Not only the
reference to imported European cloth, but also the the very fullness and
freshness of the *oriki*, with their continual quotations of Winyǫmi's own words,
suggest someone much more recent than a founding ancestor. The *oriki*
known to belong to pre-nineteenth century figures, such as the early ǫbas of
Okuku, are gnomic and obscure, and much briefer than these. It could be that
the *oriki* just quoted are modern compositions transferred back onto Winyǫmi
by well-known processes of borrowing, but this is not very likely – for they are
specific and idiosyncratic epithets, which are not used for anyone else in
Okuku. They do seem to belong to a particular figure: one who has been
conflated in memory with a founding ancestor figure, but who is more likely
to have come from the first half of the nineteenth century.

Winyǫmi is represented in these *oriki* as the head of a great household – a
household which he ruled with a hand of iron (no-one would dare pick okro
from his garden without permission) but which he supplied lavishly with food.
The reference to okro suggests that he was a great farmer, whose early and
abundant crops attracted poachers. But more important, he was a hunter who
supplied his household with great quantities of meat, so much that they could
afford to throw away the vegetable they had gathered to make their stew with.
His courage as a hunter protected not just his own family but the community
as a whole: he got rid of 'the one that was terrifying them at Gǫdǫgbǫ', and
'at Anle', both fertile cultivated areas belonging to Okuku people – that is, he
killed the dangerous animals that prevented people from going to their farms
(Johnson Onifade explained that the animal referred to was a chimpanzee,

that would follow people on the path to their farms and would make indecent
advances to the women). He is remembered for his ironical sayings. He
advises his household to commit their misdemeanours only in the safety of
their home, not outside where the consequences could be more serious; but
he goes on to suggest that it would be even better not to commit any
misdemeanours at all, for even inside the family, someone is bound to profit
at your expense when you get into trouble: 'Your own father will take a cut
of the settlement'.[14] And though he dismisses European cloth, with a down-
to-earth practicality, as flimsy stuff, the form of the words suggests that he
himself dresses up in it for show: and so, by implication, that he is a
magnificent figure, an attractive and charismatic man who would do justice
to expensive cloth.

There is a subtle balance in these *oriki* between communal values and
individual idiosyncrasy. Winyọmi is celebrated as a great provider, and as a
defender of the community; but he is also recalled as an individual with an
ironical brand of humour, a love of personal show, and perhaps a tyrannical
temper. His saying '*Dáalé mọ́ dàá òde*' ('Get into trouble at home, don't get
into trouble outside') is a clue to the tone of the whole passage. The family
represents safety and solidarity, the outside world danger and betrayal; but
even within the family, people will be quick to take advantage of your
mistakes. It is best to protect yourself by remaining aloof and irreproachable.
The *oriki* celebrates the communal solidarity of the family at the same time
as it warns that, concealed within this solidarity, is a flaw which makes
individual self-reliance essential.

Winyọmi, then, is represented as being a big man because of his wealth, his
family and his influence. His wealth is attributed to farming and, even more
important, to hunting. Lavish provision of meat is said to have made his household conspicuous (with the implication that this attracted numbers of hangers-
on). And his personal influence ('He was consulted whenever anything
happened') is ascribed to his role as communal champion. His formidable
powers, his courage, his mastery of both firearms and medicine, are the
qualities that are said to have made him a centre of attraction. He is credited
with 'people', not only in the sense of wives and children and followers, but
in the more extended sense of the adherence of the community at large.

The *oriki* recalling this period evoke an ideal of greatness which is subtle
and many-stranded. One of the finest celebrations of this ideal is in the *oriki*
of Adeọba, who reigned in the first half of the nineteenth century. He is the
last Olokuku to share the 'mythic' aura, the unlocatedness in time and
indeterminacy with respect to events in his reign, that characterises the early
ọbas, and the first Olokuku for whom we have extensive and circumstantial
oriki. The ọbas Ladile, Ọtinkanre, Olugbegbe and Oluronkẹ are remembered
in legends, often with magical themes, and in *oriki* which are brief and obscure;
and other ọbas, who appear in some accounts and not in others, are even less

well represented in the literature. Adeǫba, however, comes before us in all his
resplendence. Like the *oriki* of Winyǫmi , those of Adeǫba suggest a more
gracious era than that which followed it. They also reveal most clearly how the
big man's position was construed as being grounded in the regard of 'people',
and demonstrate the role of *oriki* themselves in focusing and re-enacting this
regard:

Adéwálé Adéǫba
Àkànní owó ǫsǫ́ ò wǫ́n
Adéwálé, ę wadúúrú yíyę tí í yęni
Oríaré Adésùre
Babaà mi àgbàlagbà lÓyè
Kò ì jó à ń gbàtę
Oríaré abijó-ranyin-lágbo
Ǫmǫ ló kǫsè ní gbòngàn
Baba sę háà lágbàlá
Wǫ́n sebí ibú lOríaré su
Àrà ló fibú ę dá, ǫkǫ Òjísàbǫ́lá
Ògòngò-gǫngǫ ní filà àrán, babaa Saóyè
Ó ní nnkan jù ǫ́n babaa Búǫ́lá ní í sę
Ó tètè rósù lágbàlá, babaa Jǫ́lásún
Baba tó kǫ́lé àrà
Àkànní tó kǫjú è sí yèyé
Adéwálé kǫ́ Bǫǫpé
Ó kǫjú è sí ilée babaa rę
Ó ní bǫ́ ǫ pé ǫ wá, bǫ́ ǫ̀ pé ǫ mǫ́ mò yà
Ęni ó pé ní í yalé Àkànní a-mére-wù-ǫ́n-gbé
Abíóyè babaà mi, Olúgbǫlá a-gbégi-jó-tǫmǫ-tǫmǫ
Ǫsǫ́ aró ò tí
Adéwálé, aró ni baba asǫ
Babaà mi, ègbè ni babaà'lękè
Ǹ bá sègbè ilękè
Àkànní, láàrin ni ǹ bá gbé
Adéwálé, ǫ yǫ nínú ęgbę́ da daa da.[15]

Adewale Adeǫba
Akanni, there's no shortage of money for adornment
Adewale, see how extremely well he befits his position!
Oriare Adesure
My father, elder of Oye
Even before he dances he gets applause
Oriare, one whose dance whirls around the circle
A child stubbed his toe in the hall
The father cried 'Ha!' in the courtyard

They thought Oriare had stumbled
His apparent fall was just a clever stunt, husband of Ojisabọla
With his jutting velvet cap, father of Saoye
Father of Buọla is someone who has more than other people
He sees the new moon early from his courtyard, father of Jọlasun
The elder who built a fine new house
Akanni who made it face Mother [Ọtin]
Adewale built 'If you have no blemish'
He made it face his father's house
He said, 'If you have no blemish, come; if you have one, then don't
    turn this way'
Only wholesome types turn into Akanni's house, one who makes
    other people want to carry the image
Abioye, my father, Olugbọla, one who takes the image and all its
    children to dance
The beauty of cloth dyed in indigo does not fade
Adewale, indigo is what gives the cloth its worth
My father, *egbe* are the best kind of beads
If I were an *egbe* bead
Akanni, I would be right in the middle
Adewale, you stand out among your peers most distinctly.

Adeọba is commended for the wealth which he spends on finery, for his splendid dancing, his spacious and well-decorated house, and for his conspicuous participation in the royal cult of Ọtin. Each of these images presents Adeọba as a figure at the centre of attention, encircled by admirers and inferiors. He is pictured as the dancer surrounded by a ring of spectators: and so commanding and charismatic is his presence, so great his reputation, that the onlookers burst into applause even before he begins to dance. When he celebrates the Ọtin festival, the way he carries the Ọtin images fills people with the desire to participate, to follow him in the procession. He is compared to the central, biggest and most conspicuous bead in a string. The singer calls on her own audience to look at this figure, and 'see how extremely well he befits his position'. The effect is to put the hearer in the role of admirer, so that by uttering the words, the performer recreates the big man's ideal situation, as the cynosure of all eyes.

These images belong to a well-established idiom, and are found in a multitude of variant formulations in the *oriki* of big men from Adeọba's time right up to the reign of Oyinlọla. Each one leads through a chain of associations with other images to the suggestion that the subject 'has people' and enjoys regard. Adeọba is wealthy, and spends his wealth on 'adornment': adornment implies that the owner has physical beauty appropriate to it, and physical beauty implies a radiant power of attraction. As he dances, his skirts whirl, suggesting voluminous cloth. Cloth is a well-known image for people: in another ọba's *oriki*, it is said that 'I could take off my robes and wrap myself in people'. It is also an image that evokes power through the suggestion of a slapping, flaunting movement in folds of the cloth – made explicit in another *oriki*: *òsánṣọ-méjì-gbá-yigi-yigi*, 'one who wears one cloth on top of another, sweeping the ground with vigorous magnificence'. Adeọba has built a magnificent house, so spacious that 'he sees the new moon early from his courtyard' (while other people, confined within narrower walls, have to wait till the moon is high in the sky before they see it). A large house indicates a large household, full of people – and this *oriki* adds the further suggestion that all these people must be beautiful. Adeọba is quoted as remarking humorously that 'If you are perfect, come; if not, don't bother to turn this way', because 'only perfect people drop in on Akanni'. The house also, of course, signifies wealth, especially as it is no ordinary house, but *ile ara*, one that is in some way novel or of exceptional beauty. A fine, well-decorated house is the physical location of the big man's achievement, the place where he is at ease, surrounded by his people and by all the evidence of his success.

Finally, the image of beads, linked with that of indigo-dyed cloth, evokes the big man's attainment in metaphors that modulate sinuously and fluently from one to another. Beads are a repository of wealth and a conspicuous display of it. They are also adornments, implying again the subject's fitness to wear them and the magnetism of his personality. These associations are present in Adeọba's *oriki*, but the image is also used to convey something more abstract. 'The glory of indigo does not fade': and Adewale's own 'glory' – both his natural adornments of grace and beauty, and his very worthiness to be adorned in cloth and beads – are likewise unfading. Just as 'indigo is the father of cloth', bestowing on it an unquestionable superiority, so *'egbe* [beads] are the father of beads' – the very best that there are. Adeọba is, by implication, as naturally superior to other people as indigo-dyed cloth and *egbe* beads are to other kinds of cloth and beads. But then the metaphor shifts: 'If I were an *egbe* bead, Akanni, I would be right in the middle/Adewale, you stand out amongst your peers most distinctly'. The beads are now conceived as a string, the most coveted place in which is right at the centre where the biggest and most beautiful beads will be put. Like the central bead in the string, Adewale is conspicuous because of his natural superiority. The effortless modulations from one metaphor to another are possible here because the performer is operating in a dense evocative field of significances, where each image is already linked with all the others through numerous strands of association, implication and memory.

The language of these *oriki* traces a circling metaphorical path. One image suggests another because they are all signs of each other. Wealth means a display of adornments; the display means the owner deserves to be adorned, because of his beauty, presence and charisma; beauty, presence and charisma mean the attention of adherents. A large house stands for wealth, but also for a lot of people. Dancing suggests cloth, cloth suggests a following, an audience suggests the dancer is exceptional. The circling style, as much as the content of the *oriki*, evokes an ideal which cannot be reduced to a single attribute. Wealth is desirable, but it is not an end or achievement in itself so much as a means by which a visible demonstration of status is effected. Power over other people is a factor in the big man's success, but this is not the whole meaning of 'having people'. 'People' are a constitutive element in the creation of a more richly-conceived position. What men hoped to attain, it seems, was not wealth as such or power as such, but a total state of sufficiency and command over their social environment, a state called *ọla*. *Ọla* is the complex, composite, shifting and sensuously realised concept that informs the ethos of *oriki*. What underlies *ọla* is the notion of recognition, of being acknowledged superior, and of attracting admirers and supporters as a result. Having people, in its widest sense, means having people who are guaranteed to go on acknowledging one. Because the relationship between the big man and his supporters was not institutionalised it had to be continually recreated.

Ọla, then, is ultimately the capacity to attract and retain the gaze of other people. Difference – the idiosyncrasies captured in Adeọba's humorous remarks and in the reference to the peculiar incident of his 'apparent fall' which he turned into 'a clever stunt' – is valued because it makes the big man conspicuous. This ability to 'stand out amongst your peers most distinctly' is the heart of the matter. The purpose of the *oriki* is to draw attention to the subject as the centre of regard in a multiplicity of ways.

4. WARTIME BIG MEN UP TO 1893

During the Ilọrin–Ibadan wars, new opportunities for self-aggrandisement appeared. Dozens of famous men are recalled from this era: almost every compound has at least one. And it is clear that the fortunes of these men were closely associated with the wars. Some of them were remembered as the head of the household who had 'led us to Ikirun' on the main evacuation of Okuku in 1877–8; others were remembered as having 'brought us back' in 1893 and supervised the resettlement and reconstruction of Okuku. But most of them were associated more directly with the actual warfare and the slave raiding for which the wars provided the opportunity. Although the war period began in c.1825 with the fall of Ọfa, almost all the stories associate the big men with somewhat later episodes, from around the middle of the century onwards.

Men attained towering powers in this period. The turbulent conditions not only gave big men greater opportunities for asserting themselves, but also, as Oroge has pointed out, increased lesser men's need for a patron (Oroge, 1971, p. 150). In the middle of the century, Fatolu the Baalẹ – one of the most senior *ọlọpaa* chiefs – became a tyrant in the town. It was he who led the faction that drove Ọba Oyekanbi out of the town and replaced him with his own friend, Ẹdun. After seven years, he changed his mind and deposed Ẹdun, recalling Oyekanbi to the throne. He conducted a reign of terror in the town which was not forgotten or forgiven for a hundred years. The office of ọba was not an enviable one, and at least one ọba-elect fled the town rather than assume it. During the same period, Oyekanbi introduced the secret punitive and judicial society, the Ogboni, to Okuku. Many *egungun* were established, among them Pajẹ, the great royal masquerade whose head-piece was acquired in a raid during the war.[16] The idiom of political struggle was *agbara* (strength) and *oogun* (medicine): great men were those who could outlast their enemies and establish a reputation for invincibility. *Oriki* of these big men emphasise not only excess of power and wealth, but also the isolation and danger of the competitive and ruthless struggle for supremacy.

In the personal *oriki* recorded for the earlier figures, Winyọmi and Adeọba, this theme is scarcely touched on. They are celebrated for their generosity, their magnificence, their idiosyncrasies, their importance to the community. But from the reign of Adeọba's successor Oyekanbi onwards, *oriki* seem to have established a pervasive idiom of personal aggression and immunity from personal attack. Oyekanbi himself is saluted as a beleaguered figure, under constant attack from enemies but able to withstand them all:

Apá ekúté ilé ò káùsá
Babaa Kóláwọlé, ẹnu yíyí kiri ló mọ
Bùtùbútù ọjà bọ́ lọ́wọ́ọ bamubámú
Oyèégóibó baba bọ́ lọ́wọ́ ìpín ìyà babaa wọn

The houserat can't control the walnut
Father of Kọlawọle, he can't get further than rolling it around the
    house
The dry earth of the market escapes the floor-beater
Oyegoibo the father escaped from the punishment planned for
    him by other peoples' fathers [i.e. his enemies]

Big men of this period could gain ascendancy through military prowess. There was no formal military organisation as in some towns. The hunters' association posted look-outs to warn the townspeople of impending raids, but the actual fighting was carried out by another group, an informal association of young men nicknamed the *ẹgbẹ Balogun*. This group would meet regularly for 'training' – which consisted mainly in instruction in the use of medicines and charms – and would go out to confront the Ilọrins on the road when they came. They also launched slave-raiding expeditions of their own, going as far afield as Omu-Aran and Irẹsa, or 'wherever they heard that raiding was good'. They would enter the victim town at night, set fire to the thatched roofs and then seize the inhabitants as they rushed out of their houses. The captives would be taken back to Okuku as slaves.

The *ęgbę Balogun* remained the only fighting organisation in Okuku. The founder and leader of the group, Omikunle, became the most conspicuous and memorable of big men of the period. He is associated with the reign of Oyekanbi and is said to have been among those who led the population to Ikirun (in 1877-8). He was a young untitled man of *ile* Aworo Ǫtin whose only advantage appears to have been the gift of leadership. He was nicknamed Balogun after the famous Ibadan leader, Ajayi, the hero of the 1878 'Jalumi War' outside Ikirun. He rallied round him young men of all compounds, who accepted his command and met at his house daily to eat and to plan their next raids. There was a core of about twenty-five men who actually fought and went on raids, but 'all the youth of the town called themselves *ęgbę Balogun*' and associated with the group, supporting them and acknowledging Omikunle's leadership. He chose his own second- and third-in-command, whom he honoured with the titles Ǫtun Balogun (Balogun's Right) and Osi Balogun (Balogun's Left). 'They were chosen for their prowess in battle'. He thus became a force to be reckoned with in the town, the real political decision-maker. The plans of the *ęgbę* would be communicated to the ǫba, but they were in no way dependent on his approval: 'They just told him afterwards what they had decided'. After many years the nickname Balogun became accepted as a real title. When Omikunle died, his younger brother Omileye in turn became the Balogun, and the conferment of the title was ratified by the ǫba. Omileye was an equally formidable war leader, remembered for riding his horse around the market and 'abusing everyone, including the ǫba'. His young nephew Aasa had to carry his sword and his luggage in front of his horse when Omileye went to war, and drummers would parade along by his side saluting him as he approached the battlefront. 'Nobody could touch him because of his medicines'. Omikunle had founded a dynasty: after Omileye's death, Omikunle's own son Omileke became Balogun. *Ile* Aworo Ǫtin has several town and palace titles – Sǫbaloju, Alala, Osǫlu– as well as the ritual title Aworo Ǫtin, the priest of the goddess Ǫtin, who was formerly also the head of the whole compound. But the new title displaced the old, and Balogun become the most important title in the compound – which is nowadays often actually called *ile* Balogun rather than *ile* Aworo Ǫtin. No other compound has ever contested it. Thus Omikunle built up for himself and his successors a position which became legitimised and institutionalised, but which began as the informal recruitment of supporters on a scale which was made possible by the disturbed conditions of the time. Like other towns in the areas of continuous warfare, Okuku seems to have produced a new kind of big man whose power was based on military leadership and whose authority in some respects overshadowed the ǫba's. [17]

The imagery of their *oriki* suggests the concentrated, threatening power possessed by this warlike dynasty. They are represented not as communal champions, as Winyǫmi was, but as magnificent, frightening forces dangerous to anyone who crossed their path:

Alẹ́sin-lóyẹ́ atìdí-gun-baaka
Baba ò-gun-bẹ̀ẹ̀kẹ̀ jánà
Kètẹ̀-kètẹ̀ Àyìndé ọ mọ́ fẹsin tẹ̀ mí
Ǹjọ́ baba Ọyáọlé ń ti ń gẹsin
Kò ì tíì fi tẹ baba ẹnìkan pa
Ó súré ń pápá ó fi ẹsẹ̀ ko idẹ
Ó rìn ń bùtùbutù ó fẹsẹ̀ ko ẹpà.[18]

Alẹsi-loyẹ who mounts a camel from the back
Father, one who mounts a mighty beast on the road
Clip-clop Ayinde, don't trample me down with your horse
Since the day that Ọyaọle has been riding his horse
He hasn't yet trampled anyone to death
He ran in the plain, he brought back brass on his feet
He walked in the marshland and brought back beads on his feet.

The horse is an image of intense and overwhelming physical power. A man mounted on a horse towers above his fellows and can, as the *oriki* suggests, easily crush them if he chooses. 'Don't trample me down with your horse' suggests an admiration that is forged out of fear. The hero has mounted and mastered the 'mighty beast' and could use it to destroy lesser men. But the horse is also an image of riches. It is a precious object in itself, an emblem of civil status more than one of warlike glory. It is associated with brass and coral beads, both valuable things and both symbols of royalty and chiefship. The violence of the image of the trampling horse is thus tempered by associations of gracious and legitimate power. But the implication that Omikunle's position was threatening to the townspeople as well as magnetically attractive is clearly there: indeed, it is the dangerous quality that makes him attractive, as a protector, in time of war.

Many of the big men from this period were recalled as members of the *egbe Balogun*, and as 'great warriors'. They were also described as being very wealthy, possessing large households with many slaves and *iwọfa*. According to Adewale of *ile* Ọlọkọ, who was one of the oldest men in Okuku, 'all the big men had slaves, usually about four or five' but 'they sold more than they kept'. Conditions were too unstable for most men to build up large households of male slaves. 'As soon as they got to the farm the slave would run away, especially if he knew where his people were so that he could go and join them'. So most of the warriors would keep only a few, 'to cut grass for their horses and to run errands', not to work on the farm. They could also augment their households without the normal delay and expense by marrying their female slaves. They would sell the rest to traders and use the proceeds to give out loans to their less wealthy fellow citizens from Okuku and neighbouring towns. With these loans they secured the services of *iwofa*, who as local people could not so easily escape. According to Adewale, '*iwofa* were very common even when slavery was rife. Everyone had them; some people had a great many, and a rich man could have as many as twenty'. The active and successful warriors who went on frequent raids thus had opportunities to enrich themselves far beyond the scope of the rest of the population. A male slave was said to sell for as much as £5 (the modern way of expressing what was then 400,000 cowries): a huge sum at a time when a load of yams fetched only 1¹/₂d (500 cowries).

Other men enriched themselves without actually fighting. Elekede of *ile* Aro-Oke, for example, was not a warrior, but he was rich from farming and he used his wealth to entertain the warriors. Whenever they returned from a raid they would repay his hospitality by selling him slaves at a special rate. He would then resell them at a profit and expand his household still further with wives and *iwofa*. Most of the big men of the period seem to have managed to go on farming despite the turbulent conditions. Old men remember that when Okuku fled for refuge to Ikirun and stayed there '17 years' (c.1877–93), the Okuku farms became dangerous. Some people would visit them and continue to grow crops there, but they always risked being captured by lurking Ilorins or even by the people of neighbouring villages, who pretended not to recognise them. According to Adewale, 'if eight men went to the farm together, maybe only three would come back – anyone who went out of the town was likely to be caught'. Others borrowed farm land from their hosts in Ikirun. Households were fragmented and families scattered. Nevertheless, most of the nineteenth century big men are remembered in words like the following:

Adekunle had a large farm and a lot of slaves [Ajala Oyeleye, *ile* Oba]

Fabiyi had a lot of money from farming

Gbangbade was very rich; he had a big farm and captured a lot of slaves in the war. [Fatoki, *ile* Oloko] He had no title but he became an important figure in family and town meetings – he knew how to organise things. He had many *iwofa*. They could not hold meetings without him [Joseph Ogundairo, *ile* Oloko]

Olanigbagbe Olowona was a very rich man. He was a warrior who used a bow and poisoned arrows instead of a gun. He captured large numbers of slaves, and sold them. They also used to get ransom money when they spared the lives of the obas of captured towns. He had a large farm and a lot of *iwofa* [Ajala Oyeleye, *ile* Oba]

Slave-raiding, then, seems usually to have been not an alternative to farming but a supplement to it, the source of labour which enabled the farmer to expand as never before. Having a warlike following and the glory of battle complemented the possession of a great household fed from a great farm, employing many more people than just the big man's own relations. The *oriki* of big men often celebrate war, wealth and farming in the same breath.

This, then, was a period of great personal danger, not only from the Ilorins who were always a potential threat, but from people of neighbouring towns and even fellow townspeople. A big man's success was manifestly at other people's expense, for the most prominent men were those who did the best trade in slaves, and this trade nurtured betrayal as well as violence. 'It was commerce. The slaves they captured could be Ekiti men or they could be local people from their own side – in which case they'd take them off quickly to another town to sell them so that their families wouldn't know'. *Oriki* of these big men articulate a philosophy of self-reliance. The individual is surrounded by enemies, and since he often does not know who they are, his best plan is to trust no-one and keep aloof. The greatest achievement is to be, like Oyekanbi, impervious to the assaults of one's rivals. But the individual is also in danger even within his own family. While Winyomi seemed to think that the family was relatively safe, the big men of the war period announced that they could trust no-one at all: 'Your worst enemy may be in your own back-yard'. This counsel of distrust belonged to a period when all relationships were capable of being converted to cash. It is likely that the influx of cash from slaves into the hands of a fortunate minority in the town greatly increased the lending and borrowing of *iwofa*. People were thus at risk not only from outsiders who might try to capture and sell them, but from their own family, who might lend them out to creditors.

The *oriki* of Bankole Gbotifayo of *ile* Aro-Isale articulate the philosophy of enemies and self-reliance in a highly elaborated form. He was a *babalawo* who was also a devotee of Sango and Soponnon. His granddaughter was the mother of Sangowemi, who knew his story well:

> Gbotifayo went to war and brought back slaves. He was a formidable medicine-man. The war took him to Ikirun, where he attracted the enmity of fellow-diviners by succeeding in diagnosing the problem of a client whom all the others had failed with. She was a woman in labour but unable to give birth. Gbotifayo revealed that the problem was that the child had been begotten by a lover, not the woman's husband, and that she would not be released from labour until she named him. The man's people hated him after this, and *nàka sí i lójú* [i.e. blinded him by using medicine against him]. By the time this happened (the Okuku people were still at Ikirun) he was old and his hair was white. But he lived a long time after that and eventually died in Oyekunle's reign [1916–34][19].

This story revolves around the idea of Gbotifayo's enemies, engendered by his own success, and his eventual survival of their attacks. Although he was a respected *babalawo,* he is quoted as taking a view of the world that sounds almost atheistic in its insistence on self-reliance:

Gbọtifáyọ̀ ó ní nǹkan   àjíbọ
Ni wọn ń pe Bánkọ́lé babaà mi
Àkàndé elékèé lèké yé
Gbọtifáyọ̀ babaà mi
Ó ní ohun tá a bá ṣe, ó ní n ni kó mọ́ọ yéni
Àkàndé baba ní nǹkan àjíbọ
Ó lé ẹ ń wá ń bọFá
Bẹ́ẹ̀ lẹ̀ ń bỌ̀sun
Ọ̀ràn wọn ò i kan tòìṣà
Ènìyàn tó wáá bọ inú ẹ ló gbọ́n, Ṣónibárẹ̀
Èké ò kuni
Ìkà wọn ò ku ọmọ ènìyàn
Ìkà ò fẹ́ a rẹrù á sọ̀
Ayọ̀délé Ṣàngódèyí Kásúmù babaà mi
Ó ló dijọ́ tí orí ẹni bá sọni.[20]

Gbọtifayọ has something to rise and worship
That's how they salute Bankọle my father
Akande, the deceiver knows his own deceit
Gbọtifayọ my father
He said, 'Whatever we do, we should understand what it is we are
   doing'
Akande the father has something to rise and worship
He said 'You worship Ifa
And you worship Ọsun
But the matter of "other people" has nothing to do with the *orisa*
People who worship their own secrets are the wise ones, Ṣonibarẹ
There is no end to the world's deceivers
Not a single person free from suspicion of wickedness
The cruel person does not want us to lay down our load'
Ayọdele Ṣangodeyi Kasumu my father
He said 'We have to wait till our Ori lifts it down for us'.

Gbọtifayọ, that is, is remembered for proclaiming that worshipping the *orisa*,
even Ifa his own patron deity, is no solution to human hostility. The only way
to deal with 'other people' is to keep your own counsel, worship your own
'inside', and be constantly on your guard, for 'there is no end to the world's
deceivers'. The only intentions you can have access to are your own:
therefore, it behoves you to know exactly what you are doing, since you
cannot know what anyone else is going to do. You must rely on your own *Ori*
(your head, luck, or destiny) to help you out of your difficulties.

A big man had to be able to defend himself and his people from attack.
Rivalry in the town between big men building up great households was
believed to take the form of anger at the survival of the rival's dependants:

Sínsinnìgún ilée wa dárí pón, inú ń béyẹ oko

The young lizards of our house are getting red heads, making the
   birds in the forest angry

Other people attack a man's household as naturally as birds prey on baby
lizards. When the lizards get too big to swallow (the mark of a mature male
lizard is its red head) the birds are furious. The fury of one's enemies is a sign
of one's own success. A big man needs to be able to defend his household –
if necessary, by violent means:

Àkàngbé ò sí ńlé, wọn nàyá è
Babaa Fágbére dé, gbogbo wọn tọ́ ọ rí ni ń bópa
Wọ́n ní, Bọ́lákànmí, ọpa bí mo ti bá ọ nàyáà rẹ 'bẹ.

Akangbe was not at home, they beat his mother
Father of Fagbere arrived, they all began to swear sacred oaths
They said, 'Bọlakanmi, may I be struck dead if I had anything
   to do with beating your mother!'

Faderera, who is the granddaughter of Bọlakanmi, commented, 'This shows
how much Bọlakanmi was feared and respected in the town. With him at
home, no-one would dare to attack the family'.

   This view of the world as pervaded by 'enemies', declared and undeclared,
whose intentions are unknown but who can be assumed to be full of malice
and envy, is deeply rooted in Yoruba culture. It is given expression in *itan*, in
Ifa stories, in the good-luck chants called *iwure*, in chants addressed to *orisa*.[21]
In their most crystallised form, 'enemies' are represented as witches,
malevolent, destructive and – according to most people – always female.
Witches are rarely exposed and expelled from the community; they are dimly
suspected, half-known, and half-tolerated for long periods. No-one can be
sure which women in their own household are witches. But the strongly
drawn picture of 'the witch' merges into a whole shadowy region of ill-
intentioned people, simply known as *aye*, 'the world'. The world can be
assumed to be hostile. Men as well as women inhabit this region, but no-one
can be sure who they are. They use their own powers, the powers of witches,
the powers of hired medicine-men, and the powers of the *orisa*, who are regarded
as being deeply embroiled in human struggles. The individual can depend
only on his or her own *Ori*, the principle of individual success, to pick his or
her way amongst this minefield of potentially harmful forces. These conceptions
are pervasive and, I have argued (Barber, 1979), appropriate to a society
driven by the dynamic competitiveness of big men, each of whom is indeed
a potential threat to all his rivals.

   But the *oriki* of the wartime big men also suggest that there was a moment
in history when this generalised mistrust became sharpened and concentrated

and found expression in extreme utterances. Suspicion of his own household ('Your worst enemy is in your own backyard') could be inverted so that the big man was represented as being himself a terrible danger to his own people. It seems that at this time power in its most nakedly violent form was needed for the creation and maintenance of big-man status. The most extreme form of power was the power to destroy, and the most extreme character was represented as one who could destroy even his own family without remorse. It became possible to suggest that the best big man – patron and protector of numerous 'people' – proved his claim to this title by menacing those very people. In the *oriki* of figures like Olugbẹdẹ, the great nineteenth century hunter and medicine man of *ile* Balogun, introduced in Chapter 2, the normal disjunctions of *oriki* style have sharpened to a violent paradox:

> Kò sí ńlé ọmọkùnrin ń dàgbà
> Ó fẹ́ẹ́ẹ́ dé ná, tọmọkùnrin óò ku pàntoro
> A gbé jẹbẹtẹ lérí Ògún, babaa Làńwò
> Òjò ṣere pèpè baba Ògúnmọ́lá
> Wò ó níhìn-ín wò ó lóhùn-ún, Baba Ògúndáre
> Àjàgbé Ọtábílápó, ó rí kowéé jóògùn ilàyà
> Àjànàkú káàde a-báni-jà-mọ́-jẹbi
> Kò rí ohun fún àlejò mọ́, ó wáá fi Fómikẹ tọrọ
> Fómikẹ mọ́jú, kò bá àlejò lọ
> Ẹ̀hìnkùlé nikú wà, baba Ògúnmọ́lá
> Bí ò bá síkú nílé, tòde ò pani.[22]

> He's not at home, the young boys are growing up
> He's about to arrive, the young boys dwindle away
> One who brings a great load [of meat] to the Ogun shrine, father
>   of Lanwo
> 'Sudden downpour', father of Ogunmọla
> We seek him here, we seek him there, father of Ogundare
> Ajagbe, Ọtabilapo, he finds a *kowee* bird to make medicine for
>   courage
> Mighty elephant, one who fights and takes no blame
> When he had nothing to give the visitor, he gave away Fomikẹ
> Fomikẹ refused, he didn't go with the visitor
> Death is in your backyard, father of Ogunmọla
> If there were no death at home, death from outside could not kill
>   us.

The protective and destructive sides of Olugbẹdẹ are brought into conjunction here without any mediation. The *oriki* hyperbolically suggest that Olugbẹdẹ is such a danger that his mere presence in the household causes the youth, who flourished in his absence, to die like flies. Indeed, the *oriki* say that even before he arrives they begin to dwindle in number. But he is a great provider: a hunter who brings great quantities of meat into the household. After Ogun has been propitiated, the family will eat the meat. The nickname 'Sudden downpour' commemorates the unpredictable violence of his character. He is a formidable medicine man who uses his powers to involve himself in fights and always come off the better – implying that he can get away with anything. But he is indispensable to family affairs, his presence always required: 'We seek him here, we seek him there' means that he is always being consulted about everything. Many people remembered Olugbẹdẹ as a protector: his medicine was so strong that no thief dared enter the town during his time. His command of *juju* was associated with the ability to see more than other people, to expose the ill-intentioned and to warn people of impending danger. In the idiom of *oriki*, it is suggested that his power could be used either for the benefit of his family or to dominate and destroy them. This does not mean, of course, that Olugbẹdẹ actually was a danger to his family, or even that people would have admired him if he had been. But the violent rhetoric does reveal that big men's power was conceived in extreme terms.

In these *oriki*, then, the many-stranded concept of *ọla* is stiffened by a paradoxical conception of power, where the capacity to protect and provide is intimately conjoined but not reconciled with the tendency to do drastic harm, even to one's closest relations. The point where the two idioms seem to be fused, as we have seen, is in the image of the horse: for the horse is both a symbol of *ọla* in its benign and generous aspects, and an engine of destruction, flattening the grass and churning up the dust under its mighty hooves. Although horses were kept for ceremonial purposes well into the twentieth century by big men, and much longer than that by the ọba, they feature hardly at all in the *oriki* of twentieth century big men. They seem to capture the contradictory ethos of one period, the nineteenth century period of war.

5. THE BASIS OF BIG MEN'S COMPETITION

When the people returned to Okuku in 1893, the buildings were in ruins and the farms completely overgrown. The fragmented and reduced population sheltered in eight temporary *agọ* while they re-established themselves. During the period of reconstruction which followed, lineages moved out of the shared shelters to build their own large enclosed compounds, after which sections of these lineages, as space became short, moved away to build their own houses nearby if the compound had enough land, or on the outskirts of the town if it did not. New parties of refugees arrived, notably the Ọtan groups who came in 1915 and established three separate *ile* in Okuku. A social history which uncovers in detail the bases of and background to the rise of big men and the role of *oriki* in the creation of their reputations can only begin in this period, with the memories of the oldest people still alive today.

It was a period of very rapid change. Patterns of residence and the division of labour, authority relations within the compound and the control of income, have all been radically transformed between 1893 and the present day. This starting point was itself a moment in flux, not a stable base line. This may partly account for the fact that people's generalisations about 'the old days', as an ideal picture, were often not corroborated by the details of their own experience. The stories told by the oldest people are also often vaguely located in time and often, apparently, already conflated with their memories of other, older, stories told to them in their childhoods about earlier periods. Nevertheless, from the collectivity of their reminiscences about their childhood houses, the organisation of the households they lived in, the arrangements made about farm land and labour, and the prominent figures that dominated the social and political life of the town, some kind of picture can be built up of the changing dynamics of the rise of big men from the early years of this century onwards.[23]

The central fact to emerge is that the competitive struggle of big men had its roots in the everyday struggle of every man to establish himself as a full social being. The town was full of individuals competing to build up a position for themselves. Those who did exceptionally well went down in memory as great men of their time. But the impression given by these reminiscences is that every compound had its own prominent individuals. Everyone had a different set of big men in memory. A few built themselves up so conspicuously that they were remembered by many people. But many others enjoyed a more limited and localised fame, among their own clients and families. The picture is of a multiplicity of individuals competing to make a place for themselves, rather than a clearly defined universally recognised category of big men and another category of followers. Every household head was a big man to his own people, while some became big men whose range reached much further. If every individual had, or potentially could have, his or her own personal *oriki*, this was because every individual was considered to have the potential for social self-enlargement. To understand the dynamics of big men we therefore need to know about the domestic, localised struggle that all men engaged in.

Oyewusi, the great wartime oba who 'brought the people back' from Ikirun in 1893, and presided over the reconstruction of Okuku after that, died in 1916. The following year Okuku was officially designated the head of the Okuku District of the Osun North-east Division, and in 1918 direct taxation with nominal rolls was introduced. But two economic changes brought by the colonial regime which had great impact on Okuku people had already got underway well before this formal imposition of administrative authority. These changes were the arrival of the Lagos–Kano railway, which reached Okuku in 1904, and the new availability of waged work – in the Public Works Department, the railways, plantations in Sagamu, or the gold and diamond mines in the Gold Coast. Both of these changed the arena within which individuals mounted their struggle for self-aggrandisement. But the way people responded to these changes was determined by the existing low-level organisational structures of domestic authority.

When the population returned to Okuku in 1893, although many of the farms had reverted to bush, the boundaries of each compound's land were clearly remembered. Some of these areas still contained virgin forest, never yet cleared, which was held in reserve for distribution to newcomers by the head of the household. Others had extensive tracts of land reserved for the use of the *baale* of the compound or for an important ritual titleholder. In some compounds the reserves of land were not used up until the 1940s; others divided their whole land immediately, between the returning elders, whose descendants then subdivided it into smaller and smaller parcels. In the early years of this century, up to the 1930s, the principal crops were food crops – cassava, sweet potato, vegetables, beans, but above all maize and yams. Palm nuts were harvested and some cocoa was planted from about 1910 onwards – it is not easy to ascertain how much[24] – as was a little kola, mainly for the personal consumption of the families at home. But most effort was devoted to growing food crops. A system of crop rotation with long fallow periods was used. Yams would be grown on a plot for one year out of three. Growing food crops did not imply permanent occupation of a plot. Although every household head had definite farmland, with clearly marked and recognised boundaries, access to fresh land for temporary use was easy. 'People just made farms wherever they liked', as one elder told me. Many people, even when they had extensive land of their own, would borrow plots from other people – often people from other compounds – both to get a wider range of soil types and to conceal the extent of their crop cultivation. Since they would only use the land for a year or two and could not claim possession or use of the permanent trees which might be scattered through it – palm trees or kola – this kind of borrowing involved no risk for the lender, and was apparently extremely common. It was not until the extensive planting of kola trees for export, inaugurated by Qba Oyinlọla in the 1930s, that land became a scarce commodity.

When the railway reached Okuku, yams could be exported to Lagos, where there was a demand for them among the rapidly expanding urban population. Because of their unwieldiness and perishable nature, it had not formerly been practicable to transport yams that distance: a four- or five-day journey on foot. Access to this market by rail suddenly made it possible for big farmers to expand their production dramatically. Up till about 1930, the issue was not availability of land, but availability of labour. As one man put it:

> Money made people important because they could borrow *iwọfa* and thus increase the number of people that they had. People who had other people to work for them were big men at that time. If their own land was finished they could easily borrow other land. [Adeleke, *ile* Jagun]

Control of labour was the key issue in the organisation of households, in the relations between fathers and sons, and in men's establishment of themselves as independent and socially recognised figures.

The compounds in which the oldest living Okuku men grew up around the turn of the century varied greatly in size. Some *ile*, even on their return from Ikirun, were already well supplied with adult, married men. In *ile* Oluọde, for instance, twenty-three grown men are remembered by name as the original members of the reconstructed lineage. 'All of them had wives': they occupied the whole of one *agọ* and later built a 'huge round house' for themselves. Other *ile*, however, consisted of a single man and his sons; a pair of brothers; or a man and a friend, often also a matrilateral relative, who built their first house together whether or not they later split into independent *ile*. But whatever the size of the compound, these households were characterised by the same kinds of tensions and generational struggles. Big houses like *ile* Oluọde soon began to split into smaller units.[25] The successive divisions were explained in terms of the need for more space, but they were also part of the fundamental process by which individuals established their own social position. Building one's own house is the culmination of a long struggle for independence and visibility, which begins in boyhood and is never relinquished throughout a man's life.

The physical building in which people live, however, is less important than the patterns of authority and obedience between its inmates. A single 'huge' house could contain several economic households, each headed by its own senior man, who commanded the labour and service of a number of younger male and female relatives. The picture of these households painted by men who were young in the early years of the century suggests that the male head of the household was virtually omnipotent:

> In those days you had to serve your father till the day of his death. The father had complete control over the family money. He was the one who got all the profit from farm products. If they were sold he could do what he liked with the money. If there was a family craft like carving or weaving, it was the same thing. He had all the money to dispose of. He only had to give us our food, and one set of new clothes every year. But before we got married, we wore only a pair of *bantẹ* (shorts); we were treated like small boys. We all slept in the *ọndẹ* (the corridors), or in the parlour of one of the big men. Only when you got a wife did you get a room, each wife had her own room and the husband could keep his things there. Work was hard. [Adedeji, Chief Ṣaiwo, *ile* Ọlọkọ]

Service did not end with the father's death:

> When he died, you went on serving his younger brother. If he had no younger brother, then you would serve your own older brother. Brothers with the same mother would serve each other till death. The father's land would be shared out to groups of *ọmọ iya* (sons with the same mother). The eldest of each group would be a father to the rest. [*ibid.*]

An unmarried son would work on his father's plot of land. From the age of about fourteen he would be given an *idabọ*, a small plot of his own on which he could work in the evenings after the main work of the day. But he could not start to claim an independent social identity until he had a wife. His first marriage was the foundation of his future existence as a social being. The father was expected to marry a wife for the son. Each son, however, had to wait his turn, and the wait was often very long:

> Who could get married in those days? There was no money. Only the old men had wives. [*ibid.*]

This picture is an ideal one in the sense that it represents the norms that the fathers upheld and tried to make their sons conform to, rather than actual behaviour. Numerous stories show that in actuality, sons often offered resistance. They believed it was the father's intention to keep them as part of his dependent workforce as long as possible, and to monopolise the women so that he could expand his own immediate household rather than provide the young men with the means to establish theirs. Their own intention was to get a wife as soon as possible and then begin to lay claim to their own share of the father's land: that is, to their right to control their own labour and that of their dependants. The testimony of the oldest Okuku men shows that in the late nineteenth and early twentieth century they often succeeded. A son did not invariably work for his father until the latter's death. Those who said they 'served' their fathers all their lives often revealed later that at a certain point this service became purely nominal, and that the son had succeeded in gaining control over the products of his own labour.[26]

Fathers were often represented as trying to block their sons' advancement. Some men, like Babalọla of *ile* Ẹlẹmọsọ Awo, appear to have bowed to their fathers' rule and waited for him to die:

> I was born before coin currency was introduced, and already had two younger brothers before the railway reached Okuku. As a boy I worked on my father's farm. The work was hard and I was often punished. One day in four I was sent to work for the Ẹlẹmọsọ Awo of *ile* Nla – I was apprenticed to him [as a *babalawo*]. My father did not allow me to leave Okuku to do paid work. I was not given a wife and even my older brother, the Alapinni [an *egungun* title], was not married till after our father's death [which occurred when Babalọla was in his late thirties]. All of us worked for our father till his death. ...About four years after my father's death I went to Ijẹbu to work as a labourer. When I got back I married my first wife. I made all the arrangements and payments myself. After that I married three more. After the second one, I moved out of the compound and built my own house.

But others were quicker to take matters into their own hands, like Samson Adebisi of *ile* Ọjọmu:

> I worked from childhood for my father on his farm. When I was about thirty my father lent me out as an *iwọfa* in exchange for a loan of £4. I

was sent to live in the house of my father's creditor, the *babalawo* Toyinbo. After three years the debt was paid and I was allowed to leave and go to Abẹokuta as a P.W.D. labourer on the roads. I spent ten months there and got £1 10s for it. When I got home I handed over the money to my father. A girl had been betrothed to me but my father did not produce the money to pay the bride price. So, I left. I joined Jacob Ajayi of *ile* Oluawo [a maternal relative] and went to Ghana with him. That was in 1930. I worked as a firewood gatherer, serving Ajayi. In 1932 I came back and paid the bride price out of my savings. It was fixed at £7 5s. After the wife had come to my house, I refused to work for my father any longer. I told him he could not expect me to continue serving him, since he had not paid the bride price or helped me in any of my difficulties. I went to the farm and seized the plot I wanted to use. I cleared it for myself without my father's consent. All my younger brothers by my father's other two wives did the same thing, one by one, after they married, until only one young boy was left working for my father. I trained as a tailor. The money from tailoring was good enough for me to marry two more wives. Eventually I moved out of the main compound of *ile* Ojọmu and built my own house at one corner of it.

These stories make clear the importance of obtaining a first wife as the essential first step in a man's career. Without a wife and some children, any attempt to claim the right to 'serve himself' would fail. Fathers could delay the marriages of their sons on the grounds that there was no money available. Marrying a wife was certainly expensive. Bride price itself, for a first wife, was quoted as costing £3 15s (in the reign of Oyewusi: i.e. before 1916) and between six and seven pounds throughout the period 1920–50. But this was a small proportion of the total expenditure. There were other gifts to be made to the bride's family,[27] as well as the *inawo*, the 'spending of money' or wedding celebration, which according to one man brought the total costs up to about £40. There were other dues and obligations in kind as well.[28] These dues were felt to be such a burden that many men regarded it as an advantage to 'take' a wife from someone else rather than marry her from her father's house. 'Taking' a wife meant paying a sum determined in court to her former husband – a sum which was quoted in many cases as being £12 10s, though one man paid £30 (in 1950) and another paid £40 (in 1937). Nonetheless these wives were described as being '*ọfẹ*' (free of charge) because none of the traditional payments or service were exacted. The average bride price alone was the equivalent of more than the cash value of a household's entire food crop consumption in a year, and the total expenditure on a marriage was many times more than this.[29] There was good reason, then, for the frequent comment that 'there was no money for marriage in those days'. Fathers did not in fact live up to their obligation to provide their sons with even a first wife.[30] The sons had to shift for themselves: and it is clear that it was the need to raise money for a wife that impelled so many of the young men in the period 1900–1950 to go away to search for temporary wage labour.

When a man had some savings from wage labour, he would return and either make his own arrangements, or hand the money over to his father in the expectation that it would be used for this purpose. Samson Adebisi's rebellion was sparked off when he realised that his father had taken the savings he dutifully handed over but was not intending to get him a wife. Samson went off for a second time, earned a lot more money, and this time paid for a wife himself. After this he felt no further obligation even nominally to 'serve' his father.

But going away to work for cash also gave a young man a practical independence from his father for as long as he was away. Most young men went alone or with friends or maternal relatives from other compounds. Though they might 'serve' such a relative if he were older, it was comparatively easy for them to detach themselves when they wished. Wage labour therefore accelerated a young man's journey to independent status in two ways, giving him experience of running his own affairs while away as well as the means to establish his own household on his return. It is not surprising that nearly every informant over the age of 40 had been away as a wage-labourer at least once in his life. The first wave of migrant workers did Public Works Department jobs, building roads and laying railway lines, and they also worked as agricultural labourers on private plantations. Almost all of this work was to the south and west, in the Abẹokuta, Ọta and Ijẹbu areas. The second wave went to Ghana, not so much to work in the gold and diamond mines as to trade among those who did. The somewhat younger men – those who were growing up in the late 1930s and the 1940s – were even more likely to go to Ghana, and tended to spend longer there.[31] Like their elders, they mostly worked as petty traders, or collected and cut firewood, though one man trained and worked as an electrician and two worked in the diamond and gold mines. Some went several times and spent many years away before returning to settle. Some never returned at all, and some only came back from Ghana when all Nigerians resident there were expelled in 1968. But among those who did return, the pattern was clear. Wage labour provided cash which gave a man a start in life. Very occasionally, it was also used later in his life as a supplement to his main income. His real career of self-aggrandisement, however, could only be conducted on home ground, and was based on the expansion of the household his earnings had helped to found.

These longer trips to more remote places made the young men less accessible; they could not be summoned home so easily. This made them more independent of their fathers than the earlier generation. They were also more likely to learn another occupation as well as farming. There were carpenters, palm-wine tappers, motor mechanics, government workers, blacksmiths, Islamic doctors, teachers, store-keepers, produce buyers, lorry salesmen, shoemakers, bricklayers, petty and long-distance traders, and drivers among them. This meant that even those who came back to work on their fathers' farms had a potentially independent alternative source of income. Many of these trades were learnt in Ghana and some were made possible by a few years at school, which they were more likely to have had than the older men.[32]

In general, the few men who did not travel to make money stayed at home for one of three reasons: they were training as ritual specialists, whether as *babalawo*, herbalists or Islamic priests; they were going further in school than their age-mates, with a view to becoming teachers or clerks (only two of the informants did this); or their fathers simply refused to let them go. Many men said they went against their fathers' will, borrowing money for the journey and simply 'running away', but a few bowed to their fathers' wishes and stayed at home on the farm.

By the time the youngest group of informants grew up, however, few fathers tried to control their sons to this extent. Young men in their twenties, with fathers still hale and hearty, said openly that they had 'freed', that they worked for themselves alone and served no-one. This generation did not travel to find paid work. Their life patterns were determined by a third great change in the economic opportunities open to the Okuku people – the advent of cocoa growing on the 'far farms', which began in 1949 and became the principal occupation of almost all Okuku men from then until the present. The fathers of these young men belonged to the first wave of pioneers who discovered the land for the 'far farms' in Ifẹ, Ondo and Ijẹṣa areas and opened the first farms. The sons lived with their fathers and worked for them on the far farms as young boys. But successful men soon needed to rent new land, often in other areas, and they often put their sons in charge of the second and third farms. Thus Sunmibare (begun in 1949) is full of farms rented or owned by middle-aged and elderly men, while Odigbo (1963) has a much higher proportion of very young single or newly-married men just starting a farm.[33] The fathers of these men may claim that the sons still serve them, but the sons usually insist that they are independent. Almost all these young men have a second occupation – barbering, tailoring, and bicycle repairing were among the most popular. This enables them to get through the first five years of the cocoa-farm, before the trees begin to fruit, without having to depend too heavily on their fathers. The urgent desire for independence can be seen in the way these young men live. They build a tiny one- or two-roomed mud house in the farm town, and live there alone or with a friend or brother. They do without all luxuries and some do not even come home for the first few years.

Changes in the pattern of domestic labour relations, then, can be seen as the eager and determined response to new economic openings by people who were engaged in a struggle for independence and subsequently for a labour force. One reason why fathers are now more willing to release their sons is that, according to Okuku farmers, less labour is required for cocoa farming than for yam farming, and another is that in a cash-dominated economy what labour is needed is easier to obtain outside the family than formerly.[34]

In the early years of the century, however, old men's reminiscences make it clear that recruiting people and building a large household was everyone's ambition, and one which men would take considerable risks and undergo great hardships to attain. Everyone, however insignificant, was engaged in the same struggle to establish themselves at the centre of a circle of 'people'. Those who were more ambitious, more determined, and luckier than their peers were able to push this process beyond the usual limits and create a position for themselves which gained acknowledgement from all or many of their fellow citizens. These men are remembered by a later generation as the big men of their time, and are celebrated in personal *oriki*.

6. BIG MEN 1893–1934

The greatest of the big men in the late nineteenth and early twentieth century was undoubtedly Abiọna, the chief Ẹlẹmọna, nicknamed Alapẹpẹsile. He was the big man most frequently remembered in the old men's stories and most widely recognised throughout the town. He was associated with the reign of Oyewusi I, which ended in 1916, but not with the period of the Ilọrin-Ibadan wars. He was famous for his enormous wealth, but it was a peacetime wealth derived in the first instance from his profession as a carver. He seems to belong, therefore, to the first phases of the reconstruction of Okuku, from 1893 until perhaps 1920.

He belonged to a small section of Ọjẹ people attached as visitors to *ile* Ẹlẹmọsọ. Wood carving was their hereditary occupation. Abiọna made enough money from it to invest in *iwọfa*. He deployed them both in his workshop and on his farm:

> He was famous because of his great wealth. He had a big farm and borrowed a huge number of *iwọfa*. [Amos Ọjẹdiji, *ile* Baalẹ]
>
> Baba Adebisi, Alapẹpẹsile, had sixteen *iwọfa* who came from Ijabẹ every four days. They carved drums. He had another seven who lived in his house. No-one was as rich as he was. He lent 1200 bags of cowries [or 1200 x 5/-, i.e. £300] to Ijabẹ to hire them.

Someone else estimated that he had one hundred and twenty-four *iwọfa*. His carving, an occupation shared by no other group in Okuku, must have been greatly in demand in this period of reconstruction, to provide door posts, heavy wooden doors, and window shutters, as well as drums, stools, chests and other objects. Many people spoke of his great farm, but as a manifestation as much as a cause of wealth. Since the local markets were restricted and the railway era had not yet got under way, it is likely that he used the bulk of his farm produce to sustain his large household. Emphasis is placed on the extent to which his numerous *iwọfa* were incorporated into his compound:

He borrowed eighteen *iwọfa* from Ijabẹ and had others who lived in his house. He was called '*Ò-yámọ-yáfá*': one who hires people Ifa and all [i.e. body and soul]. [Joseph Ogundairo, *ilé* Ọlọkọ]

During the Olooku festival, on the day of the ọba's ceremonial wrestling – a high point in the royal ritual year – Ẹlẹmọna would come out in state too. He would have a big carved chair carried in front of him by his *iwọfa*, and when he reached the palace marketplace he would have it set down opposite the ọba's chair, facing it across the market square. All his family, followers and *iwọfa* would surround him as he sat in state. The ọba's drummers would challenge him from the other side of the square:

Ẹlẹ́mọ̀nà rọra, ọba kọ́ lo jẹ!

Ẹlẹmọna, take it easy, you are not an ọba!

The Ẹlẹmọna's drummers would reply:

Èyí tí mò ń jẹ yìí, ó ju ọba lọ.

The position I hold here surpasses that of an ọba.

But the challenge was a friendly one. The Ẹlẹmọna and the ọba lived side by side, and there are no reports of the Ẹlẹmọna's involvement in the chiefly feuds which were prominent in Oyewusi's reign and even more so in that of his successor Oyekunle. Ẹlẹmọna was a title brought by the family when they came to Okuku as fairly recent immigrants. The ọba allowed them to retain it, and inserted it into the ranks of the Palace chiefs, which signified particular closeness to the ọba but no great political importance. Abiọna's position had been built up not through the chiefly hierarchy but independently of it, and his relatively lowly standing in that hierarchy did not at all affect his position as one of the most memorable of big men.

But though Alapẹpẹsile is recalled with pride and admiration for his great wealth, and is cited whenever the topic of 'the old days' arises, he figures hardly at all in the *political* history of the period. The political intrigues that characterised the reign of Ọba Oyekunle (1916–34), and to a lesser extent those of his predecessor Oyewusi (c. 1880–1916) and his successor Oyinlọla (1934–60), play a very specific role in present-day town affairs. Animosities have been inherited and must be explained; titles have been transferred, upgraded or demoted, and those who were the losers use the story of how this came about to justify their demands for the reinstatement of the status quo ante; land has been confiscated, redistributed or even stolen, and the same applies. The recollection of political history is therefore less casual and more intense than the history of neutral figures like Alapẹpẹsile. The big men that operated in this arena are remembered with a greater wealth of detail: and, significantly enough, they usually acquired more extensively elaborated *oriki*, often in language both sombre and alarming: encapsulating stories of plots, assassinations and vaulting ambition which are reconstructed in well-formed narrative already half way to becoming legend.

The accession of Oyekunle in 1916 coincided with the establishment of colonial authority in Okuku. From this moment the basis of big men's power began to shift. But initially, the colonial authorities were exploited in the political contests between big men in a manner that seemed to heighten the traditional dynamics of self-aggrandisement.

Chieftaincy disputes and matters of succession were referred to the Assistant D.O. for adjudication. The petitions and counter-petitions he received show that the British authorities often distorted the balance of power in ways that conformed to their own conception of how 'traditional' society worked. It was they who introduced the idea of *iwefa mefa* (the six kingmakers) who were to be responsible for the selection of a new ọba, as was customary in some other Yoruba towns. It was probably they who insisted that the rotation of the crown between four designated segments of *ile* Ọba should be fixed in one unalterable order, and that selection procedures should be frozen into one pattern.[35] It was they who made each compound's *baale* into its official representative, responsible for the collection of taxes from every adult male and accountable for their payment. By paying stipends of different amounts to different grades of chief (in 1935 the ọba got £120 a year, some senior chiefs got £72 and other chiefs got £24), the colonial administration added a new incentive for competitive struggle between chiefs but also attempted to fix something which had formerly been negotiable: the perquisites received by a chief formerly depended mainly on the goodwill of the ọba and were an instrument of manipulation for him. The various colonial administrators had very definite ideas about the 'traditional' order, and their selections and distortions, though often conflicting, had the same end in view, to bolster up what they saw as a fixed hierarchical system in which power flowed in one direction, from the top down.[36] The chiefs must be made to acknowledge the ọba's authority; the 'subordinate' towns must be made to acknowledge the superiority of the 'head' town in the district.

The motive for this view of the 'traditional' system on the part of colonial authorities trying to implement a system of indirect rule is obvious enough. But what is interesting is the endless difficulties and entanglements it caused them, as power brokers in the local systems perceived new ways of manipulating the rules. The failure of the colonial authorities to impose their view of the world is evident not only in the disturbing (to them) proliferation of court cases, petitions, complaints about acts of insubordination, and outrageously incompatible historical claims and counter-claims[37] but also in the oral evidence which suggests very strongly that during this period of the inauguration of colonial rule, big men and their ideology flourished as never before. The attempted imposition of alien rigidities and regularities seemed initially to stimulate a greater degree of self-aggrandisement by self-made men, who bypassed the chiefly hierarchy and challenged the ọba's authority more than ever before. In the *oriki*, there are intimations of an indigenous view of the colonial authorities, which are represented as only one factor in the all-absorbing competition between big men.

Oyekunle himself was the first man to take advantage of the opportunities offered by the ignorant but authoritarian character of colonial government. On the death of Oyewusi it was the turn of the Oyelẹyẹ branch to provide the next ọba. The chosen Oyelẹyẹ candidate asked the son of his younger cousin, Oyekunle, to go with him and the chiefs to Ibadan with the news, since his work on the railway had given him experience of the ways of Europeans and of the train journey to Ibadan. The son, Ajiboye (now an extremely old man and respected teller of history, who has often been quoted in earlier chapters) got off the train before the others and took a short-cut to the D.O.'s office. He told the D.O. that the chiefs of Okuku were bringing the wrong candidate and that his father Oyekunle was the legitimate successor to Oyewusi. The D.O. accepted this on the spot because he knew Oyekunle (having put him in charge of the Okuku railway station in 1904) and afterwards would brook no opposition to the candidate whose appointment he had endorsed.[38]

Oyekunle thus began his reign in the teeth of bitter opposition from his chiefs – an opposition which continued through most of his reign. He survived because of the support of the colonial authorities. In 1928 it was reported (Gribble to Chadwick: Handing-over Notes) that the Olokuku was an old man, 'extremely courteous but very afraid of being spoken against by his own chiefs, and appallingly suspicious of everything and everybody'. The report commented on the 'need for our influence to make the bigger towns realise they are under him', and observed that 'the chiefs in this area don't co-operate – there is constant friction, and several chiefs have been deposed at different times and some fined by Judicial Council for accepting bribes'. There were many boundary disputes, which were 'difficult to settle because of the weakness of the Olokuku'. Other comments tell the same story: the colonial authorities were constantly protecting Oyekunle against insubordinate chiefs, towns and big men. One report notes that Inịsa, a neighbouring town, was very prosperous and that the Baalẹ of Inịsa had to be warned that he was not respectful enough to the Olokuku. The Baalẹ of Ẹkọsin, another subordinate town, appeared before the Olokuku in a beaded crown and was told by the A.D.O. that he must take it off. It was reported that the Olokuku failed to impose his own candidate for Baalẹ on Okua, 'a tiny hamlet', because of his weakness. Oyekunle was clearly rather a disappointment to the British, but in the eyes of the Okuku people, his friendship with the 'European' was a great coup. His *oriki* say:

Ọbàtálá Òkè Ọtìn lÀrẹ́mú tí í fúnni léyìí tí ò wuni
Ó súré mọni ká, abọ̀rẹ́ wọ̀ntìwọnti

Ó já gùdù nínú tálà, ọkọ Asàlété

Ẹni Òyìnbó gbà níyàwó, Kólawọlé lọmọ ará oko ń fojú dì.

Arẹmu is the Ọbatala of Oke Ọtin who gives people what they
    don't want

He hastened to know all the important people, he had innumerable
    friends

He shrugged magnificently into his velvet cloth, husband of
    Asalete

The man the European took as wife [i.e. treated with lavish
    hospitality, or became exceptionally intimate with], Kọlawọle
    is the one that ignorant bushmen were rude to.

According to Ajiboye, 'they called him "Arẹmu who gives people what they
don't want" because he could do anything he liked. In his reign they brought
the court here and he was the head of it, so people had to accept everything
he said and did'. Oyekunle is regarded as having won the long drawn-out
struggle through his own cunning in getting the British on his side. By the end
of his reign most of the chiefs had come round, earning him the *oriki* 'he had
innumerable friends' – but this was seen as a result of his own strategy of
hastening to 'know all the important people', notably the colonial officers. His
whole reign is seen in terms of this struggle, and all its political personalities
are defined according to whether they were for the ọba or against him.

   This feud is seen not mainly as a contest between men occupying official
positions in the hierarchy, but more as a struggle between slippery and
unpredictable forces, construed in terms of the command of 'medicine'.
Apart from two senior chiefs – Mọlomọ the Ọjọmu and Awolẹyẹ the Arogun
– Oyekunle's principal friends were said to have been the following: Ajibade
of *ile* Jagun – a medicine man and *babalawo* but not a chief; Ogunlade of *ile*
Ọlọkọ – a member of the Ogboni society and a 'powerful man', but also not
a chief; Ajayi of *ile* Arogun – a famous herbalist and wealthy man, but not a
chief; Toyinbo of *ile* Balogun, who was given the minor palace title of Ṣọbaloju
in appreciation for his support for Oyekunle; and Idowu, a firebrand from *ile*
Ọjọmu who led the campaign against the people of Iba in the boundary
dispute. His main enemies were said to have been the chief Ọdọfin, Fadare,
the second most important town title after Ọjọmu; another Fadare, of *ile*
Oluọdẹ; Ajibade of *ile* Ọlọkọ, later made chief Ṣaiwo, one of the top six titles;
and Fawande of *ile* Baalẹ, a formidable *egungun* priest and medicine man, who
later became the *baale* of *ile* Baalẹ. Other chiefs were doubtless involved in the
feud, but they did not figure in reminiscences as active agents in it. The
contest for power was believed to have been actually fought out by those in
command of medicine, Ifa and other supernatural forces, even though chiefs
and other big men may have been behind them.

   Explanations of this feud are vague. Some people suggested that Oyekunle's stratagem to gain the throne was never forgiven. But Toyinbo's son, the present chief Ṣọbaloju, said:

It wasn't because Oyekunle tricked them in getting the throne. They settled that amongst themselves. No, it was because of the grass that they used to thatch their houses. In those days iron roofs had not come in. The town was building a new house for the ọba. Some of them were happy about it, some were not. Because as you know, no-one can be liked by everybody. There will be some who like you and some who don't. Those who didn't like Oyekunle were saying 'Why should we build a house for him?' So it became a quarrel that went on and on. They took it outside the town, they involved the Ogboni all around...

In other words, it is to be expected that the ọba or any other prominent figure will have enemies. This does not need explaining. The occasion which precipitates this latent enmity into open feuding can be explained ('it was because of the grass') and the reasons why specific people took one side or the other can also be explained. Fawande of *ile* Baalẹ, for instance, opposed the ọba because his mother was a full sister of Fadare, the Ọdọfin, who was one of the ọba's leading opponents. Fadare of *ile* Oluọdẹ opposed the ọba because he was married to a daughter of Oyelẹyẹ, the prince who was done out of the throne. He was punished in the end when Oyekunle confiscated a huge tract of his land and gave it to Idowu of *ile* Ojọmu, who had supported him. 'Some took sides out of friendship', and compounds could be split by such cross-cutting loyalties: 'Ajibade of *ile* Ọlọkọ plotted against the ọba – he just didn't like him. A few people in the compound went along with him, but others remained loyal to the ọba. The compound could even divide into three or four – every household head within the compound would do as he liked, section by section'. But the underlying presumption is that enmity is always there ('no-one can be liked by everybody') and can erupt on relatively trivial provocation. Once engaged, the struggle is pictured as deadly and implacable. Enmity does not need explaining in a society of rivalrous big men, where opposing the ọba is merely a way of demonstrating one's success, and supporting him is a way of protecting oneself against the attacks of other big men.

Of Oyekunle's supporters, the two most impressive were Ajayi of *ile* Arogun and Toyinbo of *ile* Aworo Ọtin [*ile* Balogun]. Ajayi was described as the maker of benign but very powerful medicine, a great benefactor of all mothers with sick children, and also a leading member of the Mercy of God Association in the C.M.S. Church. But Toyinbo was an even greater medicine man, a *babalawo* and the closest of all Oyekunle's confidants. His story demonstrates one of the advantages that members of his profession enjoyed in internecine intrigue: their wide-ranging contacts with fellow-professionals from other towns. They had an organisation and loyalties which transcended those of ordinary townspeople, and this sometimes enabled them to control otherwise dangerous situations. Before he became ọba, Oyekunle while on his travels abducted another man's wife from a northern Yoruba town, brought her back to Okuku and married her. Her first husband's people discovered her whereabouts and sent a party of herbalists to attack and kill Oyekunle with their medicines. They were already acquainted with their fellow herbalist Toyinbo, and stayed at his house when they arrived. During their stay they confided their intentions to him. Toyinbo begged them to wait, and promised to get the woman back for them without the death of Oyekunle. He then went secretly to Oyekunle, and told him what had been planned. Oyekunle begged Toyinbo to help him, and Toyinbo promised that if he restored the woman to her husband no-one would be harmed. The affair was settled in this way, and Oyekunle, on his accession, did not forget Toyinbo's friendship. He gave him the palace title Ṣọbaloju and made him his closest adviser. Toyinbo became indispensable to Oyekunle: all visitors to the palace had to be vetted by him before Oyekunle would agree to see them, and anything he told Oyekunle about the suspicious behaviour or intentions of people in the town would be implicitly believed. As one descendant of his put it:

> He was very powerful through medicines. He would protect the ọba from his enemies' medicines. He could tell at a distance whether visitors had bad medicines in their pockets and he could predict exactly what the medicines were. [Samuel Ọlaniyan, *ile* Ọlọkọ]

And someone else said:

> He lived in the ọba's house. He was a medicine man and he could divine anything that was going on in the town. His medicine could make anyone triumph over his enemies. He hung a mortar up by a single thread [to demonstrate his powers]. He was courageous. [Moses Oyedele, *ile* Eesinkin]

But Toyinbo was perceived as a relatively benign figure. He was known as '*A-ki-ràbàtà-nílé-àgbàlagbà*' – 'Tough and invincible one in a house of elders', but most of his *oriki* refer to more peaceable attributes:

> Omítóyìnbó ọmọ Olúlọtán
> Òyìnbó ní í fi páànù kọ́lé
> Omítóyìnbó ló folóóyọ̀ kọ́ gbàgede
> Oníméjì lAyọ̀ká
> Bi ń bá ń pAyérónbí ń mọ́ọ pỌmọogun
> Ọmọ Olúlọtán, ọmọ oókan ì í fọre, ọmọ á yàn bí eéjì.[39]

> Omitoyinbo [his full name], child of Olulọtan
> Oyinbo [short for Omitoyinbo] roofs his house with iron sheets
> Omitoyinbo built a verandah with corrugated iron
> Someone who has two [wives], someone who has Ayọka
> If he calls Ayeronbi, he'll call Ọmọogun too
> Child of Olulọtan, child of 'One [kola segment] doesn't utter good

things', child of 'It comes out right when there are two' [i.e. just
as one segment of kola alone cannot be used to do divination
and get an answer, so two wives are better than one]

Toyinbo is here being commended for his wealth – he was the first person
to roof his house with costly imported iron sheets, and was extravagant
enough to make not just a roof but a whole verandah out of them. He was said
to have boasted that a single wife was no good to him: he needed at least two,
and preferably a few more (he was 'someone who has Ayọka' as well).

The opposition, however, seemed to have more terrifying medicine men.
The most famous was Fawande of *ile* Baalẹ: the only one of the ọba's opponents,
according to one account, to survive. All the others died '*nínú ọtẹ̀*' – in the
midst of the intrigue. Fawande was seen as the leader of the faction opposing
first Oyewusi and later Oyekunle. He was a *babalawo*, as were many of the men
in *ile* Baalẹ, but he also revived the old lineage profession of entertainment
masquerading. His powers were said to have been obtained partly by
travelling and learning, but partly vouchsafed by a mysterious stranger who
came to Fawande's house in his absence and left him a package, inside which
was an *idan eegun*: a charm that gave him the power to perform magical feats.
This charm made him invincible:

One day he went to perform for a friend who was a member of the
egungun cult in Iniṣa, on the occasion of the man's father's funeral.
When he got there, there were some hostile rivals present who had
plotted with a medicine man to bring on a rainstorm to spoil Fawande's
group's performance. Rain threatened, covering the whole sky. Someone
went to Fawande inside his *egungun* cloth and said 'Look at the sky'. He
lifted up the cloth and saw that the performance would be ruined. He
heard a rumour that this was the work of malevolent people. So
Fawande went to his load and got out his own medicines. He told them
to find him a scabied dog. They searched high and low and brought him
one and he took it to the crossroads. He planted a certain medicine in
the ground and began to utter incantations. He brought out a medicine
sword, he told them to hold the dog stretched out in mid-air, and as he
uttered the last incantations he struck off the dog's head. As the dog's
head came off there was a tremendous thunder clap.

The medicine man who was making a fire to cook the rain-medicine
on inside his room was blown out with the blast and found spreadeagled
outside, dead. Then the medicine fire in his room died out and the sky
cleared. They went on with the funeral celebrations and Fawande's
troupe performed their show undisturbed. Because of this he is called:

Ó fajá eléèkúkú ṣe kisa ní Ìnìṣà.

He used a dog with scabies to do terrible things at Iniṣa.

It was these magical powers that enabled him to survive the dangerous feud
against the ọba. Like Toyinbo, Fawande owed his life to his outside contacts:

The ọba called a medicine man from another town to come and kill Fawande. But Fawande was a much-travelled man and had made friends with many herbalists in different towns. When the ọba told his visiting medicine man the names of his proposed victims, the medicine man secretly found out where Fawande lived, because he recognised the name. In the middle of the night he slipped out and went and knocked on Fawande's door. He was admitted; and he revealed the whole situation to Fawande. He said he himself would refuse to do the task given him by the ọba, but if the ọba called in a different medicine man, Fawande would be in trouble. So he gave Fawande a special prophylactic medicine to use for himself, his wives and his children to protect them. This is how Fawande and his family survived. Others kept dying but he did not. That is why he is called *A pa á pa á ò kú*: 'We kill him and kill him, he doesn't die'.

Fawande's *oriki* convey, in compressed but striking imagery, his violent and flamboyant personality. He was evidently a man of extremes and one who took unheard-of risks. His *oriki* suggest that when he danced masquerade dances, he worked himself up into a frenzy whose violence was as dangerous to himself as it was to onlookers, and ugly in its extremity. He was a formidable foe, one who would store up his evil intentions in silence till he unexpectedly unleashed them. His violence was as sudden as a thunderburst. And, unlike his fellow masqueraders, he had the bravado to build his house right up against the palace wall while engaged in a bitter feud against the ọba:

> Agídí òjè tí í jó bí alágbàálẹ̀
> Àwọnyè òjè tí í bura rẹ sán wọnyìn-wọnyìn
> Eegun pààlì tí í télẹ̀ẹ fùrò
> Ajá eléèkúkú abìlagbà ń fùrò
> Ṣéyìí tí yóò ṣe kùú'nú, ọkọ Tinúomi
> A pa á pa á ò kú, ọkọ Àasà
> Òjò sere pèpè, ọkọ Rónkẹ́
> Agídí òjè tí í bólójàá sòtá
> Gbogbo òjè ló ń kólé tí í fidí tìgbẹ́
> Ọkọ Rónkẹ́ kólé, ó fara palé ọba lọ.

> Violent masquerader that dances like a man in debt
> Greedy blood-sucking insect of a masquerader that bites himself
>   into a frenzy
> Broad flat pelvis-bone that lies above the arse
> Scabied dog lean-flanked as a whip-lash
> One who harbours schemes of revenge in secret, husband of
>   Tinuomi
> We kill him and kill him, he doesn't die, husband of Aasa
> 'Sudden downpour', husband of Ronkẹ

Violent masquerader that made an enemy of the ọba
All the masqueraders are building their houses near to the bush
Ronkẹ's husband built his house next to the ọba's palace.

Typically, these lines make references on several levels. To someone who knew Fawande's history, 'Scabied dog lean-flanked as a whip-lash' would unlock the whole story of the incident at Inisa and the dog he decapitated to avert the rainstorm. But to listeners without this knowledge, as the story-teller himself remarked, the phrase would suggest an image of Fawande himself, lean, savage, and fast-moving. 'Sudden downpour', likewise, could suggest the rainstorm that his magic prevented from falling, but it is also a metaphor for a violent, overwhelming and unpredictable personality.

The images of the blood-sucking insect, the scabied dog and the *furọ*, a ruder word than 'arse', are Fawande's own peculiar epithets, evoking his extreme and alarming personality. But idiosyncratic as these images are, they also stand for a general notion, the notion of unlimited and intensely concentrated personal power. 'We killed him and killed him, he didn't die'; 'Sudden downpour': these formulations are recognisably part of an established discourse of power. Fawande can do outrageous things and get away with it, and this is the best proof of power there is. All the details of his extraordinary and excessive behaviour, expressed in extraordinary and excessive language, contribute to his establishment as the biggest of political big men of the time, measured by a common well-understood standard.

As in the war period, then, medicine and magic is the idiom in which political struggles were thought. Contests which revolved around the retention or transfer of parcels of land; the upgrading or demotion of titles; the right of access to titles and other privileges; all these were fundamentally exercises of will by the ọba, the chiefs, and the powerful men of the town. 'Having people' in this context meant asserting a position and seeing whether you could get support for it. 'Tradition' was the gradual accumulation of outcomes of such struggles – which in turn would be used as models and justifications for future struggles – and not a set of fixed rules as the colonial authorities believed. Spiritual and supernatural force was the idiom in which the concept of will was expressed. It is not surprising that every politically prominent figure of this period was almost automatically credited with *oogun*, for this was the way power was construed.

Otẹ (intrigue or plotting) was the word used most often to describe political processes, and what *otẹ* involved was the alignment of collaborators in assertions of the will. Friendship, kinship ties, old grudges were all activated in the manipulation of these alignments; what was taken for granted was that there always would be enmity to fuel the process. The violent imagery that, in the wartime *oriki*, represented enmity as actual physical harm, is not common in the *oriki* of twentieth century men. But the idea of enemies as a pervasive, incalculable force continued into the period of reconstruction and even underwent further elaboration.

Big men of this period continue to be associated with cynical mistrust of human relations and especially of family bonds. Sentiments like these are often put into the mouths of big men themselves, confirming the supposition that it is a philosophy particularly appropriate to the process of self-aggrandisement. Domestic distrust seems not to have diminished with the ending of the wars. *Iwofa* continued to be lent and borrowed until as late as the 1930s, and in a situation where earning opportunities did not meet cash needs, loans of this kind remained a significant part of the local economy.[40] Several of the old men's biographies revealed that they had themselves served as *iwofa* within the town, and about a third of them remembered their fathers' households in the first two decades of this century as having included a number of residential *iwofa*. The sentiment that 'your worst enemy is in your own backyard' continued in the *oriki* of quite recent big men, and received even greater elaboration than in the nineteenth century *oriki*.

Big men of the early twentieth century continued to be celebrated in the idiom of unassailability, independence of spirit, and indifference to the attacks of rivals. These attacks, however, were now represented as being directed above all to the destruction of the man's reputation. After the peace, the big man's enemies were less often assassins, more often plotters and detractors. But the danger from this kind of diffuse and unlocatable malevolence was considered to be no less real. Since the big man's position depends on his reputation, malicious talk can seriously diminish and even destroy him. Ill-will and bad talk are indeed more pervasive and uncontrollable than overt aggression. So even though the concentrated imagery of violence characteristic of the war period is muted and not further developed in the twentieth century, the gracious world of Adeoba and Winyomi – steeped in *ola*, conceived almost entirely in terms of wealth, beauty, and generosity – is not recaptured either.

7. FARMING, TRADE AND BIG WOMEN

Though the railway arrived in 1904, it was not until the 1920s that the real age of yam-exporting got under way. It continued at full swing up to the early 1950s, when the mass movement out to 'far farms' put an end to it. With the railway, 'money came to Okuku', and other forms of trade followed in its wake. This gave an opportunity to ambitious women, who could not reproduce the classic pattern of big men's self-aggrandisement but who succeeded in finding alternative routes to wealth and influence.

In the 1920s and 1930s nearly two-thirds of the households on which I have information expanded their yam production by 50–150% to supply the Lagos market.[41] Some farmers were quicker to see the possibilities of the railway than others, and some had greater means to take advantage of it. These men were able to outdistance their peers by a long way. The best-remembered of these was Idowu Pakoyi, like Alapepesile a recent immigrant belonging to a small attached lineage. Pakoyi not only produced yams for sale, but moved early into yam trading, buying up surplus from local farmers and chartering railway wagons to take them to Lagos. The factors in his rise to prominence were somewhat different from those in Alapẹpẹsile's. He is said to have employed labourers more than *iwọfa*: and although labourers also lived in their employer's house as long as the job lasted, the relationship was not a semi-permanent one based on family obligation as was the relationship between *iwọfa* and master. Prices quoted in the stories about him show that his labourers' tasks were measured and paid for in precise and quite small units, and once done, the labourer would go and find another job somewhere else.[42] Labourers living in did not swell a man's household in the same way as resident *iwọfa* did. Pakoyi did have a large family ('three wives and many children') but building houses had become almost as important as marrying wives: Pakoyi built two, apart from the compound where he lived, and one of them was a prestigious 'upstairs'. Whereas at the turn of the century a large house was a sign of wealth because it was evidence of the large human population inside it, by 1950 bricks and mortar were valued in themselves.

There were new outlets for reinvestment as well as for conspicuous consumption. Other men of Pakoyi's generation who made money out of the yam trade diversified, moving into a variety of new businesses:

Oni was the first person to have a grinding mill and also to have a car. [Aderinọla, *ile* Arogun]

Adekẹyẹ was one of the first people to have a transport lorry. [Aderinọla, *ile* Arogun]

Ọsọ bought a Lister engine – the first in Okuku. [Alhajji Mustafa, *ile* Baalẹ]

Ọsọ made a great yam farm and he was also a *babalawo*. He was the first person to buy an electric saw. [Sunday Adewọle, *ile* Ọlọkọ]

But the fundamental dynamics of the process remained the same. A man built up his position by gaining command of people – whether his own household or hired labour – and investing their labour in the expansion of his farm. Increased profits and reinvestment enabled him to acquire yet more people. Whether the relationship between big man and his 'people' was one of kinship or one of payment for services rendered, the model remained a familial one. Pakoyi's large mixed household of relatives, *iwọfa* and labourers was still seen as the basis of his position. His relation to the household was that of paterfamilias, like the male household heads of the great compounds of earlier times.

New trade goods entered the town with the railway. There were successful male entrepreneurs like Adegboye of *ile* Ọba, who sold '*ọti oyinbo*' (European liquor) and became so rich that at his mother's funeral 'he got off his horse and planted money in the market like maize grains'. But Adegboye was outshone by another more determined entrepreneur – a big woman called

Ayantayǫ. She was described as *bǫrǫkììní alágbára ilú* – a highly-placed and powerful person in the town – and was known not only for her wealth but for her ability to get her own way. Like Alapẹpẹsile with his carving, she had an initial edge over other people which enabled her to get started: she inherited *dukia* (moveable property) from her mother, and was therefore *ǫlǫrǫ fúnraa rẹ* (rich in her own right). She founded her career in cash crops: but she cultivated not yams but palm nuts, and to a lesser extent kola. According to her grandson, Emmanuel Oyeleke, she specialised in palm nut production 'between 1917 and 1922', at a time when cash crops of any kind were a novelty in Okuku. Through these crops she laid the foundations for her career in other kinds of trade. The preparation of palm oil and of kola nuts for sale was women's work. This choice of crop, rather than yams, made it easier than it would otherwise have been for her to get labour, since she could recruit a female work-force; easier for her to supervise since she had experience of the work herself; and less directly threatening to the men. She employed large numbers of women from Okuku and other towns as labourers during the palm-oil season to work in the *ẹbu*, the manufacturing sites in the farm. She also employed women to wash and peel the kola. She is also said to have had male *iwǫfa* who tended the trees and harvested the kola and palm nuts.

She was a daughter of *ile* Alubata, married to Bamgboye of *ile* Ǫba, and after his death inherited by Oyewǫle who was the father of the future ǫba Oyinlǫla. She thus had influential affines. But according to Emmanuel Oyeleke, both her husbands were much older than her and died while she was still an active woman. After the death of the second, she chose to live on her own. Since she was rich, some of her children and grandchildren joined her household and worked for her. Emmanuel was one of them: he explained that 'her being rich meant that I did not have to work as hard as I would have had to on my own father's farm. Although I helped her on the kola and palm nut farms, it was not heavy work'. Like a big man, she extended patronage to her household. She took a special interest in Emmanuel, and had a song which celebrated her role as protector:

> Ẹ mǫ́ yan Ìlúfoyè jẹ
> Omǫ kékeré Àkàndé
> Ẹ mǫ́ yan Ìlúfoyè jẹ.

> Don't dare to cheat Ilufoye [Emmanuel]
> Little Akande
> Don't dare to cheat Ilufoye.

Through her help, Emmanuel became one of the first educated men in Okuku, and took a succession of jobs in teaching and local government.

But if Ayantayǫ was able to circumvent the problems of recruiting a labour force, and to a certain extent those of establishing a household, she met greater difficulties in getting hold of land for her cash-crop production. For the cultivation of palm nuts and kola it was hard to borrow land, because trees, as permanent crops, constituted the ultimate title to a piece of land. Though owners were willing to lend plots out for temporary food crops, they were very reluctant to risk lending the permanent symbols of their ownership. The importance of the tree crop in this regard is well attested.[43] Ayantayọ, according to several accounts (not, however, including Emmanuel's) simply seized the land she needed. They say she took a large piece from *ile* Baalẹ, forcing this compound to pool all its remaining plots and reallocate them so that no-one would be left entirely destitute. How she got away with this – if she did – is not clear. She had a strong link with *ile* Baalẹ, for it was her wealthy mother's compound, but the stories told about Ayantayọ suggest that her requests for land on the strength of this were turned down. Her husbands' section of *ile* Ọba was the largest and most influential of the four, and they may have intervened on her behalf; at any rate Ọba Oyekunle, who was a friend of Ọsayọmi of *ile* Baalẹ, lent a huge piece of *ile* Ọba land to *ile* Baalẹ to compensate them. But most people explain her coup by saying simply that she was 'very tough' and that 'everyone was afraid of her' – which implies that she was a witch. She hung onto the *ile* Baalẹ land for fifteen years, a feat which is still recounted with indignation by members of that compound.

From this base she moved into other kinds of trade, and her fame was as much to do with her innovations in trading as with her actual wealth. According to Emmanuel:

> She traded in meat. She was an indomitable woman (*akikanju obinrin*), and one who was awake to progress (*o laju*). All the big ọbas who came visiting knew her in the palace. She was the first person to sell European drinks in the town and the first person to build a house with an iron roof. So all the big visitors would go to stay with her. She had two horses, one white and one red, and went to the farm on them. She died around 1938....She built a house near the railway station, and opened a beer and stout shop there.

Her success, like that of the big men, thus depended not on money itself but on the influence that money could help to establish. She used her kinship, social and trading contacts to build up a clientele of 'big visitors' from outside, important people who knew her better than they knew anyone else in the town. Not only her wealth but her innovative ways of spending it (on an iron roof, European drinks) attracted important people. It is significant that she established her reputation through traditional symbols too: the two horses, 'one white and one red', were the classic marks of outstanding wealth and distinction. Ayantayọ was not afraid to compete, and to take over big men's property, methods and insignia of success when she could.

This period seems to be one which particularly favoured economic success for women. Unlike in Ibadan and Lagos,[44] the period of the wars in Okuku

does not appear to have given women scope for self-aggrandisement: there are
no memories of Okuku women thriving on the nineteenth century slave trade.
It was precisely the newness of the trade in European imports – because it had
no prior gender associations – which gave Ayantayọ an opening. Indeed, since
women already controlled the local market and had well-established trading
networks, it gave her an advantage. But there were limits on a woman's self-
aggrandisement, limits whose nature is revealed in the hints at witchcraft. A
woman's career was blocked in a crucial respect. Although Ayantayọ could
acquire wealth and networks of influence, she could never really establish a
great household in the same way as a big man. As Faderera put it:

> A woman cannot stand alone. She must be with a man, and if she tries
> to stand alone the results will be bad. The man's role is to be her
> authority, so that other people will not be able to bother her or 'touch'
> her [with medicines]. The man protects the woman. But a woman can
> be free once she's had a husband – if he dies, she will stay with her
> children and look after them and no-one will say anything.

Ayantayọ became 'free' after the death of her second husband, and established
her own household, drawing into it her children and grandchildren. But even
as a wealthy widow with children, she could not become the head of a
compound. It was her sons who expected to become the recognised household
heads of the future, with their own wives and children to support them.
Ayantayọ could attract her grandchildren to profit from her wealth and
influence, but she could not demand their labour as of right: they did not
'serve' her in the way that Babalọla of *ile* Ẹlẹmọṣọ Awo 'served' his father and
then his eldest brother until well into his middle age. And though from the
point of view of her individual dependants her position in the town was
admired and regarded as convenient and advantageous, from the point of
view of the town at large, women who tried to convert their economic success
into social and political capital on the pattern of big men were regarded as a
threat. A woman is the fountain-head of a man's household, the source of *his*
'people' in the shape of children and affines that supply him with labour and
support. A woman who tried to build up her own household would not only
be taking potential supporters away from a man; by removing her own
reproductive powers from his orbit, she would be undermining the very
foundations of his social position.

The story of another big woman of the period, Ọmọlọla of *ile* Ọjọmu, suggests
that economic success was something women did better to keep quiet about.
Ọmọlọla also made her money from the cultivation of palm trees. Unlike
Ayantayọ, she used money and persuasion, rather than force, to get the use
of the trees. But though she was successful, she did not want this known:

> She lent out money in different places and got *iwọfa* in exchange. She
> would also lend money out in exchange for the use of palm trees.
> Eventually she would get her money back but she would have had the

use of the trees until then. The profits from palm oil and palm kernels were good, so she did well, building herself up from small beginnings. She was married into *ile* Ojọmu but she worked for herself. She was rich: she had women to process the palm oil and men to clear the farms. But she had no *oriki* about it: she didn't want anyone to know that she was rich. [Samson Adebisi, *ile* Ojọmu]

Omọlọla 'did not want anyone to know that she was rich' because her wealth could not be fed into the male cycle of aggrandisement. For a man, a house full of 'people' created wealth and wealth drew in more people. Wealth spent on display enhanced reputation, reputation attracted more people and this led to greater wealth. Reputation was the medium through which men's power was constituted. But since a woman could not 'have people', in the shape of a great household of wives and children under her command, reputation could not play the creative and constitutive role in a big woman's career that it did in a man's. For a woman to have reputation at all was suspicious. It suggested a threat of encroachment into male territory. Reputation in a woman therefore almost automatically turned inside out and became an accusation of witchcraft. Successful women were almost always branded as witches. Despite Omọlọla's caution, several people who mentioned her name hinted at her frightening powers. And the only other big woman discussed in this connection was unequivocally credited with witchcraft as the source of her power:

She lived near the station beyond Matego's house – a lonely place. She was a medicine woman and the head of the witches. She could cure mad people, knew people's enemies and prescribed sacrifices. She was there in Oyinlọla's time [1934–60]. She had no family or dependants here [she came from Rẹkẹ, a town near Opẹtẹ, and was known as Iya Rẹkẹ or 'Mother from Rẹkẹ'], but she was a friend of the ọba and of Toyinbo [the great *babalawo*]. She supported the ọba. But she rarely came into the town. [Samuel Ọlaniyi, *ile* Ọlọkọ]

Women, that is, were not debarred from participating in the struggle for self-aggrandisement. Although they suffered certain disadvantages in the competition to make money, those who were sufficiently ingenious, determined and courageous could certainly do it. But when they tried to convert their wealth to public status they ran into obstacles. Ayantayọ displayed her wealth and contacts and was called a witch; Omọlọla did not dare display hers, but was suspected of witchcraft anyway, while Iya Rẹkẹ's importance was ascribed solely to her supernatural powers. As we have seen, men's power in the nineteenth and early twentieth centuries was very often conceived in terms of the possession of *oogun* (medicine). But in their case this was a source of pride. It was openly mentioned, in tones of admiration and satisfaction, and detailed narratives were told about men like Toyinbo and Fawande to show just how extensive their command of spiritual forces was. Medicine and magic were a common if not a necessary part of the composite state of social esteem, *ola*, to which every man aspired. Command of *juju* and charms is a metaphorical representation of command of resources and people. A man credited with great *juju* is a man who can protect people from enemies: it is publicly asserted and is a source of attraction to supporters.

But witchcraft was hinted at in hushed tones which suggested fear and condemnation more strongly than admiration. Far from contributing to a woman's *ola*, it branded her as a pariah, not fully human, and not fully integrated into the community. Control of spiritual powers which was creditable in a man was reprehensible in a woman. Witchcraft is represented as a power over people which is essentially secretive and destructive. It is also something innate, something that lives inside the body, connected with the woman's femaleness in a way that *juju* is not connected with maleness. A big man's success depends on command of the social environment, including women whose fertility must be harnessed to his project of social expansion. A woman who threatens to alienate her fertility to her own project of self-aggrandisement is a therefore a witch rather than merely a big woman in control of *juju*.[45]

Ayantayọ, Ọmọlọla and Iya Rẹkẹ 'had no *oriki*' about their achievements because in their careers the cycle of self-aggrandisement suffered this crucial block. Any reputation at all was likely to turn to a reputation for evil. Thus a woman had to be discreet about her networks of contact, her employees and her influence. She could not display her achievements in public, and for this reason, though there were – and still are – a number of successful and wealthy women in Okuku, they are not usually marked down in memory as people of great reputation. They are spoken of with reluctance, and with a mixture of disapproval and unwilling admiration, by other women as well as by men.

There were women, however, who could and did attain social esteem, and who had beautiful *oriki* of their own. Women's position as intermediary and as producer of children held advantages as well as limitations. This will be discussed in the next chapter.

8. BIG MEN 1934–1984

Moses Oyinlọla was installed as Olokuku in 1934. He was the first Christian ọba of Okuku, and the first to have travelled extensively outside the Odo-Ọtin area. He had spent many years in Ghana – originally as a houseboy of Jacob Ajayi, the great herbalist of *ile* Arogun. Ghana made him wealthy. He brought back with him a large, white, type of kola nut which was new to the area and which was considered greatly superior to the *abata* nuts that people grew before. Unlike the *abata* nuts which were grown mainly for domestic consumption, the 'Olokuku's kola' was exportable to the north, and was in great demand. It was Oyinlọla, then, who started the wave of kola cash-crop production which at first almost equalled cocoa in its importance to Okuku farmers, and he was at first the sole distributor to local farmers. 'If he gave you just a single nut, it was like gold'. He used this power of patronage astutely and collected many loyal adherents on the strength of it.

Oyinlọla was an immensely popular ọba, both with the colonial authorities and with his own people. Ulli Beier described him thus:

> The Olokuku of Okuku is of huge stature and has a strong face like a lion. His laugh is deep and his manner jovial. He is of unusual friendliness and hospitality. He is extremely popular in his town, and although he has had no schooling, his intelligence and judgement have earned him the admiration of a long succession of administrative officers (Beier, 1956, pp.167–8).

He was remembered by the young men of the town for his conspicuous wealth. ('His wealth was very apparent', commented one admirer.) He married seventeen wives, apart from those he inherited from Oyekunle, and was said to have had 'at least fifty children'. However, it was not the numbers of his children that impressed observers so much as the fact that he had the foresight and 'enlightenment' (*olaju*) to educate them all.[46] Today, these educated sons and daughters of Oyinlọla constitute a formidable dynasty of professionals, employed in bigger cities but retaining the dominant voice in all affairs concerning the 'progress', 'improvement' and 'welfare' of the town.

Like Oyekunle, Oyinlọla had the backing of the colonial authorities in every contest of strength against insubordinate individuals or towns. But unlike Oyekunle, Oyinlọla took the lead in these contests, leaving the colonial officers to trail behind, tidying up after him where they could. Oyinlọla needed no protection. His opponents were no match for him: there were numerous confrontations recorded in the colonial documents, and he seems to have won them all. His high-handed, intemperate manner is vividly portrayed in one document: it is a letter from one Okunade, the Native Authority Dispenser at Okuku, who was caught up in a land dispute with Oyinlọla in 1952. Okunade was rash enough to take his case to the Magistrate's Court at Ọṣogbo. Oyinlọla responded by taking out his own injunction against Okunade in the Okuku court, of which he was President. Next time their paths crossed, according to Okunade, Oyinlọla addressed him in the following terms, reported verbatim in Yoruba:

> Okunade, don't you hear that I'm calling you?.... Who do you think you are?....You bastard. I'm going to drive you out of this area. You don't want to release that land and you don't want to go. I'm telling you you *will* go, you'll definitely leave this place whether you like it or not, you'll leave this region. You liar. This is war between us.

The A.D.O. commented rather feebly 'The above is somewhat novel'; but four days later he became the instrument by which Oyinlọla's threat was carried out, by getting Okunade recommended for transfer to Ọtan.

But Oyinlọla's supremacy depended not only on the classic big man's virtues of aggression, pride, intransigence, and unassailability, but also – and perhaps mainly – on his 'enlightenment': that is, his ability to manipulate the new colonial instruments of government. In local disputes, the most important of these was undoubtedly the Chieftaincy Declaration, intended to spell out and codify forever the local systems of election to high office. In the Odo-Ọtin area, the declaration was made in 1956 by the Odo-Ọtin District Council, of which the Olokuku was chairman. Oyinlọla, well aware of the significance of this exercise, appears to have made the most of the ignorance of the colonial officers who sent out their 'questioneers' about ruling houses, order of succession and rules of election for each town in the District. Subsequent chieftaincy disputes in subordinate towns often involved bitter accusations by the losing factions that the Olokuku had fixed the succession to his own advantage.[47]

From this 'interference' Oyinlọla enlarged not only his wealth (from aspirant claimants to the various vacant thrones in the locality) but also his reputation for being able to do exactly what he wished with the full support of the bemused A.D.O. While this provoked resentment from the rebellious 'subordinate' towns, it was celebrated gleefully in Okuku. There, Oyinlọla's reign is remembered as the real golden age of Okuku. His *oriki* show how keenly he was appreciated, both as a wealthy innovator and as a headstrong, domineering overlord. The more high-handed he was, the more the praise-singers exulted:

> A-wọ́n-bí-agbọ́n
> Oróòro kò ṣe é jẹ mẹran
> Àjàlá Ọ̀kín kọ́lée mọ́tò lọ́tọ̀
> Oyinlọlá, ó kọ́ telépo
> Ó kọ́ ti aláàgbámù
> Abara hòìhòì
> Ààbà demọ dèyá
> Ọkọ ìyáláte
> Èíbó Òkè Ọ̀tìn
> Àjàlá ti dámọ lẹ́kun à-ń-ṣe-kọ́ntádíígbọ́n
> A-múniílẹ̀-kÓyìnbó-tó-dé
> Ó fidí aláṣejù bomíí gbóná
> Àjàlá gbọ́nà Ìbàdàn lọ́wọ́ aláàwîìgbọ́
> Oyinlọlá a-gba-tẹni-tó-ranpá-kan-kan...[48]

> Rare as a wasp
> 'The gall-bladder can't be eaten with the meat'
> Ajala Ọkin built a separate house for his car
> Oyinlọla, he built one for the petrol
> He built one for the lizard
> The scabby-skinned one

Staple that pins down both mother and child [i.e. the whole world]
Husband of the senior woman
The European of Oke Otin
Ajala has stopped people being insolent
One who locks people up until the white man comes
He dips the overreacher into hot water
Ajala blocked the road to Ibadan for the disobedient people
    [people who don't hear when we speak]
Oyinlola, one who seizes the goods of the man who defies him [the
    man who squares his shoulders with resolute indifference]...

While Oyekunle was *eni tí òyìnbó gbà níyàwó*, the person the European took to wife, Oyinlola has become a European himself: 'The European of Oke Otin'. His power is part of that of the colonial authorities and he is praised for using the colonial apparatus of justice for his own ends: 'One who locks people up until the white man comes'. While Oyekunle was commended for surrounding himself with friends, Oyinlola could use force to control his people. He is compared to an *aaba*, a staple used symbolically in magical charms to give the possessor power to hold people down. But while the charm is usually made specifically for the control of one person, Oyinlola holds down the whole community with a power no-one can escape. He will tolerate no opposition or resistance, and the *oriki* dwells gloatingly on what happens to people who dare offer it.

These *oriki* continue to celebrate the qualities that were made so much of in the nineteenth and early twentieth centuries. They select for special comment those aspects of Oyinlola's reign that fit the picture of the big man as tough, intransigent, domineering and ruthless. His 'progressive' aspect is referred to only briefly and indirectly, when the special house he built for his car is mentioned as a modern symbol of wealth. (He was so wealthy that he could even afford to build a house for the lizard, 'the scabby-skinned one', the last possible candidate for such a favour!) His Christianity and his interest in education are not mentioned at all. But in the comments of young men who grew up in a world dominated by Oyinlola, and who often spoke of him as one of the most important big men of their youth, his 'progressive' aspects are given more attention than his toughness:

He helped everybody and did things for people. He celebrated the Olooku festival in grand style. He was praised as '*Oyinlolá Olókukù, a-tÓkukù-so-bí-eni-sogbá*', 'Oyinlola Olokuku, one who mends the town like someone mending a calabash'. [Niniola *ile* Aworo Olooku]

He told the truth and could settle problems peacefully. [Raimi Gbadebo *ile* Ojomu]

He looked after all his children so that they all got high posts. In his time water and electricity were planned for. [Lasun Adeniyi, *ile* Nla]

He did a lot for the development of Okuku [Gustus Adebomi, *ile* Ǫtun
Baalẹ]

Oyinlọla was a new kind of big man. A fundamental change in the way
power relations were constituted, begun in Oyekunle's reign, had now
become fully established. Oyinlọla's power had a source outside the web of
support deriving from his subjects. The police, law courts and the permanent
presence of the British always ready to back up his authority gave him a
fulcrum for his manoeuvres outside the traditional client–patron relationship.
His principal characteristics as a big man were ones associated with colonial
institutions and policies: education, the law, the acquisition of 'development
goods', the manipulation of colonial bureaucracies. As a corollary of this
change, his power depended less than formerly on the ability to build up a
large household of his own (though Oyinlọla certainly did this) and more on
the creation of extended and diffuse networks of influence. Influence meant
not only providing pioneering leadership which guided the Okuku people
towards the benefits of 'modernity', but also, more specifically, it meant
manipulating local government, educational institutions, political parties and
other structures to the advantage of the town and of individual clients.

Oyinlọla overshadowed other big men in Okuku in a way no previous ọba
had done. But there were many other men considered to have been 'big'
during his reign, and they shared with Oyinlọla not only the new personality
profile but the new, institutionalised sources of power.

Some of the classic attributes of nineteenth century 'big-manism' were
still there in modified form, but some of the most prominent of them had
virtually disappeared, and a number of new ones had been added. Medicine,
for instance, the dominant idiom in which power was discussed in the earlier
periods, was hardly ever mentioned as a modern attribute. Only two of the
thirty-nine modern big men mentioned by my informants were said to have
had outstanding magical powers, one as a herbalist and one as a hunter who
protected Isalẹ Okuku from thieves single-handed and owned fifty guns.
Wealth, more surprisingly, was only once cited as the main reason for a man's
importance in the town: and this was in the case of Adebisi Olongbo, the
grandson of the famous rich man Alapẹpẹsile, chief Ẹlẹmona. What remained
a continuing and pervasive theme in these portraits was the notion of
'toughness'; but toughness now manifested itself in a rather different complex
of characteristics, associated with a different range of life chances. The
spheres of action with which it was now associated were educational
achievement; positions in local government; new professions such as plumbing
and printing, or pioneering ventures in the old occupation of farming;
leadership of all kinds, in party politics, town affairs and in the Second World
War; and 'sponsorship' of other people, which meant getting them jobs,
getting them out of trouble, and getting them sent to school. A new big man
had to use his toughness to achieve a place in the formal structures of authority

introduced by the colonial regime, and operate his patronage networks from there.

Of all these new big men, perhaps the most prominent was Tio Falohun of *ile* Baalẹ. He seems to typify the qualities most often attributed to big men by the younger generation today. He was educated and helped others to education; a local councillor who used his position to rescue people who got into trouble with the authorities; a man with friends in high places who used his influence to get people jobs; and a political leader in the 1960s who stuck to his guns when the town was almost at war with itself.

> He was always ready to help people in trouble: he would leave everything to help them. He went to school and although he only read to Standard VI he knew more than some people who have been to Grammar School. He was very generous. He had a big farm, and sent labourers there with his money. He built the Falohun house. He was called: '*Rọ̀rọ̀ àgbò tí í bí ikòkò nínú, lásán làsàn ni inú ń bí babaa wọn*' [The big ram's head that annoys the wolf (because it is too big to swallow) the miserable sods can get as annoyed as they like, it won't do them any good (i.e. Falohun's opponents can eat their hearts out)]. [Salau Abiọdun, *ile* Oluawo]

> He had influence with the Government to help anybody in his own family who got into trouble. He was made a Councillor. [Samson Ojo, *ile* Baalẹ]

> He was like the ọba of the town up here. He was always ready to help anyone in Baalẹ ward who got into trouble with the authorities. He could do this because he was an educated man and personally known to the officials – like the Health Inspector – and ready to spend money on drinks and food for them in order to persuade them to let his people off. He was a councillor. [Jimọ Abẹfẹ, *ile* Oluawo]

> He was a councillor and a leader in the N.N.D.P.. He helped people in the party who got into trouble with the police. [Lasisi Olowolagba, *ile* Oluokun]

Falohun's education gave him an official place (as councillor) and hence an unofficial network of influence among other officials. From this position he was able to build up a clientele who needed his assistance in dealing with colonial structures of authority. His following was large: 'Baalẹ ward' comprised a third of Okuku. The 'helpfulness' these clients sought required a more pacific approach to social relations than was exhibited by earlier big men. The kind of 'toughness' that was now admired did not include challenging the ọba. It was a much higher recommendation in a patron to be a friend of the ọba, and thus have access to some of the 'progress' that was being introduced under his auspices.

Big men are still a prominent feature of social and political life in Yoruba country today. Recruitment of a following is still a key component in politicians' and businessmen's success. Clients do jobs for the big man and swell his public appearances by their attendance. The big man in turn uses his networks of influence and his access to the centres of power to do favours for them. Studies done in Yoruba cities show that the patron-client relationship is fundamental to modern social organisation and outlook (Barnes, 1986 and Peace, 1979 in Lagos; Lloyd, 1974 and Gutkind, 1975 in Ibadan). But the basis and character of the modern big man's power is different from those of the war leaders, farmers, traders and medicine men of the nineteenth and early twentieth century, whose careers I have been describing.

In the first place, wage-labour, government posts and cash-crop farming introduced a new constellation of relationships around the production of wealth. Before the time when there was a market for large agricultural surpluses, a big man's 'people' both produced wealth and were wealth. They produced food and consumed it; to be wealthy was to be the centre of a very large circle of such producers and consumers. The great household was simultaneously a labour pool and an outlet for conspicuous consumption. But wage labour and government posts made it possible to accumulate wealth without the labour of others. The market for cash crops and the proliferation of other business openings made it possible to reinvest agricultural wealth directly, not through the medium of the great household. The source and the end of wealth thus became separated. Individuals could be wealthy without being installed at the heart of a 'huge house'. Occupations which required labour – as cocoa farming did – could be structured as individual or small-household operations by buying in labour as required. It was not because food-crop farming required a lot of labour that large households existed; but because the generation and consumption of conspicuous surpluses of food crops could only take place through large households.

The impact of these changes took time to be felt. In the height of the commercial yam-farming era, people still thought of wealth in terms of household. But the break-up of the great household was driven on, as we have seen, by the dynamic of individual self-aggrandisement which fired not only the successful big men who tried to build the huge households, but also all other men, at the domestic level, who strove to break away from their seniors' control. Wage labour, government posts and cocoa farming far from the parent compound gave these young men opportunities they had not had before to begin their career building early in life. The 'huge houses' holding multitudes who were at once the household head's source of wealth and his social and political support group have declined and all but vanished. 'Having people' is no longer conceived in the organic language of reproduction and nurture, in which the big man's household *produces* the people who then produce his greatness; it is more appropriately described in the language of clients, favours and services.

Secondly, there has been the shift in perspective following Okuku's gradual incorporation into the national arena. Even though many people live and die within Okuku and with aspirations focused on achievements within the town, those who have been most successful in modern terms are always those who have been away. The educated sons and daughters with jobs as doctors, bank managers, and civil servants do not live in the town. The context and source of their success – the institutional frameworks within which they operate and which give them their money and power – are far away and unfamiliar to most local people. The new influential people come back perhaps three times a year, and though they take an active interest in the welfare of the town, it is very clear that their success is not rooted in it. Local interests, opinions and support are no longer all-important to them. More generally, the mass movement to the 'far farms' has diluted the intense concentration of interest in the activities of prominent figures in the community. For nine months of the year, people are scatttered in some fifteen settlements, travelling home only rarely on brief visits, with little opportunity for the leisurely gossip which is the seed-bed of growing reputations. Reputation does not have scope to develop.

This change, however, has deeper roots in a third shift, the importance of which has already been suggested. With colonial rule, new positions became available which conferred power or influence independently of the recognition or adherence of the community. A police corporal had the power to arrest people by virtue of his appointment by the colonial authorities, not (as was the case with Omikunle the war leader) because his followers recognised and supported his right to do so. If anyone resisted arrest, external forces would be brought in to back the corporal. Even inside the community, then, positions of power were no longer created from within. Those who learnt the knack of dealing with this external source of power became the new brokers and wielders of influence. They were essentially mediators between the local system and a superordinate one imposed from above. This meant that a big man's supporters no longer *constituted* his power by their adherence and recognition. Reputation no longer had the same crucial role.

With these changes came a change in the values surrounding the big men. Personal magnificence, generosity, self-reliance, ruthlessness, destructive power and its obverse, the capacity to offer protection, were not erased from the definition of big men; but a new and apparently dominant set of values was written into it, associated with the education which was the new big men's principal avenue to power: values of Christianity, literacy, honesty, public spiritedness, helpfulness.

Thus the very grounds of *oriki*'s existence were shifting. The disappearance of the great household meant that one of the primary fields of reference in *oriki* was lost. Personal *oriki* attributed the possession of 'people' to big men by

heaping up allusions to household members, with the formula 'child of..',
'father of...' 'husband of..' Profusion was possible because the household
provided an abundant source of names and because the real, known
interconnections of these people allowed the performer to hurl their names
promiscuously together without collapsing into incomprehensibility. *Oriki
orilę* were affected too, though less directly, for the great household was the
visible embodiment and concrete manifestation of the 'lineage' which these
oriki celebrated. They placed the subject of the *oriki* against a deep, wide
background of kin, who would be acknowledged whatever form the household
took; but there is no doubt that the great household where many people
shared the same *oriki orilę* provided an image of the unity of the larger kin
group in a way that small scattered households could not.

Oriki were created in a situation where activities within the local community
were all-absorbing. Little incidents, peculiar happenings, favourite remarks,
were observed, discussed, taken up and commemorated in epithets.
Continuous interaction in a small town meant that nothing escaped notice.
The composers of new *oriki* selected some things and not others to comment
on; but the underlying presumption was that whatever the town's prominent
people did was of interest and importance. A genre that draws so much on
idiosyncrasy and difference can only thrive in a community where people are
closely observed; and one that relies so much on allusion and the unsaid can
only thrive where everyone knows everybody else or at least where there are
audiences who know what lies behind the words. When the most successful
and powerful people from the town were those who worked in other cities, and
when the whole of the active and vigorous part of the population was away
most of the year, the hothouse conditions necessary for the generation of new
oriki were removed.

Most important of all, however, is the fact that *oriki* enacted the regard of
'people' and guaranteed its continual renewal. They did not merely reflect,
but participated in, the constitution of a power based on public recognition.
An *oriki* performance demonstrates a perfect mutuality: the performer
heightens the subject's reputation, and this enhances his power to help her.
She takes on the role of quintessential supporter, whose adherence to a big
man is what makes him big. When an alternative, external source of power
enters the picture, this mutuality is broken. Supporters continue to hope for
advantages from their patrons, and patrons continue to benefit from the
adherence of supporters, the more numerous the better. The big man's
economic and political operations are still helped on by the visible presence
of his 'people', who establish confidence by producing an aura of success.
Reputation is still important and praises, therefore, continue to be sung. But
the ultimate source and guarantee of the new big man's power lies outside the
immediate community. Power is no longer created and measured by the
regard of others within the town. It is not the gaze of the community, enacted

in concentrated and exemplary form in the *oriki* singer's address, which alone lets us know that a man is important. Once power was no longer constituted in this way, *oriki* were no longer at the heart of political process. They have remained a gratifying acknowledgement of public status, a way of advertising a big patron's means and generosity: but they are no longer indispensable.

The creation of new personal *oriki* to commemorate the activities of new personalities in Okuku is now rather rare. And those that have been recently composed have perpetuated the old idioms of power, instead of creating new ones. These old idioms articulate fears and aspirations which are still very much alive in the community: rivalry, fear of enemies, the need for self-reliance. But they express only the long-established part of people's experience; the values associated with new experiences under colonialism and after are articulated in personal reminiscence and informal narrative, but not in *oriki*.

When stories about Falohun are told, for instance, only one attribution, 'The big ram's head that annoys the wolf...', is quoted by his admirers. And this epithet is a traditional proverbial formulation which asserts the subject's unassailability and the frustration of his enemies' evil intentions towards him. He has no *oriki* celebrating his education, his Christianity, or his position as Councillor. Most of the new breed of patrons acquired similar brief epithets, sometimes not much more than nicknames. Oyinlola's *oriki* were abundant, but as we have seen, they too were composed in the idiom that had prevailed at least since the mid-nineteenth century, emphasising his domineering rather than his 'helpful' side. Ọmọnijẹ, one of the few big men of Oyinlola's reign to have been given a substantial corpus of epithets, was a striking figure, ebullient, tall, handsome, and influential with the ọba. He was described as 'a big man in the church – the Secretary of the Church Association', but his *oriki* do not mention this. They emphasise his ability to get away with outrageous acts:

A-kélépo-ó-tà-ń-gbígbóná, ọkọ Oyèbọ́lá
Asọ̀rọ̀-àná-di-bá-mìíin
Ònà tí yóò jẹ mọ̀ ní í ń yán babaa Pópóọlá
Gbádéjọbí, Babalógun
Àjànàkú oníbùdó mo ríbà baba ọkọ̀ mi...[49]

One who makes the palm-oil seller sell while it's still hot, husband
of Oyebọla
One who resurrects yesterday's problem to make a new one today
He's preparing the ground for the raking in of bribes, father of
Popoọla
Gbadejọbi, the Balogun [of *ile* Ọba]
Mighty elephant of the camp, I pay homage to my husband's
father...

Fiery, rash, and acquisitive, this persona demonstrates his greatness by doing things that would be condemned in other people. Like earlier big men, he is pictured surrounded by enemies. His unassailability in the face of malicious attack is commended in words reminiscent of the *oriki* of his ancestor Oyekanbi a hundred years earlier, quoted in section 4 of this chapter: 'They gang up on the *ose* tree, the *ose* tree flourishes/They conspire around the well, and risk falling in!'. As in the *oriki* of other big men after 1893, his enemies are seen as *ẹlẹgan* ('despisers') and *ayọnusọ* ('busybodies') – the performance ends with a vitriolic attack on these types – but this idiom, as we have seen, is an extension of the earlier language of enmity. It continues to animate *oriki* chants today.

This idiom is not in any way irrelevant to present-day values and concerns. Indeed, it could be argued that in some communities ideas concerning enemies, rivalry and self-protection may actually have intensified, with the ruthless struggle for the new cocoa and oil wealth, and the alienation attendant on massive urban expansion. Nor is it anything new that *oriki* reflect only one dimension of prevailing ideology. Different Yoruba genres always, as far as one can tell, expressed different aspects of experience articulated in different models of human and spiritual relationships. Folktales did not stress the same values as *oriki*, nor present them in the same cosmological framework as Ifa verses (Barber, 1984b). However, the divergence between the *oriki* and the personal narratives now current in Okuku seems to have become wider than was the case before, suggesting that *oriki* production has reached a limit, a point where there are things which it cannot say, whole zones of social experience from which it is excluded.

The future development of the tradition may lie outside the long-established modes of performance that are the subject of this book. *Oriki* have found a new medium and a vast audience in popular *juju* music, where they are one of the stock sources of lyrics. Some of Sunny Ade's most exquisitely caressing songs are couched in the classic *oriki* idiom of medicine, violence and intransigence. But the development of the form in this case lies in the musical rather than the textual dimension. It is in other neo-traditional genres – notably the solo chants of Tunbọsun Ọladapọ and Larewaju Adepoju – that the linguistic resources of Yoruba oral poetry, including *oriki*, may be developed along new lines in a way that reconciles the long-established values with the new ones in the fulfilment of a new function. *Oriki* as a mode, a resource, a field of expression, are probably not dying out but being recycled, just as folktales have been recast and revived on the popular Yoruba stage. But the specific *oriki* tradition discussed in this book may well have lost its creative impetus.

Oriki performance flourishes in Okuku, and the new breed of big men are frequently saluted in public gatherings: but with the personal *oriki* of their fathers and grandfathers and the *oriki orilẹ* of their fathers' and mothers' lineages, rarely with new *oriki* of their own. And when new personal *oriki* are composed, it is always in the old language. Today's big men, therefore, are saluted in the idiom of an earlier age. The creation and legitimation of reputation has now become synonymous with an invocation of the past, and those who make 'progress' are hailed in the language of nostalgia.

7

DISJUNCTION AND TRANSITION

1. INTRODUCTION

Oriki mark individuality. They are imprinted with signs of idiosyncrasy through which they evoke and recall the differences between entities. But at the same time they are the means by which boundaries between entities are crossed. We have seen how the actual utterance of *oriki* opens a channel between speaker and addressee: a channel which is also a bond, both intense and all-engrossing. Through it, power flows. The individual human recipient of *oriki* experiences an enhancement, thought of as a translation beyond the normal human condition. *Egungun* are revitalised by *oriki* chanting, *orişa* are empowered. The dead are given the impetus to return and bless the living, their latent presence actualised.

Women, the principal bearers of the *oriki* tradition, are the ones who cross – as *rara iyawo* so poignantly observe – from one compound to another, and often from one town to another, when they marry. They combine two different lineage identities, in an ambiguous conjunction that is never fully resolved even on death. But if they cross boundaries between groups, they are also, as we have seen, the source of structural differentiation within them. Not only do they provide the points at which a patrilineage segments, they also introduce to their own children alternative networks of relationships which other members of that lineage do not share. They sometimes, also, import their own *orişa* which after their death will have to be taken over by someone else in the compound. The frequent statement made in *oriki*, that 'If the father is important, so is the mother', and 'Who can salute the father without first saluting the mother?' is not a mere piety. It encodes the fundamental principle of alternatives in society. It is the woman that makes differentiation possible and that offers the social actor alternative paths to pursue.

It is the disjunctiveness of the discourse of *oriki* that makes it possible for them to assert identities and at the same time to cross boundaries between individuals and groups. The discussion of *oriki* opened in Chapter 2 with the observation that they are a mode of discourse that is essentially and genetically disjunctive, an accumulation of utterances of different origins and intents, juxtaposed in performance but not fused into a single coherent statement. From this inner fragmentation the dominant stylistic features of an *oriki* text were seen to flow. Fluidity, boundarilessness and centrelessness are all made possible by the separateness and interchangeability of the text's constituent parts. It became clear, however, that an *oriki* chant is not a mere jumble of unrelated items. Chapter 3 showed that the text coheres around its subject, the present or absent addressee. Each utterance in a chant is united to all the others by a relationship of equivalence: all are alternatives to each other and to the subject's name. Chapter 4 suggested that the nature of this address, the relationship established between performer and subject, depended on precisely what the performer was doing in chanting; and that this in turn was defined by, and achieved meaning in, a particular context of utterance. And beyond this, there is a prevailing thematic homogeneity: in *oriki orilẹ* (Chapter 5), a tendency to circle around and elaborate a small number of key emblems; in personal *oriki* (Chapter 6), a preoccupation with a cluster of values each of which stands in a metaphorical or metonymic relation to all the others. Beauty means people, people means wealth, wealth means gorgeous adornment, gorgeous adornment means beauty: and out of this perpetual circle of suggestivity emerges a transcendent value, *ọla*. But the disjunctiveness and lability of the *oriki* text remain fundamental features of the genre; the very features that underpin the càpacity of *oriki* to uphold difference and simultaneously open boundaries between separate entities. We now need to look at how this is done, and how the function of *oriki* and the role of women are related.

2. CROSSING BOUNDARIES AND MERGING IDENTITIES IN *ORIKI*

When a performer utters *oriki*, she attains special access to the subject. She is felt to have touched the heart of the subject's identity. At the same time, she constructs her own identity, as the interlocutor personified. The more skilled the performer, the more repeatedly does she refer to the act of utterance itself, and include passages from her own *oriki*. The performance of *oriki* thus dramatises, and represents in heightened form, dialogue as such.

This goes beyond the mere opening of channels of communication between beings. It can involve – indeed at one level always does involve – a merging of identities or the subsumption of one identity by another. *Orisa* are saluted through the *oriki* of their devotees, and devotees through the *oriki* of their *orisa*, and this is the way in which the completeness of their mutual dependence is expressed (see Barber, 1981b and 1990b). But this is only an extreme form of what happens in all *oriki*. All *oriki* mark individuality, but all have a tendency to float, to be shared by more than one subject. An individual's 'own' *oriki* are a tissue of quotations, a collection of borrowings from diverse sources. This floating is not accidental but is a fundamental feature of the eclectic and incorporative mode of *oriki*. Individual subjects thus share with others the components that make up their innermost identity, and recognise fragments of it in other people wherever they go. There is also, as we have seen, merging between the identities affirmed in *oriki orilẹ* and in personal *oriki*. *Oriki orilẹ* belong collectively to a group, but they are usually addressed to individuals. The group emblem is thus bound up intimately with individual self-consciousness and self-display, and appears in contexts where the purpose of the performance is to enhance the individual against the background of – even at the expense of – other, rival individuals. Individual identity is constituted out of communal identity: and at the same time it is through the salutation of the individual that group identity is reaffirmed. Because there is gradual absorption of personal *oriki* into *oriki orilẹ*, individual idiosyncrasy, even the most trivial, can become part of the the symbolic self-representation of the group.

This interchange between personal *oriki* and *oriki orilẹ*, however, is better understood in the light of a process that goes on continually in all *oriki* performances: a shifting of persons. The performer fixes her attention on her subject as if nothing else in the world existed. Yet under cover of this bond, as her chant proceeds, she turns out to be sliding with often almost unmarked transitions from one subject to another. The other subjects are always related to the initial addressee, and usually of an ascendant generation, though a ṣubject's wives and *their* parents might also be included. This, as we have seen, is a technique for surrounding the subject with 'people' and a pedigree, so crucial to his standing in the town. The big man of here and now is credited with a wide penumbra of associations, in space and time, to support him. But it does not usually stop there. The singer often appears to have shifted the actual focus of her utterance, so that she is no longer attributing relationships with others to the big man of here and now, but is evoking, calling upon the others themselves – people who stand behind his shoulder: his father, his grandfather, his mother. Whether these people are alive or dead makes no difference to the style of address nor to the ease of the transition. They assume in turn the role of addressee, the singer all the while keeping her eyes fixed on the living man before her.

When the living addressee is relatively young, or when he is greatly overshadowed by the fame of his ancestors, the transition may occur almost immediately. Addressing Aṣapawo, the younger brother of the present chief Ṣobaloju and the son of Toyinbo, the Ṣobaloju before him, who was a famous medicine man and Ọba Oyekunle's confidant (see Chapter 6), Ṣangowẹmi named him as 'son of Omitoyinbo' (Toyinbo's full name) and then moved straight into the *oriki* of this great man:

> Ọmọ Ṣọbalójú ọ kú àbọ̀, ọmọ Omítóìbó ọ kú àbọ̀
> Omítóìbó ọmọ Olúlọtán, òun náà kú àfidí balẹ̀ níbẹ̀ un
> Asùnmọ́ ọmọ ọrọ̀ nÍsàn
> Òìbó ní í fi páànù kọ́lé
> Omítóìbó ló folóóyọ̀ kọ́ gbàgede...

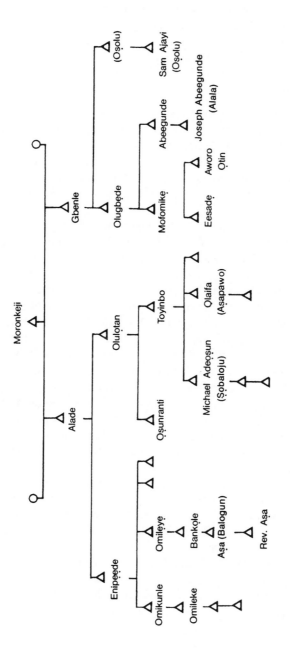

Fig. 3: Aṣapawo's ancestry

Son of Ṣọbaloju welcome, son of Omitoyinbo welcome
Omitoyinbo son of Olulọtan, I greet him too for being seated over
     there
Asunmọ child of Wealth-at-Isan
Oibo [Toyinbo] roofed his house with iron sheets
Omitoibo built a veranda with corrugated iron...

Because the occasion was the Egungun festival, when the ancestors were especially close to the world of the living, Ṣangowẹmi could picture Toyinbo 'seated over there', and address him as if he were among the living celebrants. But, as in other performances of *oriki*, the bridge to this salutation was through her immediate subject, Aṣapawo. By addressing him as 'son of Ṣọbaloju', 'son of Toyinbo', the path to the ancestral subject is opened and the transition made easy.

The ancestral hinterland the singer thus evokes is always specific to the immediate subject who is the occasion of her address. Though the purpose of an *oriki* chant is not to record genealogy, the singer may draw on detailed genealogical knowledge in order to evoke a succession of predecessors for the subject of her chant. In the performance just mentioned, Ṣangowẹmi moves on from Toyinbo to the personal *oriki* of a number of other men of the same compound but senior to Toyinbo: Olulọtan, Enipẹẹde, Alade and Moronkeji. According to Ṣọbaloju and to Ṣangowẹmi herself, the relationships between these names is as in Figure 3 (though other members of the compound gave other versions). If Olulọtan was Toyinbo's father, Enipẹẹde his father's senior brother, Alade his father's father and Moronkeji his paternal great-grandfather, then she has moved up by stages through her version of the genealogy of the lineage, with Aṣapawo as the starting point. In other performances, the paths traced back from the immediate subject may include ones that go through the mother or the father's mother or other relatives. They are usually shorter than the five generations Ṣangowẹmi evokes here, and often move laterally as well as vertically. Often a singer will evoke several different paths. The aim is not to lay out a genealogical map, but to trace the channels through which an individual acquired his accumulated fund of social attributes.

What this suggests is that although profusion of names and associations is always desirable, with often bewildering results, there is an informing principle directing the choice of attributions the singer heaps on her subject. The underlying idea seems to be that a person occupies a place created by someone who went before. Toyinbo, Olulọtan, Enipẹẹde, Alade and Moronkeji are not named just because they are ancestors of Aṣapawo; rather, Aṣapawo is seen to inhabit a social space created by them.

In the case of title and religious or other office, this space is formalised and clearly defined.[1] A title is held to be a continuous, unbroken space stretching backwards in time, successively occupied by different individuals who are, in this context, nevertheless the 'same' person. This continuous identity is affirmed by the *oriki* and by other forms of address. The head of Ẹlẹmọsọ Awo's compound, for example, was an *egungun* priest with the important title Alapinni, the most senior of the nine *egungun* office-holders. He made this title even greater by his munificence and his formidable personality. When he died, he was replaced as Alapinni by a small boy of the same family. During the biennial *egungun* festival this boy would go with the other senior priests to 'heaven' to fetch back the ancestors, and a vigil would be kept for him at home by the women of his compound. They sang:

Mé leè sùn o[2]
Mé leè sùn oorun ńkojú o
Enígbòórí baba wa ló béégún ṣeré lọ…

. I cannot sleep
I cannot sleep though my eyes are heavy
Enigboori our father has gone off with the *egungun*…

The boy is addressed as the representative of the whole *ile*, whose *oriki orile* is Enigboori. Their collective identity is concentrated in him. He is referred to as 'our father', though the leading singer was in fact the boy's own mother. The greatness of the title of Alapinni is maintained through these *oriki*, and the little boy, in occupying it, becomes an elder for as long as his role as *egungun* priest is activated (that is, till the end of the festival). In taking on the role, he takes on the attributes of a man fit to occupy that role; and, specifically, those of his predecessor who had expanded that role and imbued it with his own personality.

In the case of important offices such as ọba and Ọjọmu, the most senior town chief, it is well within the scope of *oriki* performers to trace a long chain of succession. In these cases they reverse the usual direction and start from the first office holder, working their way down through all his successors to the present incumbent. The women of *ile* Ọjọmu were able to trace the title Ọjọmu from Olongbe in the mid-nineteenth century down through seven other title-holders to the present one. In one solemn performance, the soloist marked each step with a formula signifying the death of one title-holder and the succession of the next:

Gbà eléèyun yẹ wẹ̀rẹ̀ tó foyèé lẹ̀
Ó wáá kan…

When that one stepped aside and laid down the title
It was the turn of ….

She also used another formula that showed why this succession was being invoked. She was calling on the accumulated powers of the Ọjọmu's predecessors to assist in the performance of a family ritual, for the present generation can do nothing on their own:

Ará ayé ò moròó ṣe
Ará ìsàlẹ̀ ó wáá gborò náà ṣe.

The people of the world [the living] do not know how to do rituals
Let the people of below [the dead] come and do the ritual for us.

Even when no title and no specific position is inherited, however, everyone enters a space prepared by his or her predecessors. Thus in Ṣangowẹmi's salutation of Aṣapawo, the *oriki* and the identity of Aṣapawo, Toyinbo, Olulọtan, Enipẹẹde, Alade and Moronkeji can be superimposed one upon the other, for each of these men successively occupied the space created by his antecedents. The transference is a more diffuse expression of the notion of reincarnation recognised when a new baby is named as the returned mother, father, or grandparent ('Babatunde', 'Iyetunde': 'Father has returned', 'Mother has returned'). It is not, then, just that the *alaṣeku* ('those whose deeds remain', i.e. the ancestors) are always potentially present among the living, to be evoked by the utterance of their *oriki*: it is also that they are perpetually present *in* and *through* their descendants, who occupy the spaces formerly occupied by them: and that these spaces are maintained and renewed by the performance of *oriki*.

The spaces are not neutral; they are not genealogical positions on a grid. They retain the personality of those who created them. Indeed, when there is no formal office or title involved, it could be said that the space *is* that personality, having no other dimensions. What the descendant steps into is an ambiance, a cluster of associations, a fund of symbolic resources deriving from the personality of his forebears. In this case the relationship is not one of strict or exclusive inheritance, for an individual may be felt to inhabit a composite space created by several different chains of succession, and conversely several different descendants can be seen as occupying the same space at different times. For example, on the occasion of his *egungun* festival, Aṣapawo is the one who is represented as filling the space created successively by Moronkeji, Alade, Olulọtan and Toyinbo his father; but on other occasions his elder brother Michael Adeọsun, who took over the title Ṣọbaloju, would be more likely to be the focus of attention and be hailed as the occupant of this space.

Thus the present-day individual lives in his ancestors and his ancestors live in him. This permanent presence is kept alive to consciousness in the *oriki* addressed to the living, by the continual sliding of the subject away from and through the living to those whose deeds remain.

The shifting of person in *oriki* is facilitated by the lability and polyvocality of the texts. The autonomy of the component *oriki* in a chant makes possible a continual shift and indeterminacy in the reference of pronouns. Each unit may be spoken by a different voice standing in a different relation to the subject. Not only the 'you' who is the subject, but also the 'I' who addresses the subject, are always moving their position and depth. The two 'persons' involved in the powerful dyadic communication of *oriki* never stay still. In the case of the 'you', we have already seen how the ostensible subject may almost imperceptibly be replaced by other subjects, his predecessors in the role he occupies or people associated with him in other ways. But the 'I' is even more elusive. From moment to moment the first person singular speaks from a different place.

In a performance of the royal *oriki*, Ṣangowẹmi sometimes spoke *in propria persona*, as herself, in the here and now, addressing her main listeners Ajiboye and his son Israel. From time to time she elaborated this 'I', quoting her own *oriki* to establish a full-blown image of the oral performer so expert that she excites the enmity of all her neighbours:

Èmi Àbèní ń pè ọ́, eégún-inú ọmọ Fákẹ́midé
Nítorí enlé apá ọ̀tún ò fojúu re wẹni tí ń pe lóbalóba
Ìmọ̀ràn ikà ni tòsì ń gbà
Àbẹ̀ní, ẹbọ kó jáde n tòkánkán ń rú
Kùtùkùtù tí mo ríkùn dánà sí...

It is I, Abẹni, calling you, 'inner masquerade' [genius], child of Fakẹmide
Because the householders to the right don't look kindly on a person who salutes all the great ọbas
The ones on the left are planning wicked revenge
Abẹni, the ones straight ahead desperately wish she would leave
I who from my earliest days had a mind that could follow many paths...

Even in this construction of her own persona, a shift can be observed, from speech coming directly out of her own mouth (*I* Abẹni am calling *you*) to a reference to herself in the third person ('the ones straight ahead desperately wish *she* would leave'). Soon afterwards, however, she is not speaking as Ṣangowẹmi but as a generalised transhistorical member of the public, excluded since ancient times from the privileges of the royal lineage she is saluting:

Àkànjí Ajíbóyè babaà mi jẹ́ n bá ọ délé ará Kọọkin
Tòrò Àbẹ̀bí ọmọ Anáyẹ̀ mo wáá bá yín délé Alárá
Bí mo ti pé tó, ọmọ Adémọ́lá Wúràọlá, mi ì gbọdọ̀ figbá Alárá mumi ní Kọọkin
N ò fàwo ìkòkò sebè lÓtìn

Akanji Ajiboye my father, let me go with you to the house of the native of Kọọkin
Toro Abẹbi child of Anaye, I went with you to the house of the Alara [the ọba's title before the move from Kọọkin in the

eighteenth century]
Long as I have lived there, child of Ademǫla Wuraǫla, I must not
use the Alara's calabash to drink water at Kǫǫkin
I don't use his clay pot to cook soup at the Ǫtin.

A few moments later she speaks with the voice of a member of this lineage, participating in its privileges rather than being excluded from them:

Mo dàgbà dàgbà mi ò tí bǫ̀rǫ̀ 'Mǫkǫ Ǫrǫdùn.

I became very old but I did not quickly lose my looks, 'Mǫkǫ Ǫrǫdun.

Even a chant addressed by one member of a lineage to another, where both are insiders, undergoes the same constant shifts. The 'I' changes position so rapidly and fluidly that normally the switches would not be registered by the listener except as a satisfying quality of overall texture. In the *egungun* vigil chant I have already quoted several times, the shifting position of the poetic 'speaker' is particularly clear. It is worth quoting again, at greater length:

Mé leè sùn o	1
Mé leè sùn oorun ń kojú o	
Enígbòórí babaa wa ló béégún ṣiré lǫ	
Òkú yanhùnyan ó di gbǫ́ngan	
Ìdì í mo dirù lÁgùrè	5
Nígbà tí n ò rẹ́ni tí óò gbérùù mi	
Ẹ bá n wá kékeré eégún kó gbé lé mi	
Ebi wǫn ì í pǫ̀jẹ̀	
Ebi ò yóò pa arèkú láíláí	
Kàkà kébi ó pa mí o	10
N óò purǫ́ fún ìyáá mi	
Màá ní babaà mi gbobì méjì	
Kò ní í kóbì lásán	
Ayérónfẹ́, a kó iyán rúgúdú a ní n fún baba	
Babaà mi ò nìkàn jẹ ẹ́	15
Babaà mi mìlàa jẹ ẹ́	
Èmi wáá dákǫ okòó	
Nílé Ayérónfẹ́	
Ìwǫ náà dákǫ okòó	
Ò ní mo káre mòkǫmòkǫ	20
N ò kúkú dá tẹ̀ẹ́dógbòn tán yányán	
Ǫ ṣe ní mo káre mòkǫmòkǫ	
Èmi náà lǫmǫ arùkú tí í torí baṣǫ	
Ìgbà n mo yẹgǫ̀ nígbalẹ̀	
Òkú yanhùnyan ó di gbǫ́ngan	25

Ìdì n mo dirù kalè lÁgurè
Bí okó mò mí í kẹ́
N óò lo rèé dégbèje aṣọ
Àimò mí í kẹ́
N óò lo rèé dégbèfà   30
Kíkẹ́ tàikẹ́
N óò rèé dégbèẹ́dógún
Enígbòórí, n lomọ Yáú i fi í dáṣọ...
Òní la ò yóò sùn tójúmọ́ ó i mọ́ o
Òní la ò yóò sùn nítorí omọ Babalọlá o   35
Ẹ̀kú wọn kì í hun òjè
Mo ṣebí iṣu tá a bá sun kì í hun òbẹ
Ará dá obìnrin ni ì í fi i mawo
Obìnrin ò mògbalè
Ìbá ṣe póbìnrin lè mawo   40
Ǹ bá gbénú ẹ̀kú wẹ̀kú
Ayérónfẹ́ ma gbénú aṣọ ma tún waṣọ
Ǹ bá sì gbénú agò so ilèkè...
Bí mo bá bímọ tí ò ṣe ilàwì òjè
N óò ta ìyá ẹ̀ ma wáá fi sowó ẹmu![3]   45

I cannot sleep
I cannot sleep though my eyes are heavy
Enigboori our father has gone off with the *egungun*
A disruptive corpse was put a stop to
I tied up my bundle at Agure   5
Since I can't find anyone to carry my bundle
Find me a little *egungun* to lift it onto my head.
Ojẹ entertainers never go hungry
Masqueraders will never starve
Rather than go hungry   10
I'll tell lies to my mother
I'll say my [dead] father is asking for two kolanuts
She won't bring kolanuts alone
Ayeronfẹ, she'll add a little pounded yam, she'll say I'm to
     give it to father
My father won't eat it by himself   15
My father won't eat it alone
I went and bought 20 cowries' worth of hot *ẹkọ*
In the house of Ayeronfẹ
You too bought 20 cowries' worth of hot *ẹkọ*
You said [sarcastically] well done, great expert on *ẹkọ*!   20
I didn't even buy 25 cowries' worth

So how can you say I'm a great expert in buying *ẹkọ*?
I too am the child of the masquerader who puts his head
   inside the cloth
When the costume suited me in the sacred grove
A disruptive corpse was put a stop to   25
The moment I tied up my bundle at Agure –
If my husband knows how to care for me
I'll go and buy fourteen hundred cloths
Not knowing how to care for me
I'll go and buy twelve hundred   30
The moment he takes care of me
I'll go and buy three thousand cloths
Enigboori, that's how the children of Yau buy their cloth.
Today we won't sleep until daybreak
Today we won't sleep because of the child of Babalọla   35
Masqueraders' costumes never bring retribution on the *ọjẹ*
I say the yam we roast never brings retribution on the knife
Women are impatient, that is why they cannot know the secret cult
Women do not know the sacred grove
If women were allowed to know the secret cult   40
I would wear one masquerade costume after another
Ayeronfẹ I would wear one cloth after another
And inside the costume I would wear beads...
If I have a child who doesn't become a singing masquerader
I'll sell his mother and spend the money on palm wine!   45

This chant opens with the voices of the women performers, wives and daughters of *ile* Ẹlẹmọsọ Awo, in their own persons. They announce that they will keep the vigil, hard as it may be, for the sake of their 'father', the Alapinni. The performance itself is the way they keep the vigil: they are therefore speaking as people involved in a family ceremony, announcing that they intend to do it properly. This relatively direct voice (mediated by the conventions of the form in which it is expressed, but commenting on, and arising from, the performers' real situation at that moment), returns towards the end of the excerpt, in lines 34–5, when the singers reiterate that they will not sleep that night because of 'the child of Babalọla', i.e. the Alapinni. But between and around these two points the 'I' undergoes many transformations.

In lines 4–9 the voice speaks on behalf of the whole lineage (for an interpretation of these lines see Chapter 2, Section 5), drawing attention to the occupational specialisation which marks it out, i.e. masquerading. This voice has masculine overtones, for it is the men who actually wear the costumes and who would be responsible for 'tying up the bundle' in which these are carried around. Lines 10–16, however, are clearly the voice of a child

– it could be either a boy or a girl – boasting of the trick he or she uses to get a meal out of his or her mother. The child lies to the mother that the spirit of the dead father is demanding kola, knowing that when she offers kola she will add food as well, and that the people around will help to eat it. The purpose of this unit is humorously to reiterate the theme of the ancestors with whom the lineage specialisation is so much concerned. But lines 17–22 sound like a speech from one co-wife of the compound addressed to another. The speaker protests that the other person has no right to tease her about the amount of *ẹkọ* she buys – after all, they both buy exactly the same amount. (The significance of this, however, I was unable to discover.) Lines 23–6 are spoken in the voice of a generalised male of the lineage, but lines 27–32 are the words of a wife, boasting how much she is pampered by her wealthy husband. The status of this passage as a quotation of someone's words is made clear in line 33, which rounds it up with the conclusion 'that's how the children of Yau buy their cloth', i.e. the wives who boast of the number of cloths their husbands give them are testimony to the wealth of the lineage as a whole.

Lines 34–5 are once again the singers in person, reaffirming their determination to keep the vigil. Lines 36–7 are a generalised reflection on the honour and fittingness of the profession of masquerading, and could be spoken by anyone or everyone connected with the lineage. But the next passage is distinctively a women's utterance, lamenting their exclusion from the secrets of *egungun*. The value of the secret from which they say they are excluded is enhanced by the expression of desire: 'If women *could* know the secret, I would wear one costume after another', i.e. would participate to the full in the thrilling performances of the *egungun*. The fact that by this phrase the women reveal that they *do* know the 'secret' – that *egungun* are actually human beings – is a point to which I return later. What I want to call attention to here is that the point of this passage depends on the gender of the voice uttering it: the voice represents those who are associated with *egungun* but excluded from the cult's inner secrets, and whose frustration and desire serve to heighten the cult's mysterious ambiance. This voice switches markedly in the last two lines of the passage quoted, becoming definitely male, the voice of a husband and father in the lineage. The speaker jokes that masquerading is so ingrained in the lineage and such a matter of pride to him that if any son of his fails to learn the trade he will sell his mother and spend the money on drink.

The 'I' of an *oriki* chant thus moves continually between male and female, adult and child, insider and outsider, specific and generalised persona. It occupies at times the position of the performer herself, at other times shifting completely across to the addressee and speaking in a voice that could be his. The text is all quotations, but they are not like the quotations in *The Waste Land*, identifiable fragments torn from some other context. There is no textual frame or background into which the *oriki* 'quotations' are inserted; rather, the whole performance slides endlessly around the shifting pronouns, and no voice can be identified as a stable centre, as a starting point or as a frame of reference. Bakhtin (1981, p. 69) speaks of mediaeval texts where 'The boundary lines between someone else's speech and one's own speech were flexible, ambiguous, often deliberately distorted and confused. Certain types of texts were constructed like mosaics out of the texts of others'.[4] *Oriki* go beyond what he describes; without either reverence or parody, both of which imply an authorial point of view, they simply are constituted out of the speech of innumerable, shifting others, incorporated into a single speaker's utterance.

This is possible, in the first instance, because the units of an *oriki* chant all come from different places. But this inherent polyvocality is deliberately heightened by stylistic means. Far from being subordinated to a unifying design of the performer's, the diversity of voices is overlaid and reinforced by an added indeterminacy. Shifting of persons is a positively sought effect. Even within one coherent unit, the performer often shifts position and speaks from different places, with a weaving motion that gives an *oriki* chant its characteristic rippling quality:

> Ilé kótó wọn ò ní í gbà'Gbàrí níbi wón gbé bí n lómọ
> Babaà mi òdèdè wọn ò gbOlojò lÉjù
> Yàrá kótó, Èjù Òkòmí, ò ní í gbèdín owó
> A ì í bímọ nÍràn ká pòsé owó
> Ahá kótó ni wón fi í wọnwó fáyaba[5]

> A little house can't contain all the Igbari people in the place where
>   I was born
> My father, the corridors cannot contain all the Olojo people at Eju
> A little room, Eju Okomi, will not accommodate all our money
> We never bear a child in Iran only to sigh for money
> They use little calabashes to dole out money to the royal
>   wives

This passage is a single utterance, playing with the theme of the container (the house, the passageways, the inner room, the calabash) by which the wealth and populousness of the Okọmi people are measured. But within this unit the performer varies the pronoun, from a generalised 'I' (speaking from the position of a member of the lineage) in the first line, to an implied 'you' ('my father', 'Eju Okọmi') in the second and third, to 'our' and 'we' in the third and fourth, and 'they' in the fifth. This habitual sliding from pronoun to pronoun establishes as a fully developed aesthetic feature the indeterminacy that was made possible by the oral mode of transmission and accumulation of *oriki*.

If *oriki* cross boundaries between persons, then, they do so by a continual transference and alternation of voices. The moving 'I' characteristic of *oriki* texts effects an interpenetration of person. The performer frequently speaks from the position of the addressee – as a member of his or her lineage, or, in the case of personal *oriki*, with his own words, the sayings which he is remembered by. But at the same time she always retains the powerful dyadic bond that locks speaker and hearer together for as long as the address continues. She may thus speak simultaneously *as* another person and *to* him, just as she may speak simultaneously as 'herself', the persona she constructs as utterer in the performance, and as representative of many other categories of person. The 'person' she addresses sometimes coincides more or less with the actual, living man or woman before her, sometimes with a generalised representative of the group, sometimes with other positions in the social map. These positions are never fixed in *oriki*, and the address slides easily from one position to another. Thus the capacity to open channels and effect a confluence of identities is built into the very composition of *oriki*, revealing that this is indeed what they are for.

3. DISJUNCTION AND JUXTAPOSITION

The disjunctive juxtapositions so characteristic of *oriki* need to be looked at more closely. For if *oriki* are above all a means of crossing boundaries and transcending divisions in the very act of affirming differences, then the divisions and disjunctions within the text itself are of particular significance. Gaps, like shifting persons, are not merely the by-product of a particular mode of composition and transmission: they are also a deliberately inserted stylistic feature. To the existing disjunctions, supplementary ones are added. The art of *oriki* is above all the art of handling gaps.

These gaps are discontinuities between what I have called textual 'units', and to pursue the analysis this notion of the unit must be reviewed. A performance of *oriki* is put together out of more-or-less ready-made, more-or-less internally coherent, more-or-less fixed blocks of text. A block can be identified by form and meaning: if it is stylistically patterned and semantically unified it is reasonable to treat it as one item and to assume (though with less certainty) that it originated as a single composition. These subjective identifications can be corroborated by quoting the first line. People will complete it if there are other lines that are felt to belong with it. But the definition of these blocks as 'units' is already misleading and problematic. The notion of units carries with it the implication of regularity: units in counting and measuring are after all defined by their uniformity. The conception is quite appropriate to some praise poetry: Sotho *lithoko* and Zulu *izibongo*, for instance, can be divided into units because they are made up of stanzas of a regular pattern even if of varying lengths (Kunene, 1971, Damane and Sanders, 1974; Cope, 1968). But in *oriki*, a 'unit' can be anything from a single phrase to an extended, internally patterned and subdivided passage. The nominalised phrase

Òbùmubùmu-ṣàgbá-lóṅgbólóṅgbó

One who dips and drinks, dips and drinks, and makes the beer barrel slosh noisily

is an *oriki* that stands alone, complete in itself, and it can therefore be treated as a unit. But in the *oriki orilẹ* of Omu, quoted and discussed in Chapter 5, the performer unfolds a long and elaborate textual structure before 'landing', that is, before arriving at the single key point the passage is designed to display. The whole of the passage introducing in turn the goat, the sheep, the 'mother hen/Who rejoices at the sight of maize', and the 'massive horse/Barrel-bellied', and concluding with the emblematic 'They use a great wooden dish to drink horse-broth at Omu', would have to be treated as a single unit. Lists, like the seventeen rivers of Okuku (see Note 3 to Chapter 5), and incorporated genres like *arọ* (quoted in Chapter 3) can produce even longer 'units' than this. One unit and the next may have nothing, except a putative internal coherence, to make them comparable. Structurally as well as thematically they may be quite unlike; and when passages are borrowed from other genres, remaining recognisable as such, there may be an impression of shifting modes between one passage and the next.

'Units' that are as heterogeneous as this are not easy to identify with confidence. It is not always possible to decide whether a sequence of lines really goes together, forming a coherent block, or not. People experience and remember them differently, and what to one person is an invariable sequence may not be to another. Moreover, some performers – those who are most skilful and experienced – will deliberately break up patterned sequences of text, inserting interjections of other *oriki*, or simply quoting the first line of a passage and leaving the rest to the hearer to supply. She may come back to it and treat it more fully later in the performance, or she may leave the quotation uncompleted. *Oriki orilẹ*, the best-known and most highly patterned of *oriki*, are most often treated like this. Thus even though there are a great many extensive and coherent passages in *oriki*, there is nothing that cannot be broken up. Almost any utterance and almost any *part* of an utterance can thus be juxtaposed with any other.

This is possible not just because of the autonomous origins of each 'unit', but because the *style* of *oriki* is disjunctive. There is a general absence of connectives even within semantically coherent passages. This makes the component parts of any utterance potentially free-standing; grammatically, they are self-sufficient even when semantically they are not. The following two lines from the *oriki* of *ile* Ọba are a unit in the sense of having a single total meaning; when someone says the first line people will automatically complete it with the second. Nevertheless the four clauses that make it up are left unconnected:

Mo kọ́wẹ̀, mi ì kọ́jó
Mo wáá kọ́jó tán, ijó ń yọ mí lẹ́nu.

I learnt to swim, I didn't learn to dance
I finished learning to dance, dancing was a nuisance.

The sense of the passage is this: being a member of the royal family, which 'owns' the River Ọtin and other major rivers flowing past the town, the subject is credited with having been able to swim even before he or she could dance. Having learnt to dance, however, the subject has become so good at it that she or he is never allowed to rest; thus dancing has become a 'burden' – an ironical way of saying that it was his or her pride and joy. The implication is that the subject is admired, the centre of attention, as in other similar passages discussed in Chapter 6. This passage is made up of four short sentences, and with the possible exception of *wáá* in the third sentence, which has the suggestion of '*then* I finished learning to dance', there is no connective between any of them. The sentences are just jammed up against each other, the connections implied only by the requirements of the sense.

This kind of paratactic structure is highly characteristic of *oriki*. The coherence of a succession of statements is often implied not by explicit linking but by making them *parallel* to each other in structure, and *variants* of each other in meaning.[6] Even metaphor, which is nothing if not a fusion of ideas, is accomplished most often in *oriki* by a bare sequence of statements:

Ajé funfun ní í ṣẹrí owó
Ìlẹ̀kẹ̀ funfun ní í ṣẹrí olórìṣà
Ọmọ tí mo bá wù ó bí
Èmi Àbíkẹ́ Ọmọ́tánbàjẹ́
Mo mọ̀mọ̀ ní un ni yóó ṣẹríì mi.[7]

Silver coins bear witness to wealth
White beads bear witness to a worshipper
Whatever child I may bear
I, Abikẹ, 'The child put an end to disgrace',
I say, indeed, he will bear witness for me.

The formal simplicity of this passage of *rara iyawo* conceals a comparison based on a polysemic use of *ṣẹrí*, to bear witness, vouch for or testify to. *Ajé funfun ní í ṣẹrí owó*: 'White wealth vouches for money', that is, the shining silver appearance of coins shows their genuineness and value, and they in turn bear witness to the wealth of their possessor. *Ìlẹ̀kẹ̀ funfun ní í ṣẹrí olórìṣà*: 'White beads vouch for the devotee', that is, the beads worn by the *oriṣa* worshipper testify to her membership of a cult, being a public and incontrovertible mark of her identity as a genuine devotee. *Ọmọ tí mo bá wù ó bí… un ni yóò sẹ̀rìí mi*: the child the bride hopes to have will be proof that she is a genuine wife, a complete woman, and the child, by resembling the father, will testify to her fidelity. *Ajé funfun* (white or silver coins) and *ilẹ̀kẹ̀ funfun* (white beads), both of which are shining, valuable and beautiful things, are being used metaphorically to suggest the beauty and value of the child. The relation in which these things stand to their owners, as testimonies to their genuineness, is also transferred metaphorically to the relation between child and mother. But the *form* of this passage is merely three parallel statements, the third one being elaborated at greater length and thus showing that it is the key statement, the others being preparation and support for it. Formally, the passage is identical to those discussed in Chapter 5, in which a 'slot' is prepared for a key emblem of an *orílẹ*. In those passages, the parallel sequences of statements were *not* metaphorical. For example, in the passage just reviewed, 'If a goat/Is lost at Omu…', the goat, sheep and chicken are not *metaphors* for the *orílẹ* emblem, the horse, they are rather *precursors* of it. The kind of relationship between the structurally-parallel statements is in both cases left unstated. The difference in the nature of the implied links is not visible in the form.

Parts of utterances, therefore, often have the capacity to stand alone. Sometimes they continue to imply the rest of the utterance, but sometimes they detach themselves and function differently in a new context. Rather than seeing an *oriki* text as a 'whole', divisible into a number of discrete 'parts', it might be more productive to see the performance as a process of juxtaposing elements from a repertoire of utterances which *float*: that is, elements which make sense when taken on their own but which can be brought into conjunction with other elements in variable combinations and variable contexts, acquiring new meanings in the process. Unlike in the epics which are the basis of Parry and Lord's oral formulaic theory, these recombinations are not restricted by the requirements of a narrative line. The 'units' are rarely entirely discontinuous, but they are equally rarely glued permanently together. The possibilities open to the performer are great, but her methods of combination and selection are far from random. Let me illustrate this with passages from a performance by Ṣangowẹmi in honour of Jayeọla, the father of the blind *babalawo* Gbọtifayọ discussed in Chapter 6 and Ṣangowẹmi's own great-great-grandfather. One of Jayeọla's *oriki* is *aláyà ló lògán*, 'It is the courageous person who gets the anthill'. This is a proverb-like formulation meaning 'Only a daring person can seize the opportunity to get what he or she wants'. It could be applied to other subjects than Jayeọla, but for some reason – perhaps because it was a favourite saying of his – it has become specially associated with him. This is how it occurs the first time in Ṣangowẹmi's chant:

Ọmọ Àlàdé aláyà ló lògán
Ayéṣemí abiṣuú-yagbá-oge

Child of Alade, 'It is the courageous person who gets the anthill'
Ayeṣemi, owner of yams that break the girls' calabashes

The second line commends Jayeọla (Ayeṣemi) for having a farm that produces yams so large, or in such large quantities, that they break the calabashes in which the girls carry them home. Ṣangowẹmi goes on to develop the theme of the farm: 'If you see something huge, going right down to the river, that's Jayeọla's farm...' In this passage, the idea behind *aláyà ló lògán* has nothing much to do with the idea of *abiṣuú-yagbá-oge*. They deal with separate aspects of Jayeọla's reputation. But they are held together by their similarity of form. The nominalising prefix *ab-* in *abiṣuú-yagbá-oge* is equivalent in structure and function to the nominalising prefix *al-* in *aláyà ló lògán*.

Later in the performance, however, she pairs *aláyà ló lògán* with a different second line:

Àlàdé, aláyà ló lògán
Gbogbo ojo ó máa kó tilé Agbàá lọ

Alade, 'it's the courageous person who gets the anthill'
Let all the cowards go off to Agbaa or somewhere

Here the structure of the second line is quite different from that of the first, but in meaning it is a continuation of it. The brave get the prizes: cowards should go off, no-one cares where. (This is the interpretation Ṣangowẹmi herself gave; it seems possible, however, that at one time, or to certain people, the reference to Agbaa – a town in the Ọsun area – had a more specific meaning.) Thus in each case *aláyà ló lògán* seems to 'go with' the line that follows it, the first time because it matches structurally, the second time because it follows semantically. And *aláyà ló lògán* could equally well be interjected into a passage as a free-standing epithet having no formal *or* semantic link with the lines surrounding it.

As fragments of text are juxtaposed, the skilled performer often makes temporary adjustments to accommodate them. These adjustments do not always involve structural parallelism or semantic continuity, as in the examples just given. All kinds of links can be extended. Compare the following two passages, from the same Jayeọla text:

(a) Ìjìí jà wọn ò gbọ́lọ
    Ẹ̀fúùfù lẹ̀lẹ̀ wọn ò gbókè
    Ìjí jáko ó yan
    Jayéọlá, Oyèédòkun, babaà mi akọ̀ikọ̀i ẹkùn

    The storm rages, it cannot carry away the grinding stone
    The gentle breeze cannot carry away the hill
    The monkey robbed the farm, it swaggered
    Jayeọla, Oyedokun, my father the ferocious leopard

(b) Ọmọ ìjìí jà wọn ò gbọ́lọ
Ẹ̀fúùfù lẹ̀lẹ̀ wọn ò gbókè
Bi ó wu ẹ̀fúùfù lẹ̀lẹ̀, Àyìndé, ní í darí ìgbẹ́ sí
Bi ó wu olówó ẹni ní í ránni...

Child of 'The storm rages, it cannot carry away the
  grinding stone'
'The gentle breeze cannot carry away the hill'
Wherever the gentle breeze wishes, Ayinde, it can turn the
  treetops
Wherever a master wishes he can send his slave...

Both of these passages begin with a pair of lines which are a standard formulation in *oriki* to praise unassailability: the subject, like an immoveable hill or a grinding stone, cannot be shifted by the attacks of his enemies. The first passage then proceeds *Ìjí jáko ó yan*... The link here is the similarity in sound, between *ìjìí jà* (the storm rages) and *ìjí já [oko]* (the monkey plucks [fruits from the farm]). The monkey, robbing the farm and then swaggering away with impunity, is another familiar image of the big man's power – his ability to do outrageous things and get away with it. The last line then goes with the preceding one because it is another animal image – a leopard – this time suggesting the terrifying and ferocious aspect of the big man's power.

But in the second passage, Ṣangowẹmi picks up not the sound of *ìjìí jà* but the sense of *ẹ̀fúùfù lẹ̀lẹ̀* (the gentle breeze), and she goes on to elaborate the idea of the breeze into a metaphor for a great master, whose servants bow to his behest as the trees do to the wind. Notice however that though the words '*ẹ̀fúùfù lẹ̀lẹ̀*' carry through, providing a kind of continuity, their *import* is actually reversed as she moves from one idea to the next. In the opening lines the subject is like a mountain, and his *enemies* are like the wind, powerless to move the mountain. But in the subsequent lines, the *subject* is like the wind, and his bondsmen are like the treetops which even a gentle breeze can bend. Both, of course, are images of power, but in the first it is the power to *withstand* the wind, and in the second it is the power *of* the wind, that is attributed to the subject. It is as if Ṣangowẹmi were suddenly reminded by the phrase *ẹ̀fúùfù lẹ̀lẹ̀* of another chunk of *oriki*, and veers off into it letting the word association stand as the only link. In this way the performer can take off in different directions from the same chunk of text, stringing the next bit on with the most temporary and tenuous of connections.

Sometimes utterances take on a new significance when they appear in new textual surroundings. There is a good example in another performance, this time by Faderera, where the phrase *Eléyín ní í jogún ẹ̀rín* recurs several times. This is a proverb-like expression meaning, literally, 'The owner of teeth is the one who gets the inheritance of laughter', that is, 'It's the person with beautiful teeth who benefits from laughing'. Attributed to a subject, as a free-standing *oriki* unit, it would be taken to be praise of his or her appearance and cheerfulness, embodied in a dazzling smile. But at one point in Faderera's chant, she hooked it into a context where it did other work. It became an extremely subtle image for an abstract notion of mutuality:

> Bàbáà mi Àkàndé mo ríbà orin-ìn rẹ kí n tó máa báré lọ
> Eè ní í hun mí, ìran bàbáà mi ní í ṣawo
> Ẹ̀kú dìran ọ̀jẹ̀, ọ̀jẹ́ dìran ẹ̀kú o
> Eléyín ní í jogún èrín
> Ki ní yìí dìran baba tó bí mi.

> My father Akande I pay homage to your song before I go on with
>   my performance
> It will not bring retribution on me, my father's lineage is one of
>   diviners
> The masquerade costume is of the *ọjẹ* entertainers, the *ọjẹ*
>   entertainers are of the masquerade costume
> The owner of teeth is the one who inherits laughter
> This thing belongs to the lineage of my father who begot me.

This is the performer's customary acknowledgement of her predecessors and teachers. Her performance is her father's, to whom she pays homage. She prays that it will bring no ill-effects, stating that oral performance is an attribute of her father's people. The masquerade costume belongs to the *ọjẹ*, that is the lineages associated with *egungun* entertainment; the *ọjẹ* in turn are defined as a group by their association with the masquerade costume – they 'belong' to the costume just as the costume 'belongs' to them. In the same way, having white teeth predisposes one to laughter, just as laughter displays the teeth. The skill she is displaying in performance both derives from, and is justified by, her membership of a lineage of *babalawo*. For that reason, she says, her father's spirit will ensure that she does it well and without shame.

As in the earlier example, the complex metaphorical relationships in this passage are only *implied* by the contiguity of a number of independent statements. The repetition of the key word *iran* (lineage, generation) establishes a semantic continuity between the second and third lines. It also establishes a semantic parallelism between the third and fifth lines, of the form 'The costume belongs to the lineage of entertainers..."this thing" [i.e. oral performance] belongs to the lineage of my father'. *Eléyín ní í jogún èrín*, the phrase under discussion, is inserted between these two matching lines, and this allows its abstract meaning to emerge. It functions here as an image of a kind of mutuality or self-reinforcement. Like the apparently simple but actually subtle evocation of the relations between costume, masquerader and lineage (*ẹ̀kú dìran ọ̀jẹ̀, ọ̀jẹ́ dìran ẹ̀kú*) the phrase *eléyín ní í jogún èrín* looks like a standard praise-epithet but functions as a profound metaphor for the relationship between the performer's art and her father's lineage. But a few minutes later she uses the same expression again, as an ordinary free-standing unit of praise commending the subject's attractive smile.

There is often a shifting, drifting effect in *oriki* as potentially 'free' utterances are brought into and out of contiguity with each other. There is a haunting example in the chant for the dead Ṣango priestess, discussed in Chapter 4. One passage of this text runs:

> Ẹfúntóhún alọ́tílẹ́mu
> Ọmọ a-rínú-mutí-òjó, ọmọ alọ́tílẹ́mu
> Báṣẹ́ bá mumi á tán nínú rẹ
> Àgèrè tó bá mumi á jòólẹ̀
> Oníṣàngó Àrìnké máa bómi lọ, èmi óò máa ṣọfẹ
> Ẹfúntóhún máa bómi lọ, èmi óò máa ṣọfẹ
> Báṣẹ́ bá mumi á sì tán nínú aṣẹ́
> Àrìnké bígèrè tó bá mumi á jòólẹ̀
> Amẹmu tí ń bẹ lókè Agà o, Ẹfúntóhún ní í ṣe, 'mọ alọ́tílẹ́mu.[8]

> Ẹfuntohun, one who has both liquor and palm wine
> Child of one who has the stomach for drinking liquor daily, child of one who has both liquor and palm wine
> If the sieve drinks water, it will all run out
> The woven fish-trap, if it drinks water, it will leak away
> Ṣango-worshipper Arinkẹ, go with the water, I will stay and lament
> Ẹfuntohun go with the water, I will stay and lament
> If the sieve drinks water, it will all run out
> Arinkẹ, if the woven fish-trap drinks water it will leak away
> The palm-wine drinker who is up at Aga, it's Ẹfuntohun, child of one who has both liquor and palm wine.

This passage begins by hailing Ẹfuntohun with the personal *oriki* 'one-who-has-both-liquor-and-palm-wine' and 'child of [i.e. associated with] one who has the stomach for drinking liquor daily': the *oriki* of a flamboyant, generous and wealthy figure in the town. The verb *mu* (to drink) is picked up from the second line and becomes the pivot on which the performer now turns her chant in a new direction. The next two lines are a well-known proverbial formulation to the effect that it is no use trying to keep water in an open wickerwork structure like a sieve or a fish-trap. It is used to convey the hopelessness or fruitlessness of a given undertaking. In the context of this chant, performed immediately after the death of Ẹfuntohun, it expresses a sense of loss and suggests the impossibility of imprisoning and detaining a departing soul. Life is like the water which leaks ineluctibly away. In line five, however, it is the word *omi* [water] which has become the pivotal one. The water is now pictured not as a measurable quantity escaping a small container, but as a great river which carries the dead away to the other world. The performer says farewell to Ẹfuntohun as she is swept off, promising to stay (on the riverbank) and lament her passing. She then retraces the steps by which she has arrived at this image, returning first to the sieve and fish-trap and then to the drinking of palm wine and liquor. The imagery of liquidity, of draining and flowing, establishes a consistent ambiance appropriate to the theme of loss, grief, change and death. But the way one 'unit' gives way to another seems adventitious rather than in conformity to some prior overall schema. The performer seems herself to be drifting in the stream of her own utterance, and eddies carry her now this way, now that.

So although it is a necessary starting point in the analysis, the notion of the autonomous, self-sufficient unit does not take us all that far. Almost any verbal formulation in *oriki* can be broken off, made to stand on its own, and jammed up against other formulations in a manner which positively exaggerates the discontinuity between them. In this sense the style of *oriki* is essentially disjunctive. But almost any gap, by the same token, can be bridged. The links may be solid planks of structural symmetry, laid out in parallelism and repetition. Or they may be so fragile as to look like sleight of hand on the performer's part: a single stray word, not prominent in one unit, may become the key word of the next, or a chance resemblance in sound may be enough to set her off in a new direction.

The predominant impression is of utterances that 'go together' in one way or another without having been composed exclusively *for* each other. In *oriki orilẹ* there is a higher proportion than in other kinds of *oriki* of solid and enduring bridges, producing long patterned sequences. In personal *oriki* there is a greater tendency for the links to be tenuous and for the text to seem to shift from moment to moment. There are also great differences in performers' styles: some performers produce far more gaps than others.

In the process of becoming habituated to the chanting of *oriki*, the performer becomes familiar not only with the textual materials on which she will draw but also with ways of moving on within a chant. If her materials are a repertoire of potentially or actually free-standing utterances, not grammatically linked to the utterances that co-exist with them in her repertoire, then her skill is to play with disjunction. The underlying presence of the gap is the grounds and condition of possibility of her art. It is the gap which makes her performance exciting, as she throws out one fragile and temporary bridge after another. There are no *rules* about how this is to be done. But the infinite variety and unpredictability of her practice is produced by what Bourdieu (1977) has called a 'disposition' that derives from a few basic principles.[9] Any kind of resemblance (including opposition and strong contrast) can be used to bring two utterances into conjunction: syntactic, semantic, lexical, tonal; through sound, through structure or through meaning. The resemblance can amount to almost complete identity, or it can be so faint as to be almost imperceptible. It can be in one aspect only, in several or in all. The more definite the resemblance is, the more the sequence will tend to 'stick', becoming fixed in the performer's mind and always performed – by her at least – in the same order. But even in strongly stuck-together sets of lines, the performer can break in, with interjected passages, or break off, curtailing the passage altogether.

The more skilled a performer is, the more she will produce conjunctions and juxtapositions which create tension. If too many lines resemble each other too strongly – if there is too much obvious parallelism and patterning – the performance is felt to be dull. This is why old people in Okuku would complain about young girls' performances of *rara iyawo*, which tended to consist of long stretches of highly patterned *oriki orile* without interjections or interruptions to relieve the monotony. If not enough lines resemble each other, on the other hand, the chant is said to be superficial, presumably because it is so fragmented that it seems incapable of holding any deep information. This was a comment made about Ṣangowẹmi sometimes. She broke off, interjected and changed course so much that some people felt that she never got to the heart of the *oriki*. The women whose performances were most highly regarded were the older wives who had become experts in their households and led the chanting in public and domestic ceremonies without being regarded as entertainers or professionals. These women's performances balanced difference and resemblance, disjunction and continuity, in a way that called attention to the excitement of *risk* that lay at the centre of the poetic project. There always seemed to be the possibility that the singer would come to a stop, that a gap would extend itself and, becoming uncrossable, would end in silence. This often actually happened with young and inexperienced performers. Slightly more experienced ones, instead of breaking down completely, would carry on by fits and starts as new items occurred to them. But skilful singers seemed deliberately to play on this fear, throwing up gaps in the act of crossing them. The goal seems to be to maintain an intensity of disjunctiveness. From moment to moment, the performer extends slender threads of connection which are no sooner made than abandoned, one congruence no sooner proposed than left behind while the performer moves on to another. It is this that gives *oriki* chants their characteristic weaving, shifting, fragmenting and merging quality so fascinating to listen to. Thus the mode in which the text is constructed is the means by which it fulfils its function of merging personalities and crossing gaps between beings in the act of asserting their unique individuality.

4. THE *ORIKI* OF WOMEN

Women's public faces are less differentiated than those of men. The past of Okuku is thickly populated with colourful, idiosyncratic big men, remembered in affectionate detail for their witticisms, their oddities and their achievements.

Though everyone agrees that there were big women too, their personalities rarely emerge in stories about the past. They are as if submerged in the family or cult in which they operated. At any celebration, the relative social prominence of men and women will be easy to observe. The big men, heavy, authoritative, individual, few in number, sit as if enthroned. Their faces are memorable, their names readily imparted to the visitor. They drink beer and eat pounded yam. In some other room, or out in the corridor, sit a long row of women. They will be on the floor, they will be eating *ęko*, they will be drinking Fanta or at best palm wine. They do not spring out as individual personalities. It is much harder to find out who is who. When people attempt to distinguish them in conversation, it is often through their husband or their cult [*'ìyàwó Làágbé – èyí kékeré tó sèsè kó sódò rè'* ('the wife of Laagbe – the young one who's just come to his house'), *'ìyá Ọlótìn ilé Olùọdę'*: 'the Ọtin woman of *ile* Oluọdę')]. Women undertake their public duties in large groups. At every funeral and festival, teams of women in *'ankoo'* go in procession round the town. Daughters who have married bring back groups of thirty or forty of their 'co-wives' to important family events, and no festivity can go forward without an influx of female relatives to collect firewood, cook the food and serve the guests. Women are publicly visible mainly as members of a female crowd (one reason, no doubt, why many people believe that women outnumber men in the proportion of five to one – a statistic always cited in justification of polygyny!).

However, despite their lesser social salience, women do become the object of attention as individuals from time to time. A woman can be the principal 'celebrant' on certain occasions (for instance, at a funeral, if she is the daughter of the deceased; at a festival, if she is a priestess of the cult; at a wedding, if she is the bride). On these occasions *oriki* will be addressed to her. In most cases, however, these *oriki* will be *oriki orilę* or the *oriki* of her father or other ancestors. In most modern events this is of course true of men as well: the appellation slides quickly over the here-and-now subject to layers of other subjects that stand behind him in the past. But the point is that almost all the personal *oriki* thus attributed through living people to dead ones or from dead ones to the living are the personal *oriki* of men. It is unusual to find personal *oriki* of women. If a woman is saluted through her dead mother, it will be the mother's *oriki orilę* – the *oriki* of group membership – not individual, idiosyncratic, personal *oriki* that are heard. The *oriki* that are composed for women tend to be salutations of motherhood in general, applicable to all mothers, not to differentiated individuals. Women can be praised for suffering the pains of childbirth and the drudgery of motherhood, or for producing one good son rather than thirty useless ones. The commemoration of unique personalities is not developed as it is in the *oriki* addressed to men.

But a few women do have personal *oriki*. In those that I have been able to find, there are two strongly marked characteristics. The first is that the woman's claim to fame is expressed at least partly in terms of the man she married or the children she bore. The second, however, is that apart from this emphasis, these *oriki* are not essentially different from those of men. The same conception of power, the same qualities of character are portrayed in the same idiom. The 'first' Iyalode, wife of Winyọmi of *ile* Oluọdẹ, was saluted thus:

> Dúródọlá n ló jẹyálóde nílé olórí ọdẹ
> Ìsokùnrónkẹ́ ìyákọ mi, Ògé-Ìmẹ́lẹ́
> Afòórọ̀ jorí ẹja
> Ìyákọ mi a-rọ̀-mìnì joyè Arẹ̀sà
> Kò bẹ́nikan ṣòrẹ́
> Dúródọlá tọba ní í ṣe
> Ọ̀pẹ́lẹ́ngẹ́ Olókukù Dúródọlá ọmọlójú Olúọdẹ.[10]

> Durodọla was the Iyalode in the house of the Head of the Hunters
> Isokunronkẹ my husband's mother, Ọgẹ-Imẹlẹ
> One who rises to eat the heads of fish
> My husband's mother, one who is so good-looking she takes the
>   title of Arẹsa
> She makes friends with no-one
> Durodọla takes the ọba's part
> The slender friend of the Olokuku, Durodọla the favourite wife of
>   the Head of the Hunters.

Durodọla is introduced as the Iyalode 'in the house of the Head of the Hunters', and at the end of the passage the reference is amplified to 'Durodọla the favourite wife of the Head of the Hunters'. Her position as wife and her good standing in the eyes of her husband are felt to be significant. But Durodọla is clearly also a great figure in the town in her own right. The same qualities are vaunted, and by the same rhetorical ploys, as in men's personal *oriki*. Durodọla lives in a wealthy household (she rises to eat the heads of fish, a rich diet). She is beautiful, and the beauty implies qualities of personality – calm, sufficiency, magnetism – which attracts to her a senior title. She knows her own mind, stands aloof, 'makes friends with no-one' (that is, forms no political alliances within the town), but rather stays loyal to the ọba, earning his affection.

Personal *oriki* of women, like those of men, affirm simultaneously their subject's good background and her capacity to stand out against that background, surpassing all those who surround her. A daughter of *ile* Aro-Isalẹ, said to have married the early ọba Adeọba (but possibly one of Adeọba's royal descendants), was given these *oriki*:

> Eníkẹ̀ẹ́jìnmí ńkọ́, Mogbéọlá àbẹ̀bẹ̀ ṣọ̀ṣọ́ ọmọ ọrọ̀ nÍsàn
> Eníkẹ̀ẹ́jìnmí ọmọ adókọ níbi owó gbé so
> Àbẹ̀bẹ̀ ṣọ̀ṣọ́ n tíìbí ò jẹ́ ó rókọ ní

Ó wáá ṣe kẹ́lẹ́, ó wáá bóólé Adéọba
Àrìnkẹ́ aláragbàídá
Ó yọ nínú ẹgbẹ́ da daa da
A-ṣènìyàn-lakùn-bí-ilẹ̀kẹ̀
Àìmọ̀ójó ni í jálejòó jó
Ìyá mi Àrìnkẹ́ lè jó jàlejò lọ
Ọmọ títẹ́ lewé ata
Ògògò Àrán ọmọ ekòló yọ̀
N̄bi ó wu Àrìnkẹ́ n ló ṣòfẹ́ è lọ
N ló i relé Adéọba o
Ó wáá ṣòfẹ́ rèPo
Ó wÀrìnkẹ́ iye wa ó ṣòfẹ́ rÒfà
Ó wÀrìnkẹ́ n ló ṣòfẹ́ rèJágbó
Gbà ó wÀrìnkẹ́ n ló ṣòfẹ́ è relé ọba...[11]

What about Enikẹẹjinmi, Mogbeọla, one whom we plead with to
    dress up, child of 'Wealth at Isan'
Enikẹẹjinmi, child of one who finds lovers where money is plenty
One whom we plead with to dress up, one whose family [status]
    prevented her from finding a husband
She proceeded gently and arrived at the house of [i.e. married]
    Adeọba
Arinkẹ one who has everything anyone could want
She stands out among her peers most distinctly
She's a person who stands out like the middle bead in a string
Not knowing how to dance allows the visitors to dance
My mother Arinkẹ knows how to dance better than the visitors
Child of 'The pepper leaf spreads'
Real native of Aran, child of 'The worm rejoices'
Arinkẹ can go masquerading wherever she likes
So she went to the house of Adeọba
She went entertaining to Ipo
Our mother Arinkẹ felt like going entertaining to Ọfa, so she went
Arinkẹ felt like going entertaining to Ijagbo, so she went
And when she felt like it, she went entertaining to the house of the
    ọba.

Arinkẹ's greatest achievement, as represented here, is the fact that she
married the ọba. It is for this reason that she is remembered among her
descendants. But the metaphors with which the *oriki* establish her draw on the
same things as men's *oriki*. She comes from such a good family that it is hard
for her to find a suitable husband: but eventually (by 'proceeding gently') she
outdoes all her sisters and marries the ọba himself. Like Adeọba her husband
(see Chapter 6) she is compared to a bead which 'divides the string', i.e. stands

out conspicuously amongst her neighbours, and, again like him, she is noted for her superlative dancing. With a characteristic hairpin-bend effect, her *oriki* says that normally visitors get a chance to show off their dancing because the locals, not being experts, are shy; but Arinkẹ knows how to outdance even the visitors. In this passage, even the *oriki orilẹ* shared by all of *ile* Aro-Isalẹ (and also by *ile* Baalẹ and *ile* Balogun – see the Appendix) are adapted to make a personal comment about Arinkẹ. People of Aran, whose profession is *ojẹ* masquerading, are praised for their travels: wherever they go, they are welcomed and rewarded for their performances. These salutations can be applied to any 'child of Aran'; but Ṣangowẹmi, the performer of this chant, gives the attributions a final twist. Arinkẹ can travel anywhere and be well received: to Ajasẹ-Ipo, to Ọfa, to Ijagbo (all neighbouring towns to the north and east of Okuku), but eventually she 'goes entertaining' to the ọba's palace, and stays there as his wife. Even more than the Iyalode Durodọla, Arinkẹ is remembered for the man she married; but in other respects, these *oriki* are very close in tone and imagery to the personal *oriki* of big men. There are no recognisably 'women's *oriki*'.

Durodọla was famous as the Iyalode, the chief of the women. Arinkẹ was famous as the wife of the ọba. But one of the most important arenas in which women exercised power and influence were the cults. Asked about big women of the past, chief Ṣọbaloju said:

> Those whom we can call great women in the old days were those who practised traditional religion. They could say what was going to happen, and it would happen. There were many of them, in all cults. Some were greater than others. I don't know their names. They were devotees of Ọya, of Ọsun, of Ṣango, of Enlẹ, of Orisaala – all kinds.

The apparent anonymity of this exercise of power did not prevent people – men as well as women – from recognising its existence. Within the cults, great women devotees of the past are frequently commemorated in *oriki* performances. The idiom in which this is done is highly significant. Ẹrẹ-Ọsun, one of Ṣangowẹmi's age-mates and a skilled performer, was a member of the Erinlẹ cult. One of her predecessors in the cult was Awọrọka, whose role as ancestress of a large body of people has already been discussed in Chapter 5. The scattered descendants of Awọrọka recognise a relationship with each other through their common descent from her, though being a woman she did not create 'place' in a patrilineage which any of them could step into. What she did create, however, was cult responsibilities and powers. Awọrọka was Ẹrẹ-Ọsun's mother's mother, and Ẹrẹ-Ọsun describes her inheritance in the following terms:

Awórọká nì ń kì un
Òìsà tí ń bẹ lórí Awórọká nì ń kì un
Àwọn wáá lọ sídìí òrìsà àwọn

Wọ́n wáá lọ ní mìnimìni
Wọn ń lọ mínimíni
Olórí enímọ̀jèsí
Àwọn ló kọ́ n lÉnlẹ̀ ńlẹ̀ omi
Ó wáá lọ sọ́run kò dé mọ́ ẹbọra tọ́ ọ rí n ni ń báá jẹ
Àwọn ọ̀gá oníwòròògún o o o
Àwọn náà ló kọ́ mi ní òrokòto
Ó wáá dení
Ó dèjì
Ó dẹ̀ta
Ọ̀gá oníwòròògún tí ń bẹ lOyè-mokò
Ńlée Kọọkin
Àyàbù lọ́nà tèrò
Adébínpé
Alénrúurú orin lẹ́nu
Pààkáa bótèbótè
Adébínpé alónírúurú orin lẹ́nu
Àwọn ló kọ́ mi níwòròògún n ò ní í ṣiṣe
Mo kéré nnú òníwòròògún o
Àwọn náà ló rán n lóde n ò ní í ṣòde lọ...

Aworọka is the one I am saluting
It's the *orìṣa* upon Aworọka's head [i.e. that devolved upon her]
   that I am saluting
Then she went to the shrine of her *orìṣa*
She went dressed very neatly
She went all spick and span
Head of all the lesser cult members
It was she who taught me about Enlẹ at the bottom of the water
Then she went to heaven and didn't come back, she's dining there
   in the company of that spirit that you know of
She, the master of the praise-singers
It was she who imparted to me the gift of the gab
There was one
There were two
There were three
Masters of praise-singing at Oye-moko
In the town of Kọọkin
Where travellers stop to drink
Adebinpe
One who has all kinds of songs on her lips
Little masquerade that frays its lips with talking!
Adebinpe, one who has all kinds of songs on her lips

> She was the one who taught me praise-singing, I will not make any mistakes
>
> I am small among the praise-singers
>
> It was they who sent me out, I will not make any mistakes in my outing...

At the beginning of this passage the importance of inheritance of the *oriṣa* itself is referred to. Aworọka, a former devotee of the cult, now dead, is saluted in conjunction with her *oriṣa*, a manifestation of Erinlẹ: and it is explicitly stated that this manifestation was 'on her head', i.e. devolved upon her from some even earlier member of the cult. Aworọka was keeping open a place in the cult, a place now occupied by someone else. It is not just a slot in the cult membership that Aworọka left behind to be filled, but a relationship with the spiritual world – a relationship which her successor has a duty to maintain. And the second crucial feature of this situation is the fact that Aworọka is remembered, above all, for her gifts as a praise-singer. She is not just a matriarchal figure in the cult (*olori onimọjesi* – literally the head of all the mothers of toddlers, i.e. other female cult members); she is also *ọga oniworoogun*, the master of the vocalists. Ẹrẹ-Ọsun acknowledges Aworọka as the one from whom she has inherited place: the place belonging to a leading vocalist in the cult. She pays tribute by saying that Aworọka taught her everything, and that she herself is a novice. It is only by the good will and protective beneficence of Aworọka and the other expert vocalists of former times (she prepares at one point to name two others, but does not do so) that she can carry out her assignment without mishap.

It is common in all *oriki* performances for the performer to acknowledge his or her teacher. But the text just quoted goes further than this. It suggests that the cult itself is conceived in terms of great chanters. Ẹrẹ-Ọsun of this text was not a specialist performer who would routinely pay homage to her predecessors in the praise-singing profession. Neither was her subject, Aworọka. Aworọka's prominence arose rather from her position as a senior member of the Erinlẹ cult. But her position in the cult was conceived in terms of her mastery of the cult chant. The past of the Erinlẹ devotees, that is, is seen as the transmission not so much of title or office but of a capacity to communicate. The great devotees are those who can best cross boundaries between mortal beings and spiritual ones.

If women 'are not interested in being known' in public, one reason may be, as suggested in Chapter 6, that in women's careers reputation cannot play the same role in the cycle of self-aggrandisement as it does in men's; it is therefore dangerously liable to turn sour, to become a reputation for evil. But an underlying, less easily elicited explanation is that women's power is acknowledged but not made visible in the development of public personality, as among men, because women are above all the mediators and the knowers.

If it is they who link compounds through marriage, it is also they who are in charge of the channels of utterance through which powers flow between beings. So when women do have *oriki*, these *oriki* dwell on the woman's mediating role as wife or mother; or on her mastery of the oral arts that open the boundaries between humans and spirits, living and dead. A master of the vocalists does not need to be a publicly recognised figure, for it is her activity which creates the conditions of possibility for the development of all public personalities and for their enhancement through contacts with the spiritual world.

But women who do have their own *oriki* participate in the public idiom of power and grandeur. There is no women's style, no special womanly content. Women can be as tough, proud, magnificent, and rich as men. Their *oriki*, though not as extensive as those of men, affirm that they can do what men do. Oya is called '*Obìnrin gbònà, okùnrin sá*': the woman blocks the road and men flee. If *orisa* are created by the same process as big men (see Barber, 1981b), then mighty female *orisa* tell us something about the way human female power is construed. Unlike in many traditional African cultures, the Yoruba world is not dichotomised into clearly distinct male and female sectors. The rigid pairs of correspondences that appear in so many accounts of African cosmology[12] are not on view here. The house is not divided, nor is the mental world carved into male and female domains. Gender classifications are not organised in a fixed schema: they are ambiguous and fluctuating.[13] This, again, must be understood in terms of the importance placed in the culture upon the maintenance of a multiplicity of differences and alternatives.

5. PROFUSION AND DIFFERENCE

Okuku, like other Yoruba towns, was and is a highly differentiated society. The traditional political structures, as we saw in Chapter 6, are hierarchical, and day-to-day life is based on the fundamental and radical distinction between a person's inferiors and his or her superiors. There was highly developed occupational specialisation, and goods were produced for trade far afield as well as for domestic consumption. Blacksmithing, carving, drumming and weaving were, and to some extent still are, the inherited occupations of particular *ile*, providing, as *oriki orile* show, one of the cornerstones of their identity. Personal *oriki*, as we saw in Chapter 6, make much of individuals' excellence in specialised skills: there are *oriki* for brilliant diviners, exceptional hunters, and outstanding masqueraders and medicine men. There was marked differentiation through cult membership, which set up strongly solidary groups that usually cut across membership of an *ile*. There was not one single mode of self-aggrandisement to which all big men conformed, but a variety of routes to position in society, all of which would be cited by the big men's admirers with equal satisfaction. The big man could be a war leader like Omikunle, or a leader of civic action like Idowu who, though young and untitled, led the opposition to Iba during the boundary dispute through sheer nerve and bravado. He could make his way in the world through diplomacy, like Aaṣa, Oyinlọla's messenger who was given a high title as a reward for his indispensable tact. He could be wealthy but uninvolved in intrigue, like Alapẹpẹsile, or a powerful intriguer not noted for his wealth, like Fawande. He could gain a following through his powers as a hunter and defender of the community, like Winyọmi and Olugbẹdẹ, or because he could cure people's illnesses, like Ajayi of *ile* Arogun. If there was a historical shift in what was regarded as the ideal, one thing that remained constant was the profusion of alternative avenues to greatness. All the horizontal differences are vigorously advertised. Big men advertise their unique personalities, cults insist that they are different from other cults, *ile* affirm that they do not resemble other *ile*. In every domain there is an insistence on difference and division.

The principle of vertical social inequality is represented in *oriki* in a formulaic pattern which is taken completely for granted, so that it normally would scarcely call attention to itself: the triad *ẹru/iwọfa/ọmọ bibi inu* (slave/bondsman/free-born child). This schematised tripartite structure stands, in an oblique way, for hierarchy itself rather than for the actual social divisions that are most significant in real life. But if hierarchy is 'automatised' in formulas like this, it is also consciously reflected upon and affirmed in *oriki* chants. Social difference is represented as a fact of nature; inequality is represented as a feature that humanity shares with the whole of the known world, whether natural or cultural:

> Sányán ni baba aṣọ
> Àlàárì ni baba ẹ̀wù
> Yánkàtà ni baba àgbàdo
> Ìyànrìngobí baba 'yánrin
> Kètènkèrí baba odòkódò
> Bá à bá ní í purọ́, ọkùnrín pọ̀ juraa wọn lọ

> *Sanyan* silk is the best of all cloths
> *Alaari* cloth makes the best of all gowns
> The giant-grained maize cobs are the best of all maize
> The *iyanringobi* vegetable is better than ordinary *yanrin*
> Ketenkeri river is the father of all rivers
> If we are not to tell a lie, some men are greater than others.

Baba, which means 'father of...' also implies 'superior to...'. Thus an inevitable relationship, that of parenthood, is subsumed into, and made to stand for, a larger notion of hierarchy. Fatherhood appears as a specific case of a universal, inescapable vertical stratification which embraces nature [rivers as the superiors of their tributaries, the large *iyanrin* plant (*Lactuca capensis*) as the best of its type], cultivated crops (big-grained maize as superior to small) and human artefacts (high-grade *sanyan* as the best kind of silk, robes of red-dyed *alaari* cloth as the best of all robes). Against this backdrop the conclusion that 'some men are greater than others' appears inevitable.

Since the work of *oriki* is to effect *transitions* in status – to enhance the social size of their subject (in the case of a big man by confirming his claims to the regard of his following of 'people') – philosophical statements endorsing hierarchy must be understood in a dynamic not a frozen way. By asserting that 'If we are not to tell a lie, some men are greater than others', the performer is launching a very strong claim for her subject. She is asserting that he is important by nature, because he just *is* greater than his rivals. This statement is part of the competitive struggle. It does not indicate a fixed scheme of social relationships, it indicates that once a big man *has* succeeded, the *oriki* singers will go to all lengths to legitimise and uphold his position.

But such statements about social inequality can also be read on another level, as an aspect of the permanent commitment, in *oriki*, to social and cultural *diversity* in every form. *Oriki orilẹ* are entirely dedicated to establishing and maintaining symbolic differences between social groups. Emblems of identity are inevitably assertions of difference. Personal *oriki* attempt to capture the distinctiveness of the individual, enshrined in idiosyncrasies and trivialities, as well as his conformity to public ideals. Each collection of personal *oriki* is like a thumb-print, confirming the possessor's common humanity and accountability to society while marking down his individual irreducible uniqueness. *Oriki* are positive and affirmative about difference. They often express a kind of gleeful delight in non-conformity. The masquerading lineage, for instance, rejoices in being released from the tedium of the normal agricultural cycle. While most of the population is bending over the soil, the masquerader is 'pointing his head about inside the cloth'. This alternative source of income gives him the freedom to neglect farm-work and, with characteristic exaggeration, the *oriki* suggests that he never does a stroke:

Apáà mi ò kúkú roko
Ẹ̀yìn mi ò tiẹ̀ bẹ̀rẹ̀
Bẹ́ẹ̀ ni mo fẹ́ ohun tó dùn ún lò
Bénìyàn ò mú mi lápá mú mi lẹ́sẹ̀ n ò lè tú gaga eéran
Gbogbo àgbè, Ilọ̀kọ̀í, ti lé ìdíhàn tán
Enígbòórí, mo lémi ń ṣorí gogo lábẹ́ aṣọ...[14]

My arms are not accustomed to farm-work
And my back does not bend
But I do want things that are nice to use
If I'm not seized hand and foot
I can't pull up a single stalk of *eeran* grass
All the farmers, Ilọkọi, have finished their mulching
Enigboori, while I am pointing my head about inside the
    masqueraders' costume...

This sense of being different, of being out of step, is protected by an assertion that masquerading cannot do any harm to a lineage traditionally associated with it. The implication is that each social group is best served by its own inherited body of practices. Masquerading would not necessarily suit other people, but it suits the Enigboori:

Ẹ̀kú wọn kì í hun òjè
Mo ṣebí iṣu tá a bá sun kì í hun ọbẹ.

The costume never brings retribution on an *ọje* masquerader
I maintain that the yam we roast never brings retribution on the
    knife.

It is an axiom of this culture, expressed in other genres as well as *oriki*, that the town's work is composed of a range of different specialisations, each of which has its own characteristic implements and techniques and each of which provides its practitioners with a separate path to success. An Ifa verse says:

Ojúmọ́ mọ́, olówò gbówòo rẹ̀
Rànwú-rànwú
Wọn rèé gbé kẹ̀kẹ́
Rokoroko
Wọ́n kọ́kọ́ roko
Jagunjagun
Wọ́n gbápata ogun
Hunṣo-hunṣo
Wọ́n bẹ̀rẹ̀ gbáṣà
Bójú bá mọ́ mo mọ̀ gbáròyéè mi
Àròyé lèmi óò ṣe là nílé ayé.[15]

Day breaks, the trader takes up his trade
The spinners
Go to take up their spindles
The farmers
Take their hoes to the farm
The warriors
Take up their war shields
The weavers
Bend to take up their combs
When day breaks I begin my talking
Talking is how I, for my part, will get rich in the world.

'Talking' here refers to the *babalawo*'s command of divinatory and incantatory utterances. People all have their own métier, their own chosen route to achieving the same common goals of wealth and honour. One of the functions of Ifa is indeed to direct people to the specialisation that will best suit their *Ori* (luck, destiny) and will best reward them. There is no suggestion of caste, of a generally agreed ranking of the various occupations. Each is best for its own practitioners.

The same attitude informs people's attachment to their *oriṣa*. Difference between spiritual beings is significant not so much for the production of a comprehensive 'cosmology' as because what is good for one devotee may not be good for another. Indeed, the efficacy of the relationship depends precisely upon its particularity. It is because this *oriṣa* is 'mine' that it will bless me. Devotees go out of their way, in *oriki*, to deny their association with other people's objects of devotion. The Ọtin worshipper says she will have nothing to do with children given by medicine men and herbalists, all she wants is children from Ọtin, the Cool Water. The masquerading lineages say they don't get their children from Ifa but from *egungun*:

> Ògbórí me ì í yà lójú ọpọ́n
> Eégún ní í yamọ lọ́wọ́ọ wa.

> Ogbori, I never appear in the utterances of Ifa
> It is *egungun* that provide us with offspring.

The *oriṣa* themselves are credited with similar differences in their spheres of interest and in their tastes. Each has its own special food, for instance, and the different preferences of a list of four or five *oriṣa* are often cited in *oriki* and Ifa literature. The attitudes underlying these and other discriminations made in *oriki* are summed up in the well-known formulations dealing ostensibly with personal appearance, but with an application that goes well beyond it:

> Dúdú ẹlú yẹlú
> Pupa epo mépo lára.

> The darkness of indigo suits the indigo
> The redness of palm oil is what palm oil is used to.

and

> Kúkúrú ọká yọká
> Èjòlá fi gígùn ṣe rògbòdò.

> The shortness of the viper suits the viper
> The python combines length with hefty roundness.

In other words, every species, and by implication every person, has its own qualities which suit it but which would not suit others. What seems to be suggested is that beauty lies precisely in contrast. The difference between the palm oil and the indigo, the viper and the python, allows the proper beauty of each to be seen. Viewed from the standpoint of an individual, what he or she is, has and does is the best; her own *oriṣa* surpasses all others, his family occupation makes his family unique. But these elements are not fitted into a *general* cosmological hierarchy shared by the whole community. The whole point is that each individual and each group should be different and should have their own characteristics and properties. The contrasts are maintained because each individual, cult or lineage vigorously upholds the merits of its own properties.[16] *Oriki*, as a concatenation of independent 'voices', are a perfect embodiment of this ideology.

Furthermore, there is glory in profusion. The more contrasting and contesting elements the better. The value placed upon profusion is evident in every aspect of *oriki*. It is seen in the incorporation of materials from diverse sources; in the frequent lists (of names of rivers, uses to which palm trees can be put, etc.) and chain-like *arọ* sequences; in the constant repetition and recycling of elements to give them more mileage. Some of the motives underlying this impulse to multiplication have been discussed. If *oriki* are equivalents to names, and names imply qualities, reputation, and regard, then the more *oriki* attributed to a person the better. The sliding movement from the subject's own *oriki* to those of a host of other people provides the subject with a plenitude of 'people', the basis of social position. Similarly, in *oriki orilẹ*, if *oriki* represent the glory of the lineage, the more that is said the better; and if they represent lineage *connections*, as they also do, then the more lines of affiliation and descent the better. The mother's *orilẹ*, the grandmother's, the wife's and even the wife's mother's provide valuable lines of connection to potential influence and aid. Thus the continual proliferation of 'heads' of *oriki orilẹ* within a chant addressed to a single subject.

The impulse to profusion is inscribed in the innermost form of *oriki*. The most common rhetorical structure in *oriki* is a sequence of parallel cases, usually concluding with the key one. The nature or importance of (d) is established by the comparable, though in some respects contrasting, cases of (a), (b) and (c). Sometimes these sequences are based on standard lexical sets (okro/egg plant, vulture/hornbill, and so on) but sometimes they introduce original and wide-ranging comparisons. In a text of *rara iyawo*, one sequence juxtaposes humans, animals and artefacts to make a single point:

> Ìbí ní í jọlá ìbí
> Ẹni a bíni mọ́ ní í jọlá ẹni
> Ahere ń jọlá tiẹ̀ lóko
> Gòngò ń jẹ tirẹ̀ láàtàn
> Àgbẹ̀dẹ ń jọlá ẹmú
> Èmi mọ̀mọ̀ ń jọláa mọ̀mọ́ọ̀ mi
> Ire lónìí orîì mi àfire.[17]

The family enjoys the privileges of the family
Someone born among us enjoys the privileges of being one of us

The farm-hut enjoys its own privileges in the farm
The *gọngọ* worm enjoys his in the dung-hill
The forge enjoys the privileges of the pliers
And I enjoy the privileges of my mother
May good luck attend me today.

Thus to establish a claim, it is placed in parallel with several other statements of the same structural form. The existence of these parallels creates a rhetorical climate in which the real claim can be accepted as incontrovertible. The passage above boils down to 'Everything in creation enjoys the privileges of what pertains to it; I enjoy the privileges of my relationship to my mother'. This rhetorical strategy has the effect of continually reiterating the variety of the world and the separateness of its components: every entity or being has its *own* domain, and pays no attention to the domains of others. The paratactic structure bears this out. There is no attempt to unite the farm-hut, the worm, the forge and the mother into a single 'scene': each is a separate instance of a universal principle, and that principle is 'each unto his own'.

The disjunctive style of *oriki* makes possible the fullest expression of this principle. The chant does not subordinate one element to another or any elements to an overarching design which assigns each a determinate place in relation to the others. The chant is rather held together by the suspension of contrasting elements in juxtaposition with each other. As the chant proceeds, each element asserts itself and then drops out of sight as it is succeeded by another. Each, in turn, is centre stage, just as each big man, for as long as the performer addresses him, is the centre of attention. Though performers are adept at making their materials do different things, according to the nature of the occasion, these materials still retain a certain irreducible independence from the performer's intent and from each other. This allows something very interesting to happen. Though *oriki* may ostensibly be dedicated to upholding social difference in the interests of the successful, the voices of the downtrodden may still momentarily surface and assert themselves – partially but never fully co-opted into the project of the chant as instrument of social aggrandisement. The result is a most profound irony. In Ṣangowẹmi's salutation of Jayẹọla that was discussed earlier, the privilege of the big man Ayẹṣemi (Jayẹọla) is contrasted with the suffering of his servant, the *iwọfa*:

'Bi ó wu ẹfúùfù lẹ̀lẹ̀, Àyìnlá, ní í darí ìgbẹ́ sí
'Bi ó wu olówó ẹni ní í ránni
Olówó wáá mọbi ẹ̀gún, ò ro
Ni wọn ń ki Jayéọlá babaa wa
Babaà mi, ìwọ̀fà tibi ẹ̀gún bẹ̀rẹ̀
Bótutù bá ń pàwọ̀fà, Àlàdé,
Wọ́n á ló kó ìṣe ẹ̀ dé
Bí ń bá ń ṣọmọ Ayéṣemí, wọ́n á gbọn epo ra á gẹdẹ.

The gentle breeze, Ayinla, can turn the treetops whichever way it
　likes
One's master sends one wherever he wishes
The master knows the thorny patch, he doesn't hoe there
This is how they salute Jayẹọla, our father
My father, the *iwọfa* bends his back over the thorny patch
If the *iwọfa* starts shivering, Alade,
They'll say he's up to his tricks again
If it was the child of Ayẹṣemi they would rub him lavishly with
　palm oil.

As Ṣangowẹmi asserts, the purpose of her performance is to enhance the
reputation of Jayẹọla – 'This is how they salute Jayẹọla, our father' – and in
this context the misery of the *iwọfa* only serves to intensify our apprehension
of the master's well-being. The master is someone who does not need to do
the hard, painful work on the farm, for he has other people to do it for him.
The master's life is one of affluence and ease; any little ailment, and the
master's children will be tenderly cossetted. The distance between the
master's comfort and the *iwọfa*'s wretchedness is a measure of the master's
greatness. Nonetheless, these lines speak with the voice of the *iwọfa*. 'If the
iwọfa starts shivering...they'll say he's up to his tricks again': when the *iwọfa*
is ill, he will be accused of malingering, and the unfairness of this comes across
clearly. These lines sound as if they could have originated as an *iwọfa*'s lament,
protest, or ironical comment on his condition of servitude. They have been
co-opted into the *oriki* of a big man, but the accent of disaffection is still heard.
If, as Bakhtin said, one's language is never fully one's own, but in using it one
strives to appropriate it, in *oriki* one's own utterance may be appropriated by
others but can never be completely assimilated by them.

　　Women's voices sometimes come across with a similar double-sided
effect. Consider the words of the women's *egungun* vigil chant, already quoted:

Ará dá obìnrin ni ì í fi mawo
Obìnrin ò mọgbàlẹ̀
Ìbá ṣe póbìnrin lè mawo
Ǹ bá gbénú ẹkú wẹkú.

Women are uneasy [or frustrated, fed up], for they cannot know
　the secret
Women do not know the sacred grove
If only women were allowed to know the secret
I would wear one masquerader's costume after another.

Women's exclusion from the secrets of the *egungun* cult is what gives this cult
its authority and mystery. As I have argued elsewhere (Barber, 1981b), 'the
secret' is at the centre of the sacred in Yoruba religious thought, and human

collusion in maintaining the secret is indispensable. On the eve of the great biennial *egungun* festival, women keep watch for their husbands, the priests of the cult, and uphold their spiritual glory by asserting that they themselves can know nothing about it. The voice is the voice of a woman, not a man, and speaks with accents of loss and desire: 'If only women were allowed to know the secret/I would wear one masquerade costume after another'. But, as with the *iwofa*'s lament, the sense of sorrow or grievance has been co-opted (by the women themselves) to the greater glory of the male 'secret'. The ambiguity of the text is revealed in the expression *ará dá obìnrin ni ì í fi mawo*. The grammatical construction of this sentence suggests a translation 'Women are impatient/restless/unreliable, that's why they can't know the secret' – a male perspective on the exclusion of women. But the performer, Ẹrẹ-Ọṣun, told me it meant 'Women are fed up/frustrated *because* they cannot know the secret' – a female perspective.[18]

This passage, however, reveals a further and more profound irony, bordering on paradox. Women assert that they cannot know the secret, but in the same breath they reveal that they *do* in fact know it: 'I would wear one masquerader's costume after another'. *Egungun* costumes have human beings inside, and this is the 'secret' that women collude in pretending not to know. Because of the continually shifting voices in *oriki* chants, the performers can go on to give, in the voice of a young boy of the lineage, graphic details of the experience of wearing an *egungun* costume:

> Àròyé iṣẹ́ bàbáà mi ni
> Ìyáà mi ò tètè mọ̀
> Ó wáá yan ẹ̀kọ dè mí
> Ó ṣeb'óko ni mo lọ
> Kò mọ̀ pábẹ́ ọdán n mo wà bí ẹ̀gà
> Tí mo ń ti ń ṣawo ẹnu
> Mọ́ jọ́ọ̀bùn ọ̀jẹ̀ ó bá mi rẹ̀kúù mi
> Bọ́bùn ọ̀jẹ̀ bá n gbágò wọ́n á bà mí láṣọ jẹ́
> Eléyùn-un nìì á wáá sorí palagún lábẹ́ aṣọ
> Bí kékeré Ògbórí bá ti gbágò á mọ̀ọ́ yan
> Bí àgbà Ògbórí ti gbágò á mọ̀ọ́ rìn
> Bí kékeré Ìlọ̀kọ́ bá gbágò yóó wù ọ́
> Enígbòórí, eyín á wáá fun kinkin lábẹ́ aṣọ.

> Vociferous talking is my father's work
> My mother was slow to realise
> She went and bought *ẹkọ* to keep for me
> She thought I'd gone to the farm
> She didn't know that I was under the fig-tree like a weaver bird
> Where I was chattering interminably
> Don't let a dirty *ọjẹ* wear my *egungun* costume

If a dirty ọjẹ wears my outfit he'll spoil my cloth
That one has a misshapen head under the cloth
If a little Ogbori puts on the costume he'll know how to swagger
If an old Ogbori puts on the costume he'll know how to walk
If a little Ilọkọ puts on the costume he will delight you
Enigboori, his teeth will be shining white under the cloth.

The woman in this scene, the mother, is in ignorance of what her son is really doing. She thinks he's working on the farm, but he is really with his father's band of entertainment masqueraders performing *iwi*, the *egungun* chant, in a public place ('under the fig tree', which usually marks a market). The boy makes a sharp distinction between the *egungun* costume and the person under it which exposes the 'secret' in unmistakable terms. Because of the multiple, shifting, voices of *oriki* it is possible for a woman to utter words such as these in the persona of a boy. She maintains an appearance of proper collusion in the 'secret' (in her role as a woman, she is like the mother, ignorant of the masqueraders' activities) while at the same time opening a crack in its facade which women as well as men can see through.

In these ways horizontal difference and vertical hierarchy are simultaneously upheld (by being built into the structure of *oriki* as well as being explicitly stated) and ironically subverted. At the heart of the world view proposed by *oriki* there is an irresolvable paradox. When human and cultural differences are represented as parallel to natural differences, this is usually taken, in sociological literature, as a strategy of legitimisation. It suggests that the human order is naturally and inevitably as it is, that it could be no other way. Berger and Luckmann (1967) suggest that this process of legitimisation creates a world view which encloses the people like a dome, allowing no prospect of an alternative. Bourdieu, similarly (though from a somewhat different perspective), argues that in societies without class there can be no 'orthodoxy' because there is nothing to contrast it with, no possibility of heterodoxy: there is therefore just 'doxa', the way things naturally are (Bourdieu, 1977). The disadvantaged groups in Okuku are not conscious of themselves as classes and do not articulate an alternative view of the world. But the 'view' articulated in *oriki* is itself heterogeneous, full of contrasts and alternatives, and as we have seen offering possibilities of different interpretation according to the standpoint of the speaker. A central instance of this essential polyvocality and ambivalence is, precisely, the way the relationship between culture and nature is represented. Natural models are continually used to represent human stratification and differentiation. But look at this passage, which expresses human religious specialisation in terms of the differences between birds:

Ìran agbe ní í paṣọọ rẹ̀ láró
Ìran àlùkò ní í paṣọọ rẹ̀ lósùn

Ìran Olóya ní í lo àyán
Mo sebí ìran-àn mi ní í sawo.

The Blue Touraco's lineage is the one that dyes its cloth in indigo
The *aluko* bird's lineage is the one that dyes its cloth in camwood
The Oya devotees' lineage is the one that wears *ayan* beads
But my lineage is the one that goes masquerading.

At the same moment that the Oya cult is represented as being 'naturally' different from the *egungun* cult, the touraco and *aluko* birds are represented as being *culturally* different from each other. Not only do the birds have 'lineages', like people, but they also wear clothes which they dye in blue and red, respectively. If human differences are legitimised as natural, at the same time the whole of nature is brought within the sphere of the cultural. The whole known world and all its categories is a cultural artefact. In this moment, the text seems to contain a hidden acknowledgement that divisions, difference (and by implication, hierarchy) are not naturally given, in-born characteristics but social products. They could therefore be changed.

This is not an isolated or atypical perception. As I have argued elsewhere, a similar moment of inversion and paradox seems to me to lie at the heart of the whole of traditional religious practice. The intense and fervent communication between devotee and *orisa* is founded on the acknowledgement that 'man makes god'. *Oriki* are the central channel through which this acknowledgement is articulated. Similar ambiguities are found in all areas of thought. Each statement is shadowed by its opposite. The outcome is a kind of permanent suspension of resolution. 'In every voice... two contending voices, in every expression a crack, and the readiness to go over immediately to another contradictory expression' (Bakhtin, 1984a, p. 30). Every institution and every entity is represented as being at once fixed, 'natural', beyond human intervention; and as malleable, the outcome of an exercise of choice.

The ideal of choice is used to flatter subjects. In *oriki*, qualities we would think of as inevitable, as 'natural' par excellence, are attributed, hyperbolically and amusingly but still with serious intent, to the free will of the subject:

Ìgbà tó wùjòkún ló i dú ìdú òjé
Ó wáá wu Babalolá Omítótán ó dúdú tán ó feyín seke.

It was by choice that the *ijokun* plant became as black as lead
And by choice Babalola Omitotan became perfectly black with
   teeth as white as gristle.

Both nature (the *ijokun* plant) and human beings (Babalola) are black because they have chosen to be so.

Difference is what creates opportunity and the scope for choice, as this quotation from *iyere Ifa* demonstrates:

Bólókó bá ṣegba
Olóbò làyèé gbà
Àìjọ ẹranko làyèé gbẹkùn.

If there are two hundred people with penises
It's the one with a vagina who has scope
Not being like other animals is what gives scope to the leopard.

In *oriki*, to summarise observations that have been made in this and earlier chapters, the following features are found. Utterances are juxtaposed without one being subordinated to another. The discreteness of the elements in *oriki* is heightened by supplementary stylistic disjunctions. The 'I' of the utterance moves continually, speaking with different voices, which are not 'placed' in relation to each other or to the self-presentation of the performer. The text is like a tissue of quotations, but quotation is never distinguished from context – it is *all* quotations – and these quotations modulate fluently and sinuously from one to the next within the prevailing mode of attribution. There is no overall design, no dominant 'authorial voice' in relation to which other voices are calibrated, no framework within which the disparate elements are assigned a determinate place. These features are what keep open the possibility of alternative states. While affirming 'the way things are', *oriki* statements contain the seeds of their own opposite. *Oriki* are the *means* by which any given state is transcended. It is clear that the withholding of a fixed framework, of a single 'point of view' from which the world can be regarded, is what makes this perpetual motion of transcendence possible. *Oriki* easily accommodate, indeed their mode encourages, the juxtaposition of opposites. These opposites are contained in one place and held together by a kind of surface tension, the thinnest of skins. Within the transparent integument – the 'bag' of *oriki* into which all kinds of materials are thrown – continual transformations and modulations take place. *Oriki* never criticise the community's 'orthodoxy', for as Bourdieu suggests, they cannot. But they always hold open, by the oppositions and contradictions embedded in them and deliberately held unresolved and suspended, a tiny 'loop-hole', as Bakhtin (1984b) put it: the possibility of things being otherwise.

This is the context in which women's powers are construed. There are few situations in which women are told they *cannot* pursue a certain course because they are women. It is said that they do not *choose* to pursue it. Despite the heavy disadvantages that weigh down an ambitious woman, if she decides to become something, it is accepted that she can do so. Comments about Ṣangowẹmi's mother Fakẹmide, the *babalawo*, were illustrative of a general attitude to the flow of power and the acquisition of status. Fakẹmide was the granddaughter of Gbọtifayọ, the renowned *babalawo* and herbalist. Gbọtifayọ had sons and grandsons who could have taken over his position. But Fakẹmide became a fully fledged member of the diviners' association, doing consultations for clients, chanting *iyẹrẹ Ifa* before the ọba during the Ifa festival vigil in competition with all the male *babalawo*, and travelling far afield in search of greater knowledge. Her *oriki* call her '*Ọmọ Ṣónibárẹ́ tí í tún Ifá rọ lẹ́nu ọmọ awo bí agogo*', 'The child of Ṣonibarẹ who re-forges Ifa in the mouths of trainee diviners like a bell': not only does she know Ifa, but she has apprentices of her own whom she instructs and corrects. When I tried to discover how people accounted for this extraordinary behaviour, no-one ever suggested that there was anything odd about it.[19] Men and women alike asserted that no code was transgressed by her actions and that no disapproval was directed at her. According to Ṣọbaloju, who had himself been a *babalawo* before his conversion to Christianity in 1927:

> She learnt Ifa. If a woman goes to school she becomes an educated person; if she learns Ifa, she becomes a *babalawo*. Her father was a *babalawo*, so was her husband, so she picked it up little by little from them. There was never a time when the association of *babalawo* said she had no right to participate in their activities. She would go to the cult house and participate in meetings just like the others. They would ask her about a certain verse of Ifa: if she answered correctly, they would accept that she was a *babalawo*. The verses she learnt were the same as those of the other *babalawo*. Once she learnt them, she was a *babalawo*. Then she also had the right to examine other people on their knowledge, just as they had examined her. Both men and women would come as clients to consult her.

When I asked why there were not more female *babalawo*, he said, 'They aren't interested. If a woman was interested, there'd be nothing to stop her. The *babalawo* would actually be happy! You, for instance, could become a *babalawo*, and I would teach you.' Ṣọbaloju speaks like an existentialist. A woman becomes a *babalawo* by choosing to be one; once she acts as a *babalawo*, she is one. There was no alternative Ifa for women – Ṣọbaloju stressed that she was a *babalawo* just like the men, doing the same ceremonies, reciting the same verses, and offering consultations to the same range of clients. In this philosophy, women are not debarred from the man's world. In a political and social universe where power is construed in terms of the exercise of will, anyone who exercises that will can attain power. Power flows through any channel that is opened to it.

Most women, however, do not 'choose' to compete in male arenas of self-aggrandisement. Faderera learnt *oriki* from her famous father Awoyẹmi, but not Ifa verses. 'That's not our way', she said: that is, that is not the route women choose to take. If they do compete with men, no-one will denounce them: but if they succeed, people are likely to hint at witchcraft. Ṣangowẹmi's mother, like Ayantayọ and Ọmọlọla, was feared for her alleged witchcraft. In reality, therefore, women's freedom of choice is more limited than the culture declares. Like Babalọla's or the *ijokun* plant's freedom to choose to be black, it expresses a cultural principle which it is not always possible to put into practice.

But women do operate the very channels through which power flows. This does not mean that they are invisible or self-effacing. In the dramatised dialogic relation between performer and recipient of *oriki*, the performer is as present, as much the centre of attention, as the recipient. As Ṣangowẹmi boasts, the command of oral art is itself a power: a power that is vouched for, just as the big man's is, by the envy and hostility of other, inferior people. But hers is a power based on knowledge and intelligence. In her own *oriki* she is called '*eegun-inu*', one like a masquerade inside, that is, a brilliant mind, a genius. And she adds:

> Kùtùkùtù tí mo ríkùn dánà sí
>
> I who from my earliest days had a mind that could follow many paths.

Having much knowledge of *oriki* is equivalent to having many social connections, the prerequisite of successful social navigation. As Faderera said, amplifying a well-known formulation:

> Kò sí orílẹ̀ a ò mẹwẹ
> Kò mọ̀mọ̀ sí orílẹ̀ a ò mòwè
> Kò sí orílẹ̀ wọn ò bí mi dé
> Wọ́n bí mi nídìí ìyá bẹ̀ẹ̀ wọ́n bí mi nílée baba...
>
> If there were no *orilẹ* we wouldn't recognise itching beans
> And if there were no *orilẹ* we wouldn't recognise bean sprouts
> There is no *orilẹ* that I was not born into
> I was born on the mother's side, I was born in the father's house...

It is not just men who operate their social strategies through connections made possible by women. As Faderera's words show, women also enjoy a power of manoeuvre through their knowledge.

The 'many paths' of social knowledge that Ṣangowẹmi alludes to are paths traced by *oriki*. They lead into the thicket of contemporary social relationships and back to influential forebears, 'those whose deeds remain'. They are paths that are kept open to allow the flow of power and beneficence between beings. They join a big man and his 'people', swelling his persona through the appropriation of multiple other personalities, and creating, in paradigmatic form, the dialogic bond between them. They run from the living individual straight back to the moment of origin, when social difference was installed.

They allow the past to inhabit the present, perpetually accessible and contiguous. They are paths that are not always easy to follow; but they are marked along the way with clues to their own decipherment, for *oriki* themselves tell us what *oriki* can do.

APPENDIX

Ile in Okuku

NOTES

1. This table was compiled mainly from information given by the head of each *ile*, in some cases supplemented by other elders from that or other *ile*.

2. It cannot be emphasised too strongly that this table should be read as a map of possibilities and not as a fixed or exhaustive scheme of relationships. It represents the state of my knowledge at the time I left Okuku in 1977, which was uneven, and most detailed in the case of those compounds I was closest to. More importantly, the definition of *ile* and the nature of the relationships between them varied not only from case to case, but also from moment to moment. The picture also varied according to the perspective of the viewer.

3. *Ile* which were always or almost always acknowledged as independent units are written without parentheses; those which are attached to a 'host' group are written in parentheses after the group to which they are attached. No attempt has been made, however, to indicate the degree of closeness or independence in this relationship, which varies from semi-autonomy to virtual absorption.

4. Following local custom, the *ile* numbered 1-7 follow the order of titles owned by each compound from ọba down through the six 'kingmakers', while the rest of the *ile* are presented roughly in order of perceived importance, according to a variety of criteria including size, seniority of title, and presence of prominent men among them.

5. Although in almost all cases the town of origin was readily named, together with the *oriki orilẹ̀*, the period at which the group arrived was often described in vague or contradictory terms. When no information at all was forthcoming, the relevant column has been left blank.

6. The historical periods referred to are as follows:

Period I: from the foundation of Kọọkin (seventeenth century?) to its sack in the Ijẹsa Arara war (c. 1760).

Period II: from the sack of Kọọkin and foundation of Okuku (c. 1760) to the fall of Ọfa and involvement in Ilọrin wars (c. 1825).

Period III: period of Ilọrin-Ibadan wars (c. 1825 to 1893).

Period IV: from the resettlement of Okuku (1893) to the death of Oyewusi I and beginning of colonial administration (1916).

Period V: colonial and post-colonial period (1916 to the present day).

7. Population numbers for each *ile* were estimated from the 1977-8 electoral register, but since they are not reliable it would not be helpful to publish them. However a rough indication of size may be useful. Of the fully-independent *ile*, the two largest had about 2000 male and female adult members (1a, 8a); two had between 1500 and 2000 (5a, 9); several had nearly 1000 (2a, 4a, 6a); most of the rest had 200-650. Some 'attached lineages' had 100-300 members (1b, 14b, 14c, 21b) but most had less than 100. Several independent *ile* however, also had less than 100 members.

8. Senior town titles (*ilu ọlọpaa*) are italicised. Religious titles which are exceptional in belonging to specific lineages are in parentheses. Of the junior town titles (*ilu aladaa*), and palace titles, only those which have become firmly associated with particular lineages are listed.

Name	Identified with	Oríkì orílẹ̀ (first lines)	Origin	Period of arrival	Co-op-eration	Forbid-den to marry	Cohabi-tation	Access to titles
1a Ilé Ọba	—	Ọ̀kín Ọmọ Olóòórò Ọmọ a-ríbi-le Ọmọ a-wàyè-jà	Arámako → Ìmẹ̀sì	Period 1 (foun-ders)	1b, 1c	1b, 1c, 3	—	Ọba
1b (Ilé Awóyemi)	1a (matrilateral connection)	Abe Ọmọ Eésà Ọmọ Bàrà Ọmọ a-lé-bi-ojọ Ọmọ ò-dunlẹ́-bi-òjò	Ọlà → Ọ̀yán	Period III (reign of Edun)	1a, 1c	1a, 1c	—	(Àràbà)
1c (Ilé Ọ̀pàlékè)	1a (matrilateral connection)	Ọ̀lá Ọmọ Alárán-án Ọmọ Asọ̀sùn Ọmọ a-dókọ-nìbi-owó-gbé-so	Àrán-Ọ̀rin → Unknown town near Ilorin	Period II?	1a, 1b	1a, 1b 4a, 8a, 17	—	(Àràbà)
2a Ilé Ọjọmu	—	Amọ̀ Ọmọ a-rókè-mú-gùn Ọmọ a-róba-tún-yan Ọmọ ọba a-ṣẹgì-amọ̀)	Ọ̀fà	Period I?	2b-i	2b-i 13	Formerly 2b-i. Now all sections have own buildings. 25 (ceased)	Ọ̀jọmu
2b (Ilé Awógidé)	2a	Ògán Ọmọ Olúpo Ogudu Àjàsẹ́ a-yólẹ̀-doyè	Àjàsẹ́	—	2a 2c-i	2a 2c-i 5d,15	See above	—

2c (Ilé Bélò)	2a	Ọ̀pó Ọmọ Ọ̀pómúlérò, Mọjà-alekàn Bó bá di orún ojà ní Jàágùn Olúkúlùkù ní í mọ́ọ mạ́sọ tiẹ̀	Ọ̀yọ́	—	2a-b 2d-i	2a-b 2d-i, 5a, 24	See above	—
2d (Ilé Olúawo Onifá)	2a	Ọmọ Akinnú Ọmọ òrìṣà ṣiṣẹ́ Ọmọ Ìrókò tẹkẹ́ Abíòṣẹ́ Oba Oriarẹ́ Adésùre Sẹsẹ Ìkòyí ọmọ agbọ̀n'yun	Ìkòyí → Fàjì	Period IV	2a-c 2e-i	2a-c 2e-i, 22	See above	(Olúawo Onifá)
2e (Ilé Ọ̀kéwoyè)	2a	Ọ̀gbin Ọmọ Ológbojò Ọjọ́ àyíkí Ọmọ Awẹ́ IÈsà	Ọ̀gbin	—	2a-d 2f-i	2a-d 2f-i	See above	—
2f (Ilé Ọ̀kéyẹbi)	2a	Àgàn Ọmọ Olópondà Ọmọ ẹranko yáyo	Tápà → Ìgbàyè	Period V	2a-e 2g-i	2a-e 2g-i	Now with 2g	(Ọ̀nà Mọgbà)
2g (Ilé Akódá)	2a	Ọgùn Ọmọ oba iyàwó ológun Ọmọ tó bá dijọ́' jà Ẹ bá n ránni sí Asabari Bó bá dijọ aré ẹ ránni sólógun	Ìmẹ̀sì	Period V	2a-f 2h-i	2a-f 2h-i, 19b	Now with 2f	—

Name	Identified with	Oríkì orílè (first lines)	Origin	Period of arrival	Co-op-eration	Forbid-den to marry	Cohabi-tation	Access to titles
2h (Ile Òkègbohun)	2a	Àró Omo Orò	Òtà	—	2a–g 2i	2a–g 2i	See 2a above	(Alág-bàáà)
2i (Ilé Sùmánu)	2a	Èèkan Omo olówé Omo Elérin	Èrin-ilé	Period V	2a–h	2a–h 10b	See 2a above	—
3 Ilé Òdòfin	—	Òwá Omo Olójonwòn Omo Ikújènrá Omo Agbósòkun Làgbáì omo abúrókò-lówó-lówó	Òjè	Period I	—	1a, 20, 28	—	Òdòfin
4a Ilé Baálè	—	Òlá Omo Baálè Baálè a-dáwonwon-sésin-lénu Omo olódan méje lókè Àgádángbó	Arán-Òrin	Period I	4b, 8a & b, (ceased), 15 (ceased)	1c, 8a, 17	15 (ceased)	Baálè (Aláràn-án)
4b (Ilé Awódélé)	4a (matrilateral connection)	Amò Ògógó òkú ò gbórí Mo sa kéké mo i jèwe Apínni Mo bàbàjà mo i jèwe Agùrè Ìgbà mo wá wó gònbó, mo i jèwe Ìgbórí Njó ti olúogógó ti kú, n ò róbè re jé mó	Òyó ↓ Èrin-ilé	—	4a, 8a (ceased)	4a	4a	—

							Sáwò (Olúodẹ)
5a Ilé Olókò	—	(i) Erin Omo olówó fújà Omo akiti olú Omo kankan bí eyín erin (ii) Òpó Omo Òpómúléró, Moja-àlékàn Bó bá di orún ojà ní Jáàgún Olúkúlùkú ní móo máso tiè	Ìwátá ↓ Òyó	Period I	5b-d	2c, 5b-d 24	—
5b (Ilé Ògúntáyò)	5a	Àgbè Omo Yánbíridolú Elégbà mo di pèlé Omo ojú oró ò jé esé ó tómi	Ìkòyí → Òfà → Ìkìrun	Period V	5a,5c,5d	2d, 5a, 5c, 5d, 8b, 22	—
5c (Ilé Òrìsàléyè)	5a	Níní omo erè lÁpà Ará ìdí ògbàgbá Ará Omi-efun Mo dadì kalè orò lÁpà	Apà	Period V	5a-b, 5d	5a, 5b, 5d	5a
5d (Ilé Olàdípò)	5a	Omo Olúpo Ògudu Àjàsé a-yólè-doyè	Àjàsé ↓ Ilúdùn	Period V	5a-c	2b, 5a-c 15	5a
6a Ilé Nlá	—	Òkín Omo Olófà-mojò Omo Olálomi Omo abísu-jóóko Ìjàkadi lorò Òfà	Òfà	Period I	9 (ceased) 18 (ceased)	6b, 9 18	*Inúrin*

Name	Identified with	Oríkì orílè (first lines)	Origin	Period of arrival	Co-operation	Forbidden to marry	Cohabitation	Access to titles
6b (Ilé Pàkòyi)	6a	Òkin / Ọmọ Olófà-mọjò, etc.	Òfà	Period V	6a	6a, 9, 18	6a (ceased)	—
7 Ilé Olúawo/ Ilé Arógun	Female line incorporated	(i) Male line: (a) Òwé / Ọmọ a-mÒgúnún-dé nírè / (b) Epo / Aşẹbu-àgbà / (ii) Female line: / Àró / Ọmọ Àró nílalà / Ọmọ Adéoba	(i) Ìrè → Ìrẹsà (ii) Ìjẹsà	Period I	14a, b, c (ceased) / 23 (men only)	14a, b, c / 20, 23	23 (ceased)	Arógun (Olúawo Onişẹgun)
8a Ilé Awòrò Ọtin / Ilé Balógun	—	Òlá / Ọmọ Aláràn-án / Ọmọ asòsùn / Ọmọ a-dókọ-níbi-owó-gbé-so	Isàn (Àrán-Òrin)	Period I	4a (ceased) / 17 (ceased)	1c, 4a / 17	—	Balógun / Alàlà / Oşòlú / Sòbalójù / (Awòrò / Òtin)
8b (Ilé Àyàndìpè)	8a (matrilateral connection)	Àgbé / Ọmọ Yànbírídolú / Elégbà mo di pèlé / Ọmọ ojú oró ò jẹ ẹsẹ ó tómi	Ìkòyì	—	8a	5b, 8a / 22	8a	—
9 Ilé Olúọdẹ	Female line incorporated	Òkin / Ọmọ Olófà-mọjò, etc.	Òfà	Period I	6a (ceased) / 18 (ceased)	6a, 6b / 18	—	Olówóẹyin / Sàbà / Olúkòtún / (Oluọdẹ)

10a Ilé Ọ̀dọgun	—	Omọ Ajíbọ́rọ̀ Omọ a-jowú-yoko-lẹ́nu Òkò tẹ́ me i'lẹ̀, ng ò wẹ́ni Ọjọ́ kan ọ̀jọ̀ kan tí wọ́n mólẹ̀ nfrésẹ́-ilé	Òkò → Ìgbajà → Akúnyún	Period IV	10b 11 13 (ceased)	10b 11	11 (ceased) 16 (ceased)	Ọ̀dọgun
10b (Ilé Agbore Olóriṣàdé	10a	Omọ Olówé Omọ Elẹ́rin	Ẹrin-ilé	Period V	10a	2i, 10a 11	10a	—
11 Ilé Limómù	10a (ceased)	Epo Omọ Epo Omọ a-ṣẹ̀bù-àgbà Omọ kẹkẹ́ etí'jà mẹ́rindinlógún Kẹkẹ́ subú Kẹkẹ́ dide Kẹkẹ́ ni ó gbọ́jà gbẹ́ sí	Ìrẹsà → Òfà	Period IV	10a	10a, 10b	10a (ceased)	—
12 Ilé Àràrọ̀	—	Ọ̀gbó Omọ a-jí-jÈèsà Omọ olówó ńlá tí n bẹ lóde Isálúpo Omọ olórọ̀ jiìngbinni tí ń bẹ lọ́sàa'yọ̀	Odè (Ìjẹ̀bú) → If ẹ̀	Period II	13 (ceased)	13	13 (ceased c. 1920)	Ṣọbalojú
13 Ilé Ọṣọ́lọ̀	—	Amọ̀ Omọ a-rókè-mú-gùn Omọ-a-rọ̀ba-tún-yan Omọ ọba a-ṣẹgi-amọ̀	Òfà → Akúnyún	Period IV	10 a (ceased) 12 (ceased)	2a, 12	12 (ceased c. 1920)	Ọṣọ́lọ̀

Name	Identified with	Oríkì orílẹ̀ (first lines)	Origin	Period of arrival	Co-operation	Forbidden to marry	Cohabitation	Access to titles
14a Ilé Jagun	—	Ògbó Ọmọ akutí otí Gbongbon nigboro Ọmọ a-lé-mu-lé-rà LÉgbàá Òsòdí ọmọ ẹbiti pẹyẹ nínú oko	Ìrégbà → Ìkirun	Period I or II	7 (ceased) 14b & c, 20 (ceased) 23 (men only)	7, 20	—	Jagun
14b (Ilé Ṣàngódìrin)	14a	Ọmọ Olómù apèran Ọmọ olóró agogo Ìjà ewú ni wón jà lÓmù Wón fúnra wọn lówó wón fúnra wọn lómọ	Akunyún	Period IV	14a	7		14c—
14c (Ilé Ológemo)	14a	Eẹ̀kan Ọmọ Olúfón-adé Àrè Òṣèlú ọmọ kelu ogbadun nífón Olóìṣà ọmọ akẹyẹ tí dádé orí igi Àrè Òṣèlú mo nìyò mo jàtẹ́ Mo lépo nílé mo jìlá ń funfun	Ifón → Ipẹ̀ẹ́	Period IV	14a	7	14b	—
15 Ilé Aláwẹ̀	—	Olúpo Ògán Òkò mòjẹ Ọmọ Ògúdù Àjàsẹ́ Ọmọ a-yólé-doyè	Àjàsẹ́ → Akunyún	—	4a (ceased)	2b, 5d	4a (ceased)	Aláwẹ̀
16 Ilé Olóyàn	—	Ẹ̀ná Ọmọ a-rókè-mú-gùn Ọmọ a-róba-tún-yan Ìkòtún ọmọ a-rókè ọmọ Ẹ̀ná	Ìkòtún	—	10a (ceased)	—	10a (ceased)	Olóyàn

			Áràn-Òrin					
17 Ilé Àró-Ìsàlè	—	Òlá Omo Aláràn-án Omo asòsùn Omo a-dóko-nibi-owó-gbé-so	Áràn-Òrin → Ìlorin	Split off from 8a in the 19th century	4a (ceased) 8a (ceased)	1c, 4a, 8a	—	Áró rotated with 18
18 Ilé Àró-Òkè	—	Òkin Omo Olófà-mojò Omo Olálomí Omo abisu-jóóko	Òfà	Split off from 9 and 6a in the 19th century	6a (ceased) 9 (ceased)	6a, 6b 9	—	Áró rotated with 17
19a Ilé Elémòsòó	—	Èdú Bí mií rígún, mií lè sèbo Bí n ò rákàlà, ng ò gbodò sorò	Ìkólé	—	19b	19b	—	Elém-òsòó
19b (Ilé Elémòsòó Awo)	19a	Ògún Ayérónfè ará Ògùnmòso Omoba iyàwó ológun Omo tó bá dijò'jà E bá n ránni sÁsaberi	Ìjèsà → Òyó → Ìséyin	—	19a	2g, 19a	—	(Elém-òsòó Awo)
20 Ilé Olúókun	—	Agbó-ojè Omo Olójonwòn Omo Ikújénrá Omo Agbósòkun	Òjè	Period III	7 (ceased)	3, 7, 14a, 28	—	Olúókun

Name	Identified with	Orikì orílè (first lines)	Origin	Period of arrival	Co-op-eration	Forbid-den to marry	Cohabi-tation	Access to titles
21a Ilé Aṣípa	21b	Olóyè	Ìgbéti → Àràn-Òrin	—	21b	21b	21b	—
21b (Ilé Àwòrò Ètuè)	21a	Olóyè	Ìgbéti → Imúléke → Ìgbàyè	Period V	21a	21a	21a	—
22 Ilé Alubàtá	3	Àgbé Ọmọ Yánbirídolú Ẹlégbà mo di pèlé etc.	Ìkòyí	—	—	2d, 3, 5b, 8b	—	—
23 Ilé Ẹlégbèdé	7, 24, 25 26, 27	Ìkó Ọmọ Okunọlà ọmọ olókùn ló lẹsin Ìgósùn ọmọ Àbón Ọmọ a-siwo-mojú-le-koko Ọmọ pakutaa kosùn IÉjin	Igósun → Òtan	Period V	7 (men only)	7	7 (ceased)	—
24 Ilé Àgó	25, 26, 27, 29	Ọpó Ọpómúléró, mojà-àlekàn etc.	Òyó → Òtan	Period V	—	2c, 5a	—	—

303

25 Ilé Obaálé	24, 26, 27, 29	Ògé Òkòmi omo oyè nfràn Oníràn omo orí re tí i sunkún ate Òkòmi tí mo gbélè wú sègi Mo ka' kùò wayùn nfràn	Ipèé → Ìgbósun → Òtan	Period V	—	—	—	2a (ceased) Obaálé
26 Ilé Eésinkin	24, 25, 27, 29	Èèkan/Èdú Omo Olówé Omo Elérin	Èrin-ilé → Òtan	Period V	—	27	18 (ceased) Eésinkin	
27 Ilé Àwòrò Olóòkù	—	Èèkan Omo Olówé Omo Elérin, etc.	Èrin-ilé	Period I ?	—	26	—	Obálá (Àwòrò Olóòkù)
28 Ilé Elémònà	19a	Òwá Omo Olójonwòn Omo Ikújénrá Omo Agbósòkun	Òjè	—	—	3, 20	—	Elémònà
29 Ilé Òtún Baálè	24, 25, 26	Omo Olúfòn-adé Omo Kéisà Omo aládé-sésé-efun Ajamapo ojú ò léjè Omi gbéré ni ojú rí sun	Ifòn → Òtan	Period V	—	—	—	Òtún Baálè

NOTES

Notes to Chapter 1

1. It would be neither accurate nor desirable to draw strict lines between history, the social sciences and folklore. This study is based on the assumption that only an integrated approach can advance our understanding of literature in society/ society in literature. However, in order to clarify my aims, it is helpful to place this study in the tradition of anthropology that sees 'the text' and representations of 'the past' in dialectical relation to social forms, rather than as the sole end of study in themselves. Oral historians, in the attempt to use representations of the past as a source of data, necessarily tend to discount those of their features that are most bound up with contemporary social interests and conventions and therefore most likely to be 'biassed' or 'corrupted'. Folklore, though a broad and eclectic field accommodating a great variety of approaches, does tend either to focus fairly closely on the text-in-performance or to see the text as exemplar of widely-distributed motifs and structures. If the former, only the social forms and processes most closely implicated in performance are integrated into the picture, and the larger society appears as 'background'. If the latter, social forms and processes do not need to be included in what is essentially a classificatory project. Studies which look at the way social forms produce, and are produced by, 'the text' and representations of 'the past' have usually in fact belonged in the anthropological tradition. In African oral historiography, such studies include Cunnison (1951) and Bonte and Echard (1976).

2. See especially the work of Victor Turner (1967, 1968, 1975), who achieved a breakthrough in the study of ritual action by treating it as dramatic text.

3. Henrietta Moore (1986) has shown brilliantly how a textual interpretation, drawing heavily on current literary theory, can be brought to bear on the social construction of space.

4. In Geertz's formulation (Geertz, 1973), culture itself has become a 'text', and the anthropologist's task is to 'read' it. The kind of interpretative anthropology represented in different ways by Turner, Geertz and Moore is not, of course, incompatible with a closer anthropological scrutiny of actual literary texts, and may be an inspiration to it.

5. Vološinov is believed by some scholars to have been one of several pseudonyms used by Mikhail Bakhtin. See Clark and Holquist (1984) on the disputed texts, and the arguments for regarding them as Bakhtin's work. I refer to these disputed texts by both names, without wishing to suggest that I am competent to judge their authorship myself. As will be seen in the next chapter, Bakhtin, like 'Vološinov', has a great deal to offer the interpreter of *oriki*-type texts.

6. According to J. L. Austin, every utterance is an 'illocutionary act' – for instance, the act of asserting, complaining, reminding, persuading and so on – and if it is successfully performed, it is also a perlocutionary act, that is, it has the intended

results. But to be successfully performed, the situation must be appropriate and the utterance must conform to the conventions that define what counts as an example of that speech act (Austin 1962). The context of utterance is thus inseparable from the utterance itself. The importance of context was redefined and analysed further by H. P. Grice (1975); see also John R. Searle (1969).

7. Pratt (1977) approaches the question from the point of view of the audience, suggesting that literary texts arouse greater expectations than most utterances, and are therefore accorded greater attention. She argues that literary texts, in common with a number of other kinds of utterance such as anecdotes, jokes and so on, are 'display texts' which require an audience to suspend the normal rules of conversational turn-taking and yield to them an unusual amount of time and concentration. Richard Bauman (1977, 1986), from a performance theory perspective directed specifically to oral texts, proposes that what distinguishes oral literary performance from other speech genres is that the performer accepts the responsibility to display verbal skill beyond the requirements of normal conversational exchange.

8. Pierre Macherey (1978) suggested an inverse and complementary model of literary discourse's power to articulate what is otherwise unspoken. He said that in attempting to impose coherence on the ideological materials of daily life, gaps and flaws break through the smooth surface of the text in the places where something 'cannot be said'. Because of the requirement that a literary text should be a unified whole, these 'silences' are always significant; they unwittingly throw up the inherent limits of the ideology to view. This view of the relations between ideology and text was differently developed in the deconstructive criticism of Derrida, de Man and others. Though Macherey's version of the theory has great attractions for the analysis of certain kinds of text (notably post-Renaissance, written, European works), its applicability to *oriki* is doubtful, for the same reason that deconstructive criticism is inapplicable: see Chapter 2.

9. For some suggestions about how these techniques are used in the interpretation of Ifa divination verses, see Barber (1990a). Etymology quickly became the stock in trade of academic as well as traditional enquiry: see for example the Revd. Olumide Lucas's method of tracing Yoruba origins back to ancient Egypt (Lucas 1948).

10. Howard Bloch suggests that twelfth and thirteenth century France was such a time and place. The subsequent rise of historical and scientific enquiries led to a reorganisation of the fields of knowledge and literature lost its role as the key organising discourse. But for a time it was a 'privileged forum', and a 'key to the anthropology of the age', offering 'a unique opportunity for an anthropology based upon the practice of the text' (Bloch, 1983, p. 14).

11. Useful as this suggestion of Ong's is, it comes from a theoretical background which has rightly been criticised – one which proposes 'oral society' and 'literate society' as polar opposites and sees the whole of human history as the slow but inevitable and unilinear passage from one to the other, powered by the intrinsic properties of writing rather than by the social and political factors that determine how literacy is used. For a well-balanced and cogent assessment of this position, see Finnegan, (1988).

12. See for instance accounts of patrons and their clients in Lagos by Barnes (1986) and Peace (1979), and a more general discussion of patronage among the modern elite by Lloyd (1974). For a discussion of concepts of relative status among the Yoruba, see Bascom (1951).

13. I am indebted to Graham Furniss for suggesting this way of putting it: see Furniss (1989, p. 26).

14. This is asserted especially of *oriki orilẹ*: see for instance Babayẹmi (1988, p. 23–4).

15. Most of the many studies of Yoruba social structure have dealt with larger towns: e.g. Ọyọ (Morton-Williams 1960a, 1964, 1967), Ijẹbu-Ode, Ado-Ekiti, Iwo (Lloyd, 1958, 1960, 1962), Ifẹ (Bascom 1942, 1951), Oṣogbo (Schwab 1955), Ibadan (Lloyd *et al.* 1967), Lagos (Aderibigbe, 1975), Ilẹṣa (Peel, 1983). Research has been done with smaller towns as the base: for instance Awẹ (Sudarkasa 1973), but much of this work has remained unpublished: e.g. Guyer (1972), Clarke (1979), Schiltz (1980), Francis (1981).

16. Performance theory focuses not on a literary text *per se* but on the 'performance event', thus making it possible to include in the analysis many non-verbal features of the performance: the vocal style of delivery, dramatic action, pacing and timing, interaction with an audience, the use of responsive and creative variation, and so on. It directs attention to the processual and emergent qualities of oral texts instead of reifying them as verbal artefacts. A comprehensive description of the elements of 'performance' is given in Finnegan (1970). Some important contributions to the field are: Abrahams (1977), Ben-Amos (1975), Bauman (1977, 1986), Ben-Amos and Goldstein (1975), and Bauman and Sherzer (1974). One of the most far-reaching and illuminating extensions of the notion of performance is found in the work of Tedlock (1983).

Notes to Chapter 2

1. *Itan* and their relationship to *oriki* in Okuku will be discussed in detail in Chapter 3. For a general discussion of *itan* throughout the Yoruba-speaking area, see LaPin (1977), and for a discussion of Ijẹṣa examples see Peel (1984).

2. *Alọ* are rarely told nowadays. In the three years I spent in Okuku, I never heard a spontaneous session of story-telling in the town itself. But once when I was staying at Odigbo, one of the Okuku farm towns south of Ifẹ, the family I was staying with told *alọ* in the evenings after supper. There was no electricity in Odigbo, and no school, so the children, instead of doing their homework, were sitting around waiting to join in. Apart from that, children are told *alọ* at school, or made to read them (much of the *Alawiye* Yoruba reader series is based on folk stories), but their parents will probably only tell them if specifically asked to do so by a researcher. However, there is widespread latent knowledge of the stories, which resurfaces in other genres, such as modern popular theatre. For detailed and illuminating analysis of *alọ*, and many examples in Yoruba with English translation, collected from all over the Yoruba-speaking area, see LaPin (1977). For a large collection of Yoruba texts of one type of *alọ*, the tortoise trickster tale, see Babalọla (1973a, b).

3. For studies of *ẹsẹ Ifa* and the Ifa system of divination see Abimbọla (1975a, 1976, 1977), Bascom (1969), and McClelland (1982).

4. For accounts of *eleegun ọjẹ* (also known as *apidan, agbegijo* and *alarinjo*), see Götrick (1984) and Adedeji (1969a, b, 1972, 1978). For a description and analysis of the *iwi* chant, see Ọlajubu (1972).

5. Among the conspicuous, widely known and well-documented *oriki*-based chants are the hunters' chants *ijala* (Babalọla, 1966a) and *iremoje* (Ajuwọn, 1982), the masqueraders' chant *iwi* (Ọlajubu, 1972), the brides' chant *ẹkun iyawo* (Faniyi, 1975), the Ṣango devotees' chant *Ṣango pipe* (Iṣọla, 1973). There are also countless localised chants based on *oriki* of one kind or another: see Babayẹmi (1988, pp. 2-3) for a comprehensive list.

6. This kind of *oriki* has been labelled *oriki bọrọkinni* (the *oriki* of notable people,

people of high standing). See S. A. Babalola's *Awọn Oriki Bọrọkinni* (1975), which contains a selection of personal *oriki*, mostly from nineteenth-century Ibadan.

7. For a fuller discussion of *akija* see Barber (1979, pp. 185–6, 308–12).
8. From a performance of *rara iyawo* by Susannah, wife of Ẹlẹmọsọ Ogun of *ile* Odọgun, recorded 1976.
9. '*Àwọn orikì orílẹ̀ náà kún fún ààbọ̀ ọ̀rọ̀ – ọ̀rọ̀ tí à í-sọ fún ọmọlúwàbí tàbí ọmọ̀ràn, tí sì í-dé'nú rẹ̀ tí í-d'odidi*' (Babalola, 1966b, p. 13). My translation.
10. Yoruba scholars such as Babalola (1966a), Ọlajubu (1972), Ọlatunji (1973, 1984), and Ajuwọn (1982) did not of course have the *experiential* difficulty with *oriki* that I did in my first encounter with them: that is, the feelings of discomfort and bewilderment which were clearly as much the result of my sheer unfamiliarity with the culture as because of any theoretical literary preconceptions. Their work shows their intimacy with, and appreciation of, the *oriki*-based chant form. However, the critical language and analytical tools needed to create a *poetics* of *oriki*-based texts have not yet been developed. I suggest that this is partly because formal literary education in Nigeria has always been resolutely writing-oriented and modelled on mainstream European conceptions of literature. The meta-language available, with the deep freight of assumptions it carries with it, just is not appropriate. See Yai (1989). For further discussion and examples see note 17 below.
11. Roger Fowler quotes the linguist C. F. Hockett as being of the opinion that 'a poem is a long idiom' (Fowler, 1966, p. 20).
12. See for instance the immense critical effort that went into reconstituting *The Waste Land* into a smooth, seamless 'whole' by filling the gaps and fractures with other levels of meaning, clearly documented in Cox and Hinchliffe (1968).
13. This characteristic of *oriki* chants has been well described by Isọla (1973) in the case of *Sango pipe*, the *oriki* of the *orisa* Sango. Different chanting modes tend to favour different formulas for changing tack as well as for beginning and ending a performance, as do individual performers.
14. See Ọlatunji (1979) for an account of how a skilled performer might approach a well-known theme from an unexpected angle, causing delight and astonishment when he or she finally reveals what it is.
15. Some of the key texts expounding these ideas are Barthes (1975, 1979), Derrida (1976, 1979) and Miller (1979). For clear exposition and critical discussion of them see Culler (1975, 1981, 1983), Belsey (1980), Norris (1982) and Eagleton (1983).
16. 'Composition in performance' (Lord, 1960) describes the way oral performers create/recreate a text in the act of performing it, by means of a stock of formulas combined with metrical rules. It has probably been the single most influential notion in the study of oral literature, and has had revolutionary implications for the analysis of the Bible, Old English literature, and many other historical genres, as well as for contemporary oral traditions. However, the tendency to regard composition in performance as a single technique by which *all* oral texts are constructed has been criticised (e.g. Finnegan, 1988) and, in a study of a Xhosa 'praise-poetry' tradition not unlike *oriki*, Opland (1983) has shown that the approach yields little when applied to non-narrative poetry. It works best on genres which are both narrative and metrical, like Homer and the Yugoslavian epics which Parry and Lord did their own research on. Other aspects of Parry and Lord's approach, however, which have been less highlighted by subsequent scholarship than the search for 'formulas', have enduring value for our understanding of non-narrative genres and indeed for other cultural behaviour than the generation of literature

(see Bourdieu, 1977. p. 88). For further discussion see Chapter 7.

17. In the detailed and well-researched Oxford Library of African Literature series, for instance, where Southern African 'heroic poetry' is particularly well represented, the aesthetic preference of the authors for unified, regular, boundaried forms is clear. In their commentaries, they tend to play down the fluidity and irregularity which is evident in the texts. Cope, on Zulu *izibongo* (Cope, 1968) and Kunene, on Sotho praise poetry (Kunene, 1971), focus on the formal regularity and internal coherence of each 'paragraph' or stanza, paying less attention to the indeterminacy of the relations *between* these units. Damane and Sanders, also writing about Sotho heroic poetry, declare their preference for 'poems' which are 'logical and straightforward... balanced and well-rounded', and observe that though the ordering of stanzas often appears arbitrary, sometimes, 'with a little imaginative effort, it can be seen to follow a definite train of thought' (Damane and Sanders, 1974, p. 36). These preferences for order and unity were in part a rejection of early ethnocentric depictions of Southern African heroic poetry as a mere untutored outpouring (e.g. Van Zyl, 1941) but also clearly end up reaffirming a European view of what a literary work should be. Schapera, writing about Tswana praise poetry, has no difficulty in acknowledging that these 'praise poems do not seem to have any consistent unity of structure' (Schapera, 1965, p. 10), but his analysis is brief and does not propose any view of how this poetry does work. Though *oriki* chants are even more fluid and irregular than the Southern African praise poetry, Yoruba scholars have been less concerned with the question of form. Ọlajubu (1972), however, argues that *iwi* chants have a regular overall structure, basing this view on the presence of opening and closing formulas. Ajuwọn calls *iremọje* 'poems', but devotes little attention to their textuality, beyond the comment that they are 'characterised by cumulative linear verse lines which consist of a free combination of accepted traditional formulae' (Ajuwọn, 1982, p. 10). S. A. Babalọla (1966a) also calls *ijala* texts 'poems', but his attention is much more on the properties of poetic language itself, and his treatment is the best and richest discussion of any mode of *oriki* performance yet to appear.

18. S. O. Babayẹmi (1988) suggests the use of *oriki orilẹ* to trace the movements and dispersion of the groups of people claiming the same origin. The fragments of large groups of people could be mapped out over a wide area, and, in conjunction with *itan* explaining the groups' movements, some kind of historical demography could be attempted. Such a study, which would involve a large-scale comparative exercise of collection and collation, would indeed be very valuable, but has yet to be undertaken.

19. This is admittedly a large assumption, and there is no evidence either to support or to refute it. Babalọla's dating is probably too specific: he says '*Ìtàn àwọn baba-ńlá àti ìyá-ńlá tí à ń sọrọ bá wọnyí yíó lọ sẹ́hìn sẹ̀hìn dé aiyé àtijọ́ gan-an kété lẹ́hìn tí Ọ̀rányàn tẹ Ọ̀yọ́ ilé dó, èyíinì ni ní nkan bí i ọdún A.D. 1250*' [These stories of our male and female ancestors that we're talking about go back into the distant past to the time immediately after Ọranyan founded Ọyọ Ile, that is to say about 1250 A.D. (my translation)]. But the topicality and allusiveness of so many of the references suggest a contemporary context in which all the circumstances surrounding the formulation and giving it meaning were present in people's minds. It is likely, then, that *oriki* were usually composed soon after the events they allude to.

20. See Chapter 6 for examples.

21. My translation of '*Fẹ́rẹ́ fẹ́rẹ́, ni oriki náà yíó maa yán ìtàn àtijọ́; àlàyé kíkún yíó sì kù sí ọwọ́ iwádìí àti itọpinpin-ọ̀rọ̀*'.

22. As David Henige points out, this kind of apparent triviality has long troubled the oral historian: Robert Lowie complained that 'oral tradition tends to remember

only the insignificant and fails to record "the most momentous happenings"'(Henige, 1982, p. 17).

23. Cf. McCaskie (1989, p. 85) on Asante hermeneutics.

24. In this fascinating analysis, Tedlock suggests that the anthropologist's impulse to separate the narrative into two components, an authentic text and a secondary commentary, does not correspond to the Zuni view, in which the telling of a story of origin is 'simultaneously something new *and* a comment on that relic, both a restoration and a further possibility' (Tedlock, 1983, p. 236). 'For the Zuni storyteller-interpreter, the relationship between text and interpetation is a dialectical one: He or she both respects the text and revises it. For the ethnologist that relationship is a dualistic opposition.' Tedlock's emphasis on the unity of 'text' and 'commentary' is highly pertinent to the case of *oriki*, and the difference between this and the Zuni example seems to be only a matter of degree.

Notes to Chapter 3

1. Unfortunately no new map has been issued since the construction of this road; Map 3 therefore shows the old road as it was when I first went to Okuku in 1974.

2. The seventy-five men from whom life stories were solicited in Okuku had had, at one time or another, a total of 172 wives between them. Of these, seventy were from towns other than Okuku. These women came from twenty-nine different places – some as far afield as Abẹokuta, Ilọrin, and even the mid-West and Ghana – but mainly from towns in the Odo-Ọtin District. The most heavily represented towns were Okuku's nearest neighbours Ijabẹ, Inisa and Ekusa. As the informants were selected to represent three age-ranges (over 70; 40-69; 20-39) and as the proportion of outsider wives was about the same in each group, it seems reasonable to suggest that this marital relationship with the neighbourhood is a well-established and continuing custom.

3. Okuku is traditionally said to have '17' festivals. The ones I observed during my stay there, in order round the calendar, were: Olooku (May/June); Esilẹ (same time as Olooku); Orisa Oko (July); Ori Oke (July/August); Ifa (August); Ọsanyin (August); Otin (October); Ọsun (October); Erinlẹ (October); Ṣango (November); Gbẹdẹgbẹdẹ (November); Ogboni (December); Ṣọpọnnọn (January); Oya (February/March); Egungun (March/April); Ogun (same time as Egungun).

4. For a description of this festival, and a speculative assessment of its origins and political significance, see Beier 1956.

5. One elder of *ile* Ọba, Oyelẹyẹ, said that there were four *orisa* belonging to the royal family, brought by the ọba Alao Oluronkẹ from the old town of Kọọkin. Each belonged to a different ọba of this early period: Ifa to Olugbegbe, Ṣọpọnnọn to Ọladile, Orisala to Oluronkẹ Alao, and Otin to Ọtinkanre. For further discussion of these ọbas, see the next section of this chapter.

6. Berry (1975, 1985) provides a broader perspective on this kind of migration, which is characteristic of large areas of northern Yorubaland.

7. Ọsun Div. 1/2 File no. 294, *Intelligence Report: Okuku District*, 16/12/1935.

8. According to an Intelligence Report, a motor road from Ikirun to Okuku was 'under construction' in 1936 (Ọsun Div. 1/2 Os 294), and by 1940 it had reached Ọfa, ten miles beyond Okuku.

9. Ọyọ's sovereignty ended probably some time between c. 1825, when the Ilọrins entered Ọfa, and 1831-3, when the city of Old Ọyọ was sacked (Law 1970). The form it took is unclear: the only reference to it that I came across was in the legend about Olugbegbe, the magical ọba who turned into a leopard (see below). The Alaafin was said to have interested himself in Olugbegbe's case to the extent of

trying personally to get rid of him, but without success. There are indirect and ambiguous references in stories to the role of Ilọrin during its period of overlordship. In Oyelẹyẹ's version of the story, Adeọba, who may have begun his reign around 1830, was said to have been called to the throne and to have come 'from Ilọrin' – though what he was doing there was not explained. In the same narrative, Adeọba's successor Oyekanbi was driven away from the town and took up residence in Ọfa, by then an the Ilọrin outpost, from where he was recalled seven years later. Though the Ilọrins are always referred to as the enemy, nevertheless more than one old man recalled that slaves captured by Okuku men would be sold off 'to Ilọrin'. The *ajẹlẹ* system is remembered well. Some *ajẹlẹ* settled in Okuku, attaching themselves to host compounds, and their descendants are still known to be '*ọmọ ajẹlẹ*', children of the *ajẹlẹ*. For more information about the *ajẹlẹ* system, see Awẹ (1964b). According to colonial records (Schofield, 1935), Ibadan also extended to Okuku the system of assigning the town to an Ibadan chief (*baba ogun*) who acted as their patron.

10. This characteristic of *itan ile* as exclusive to the groups that own them, and symbolic of their identity, has been discussed by Lloyd (1955, p. 237).

11. A possible exception to this is Olugbegbe, the leopard king, from whom a discreet distance is maintained.

12. This of course is a widespread phenomenon in Africa and elsewhere; a thoughtful and influential early treatment of it is Cunnison's discussion of the 'historical notions' of the Luapula (Cunnison, 1951). Sahlins has recently extended the discussion in an inspiring essay (Sahlins, 1987).

13. A similar process of progressive conflation of historical 'landmark' incidents was noted by J. D. Y. Peel in Ilesa (Peel, 1984).

14. The 'official' version of Okuku history (as published in the publicity for the present Olokuku's coronation) assigns dates, something my own narrators never did for any event before the twentieth century. The dates are based on reign lengths and go back to Adeọba. As Henige (1982) has convincingly shown, such dating must be treated with great caution, and in most of my discussion of the nineteenth century, here and in Chapter 6, I have deliberately left things vague, as did Ajiboye, Oyelẹyẹ, Adeọsun, Adewale, and many other Okuku elders who told me stories of the past.

15. Beier's version of Okuku history, culled from unnamed 'praise singers' of the town, corresponds in all salient points to the summary given here. He observes that 'The praise singers of Okuku list fifteen Obas. There is agreement on the order of succession only among the first two and the last six rulers. There is disagreement about the order in which the intervening obas reigned'(Beier, 1982, pp. 38-9). Versions I collected did not even agree about the first two, nor on which ọbas were to be included in the early period.

16. It is noteworthy, in view of prevailing assumptions about Yoruba kingship ideology (e.g. Smith, 1969, Kenyo, 1964, Beier, 1982), that none of the elders who told me *itan* of Okuku ever traced the story back from Aramọkọ to ultimate origin in Ifẹ. However, the Olokuku himself, Ọlaọṣebikan Oyewusi II, an educated man, did; and this is also reflected in the 'official' version of the history presented for public consumption by the ọba and the educated elite.

17. Estimated dates for the foundation of Oṣogbo vary widely. Schwab, who did field-work in the town in the 1950s, places it 'at about 1800' (Schwab 1955, p. 355) which must certainly be too late and probably the result of the kind of foreshortening of past time by local narrators discussed above. Akintoye (1971, p. 30) estimates the late seventeenth century, whereas Peel in his account of the expansion of the

Ijẹṣa (Peel, 1983, p. 21) puts it further back, in the late sixteenth century.

18. When the colonial authorities established Okuku as the head of one of the twelve districts of Ibadan Division of Ọyọ Province (1914–34), they listed the following towns as subordinate to Okuku: Ijabẹ, Igbaye, Okua, Ẹkọsin, Faji, Iyẹku, Ekusa, Agboye, Ila-Odo, Iniṣa and Ọyan. Elders of the royal family of Okuku, however, claimed that in addition to those listed, Okuku also had overlordship over Ore, Ọpọnda, Ọpẹtẹ, Imuleke, Iba and Aṣaba, making seventeen in all. It claimed authority over them by virtue of having granted the land to them when they first settled. Some of those listed were satellites of others – Imuleke, for instance, was subordinate in the first instance to Igbaye, having been founded by Igbaye people, Faji was subordinate to Ẹkọsin and Aṣaba was subordinate to Ọyan. Some of these towns formally denied being subordinate to Okuku, notably Iniṣa and Ọyan, which were rapidly outgrowing Okuku (according to Schofield, in 1935 Ọyan was already more than twice the size of Okuku, and Iniṣa was not far behind). Others, like Iba and Igbaye, with whom Okuku was engaged in land disputes, told stories of origin in which they claimed to have preceded Okuku to the area. Nonetheless, Okuku clearly did have a ring of smaller subordinate towns around it, and these in turn sometimes had even smaller subordinate hamlets. For towns of origin claimed by each *ilé*, including moves from one town to another before arrival at Kọọkin, see Appendix. After the establishment of Kọọkin, new towns were also created in the area by outward expansion. Eko-Ende and Ijabẹ are both acknowledged as settlements founded by princes of the Kọọkin royal family, and to this day they claim the same core *oriki* relating to origins in Aramọkọ and the cults and customs established at Kọọkin, notably the relationship to the River Ọtin.

19. Johnson (1921) mentions an 'Ijesha Arera War' between Ọyọ and the Ijẹṣa at a much earlier period, in the reign of Ọbalokun, which according to Law's calculations must have been some time in the early seventeenth century. J. D. Y. Peel (1983) refers to the incursions northwards into Igbomina territory by Ilẹṣa in the eighteenth century. Kọọkin was further to the west than the towns known to have been the object of Ilẹṣa's interest, but only by about twenty miles. The Arọkin – the oral historians and praise-singers of Ọyọ – mentioned the 'Ijẹṣa Arara' in an interview with them in 1988. They said that Ṣango sent Timi to Ẹdẹ in the hope that he would be set upon by the Ijẹṣa Arara who had the habit of ambushing people on the road. This story identifies the Ijẹṣa Arara with the earliest, mythological era of Ọyọ history, but the Arọkin went on to suggest that the warlike Ijẹṣa Arara were a permanent feature of that area. Their account is therefore no help in dating the fall of Kọọkin. The problem of written sources re-entering oral tradition is of course well known to oral historiographers: see David Henige's 'The Disease of Writing', in Miller (1980).

20. For detailed accounts of the events after Alaafin Abiọdun's death in c. 1789 up to the fall of Old Ọyọ in c. 1835/6, see Johnson (1921), Law (1977), Akinjogbin (1965). For discussion about the chronology of these events, see Akinjogbin (1966), Law (1970), Abdullahi Smith (1983).

21. Sources on which this brief summary is based include Johnson (1921), Ajayi and Smith (1964), Akintoye (1971), Law (1970, 1977) and Atanda (1973). All information relating specifically to Okuku, however, is derived from oral sources.

22. According to Lloyd (1960, p. 233), 'Deposition could only be effected by death and never by exile or abdication, for only by the death of one ọba could his successor perform the consecration rituals necessary to validate his own rule'. Though Lloyd is speaking specifically of Ado-Ekiti, the reference to consecration rituals applies to Okuku. Only the turbulence of the war period and perhaps the uncertainty as

to which town was Okuku's overlord explains how Oyekanbi got away with it.

23. J. D. Y. Peel (1984) has proposed a concise and well-formulated rebuttal of the 'presentist' theory of oral societies' accounts of the past, and offered in its place a dialectical view of the relations between present action and past precedent: on the one hand, present-day actors are guided by their conception of the past and attempt to make on-going events conform to it; on the other hand, when the 'perturbations of history' result in a radical departure from these precedents, people then attempt to revise history so as to maintain a sense of its unbroken continuity with the present. This picture of the 'past in the present' is one of continual mutual adjustment between action and representation. To this model, with which I am in agreement, my analysis suggests the addition of a further point, that is that the discussion needs to take more account of the *medium* in which Yoruba representations of the past are formulated. As I have shown, the episodic and unconnected character of *itan*, existing as they do in a symbiotic relationship with the disjunctive discourse of *oriki*, shows that like *oriki*, *itan* do not attempt to present a total, consistent overview of the past. There is therefore always a large reserve of *latent* information, of dormant precedents which are not ironed out and brought into line with current practice. In this respect, the repertoire of representations of the past is much more like what is usually associated with a literate, archival culture, where texts may be left lying for decades until they once again suit some new political or social purpose. It also means that there is always material for oppositional views to work on.

24. In Okuku, it is said that the Eesa was banished on a wrongful charge of adultery with the ọba's wife, who had taken refuge with him after a quarrel with the ọba. He thereupon went and founded Inişa. In Inişa itself, a different story is told, ascribing the foundation of the town to a hunter unconnected with Kọọkin, who was later joined by the Eesa. Similarly, the ruling house of Iba is reported to have claimed this town's independence, asserting that their forefathers came from Ife long before the foundation of Kọọkin (File 60/1923, Osun Div. 2/2, document dated 11/9/1936).

25. A passive prefix à- followed by two syllables, the word's tonal pattern being either low-low-high or low-high-high.

26. This process of accumulating personal *oriki* has been well described by Babalọla (1975).

27. *Egbo* is made from mashed boiled maize; *ẹwa* usually refers to boiled beans, but here means a mixture of boiled beans and boiled maize.

28. See Adeoye (1972), Oduyoye (1972) and Sowande and Ajanaku (1969) for excellent discussions of the structure and meaning of the various categories of Yoruba names.

29. From a performance by Faderera, daughter of *ile* Awoyẹmi, wife of *ile* Ọlọkọ, at the grave-shrine of her grandfather Awoyẹmi, during the Egungun festival of 1975.

30. *Èèwó*: according to Babalọla, 'mashed, boiled yam pieces mixed with palm oil' (Babalọla, 1989, p. 170).

31. In Okuku there are four main types of *egungun*. The *eegun rere* (good *egungun*) belong to compounds rather than individuals; they wear large, square sack-like robes of dark blue material, do not carry a mask, and behave in a mild and co-operative way. They seem to represent the benign aspects of the collectivity of a compound's ancestors. The *eegun nla*, or great *egungun*, were founded by individuals, and each remains in some sense the alter ego of its founder, though with the passage of time becoming the property of a compound or a section within a compound. They are flamboyant and individualised figures, with colourful costumes and carved masks,

their own names and *oriki*, and a tendency to be ferocious. There are small *egungun* called *pakaa* carried by young boys for fun. Finally there are the *eegun ǫje*, entertainment masquerades, who perform as a group on special occasions. The now disbanded Okuku group has already been mentioned. The categories of *egungun* vary from town to town; for a useful survey, see Drewal (1978) and the articles by Houlberg, Drewal and Drewal, Pemberton, Poynor, Adedeji and Schiltz in the same volume.

32. From a performance of *rara iyawo* by Susannah Faramade, married into *ile* Arogun (1976).

33. A comparison of any two collections of *oriki* – such as those compiled by B. Gbadamǫsi (1961), S. A. Babalǫla (1966), C. L. Adeoye (1972), or S. O. Babayęmi (1988) – shows that there is no such thing as a complete and discrete corpus of units for any *orilę*. Although each informant and collector tends to treat his or her own collection as definitive, there are wide variations between one collection and the next. In some cases, the same units of *oriki* can be attributed to two or three different *orilę* by different authorities. Even within the context of one community, variations occur. No performer could ever claim that her own repertoire of units for a given lineage/clan was exhaustive. Other performers will know a different range. Some units, which could be regarded as the core *oriki orilę* for each kin group, will be known by all performers, but these turn out to be a surprisingly small proportion of the total range.

34. For a full discussion of *arǫ* narratives see LaPin (1977, pp. 66–72).

35. In some cases, it is not clear in which genre a piece of text originated: there are formulations which are shared by several genres. The Ifa corpus – the other great Yoruba poetic genre – is also incorporative, though for different reasons and in different ways. [See Barber (1990a) for this.] Thus passages may be shared by both Ifa and *oriki*, and who borrowed from whom is a matter of speculation.

Notes to Chapter 4

1. From a performance by Iyabǫ, daughter of *ile* Ǫlǫkǫ, February 1976.

2. Johnson Onifade of *ile* Oluǫdę.

3. From a performance by Elizabeth, Olumide, Yęmisi, and Ibiyǫ, all daughters of *ile* Ǫlǫkǫ, February 1978.

4. This is not to say that all specialist/professional performers produce chants as fragmented and eclectic as Ṣangowęmi's. Visiting *akewi* whose performances I recorded were generally in fact more coherent. However, they, like Ṣangowęmi, were entertainers in a way that the *obinrin ile* were not, and their performances reflected this. The general point holds, which is that the knowedge of the *obinrin ile* is more restricted to particular bodies of *oriki orilę* and personal *oriki*, but is also 'deeper'.

5. For another description of Yoruba betrothal and marriage procedures, based mainly on the Ęgba but incorporating references to other Yoruba groups, see Fadipę (1970, pp. 69–86). Though this account is very detailed, it contains no mention of *ękun iyawo*, confirming the suggestion of Faniyi (1975) that this is principally an Ǫyǫ genre.

6. Nowadays only brides of special categories are stripped: these categories include twins, the *arugba* or ceremonial calabash carrier of the Ǫtin cult, and daughters of *ile* Ǫba. Other girls undergo a token washing of the feet only.

7. For detailed descriptions of the hierarchy within Yoruba compounds, see Bascom (1942), Schwab (1958) and Fadipę (1970, pp. 114–34).

8. From a performance of *Erinlę pipe* by Ęrę-Ǫsun, daughter of *ile* Ǫdǫfin, married

into *ile* Elẹmọsọ Awo, May 1977.

9. A similarly ambiguous attitude to marriage is expressed in the wedding songs of the Limba, though in a less elaborated and eloquent form (Ottenberg, 1989). Faniyi (1975) also gives examples of the expression of fears and anticipation of joys in *ẹkun iyawo* from Ọyọ. In the interesting cases described by him, brides would sometimes engage in chanting contests if they met on the road (Faniyi, 1975 pp. 691–2), and were sometimes able to improvise verses on the spot (Faniyi, 1975 p. 693), something I never saw in Okuku.

10. From a performance by Susannah Faramade, wife of Joseph Ajeiigbe Faramade of *ile* Arogun, February 1976.

11. *Ibid.*

12. *Ibid.*

13. *Ibid.*

14. *Ibid.*

15. *Ibid.*

16. From a performance by Omiyiọla, Iyaa Laagbe, daughter of *ile* Ọba, wife of *ile* Aṣipa, February 1978.

17. From a performance by Adedigba Akindele, daughter of *ile* Oluọdẹ, February 1975.

18. From a performance by Motunrayọ, daughter of *ile* Ọdọfin, February 1975.

19. For an example of such a treatment of the Lagbai passage see Chapter 5.

20. For a fuller text of the Ikoyi *oriki*, which revolve around the twin themes of warfare and thievery, see Chapter 5.

21. The details of the ceremony were as follows. The family had to provide objects for sacrifice: 55 *kọbọ* (the modern equivalent of 22,000 cowries); a large billy-goat; one cock and one hen; a tortoise; a snail; chalk; camwood powder; shea-butter; twenty naira. As is the usual practice, the body was washed with hot water and dressed in men's trousers put on back to front. Her head was then shaved and the *osu* (or *oga* as the Oniṣango called it) was cut off and put in a calabash. All the animals except the goat were killed without the use of any instrument, and their blood was poured on her head. Other medicines which had been prepared at the Baalẹ Ṣango's house were brought and piled on her head. White cloth was put over her face and marked with blood to look like a face. The corpse was sat up and draped in cloth. Then everyone was allowed to come in and look, and give money to the children of the deceased.

22. In some chants that I recorded, the refrains were quite different from each other and changed every few lines, yet the chorus always seemed to know which one to sing. This remarkable unanimity has been commented on by Akinwumi Iṣọla (1973).

23. For a fuller quotation and analysis of this passage see Chapter 7.

24. An *egungun* priest, and therefore expert on the spirits of the dead, told me '*Àgbèdẹ lọnà ọrun nítorí pé iyá tó bí Ògún ló bí eégún*' (The smithy is the road to heaven because the mother of Ogun [*orisa* of blacksmiths] is also the mother of Eegun [Egungun]). This use of puns and invented etymological links (here, the similarity of sound in 'Ogun' and 'Eegun') to explain relationships amongst spiritual beings was a very common discursive strategy.

25. There is also a story told in explanation of the *oriki* 'Mọja-Alekan', which says that the ọba of Iwata was a carver from whom the Alaafin commissioned 200 houseposts (Professor Wande Abimbọla, personal communication).

26. On the occasion when this chant was recorded, the ceremony was being performed in honour of Yọoye, a daughter of *ile* Ọlọko who had married into *ile* Oluọdẹ. Normally, when the deceased is a woman, the *oro ile* is performed in her own (i.e. her father's) compound, but the burial itself and the dancing, spending of money

and serving of food that follow take place in her husband's compound. However, in this particular case the woman was not buried in her husband's compound, *ile* Oluọdẹ, but in her father's, *ile* Ọlọkọ. This was because her husband had died long before and she had no surviving children to keep her in *ile* Oluọdẹ, and she had therefore moved back to *ile* Ọlọkọ to live. The whole ceremony was performed in *ile* Ọlọkọ.

27. Orisa Oke could mean either the Hill deity (whose cult, in Okuku, belongs to *ile* Ọjọmu, a compound related by origin in Ọfa to Abọyarin's compound *ile* Nla); or 'the Orisa Above', i.e. God.

28. For the various categories of *egungun* recognised in Okuku, see Chapter 3, Note 31.

29. This was the explanation given me by several participants in one such ceremony. However, a *babalawo*, Aṣapawo, gave a characteristically more complicated explanation, involving a story about a man with three wives who, after his death, all told lies about him. One said she had given him all her savings; the second said he never bought anything for her, and that all her clothes were bought with her own money; the third complained that he had never given her a child. The dead man's friend told them he would make the dead man come alive on the seventh day and they should repeat their stories in front of him. Then he wrapped a banana stem in cloth – the kind that the *eegun rere* wear nowadays – and buried it in place of a corpse. He told each of the wives to bring an egg, a ball of cotton and 1s 8d and place them on the heaps that had been dug on the path. But all the while, the husband was not dead at all, he was hiding in the rafters watching the behaviour of his wives. After the 'burial' he burst out and confronted them with their lies. This is why there is a prohibition against lying about a dead person, and why there is always a ceremony at the funeral in which people with grievances against the dead, or debts owed to them by him, are asked to come forward. The objects the women were told to bring were presented as an offering, so that what they had done would not rebound on them fatally; they were also symbolic. The egg is something cool and delicate, which Ọbatala moulded with great care; it is also the offering we make to witches. Its purpose was to prevent the household becoming 'hot' (painful, full of trouble) for the wives. The ball of cotton was offered so that the wives' loads would not become too heavy for them, i.e. so that their problems would not become intolerable. This explanation makes use of a pun on the words *òwú* (cotton) and *wúwo* (heavy), as well as of the fact that a ball of cotton is itself light. The money was for the dead to take with him to the other world; but it was also given in the expectation that the dead would repay those who gave him the money many times over.

Notes to Chapter 5

1. S. A. Babalọla (1966a), showing how *ijala* chanters use formulaic utterances to correct each other's performance, significantly uses *oriki orilẹ* as his example.

2. In *Dance and Society in Eastern Africa*, Ranger describes the Beni dance as a 'trace element' (1975, p. 6) and as 'a good decoder' (1975, p.165), in the sense that tracing the history of the growth and spread of this popular dance form reveals aspects of popular consciousness and popular organisation which might not otherwise be accessible.

3. *Oriki orilẹ* of *ile* Ọba, Okuku. This is the version that everyone knows. Ṣangowẹmi, always given to even greater profusion than other performers, attributed no less than seventeen rivers to the Okuku royal house in her version.

4. As in many other African cultures, 'farm' is a Janus-faced mediator between

'settlement' and 'forest', 'civilisation' and 'the wild'. Depending on the frame of reference, it can be positioned on either side. This is revealed in everyday idioms. *Ara oko* (literally, person of the farm, farm-dweller) is an abusive expression meaning 'bush-man', 'boorish, uncultivated person'. Similarly *eranko* (animals of the farm) means wild as opposed to domesticated animals. However, *oko* (farm) is also used as a metaphor for any place of productive (i.e. civilising) work: a carver goes to *oko ọna,* the 'farm' of carving, and the trader goes to *oko owo,* the 'farm' of trading, i.e. goes on a trading trip.

5. This is not the only transformation that is taking place, of course. The trees are represented as animate beings themselves, waiting for Lagbai's arrival and wondering which of them he is going to cut down. Trees are inhabited by spirits, who have to be propitiated by the carver before he cuts. But they are spirits of the bush, not part of the human community. When the carver has produced an image, this image is likely to be used in religious ceremonies in which spiritual powers are invoked. But this time they will be *orișa,* gods who, even if not once human themselves, are at least in communication with humans and responsible for the foundations of human culture. Thus on the spiritual level too the nature: culture transformation is repeated.

6. *Apá:* Afzelia Africana (Abraham, 1958, p. 57).

7. *Ìrokò:* 'African teak', Chlorophora Excelsa (Abraham, 1958, p. 316).

8. Since the status order is slave–bondsman–freeman, one would expect the value of the carvings to be similarly ordered from smallest to biggest. The reversal which makes the value of the bondsmen's carvings less than that of the slaves', is however a characteristic rhetorical pattern in *oriki* and in everyday figures of speech.

9. According to S. O. Babayẹmi (1971), Ọla, though attacked in the early nineteenth century, still exists. The people of *ile* Awoyẹmi however do not refer to this, saying that Ọla was destroyed in the 'Fulani war'. Further investigation is needed to establish whether it was one of the many towns that were destroyed and then rebuilt, often on a new site; whether it was a different Ọla; or whether *ile* Awoyẹmi simply lost contact and lacked information about it.

10. Facial marks in certain circumstances can also indicate status. The royal lineage of Ọyọ, for instance, had different marks from other Ọyọ lineages: see Abraham (1958, p. 300). It seems likely, however, that the *primary* signification of the royal marks is the royal lineage's place of origin; because they are a high-status lineage, the marks also take on that significance.

11. From a recitation of *oriki orilẹ* by Oketundun, daughter of *ile* Ọlọyan, married into *ile* Ọba.

12. S. O. Babayẹmi suggests that this incorporation of an outsiders' view is characteristic only of *oriki orilẹ* of towns outside the central Ọyọ area. He points out that the *oriki orilẹ* of Ifẹ have the same perspective as the Omu ones. In his view *oriki orilẹ* were not characteristic of the outlying areas, and can be assumed to have been made up for the townspeople by people from central Ọyọ. (Babayẹmi, personal communication and 1988). This does not conflict with my general point that all *oriki orilẹ* are about insider–outsider relationships because they are exercises in *self-presentation* to outsiders.

13. From a recitation of *oriki orilẹ* by Iyaa Lajire, daughter of *ile* Ẹlẹmọsọ, married into *ile* Oluọdẹ.

14. *Ibid.*

15. It is possible that early Northern Yoruba towns were more like the towns of Ijẹbu and Ondo today, where emblems of lineage membership are diffuse and of less importance than emblems of town membership. According to E. Krapf-Askari, in

these towns 'the same facial marks are … shared by all *ara ilu* of a single town, only the royal lineage bearing additional distinguishing scars; *oriki* and food taboos, along with land and priestly titles, descend through women as well as men…' (Krapf-Askari, 1969, p.75).In a situation like this, the most strongly demarcated unit would be the town: in Northern Yorubaland one can add *oriki orilẹ* to the 'facial marks' Krapf-Askari refers to. Lineage *oriki*, being claimed equally by descendants through females and through males, would not demarcate agnatic corporate groups and would have a less powerful identifying function than the town *oriki*. However, a less radical hypothesis would account equally well for the importance of *oriki orilẹ*.

16. For explanation of these terms see Section 3 of this chapter.

17. Three of these towns, mentioned by Babayẹmi (1971), were Igbori, Ogbin, and Ojẹ, all of Tapa (Nupe) origin and all intertwined in the *oriki orilẹ* of *ile* Ọdọfin in Okuku: probably a case of conflation as in the Ọyọ example discussed. The sack of Ọyọ by the Nupe is supposed to have taken place in Alaafin Ajaka's reign. Since this ọba belongs to the same kind of mythical, non-chronological era as the ọbas of Kọọkin, in which the accounts vary greatly, any attempt to assign him to a period – even to the nearest century – must be considered highly speculative.

18. I am grateful to Professor W. Abimbọla for telling me this story.

19. According to the *Iwe Itan Ọfa* by Ọlafimihan (1950), Ọfa changed its site nine times before the nineteenth century. Babayẹmi (1968, 1971) is my source for the status and location of these towns.

20. Schwab speaks of '*oriki idile*' (the *oriki* of descent groups – not a phrase in common use in Okuku), which are supposed to trace the relationships of all the members of the lineage and 'serve to define the structural relations of persons and groups within a lineage' (Schwab, 1955, p. 354). The way genealogical relationships are actually treated in *oriki* is very different, as will be shown in the next chapter.

21. As is common in Yorubaland, all compound land, if a group within the compound dies out, reverts to the compound as a whole for redistribution by the compound head. None of the land belongs absolutely to any segment, nor have they the right to sell it; but it is usually regarded as theirs as long as they and their descendants survive to claim it.

22. From a performance by Faderera, daughter of *ile* Ọba/Awoyẹmi, wife of *ile* Ọlọkọ, at the family celebration of the Egungun festival, 1975.

23. Schwab points out that there are two simultaneous principles of cleavage. He distinguishes the *isọkọ*, a segment descended from a common male ancestor, from the *origun*, a segment differentiated by reference to the mother: Schwab (1955, p. 353).

24. In his discussion of Yoruba medicine, Buckley describes the compound as 'an enclosure containing a male lineage' where 'the men encounter, coming from the outside, a flow of women': an inversion of the Yoruba model of the healthy body and therefore, according to Buckley, regarded as a potential threat to the integrity of the corporate group, while at the same time being essential for its survival. Women make links with the outside world which are both dangerous and necessary (Buckley, 1985, p. 168).

25. From the funeral chant by Iwẹ, daughter of *ile* Baalẹ, discussed in Chapter 4.

26. From a performance by Iya Lajire, daughter of *ile* Ẹlẹmọsọ, married into *ile* Oluọdẹ.

27. *Ibid.*

28. In other versions the river is given as 'Agunlọfa' and '*irúnmọlẹ̀ lÓfà tí gbogbo ayaba ń pọn ọ́n mu*' [the spirit at Ọfa from which all the royal wives drink.] This *oriki* is probably to be associated with Ọlafimihan's reference to a river flowing by Ọfa-

Igbo-Oro, one of the early Ọfa settlements, which was so good that only the wives of the Ọba Okunmolu were allowed to use it, and which was called Odo Ayaba, the river of the royal wives, up till today (Ọlafimihan, 1950, p. 5).

29. The verse, performed for me by the Araba of Okuku, Akanbi Ọpaleke, has been included in LaPin's collection of narratives (LaPin, 1977, pp. 139–42).

Notes to Chapter 6

1. *Àtin-in* mat: a mat characteristic of Ijẹṣaland. *Òré* mat: a highly valued type of mat found widely in Yoruba country, often included in a bride's 'dowry', i.e. the collection of household goods she takes to her husband's house for distribution to her husband's people (see Chapter 4).

2. People remember the main names but do not bother much about the relationships between them, even in the generation immediately before their own. People often skip a generation, calling themselves the grandsons or granddaughters of people who were actually their great-grandparents. There are considerable differences between the genealogies produced (on the demand of the anthropologist) even by full brothers – and regarding even their own father's generation! These variations seem in most cases not to be the result of political or other interests at work so much as a lack of use for detailed distinctions. Only when one branch of a lineage was traced through a daughter do people bring up ancient genealogical issues in chieftaincy contests (see Chapter 5). The royal family is somewhat more rigorous in its genealogies, at least in its accounts of the last three generations, because of the rotation of the crown between segments whose relationships have to be accounted for. But even here there are considerable divergences between one version and another, as was shown in Chapter 3. Chieftaincy contests which the colonial authorities collected evidence about in Ijabẹ (Ọṣun Div 1/1 File 175 vol. II, 1933), Okua (Ọṣun Div 1/1 886D/2A, 1957) and Iniṣa (Ọṣun Div 1/1 2173, 1953), show that this degree of malleability was common in the area. There is little interest in genealogies, in general, in this area. There is no formal oral genre for the preservation of genealogical knowledge and such knowledge is rarely called for.

3. For details of Ajayi's leadership during the Ikirun campaign, see Johnson (1921, pp. 428–34), Ajayi and Smith (1964, p. 45) and Akintoye (1971, pp.98–101).

4. According to Fadipẹ (1970, pp. 180–9), domestic slavery among the Yoruba was 'mild'. The right of slaves to emancipate themselves by payment of a standard fee was universally recognised; slaves were allotted their own farmland to work on after they had finished their day's work for the master; they were treated like members of the household and often eventually absorbed into it if they did not buy their freedom; and no stigma attached to children of female slaves. On the other hand, he reveals that the slave could hold no property, and that the master had the right to beat him to death! Oroge (1971) also stresses the mildness of the slaves' treatment and the high positions of power and privilege which some slaves attained. Law (1977, p. 206) postulates that by the early nineteenth century a more exploitative form of slavery had developed alongside the relatively benign patriarchal form described by Oroge.

5. Oroge's study (1971, p. 419) implies that the institution of *iwofa*, though an 'age-old...system', was of little economic or social significance until the suppression of domestic slavery, in the late nineteenth and early twentieth centuries. Oral texts however hint that it was an important institution well before this period.

6. According to Okuku people, one slave out of the total captured by the members of a compound on any expedition would also be given to the *baale*. A similar custom

is mentioned in passing by Fadipẹ, in his detailed but generalised description of Yoruba social structure, when he says that of the slaves captured in a campaign by the members of a compound, 'one or two were sure to be passed on' to the *baale*, and also that the ọba would take a 'certain percentage' (Fadipẹ, 1970, pp. 111,181). Johnson describes a complicated set of rules operating in Ibadan, by which free-born soldiers would hand over to their 'captains' either one- or two-fifths of their captives and keep the rest, but slave-warriors would hand over three- or four-fifths (Johnson 1921, p. 325). According to Lloyd, 'One-third of all war booty was handed over to the ọba, and a further third to the chief under whose jurisdiction the captor lived' (Lloyd, 1960, p. 229). The details of the system evidently varied from place to place, but the principle remained constant.

7. Michael Adeọsun, the present chief Ṣọbaloju, said that in the old days the new ọba would be chosen from among the competing candidates in a secret meeting of all the chiefs, using Ifa divination. 'But everyone present would be told, "You mustn't breathe a word of this outside". So all the chiefs and *babalawo* would keep quiet, and all the contesting princes would be sending presents, bringing food, and even holding feasts for the chiefs, not knowing that Ifa had already chosen one of them. That's how the chiefs got their share of the good things arising from chieftaincy'.

8. For a detailed description of the selection and installation of the ọba of Okuku, with special reference to Ọlaọṣebikan Oyewusi II, see Beier (1982, pp. 14–22).

9. So memorable was Oyekanbi's achievement in 'making six *ilari* in one day' that the names of all six are recorded in his *oriki*:

Gbà ó wá làlàrí tó la mẹ́fà lóòjọ́
Ó la 'Kú-ò-mọ̀nà
Ó la 'Kú-ò-yalé
Ó la 'Kú-yẹ̀
Ó la 'Pèjìn
Ó là'Jòbọ
Ó la 'Gbéjó, n ló wáá rígbá ńlá mutí baba 'lóya
Abìlàrí dógba jálẹ̀ baba Apèjìn...

When he made six *ilari* on a single day
He made Ku-o-mọna [Death-doesn't-know-the way]
He made Ku-o-yale [Death-doesn't-come-to-this-house]
He made Ku-yẹ [Death by-passes]
He made Apejin
He made Ajọbọ
He made Gbejo, the one who had a great dish to drink liquor
     from, father who is a devotee of Ọya
Owner of *ilari* who are exactly alike, father of Apejin...

According to Ajiboye, a descendant of Oyekanbi, 'the *baale* of each compound would hold a compound meeting after the accession of the ọba, to decide who to send from the compound to be an *ilari*', but if the ọba was unpopular they might not bother. He added that 'The *ilari* shaved half his head and plaited the unshaven half into a point like a woman's. After six months, when the hair had grown back, he would shave the other side. This was to make him immediately recognisable as the ọba's messenger, so that if he were sent to fetch someone, that person would know that it was a serious matter; he would be frightened and obey at once.' [According to Johnson (1921, p. 76) the provincial kings of Oyọ were allowed only one *ilari* each, and according to Oroge this rule was still in operation in the mid-nineteenth century (Oroge,1971, p. 80). Oyekanbi's action may have been made so much of because it was a decisive act of defiance. But it is equally likely that 'rules' emanating from the capital were unknown or disregarded in small towns like Okuku. The rule that provincial ǫbas could not wear fringed beaded crowns, *ade* (Law ,1977, p.98) certainly did not hold in Okuku, where the undoubtedly ancient collection of such crowns is one of its most famous possessions (see Beier, 1982).]

10. Robin Law (1977, p.62) observes that 'Political power normally lay with the senior "chiefs", or holders of titles (*oloye*). However, generally speaking, these men were given senior titles in recognition of their power; political power does not derive from possession of a title'. This account corresponds to some cases in Okuku, but not all; the amendment made by Peel (1983, p. 266), to the effect that title is not merely a ratification but also a source of power, is a valuable one. Law is surely right, however, to stress that 'Power was based ultimately on the control of resources, *more specifically on the allegiance of followers and the accumulation of wealth – 'men and means', to use an illuminating phrase of Samuel Johnson'* [*ibid.*: my italics]. Whether chiefs got their titles mainly because they were already big men, or expanded their position significantly only after getting a title (and both these things happened in Okuku), the principle of their success was the same: men and means, i.e. building up wealth by having 'people', and attracting 'people' by having wealth.

11. The genealogy, however, is only four generations deep: Winyǫmi is represented as the great-grandfather of the oldest men of *ile* Oluǫdę living today. The greatest foreshortening of the genealogy occurs between the third and the fourth ascendant generations, for Winyǫmi's 'sons' Ǫlǫmi, Ogunṣǫla and others did exist within living memory.

12. The first systematic use of firearms in Yoruba country has been estimated to have been around 1820 by Ajayi and Smith (1964) and Akintoye (1971). Alan Richards says that a few guns reached the Ǫyǫ area in the eighteenth century, but that it was not until the early 1850s that 'guns had become the standard weapons of most Yoruba warriors' (Richards, 1983, p.83). The reference to the gun, however, might well have been added to an older story anachronistically.

13. From a performance by Okeyǫyin, wife of Daniel Ogundiran, Chief Ṣaba, of *ile* Oluǫdę (March 1978).

14. Fadipę, writing in 1939[1970], says 'Before the establishment of colonial rule, the *baale* had many opportunities of turning to his own advantage the misfortune of members of his compound', notably by taking 'an extra percentage' for himself on any fine he imposed on offenders (Fadipę, 1970 [1939], p.111).

15. From a performance of the royal *oriki* by Abigail Ǫlatundun, daughter of Oyekunle branch of *ile* Ǫba, married into *ile* Ǫlǫkǫ. For a comparison of this passage with the *oriki* of the warlords of Ibadan, in the context of an analysis of changes in social structure and ideology in the nineteenth century, see Barber (1981a).

16. For a discussion of the different categories of *egungun* in Okuku, and the way in which 'big *egungun*' like Paję are founded, see note 30 in Chapter 3.

17. Historians have noted the rise of a new kind of big man in a number of war-ridden areas in the nineteenth century. Akintoye describes how the warboys of Ekiti raised private armies, and went on raids not instigated by their ǫba; they constituted 'new pockets of power and prestige which were frequently in conflict with, and potentially threatened, the position of the ǫbas'. But because of their ability to resist Ibadan 'these new men were generally welcomed and adored' (Akintoye, 1971, p. 77). Awę describes vividly the scale of operations of the military leaders in Ibadan (Awę 1964a). Although the Olokuku's household expanded with wartime access to an increased supply of slaves, the actual power of the ǫba probably

diminished. Lloyd shows clearly that this was the pattern in a number of larger nineteenth century kingdoms (Lloyd, 1971).

18. Recited by the late Ogunbuyi, Iyalode of Okuku, married into *ile* Balogun.

19. Gbọtifayọ was remembered by the present Chief Alawẹ, Samuel Ayantunji, as an ancient, blind *babalawo* to whom he was sent to learn Ifa as a child – around 1910–15.

20. From a performance by Ṣangowẹmi, addressed to members of *ile* Aro-Isalẹ, descendants of Jayẹọla and Gbọtifayọ his son, May 1975.

21. For further discussion of this complex of ideas, illustrated with samples of all these genres, see Barber (1979, pp. 233–45)

22. The story and *oriki* were told by Ọjẹyẹmi of *ile* Baalẹ. Ọjẹyẹmi was a former *ọjẹ* masquerader, a title-holder in the *egungun* cult and an accomplished *akewi* (performer of *iwi*, the *egungun* style of chanting), hence his unusual knowledge of *oriki*. He was a most brilliant interpreter of the meaning of words, *itan* and *oriki*. He was a philosopher. Sadly, he died before he reached old age.

23. This information is based on interviews with seventy-five men, divided into three age groups with twenty-five in each: the old men (over 70); the middle-aged (40–69); and the young (20–39). These age divisions are of course approximate, as few of the older men knew their exact age. I made no attempt to obtain a statistically random sample, for the most important thing was to talk to people who were willing and able to give a detailed account of their earliest memories – and they tended to be the people I knew best. I talked to more people from the compounds around the house where I stayed (*ile* Oluọdẹ, *ile* Ọlọkọ, *ile* Baalẹ, *ile* Oluawo) than from 'downtown Okuku'; and to more people who supported the ọba in the chiefly feud than to those who opposed him, for my honorary adoption by *ile* Ọba made this inevitable. The information is supplemented by numerous other interviews and informal discussions I had with certain very nice old men, like Johnson Onifade, Adewale baba Ọlọsun, Joseph Ogundairo, Michael Adeọsun and others. Attempts to question women about household, land, labour and residence invariably led to a referral to the husband. But women's informal comments and reminiscences about their own grandfathers and great-grandfathers, especially in connection with their *oriki*, were illuminating and are included.

24. In the first extant report on the Iba–Okuku boundary dispute which began around 1910, the A.D.O. sent from Ibadan in 1921 was under the impression that the problem concerned the planting of palm trees in an area beside the River Ọtin claimed by both towns. He observed that 'no dispute apparently arose until 1910 (possibly when palm trees became to be known more and more as profitable possession)' and also that there were 'some 60 farmers from Iba, with farms inside the disputed Area', all of which were planted with palm trees. 'Both the Eburu [Baalẹ of Iba] and Olokuku contend that they each have been reaping the Palm Trees'. He adds 'I believe there is some Iba Cocoa in the Area, but the rains and flooded condition of the Streams forbids a more detailed sketch of the actual farms and crops' (R.H.Lapage, 21–26 September 1921). However, subsequent reports speak only of cocoa on the disputed land (e.g. Resident to D.O. Ibadan 1923, A.D.O. to Olokuku 1924); they say that 'all [the Iba farmers and chiefs] admitted that they had planted the cocoa since 1914' (Senior Resident to Secretary of Southern Provinces, 1923); and list twenty Okuku farmers whose land was alleged to have been overplanted with cocoa by Iba people. It is also made clear that Iba people had also planted cocoa on other land whose ownership was not disputed. It seems likely that the problem arose because the Iba people were quicker to embark on cocoa farming than the Okuku people, whose own accounts of the

period speak overwhelmingly of yam farming rather than either cocoa or palm trees. But at least two women were involved from an early date in palm tree farming: see section 7 of this chapter.

25. 'Three years after the influenza epidemic' (i.e. in 1921), seven members of *ile* Oluodẹ – a set of five brothers and another pair related to the first through a maternal link – moved out to build a separate house 'because there was not enough room any more'. The new house was also 'huge' and 'had seventy rooms'. Seven of these were occupied by the matrilaterally-related pair of brothers, who stayed for fifteen years and then moved out to build their own house. Throughout the 1940s and 1950s the remaining five brothers – or their sets of grown-up sons – one by one moved out or rebuilt their own sections of the compound as separate buildings. Chief Ṣaba, for instance, the son of the eldest of the five brothers, rebuilt his father's section of the compound in 1940 as a 'long house with a parlour' for himself and his full brother. In 1971 he moved further up the road to a new site and built an 'upstairs' – a square two-storeyed house – for himself, his wives, his two grown sons, and his apprentices. The others did the same, so that now *'ile* Oluodẹ' consists of about twenty buildings. Only one man was eventually left on the original site in the centre of town: and he is in the middle of pulling down the remains of the old compound and putting up a storeyed house there.

26. Eleven of the twenty-five oldest informants said they stopped serving their fathers once they had married and got children of their own. They obtained their own share of their fathers' farms before his death, and had complete control over its use and produce. Even less often did sons continue to serve their uncles or older brothers very long after the father's death. If the sons were young, they might work for a senior relative for a number of years, but eventually the farm would be divided and only sons of the same mother would continue to work together in groups. Often even these, the closest units in the system, would split up before their deaths. Even some of the very oldest men, those who were young boys before the beginning of this century, said that as children they worked not for a group of men – as might be expected if the ideal were realised – but for a single man: their own father or, if he had died, his nearest male relative. This means that even as long as eighty years ago, full brothers did not necessarily conform to the ideal of staying together and serving the eldest among them all their lives. Only four out of twenty-five of the oldest men said they worked for a partnership. Three of these partnerships were pairs of full brothers, and two of them broke up before the partners' deaths. The fourth was not a real partnership, for though the brothers did not divide the farm, each of them worked separately on it.

27. At the *iṣihun* ceremony one man paid £1 1s; at the *parapọ* ceremony several men said they paid £2 10s; some paid for a sacrifice (£2 10s).

28. A man owed the woman's father one day of *ọwẹ* labour every year, or every other year, throughout the period of betrothal. This involved the recruitment of a large body of age-mates and friends from his compound – it was said that less than forty people would not be acceptable – to do a full day's work. He also gave the father a parcel of yams (one man said nine yams made a parcel) and a basket of maize one, two, three or even four times a year, as well as a chicken for his annual festival.

29. During this period, the average area cultivated for the food for a household was between 2000 and 8000 yam heaps, that is, between two-thirds of an acre and 2 and two-third acres. Two thousand yam heaps were estimated to yield 20 *ofaaṣu*, that is, twenty lots of 120 yams; and around 1930 one *ofaaṣu* would fetch 5/- in the market. These figures are of course approximate and based on memory rather than record, on individual reminiscences rather than statistics.

30. Among the twenty-five oldest informants, only nine said their fathers paid the first bride price for them. Seven more said their fathers made all the arrangements but left it to them to produce the money. The son's obedience did not seem to affect the father's readiness to meet this obligation. Out of the fourteen men who said they 'served their fathers till death', only four were given wives by their fathers.

31. While the oldest group of twenty-five informants spent a total of forty years between them in Ghana, the middle group spent a total of one hundred and forty-four years. They also spent more years away from home altogether – whether in Ghana or elsewhere – averaging more than nine years each in contrast to the older men's seven.

32. Of the twenty-five oldest men, three went to a Christian school and one to *ile Kewu*, the Islamic school. Of the twenty-five men in the middle group, five went to Christian school and two to *ile Kewu*.

33. For a discussion of the different age ranges of cocoa farmers in farm towns founded at different periods, see Berry (1975, pp. 160–4).

34. However, as Sara Berry has shown (Berry, 1975, pp. 126–52), labour shortage was still the main constraint on cocoa farmers. She found that this problem was often solved by hiring wage labourers who were themselves young cocoa farmers, whose trees had not yet started to bear fruit and who were therefore in urgent need of cash. As well as the secondary occupations such as barbering, tailoring, etc. that I have already mentioned, wage labour on neighbours' farms was certainly an option some Okuku men took up.

35. Since the genealogy is, as we have seen, easy to revise, present versions do not demonstrate when this rotation was instituted or to what extent it really ever operated. The number and order of segments was finally fixed only by the Chieftaincy Declaration of 1956. Before this, four segments appear to have *contested* the throne but only three ever succeeded in getting their candidates in. Moreover, the order of rotation was certainly not immutable. Even in the colonial period, each chieftaincy contest saw vigorous campaigns staged by segments out of turn, no doubt in the belief that if the candidate was attractive enough the order would be overridden. According to Michael Adeọsun, the present chief Ṣọbaloju, rotation between segments in a set order only came in in the time of Oyinlọla, but he attributed this not to colonial intervention but to the Okuku chiefs' wish to imitate the Ibadan system.

36. When Oyekunle died in 1934, the six 'kingmakers', together with the Iyalode and the Ṣọbaloju – Oyekunle's closest confidant – wrote to the Assistant D.O. at Oṣogbo to say that they wanted Moses Oyinlọla to succeed him, 'but we have not ready yet we are making the funeral of the late, we only hint you aforehand because many of our people will be given you trouble that they like the post'. A week later the A.D.O. hurried over to Okuku to supervise the selection process, and then reported approvingly to the D.O. at Ibadan that 'In the presence of the chiefs, the members of the late Olokuku's family and people of Okuku and some representatives of neighbouring villages, Moses Oyinlọla was unanimously elected to become Olokuku....' (30/10/1934: Oṣun Div 1/1, File 175, Vol II: *Chiefs:Okuku District:Matters Affecting*). This drew a stinging reply from the Resident himself: 'An Olokuku should be 'selected' by the chiefs and not 'elected' by the people'. The A.D.O. was responding to the flexible and consensual aspect of the process of selection, the Resident to the privileged position of the chiefs who made the final choice among candidates who had already competed to win popular favour. The A.D.O.'s democratic leanings were quashed, for the dominating tendency in colonial rewriting of tradition was to make the hierarchical and fixed elements

prevail over the open and competitive ones.

37. There is a wealth of detail on such disputes in the colonial records. See for example the reports in Ọṣun Div. 1/1, 1933–38, *Chiefs: Okuku District* 326. 175/Vol. II, and 1948–53, *Chiefs and Chieftaincy Disputes* 326.175/Vol II.

38. This at least is one of the versions of the story that circulated. Ajiboye's account of this adventure is too long to quote in full, but it includes some episodes that shed an interesting light on local perceptions of the colonial authorities. When Ajiboye saw the '*oyinbo agba*' (the senior European) in Ibadan, this man sent for the '*oyinbo kekere*' (the junior European), the one who had visited Okuku. The junior European confirmed that he knew Oyekunle very well, that Oyekunle was the one who always came to see him and brought him eggs when he visited Okuku, whereas he didn't know Oyeleye at all. The senior European then wrote three letters, to Ibadan, Ikirun and Ọyọ, announcing that Oyekunle was to be the next ọba. When the letter was read out in Okuku – by a literate forest guard, a stranger working there – there was uproar. They said a European had never made an ọba before, ọbas were always made by themselves in the marketplace of Okuku, and that their choice was Oyeleye. They went to Ikirun to tell the European this when he arrived, but the European insisted that he would install Oyekunle. So the chiefs decided to install Oyeleye before the appointed day. When Ajiboye heard rumours of this he ran all the way to Ikirun, found that the junior European had left for Oṣogbo, ran all night and reached Oṣogbo just in time to glimpse the European leaving in his car [*sic*], learnt he had gone to Ogbomọṣọ so ran all day and reached Oko just as night fell. At dawn he found people to take him to Ogbomọṣọ to look for the European. When they had found him and explained the situation the European said 'WHAT!!' He wrote three letters on the spot and sent them to Ibadan, Ikirun and Ọyọ. He told Ajiboye to start walking home and promised that before he got there the Europeans would have arrived. Just as Ajiboye reached Okuku, the people from Ibadan, the Europeans and the African officials arrived. It was the day of the installation. The European sat down in the market and called all the chiefs, all the heads of the subordinate towns, and all the supporters of both contestants. The he asked 'Does the choice of Oyekunle please you?' They said no. Then he read the letter out to them and said 'That's that. That's what the Government says'. They installed Oyekunle that very day. His supporters danced and started singing '*Ẹni òyinbó gbà níyàwó tí ará oko fojúdi*' (The person the European took to wife, when the bushmen insulted him) This became part of his *oriki*.

39. From a performance by Ṣangowẹmi, on the occasion of Ṣapawo's *egungun* feast, further discussed in Chapter 7.

40. I am indebted to John Peel for suggesting this way of putting it.

41. As was mentioned in Note 25 above, before the Lagos era, most farms were recalled as being 6d-2/- *ebe*, that is 2000–8000 heaps or two-thirds to two and two-third acres. After Lagos selling came in, the farms were in many cases said to have increased to a size between 3/- and 5/- *ebe*: that is, four to six and two-third acres. The middle-aged group, speaking of their childhoods in the 1930s and 40s, remembered farms as big as 5/- to 10/- *ebe*: that is, six to thirteen and a half acres.

42. Prices quoted for labourers' wages in Pakoyi's time include the following examples: 'Labourers' fees were 4d for building 200 heaps, 2d for hoeing 200 heaps, 1$\frac{1}{2}$d for mulching 200 heaps' (Amos Ọjẹdiji, *ile* Baalẹ). This informant added 'They came from Ilọrin, and stayed in the house of the host, but only until the job was done'.

43. A story told by Mohammed Akanbi of *ile* Ọlọyan, about an incident in Oyinlọla's reign, illustrates this. Mohammed's grandfather Faliyi had had a great friend

Morakinyọ in *ile* Aṣipa, whose farmland adjoined his own. Faliyi lent part of his own land to Morakinyọ to use for food crops. One day when they were working near to each other in the farm, Faliyi offered Morakinyọ some kola nuts and after they'd eaten a few, Morakinyọ jokingly said 'Why don't we plant one so that we can eat it together in the future?' Faliyi took this as a symbol of their friendship and agreed. In due course the seed grew into a tree and both men ate the fruit. Years later, after Faliyi's death, Morakinyọ's son claimed that Morakinyọ had planted the tree there and that that meant he had a right to all the land between it and the (former) boundary of *ile* Aṣipa's land. The matter became a big court case and because Oyinlọla had a grudge against *ile* Ọlọyan, for a quite unrelated reason, he supported *ile* Aṣipa. *Ile* Ọlọyan lost the land on the grounds that the person who plants a permanent crop has title to the land on which it is planted.

44. Two notable nineteenth century figures were Madame Tinubu of Lagos and Ẹfunṣetan of Ibadan. Both built up formidable households of followers and slaves, and Madame Tinubu was herself deeply involved in the slave trade. She was eventually driven out of Lagos by the ọba Dosunmu at the instigation of the British Consul (Biobaku, 1960; Oroge ,1971, pp. 181–3). Ẹfunṣetan was also defeated by the male chiefs of Ibadan, led by Latosisa, and expelled from the city (Johnson, 1921, pp. 391–4). The importance of these figures in popular memory is attested by the success of the Yoruba-language play *Ẹfunṣetan Aniwura* (Iṣọla 1970), later made into a popular film by a travelling theatre company, and an English language play about Madame Tinubu, also by Akinwumi Iṣọla.

45. In the considerable body of recent work on Yoruba witchcraft, all the elements of this picture have been touched on. Beier (1958), Hoch-Smith (1978), the Drewals (1983) and others have related notions of witchcraft to female fertility, pointing out that the ambivalence towards 'witchcraft' powers derives from the ambiguous power women have, either benignly to produce offspring or malignly to interfere with their production. Belasco (1980), on the other hand, argues that women were accused of witchcraft because their control of local trade aroused male jealousy: men produced goods, women merely manipulated them and yet came out rich from it. Marc Schiltz, in a recent perceptive paper (1987), has suggested that economic success in women created an anomalous and unlocatable power, one which could not be exercised through the normal channels of household patronage and redistribution. It was a power that had no 'natural' outlet, and was therefore regarded with suspicion and, if it went too far, interpreted as witchcraft. Regarded from the perspective of the dynamics of self-aggrandisement, all these notions can be related. Men can convert wealth to reputation; in women, reputation means they are encroaching on male territory, and is therefore almost certain to be evil. The Drewals, in my view, exaggerate the benign aspect of the 'mothers'' powers. What people said in Okuku corresponded much more closely to the account of witchcraft given by Peter Morton-Williams (1956a, 1956b, 1960b, 1964). When a woman is released by her husband's death from the obligation to swell his household, she is given licence to live on her own; but this transition makes her not only useless from the point of view of the expansion of men's power, but also potentially a rival to male household heads. Older women are more likely therefore to be 'witches' than young ones.

46. For a full discussion of this concept, central to modern Yoruba notions of 'progress', see Peel (1978).

47. See the account of a chieftaincy dispute in Okua, one of the subordinate towns, in 1957 soon after the Chieftaincy Declaration had been made (Ọṣun Div 1/1 886D/2A).

48. From a performance of *iwi* by Ojeyemi of Ekusa, an itinerant professional *akewi*, well known in the locality and beyond through his radio performances and commercial records.
49. From a performance by Janet Bolatito, Iya Denle, wife of *ile* Oba, Edun branch.

Notes to Chapter 7

1. Palace titles could be passed from father to son. Michael Adeosun, the present chief Sobaloju, is the eldest son of Toyinbo, the previous incumbent. Junior town titles of the *aladaa* grade could also be inherited in the same way. Some important religious titles were ritually required to pass from father to son – the priesthood of Olooku, for instance (also noted by Murray, 1950) – while most could be taken over by a variety of successors, and 'place' in a cult could switch gender or skip a generation. But senior town titles of the *olopaa* grade tended to rotate between segments of the lineage that owned it, in the manner described by Lloyd (1955) – especially when the lineage was large. In these cases, the title was certainly seen as a continuous 'place' successively occupied by different individuals all of whom took on the identity of the office; but at the same time, each of these individuals created a personal place, expressed in *oriki* and *itan*, which would be taken on not by other segments of the lineage but by his own descendants.
2. *Mé leè sùn*: a dialect variant of the standard Yoruba *mi ò lè sùn* or *mi ì lè sùn*.
3. The leader of this performance was Ere-Osun, daughter of *ile* Odofin, married into *ile* Elemoso Awo, on the occasion of an *egungun* festival vigil. Each line was repeated by a chorus of other *obinrin ile* and *omo-osu*.
4. This is an example of the way *oriki* converge with Bakhtin's concerns in an oblique way that raises questions rather than answering any. Bakhtin's argument, in the essays published as *The Dialogic Imagination*, was that polyvocality, the frequent and easy incorporation of the voice of the 'other', was the product of culture contact, exposure to other languages or registers of language. That is when the enclosing, limiting orthodoxy of the patriarchy is breached and people realise that the patriarchal language is not the only one. Polyglossia is associated in Bakhtin therefore with joyous liberation, with mockery and satire, and with a new self-consciousness. In *oriki*, the quotations are seamless. They do not become an object of representation, as in parody, and cannot therefore be seen as a chink through which self-consciousness and criticism may enter discourse. However, as I argue here, they do nevertheless represent in some sense a deferral of ideological closure. Alternatives and opposites are held in juxtaposition without being resolved or subordinated to a higher unity. Formally, they represent the extreme end of the range of possibilities Bakhtin outlines, and indeed go further in polyvocality than any of the European texts he examines.
5. From a performance by Oni Okekanyin (Iya Olose), married into *ile* Obaale, on the occasion of the funeral of her co-wife Adeboyake, April 1977.
6. Olasope Oyelaran, in an illuminating paper (1975), argues that syntactic parallelism, not stress, is the basis of 'rhythm' in Yoruba oral poetry, and that it 'pre-conditions any other factor, including logical or sense parallelism'.
7. From a performance of *rara iyawo* by Susannah Faramade, wife of *ile* Arogun, February 1976.
8. From a performance by Sangowemi supported by a chorus of women devotees of Sango, on the occasion of the funeral of Arinke, wife of *ile* Baale, discussed in Chapter 4.
9. In his exposition of the idea of 'habitus' or 'systems of durable, transposable *dispositions*', Bourdieu (1977, p. 72), re-examines the oral-formulaic theory of

Parry and Lord. The important thing to Bourdieu is not the idea of the formula itself, as in many subsequent applications of the approach, but the way the Yugoslav poets learn to use it. The *guslar* gains his practical mastery of formulaic composition 'through sheer familiarisation, "by hearing the poems", without the learner's having any sense of learning and subsequently manipulating this or that formula or any set of formulae: the constraints of rhythm are internalised at the same time as melody and meaning, without being attended to for their own sake' (Bourdieu, 1977, p. 88).

10. From a performance by Okeyọyin, wife of Daniel Ogundiran, chief Ṣaba, of *ile* Oluọdẹ, March 1978.

11. From a performance by Ṣangowẹmi in honour of members of *ile* Aro-Isalẹ.

12. See, for instance, Stenning (1959) on the Wodaabe pastoral Fulani; Okonjo (1976), Van Allen (1972, 1976), Ifeka-Moller (1975) and Amadiume (1987) on the Igbo; Edwin Ardener (1975) on the Bakweri; Moore (1986) on the Marakwet.

13. Little systematic work has been done on this fascinating question – perhaps because scholars of the Yoruba do not see any striking classificatory dichotomies to investigate. The questionnaire on male/female stereotypes administered by Asuni (1987, pp. 272–85), despite its methodological limitations, confirms that the whole range of qualities ascribed to men can also be ascribed to women; the proportions and order of importance vary, but it seems to be granted by Asuni's informants that any man or any woman *could* appear anywhere in the range of personality types.

14. From the *egungun* vigil chant led by Ẹrẹ-Ọṣun, discussed in Section 2.

15. From an Ifa song performed by Adewale, Baba Ọlọṣun, one of the *babalawo* of Okuku, on the occasion of Araba's feast during the annual Ifa festival (August 1976).

16. In their brilliant analyses of Yoruba masquerade art, H. J. Drewal (1978) and H. J. and M. T. Drewal (1983) have used the term 'seriality' to describe the fundamental organising principle of Yoruba arts, which produces a structure 'in which the units of the whole are discrete and share equal value and importance with the other units and in which the autonomous segments evoke, and often invoke and activate, diverse forces' (Drewal and Drewal, 1983, p. 7). Though their focus is on the visual arts, they themselves indicate that 'seriality' is also the underlying principle of 'praise poetry, invocations, incantations' (*ibid.*).

17. From a performance of *rara iyawo* by Susannah Faramade, wife of *ile* Arogun, February 1976.

18. Henrietta Moore's discussion of Marakwet representations of space is helpful here. She argues that rather than having an alternative, autonomous model outside the dominant male culture, Marakwet women have a different location *within* a shared system of representations. There is a 'negotiability of meaning' which 'permits the expression of the female perspective within the spatial medium' (Moore, 1986, p. 186). Yoruba culture, like Marakwet culture, is biased towards the male; but as the foregoing discussion will have made clear, Yoruba culture offers women much greater scope to choose and make their own position within a range of alternatives. Women in Yoruba towns are far from 'invisible', and male/ female cultural dichotomies are, as we have argued above, porous and malleable.

19. One man said that it was not uncommon for women to become *babalawo* 'up towards Ogbomọṣọ and Ọyọ', but knew of no other examples by name. The existing literature on Ifa gives the overwhelming impression that it is an exclusively male cult. However, one documented example of a female *babalawo* is the Iyanifa Mopelọla Fawẹnda Amọkẹ of Ọyọ, now 80 years old, whose photograph appears

in González-Wippler (1989). According to Bayọ Ogundijọ of the University of Ifẹ, the Iyanifa was initiated into the Ifa cult 45–50 years ago, after learning Ifa by the same system as male diviners. Like them, she travelled to other towns to extend her knowledge, gave consultations, and attended meetings of the association of *babalawo* until old age prevented her (personal communication).

BIBLIOGRAPHY

Abimbọla, Wande (1975a) *Sixteen Great Poems of Ifa*. UNESCO.

Abimbọla, Wande, (ed.) (1975b) *Yoruba Oral Tradition*. Department of African Languages and Literatures, University of Ifẹ. Ifẹ African Languages and Literatures Series no. 1.

Abimbọla, Wande (1976) *Ifa: an exposition of Ifa literary corpus*. Ibadan: Oxford University Press.

Abimbọla, Wande (1977) *Ifa Divination Poetry*. New York: NOK.

Abraham, R. C. (1958) *A Dictionary of Modern Yoruba*. London: University of London Press.

Abrahams, Roger D. (1977) 'Toward an enactment-centred theory of folklore', in *Frontiers of Folklore*, ed. William Bascom. Boulder: Westview Press for the AAAS.

Abu-Lughod, Lila (1986) *Veiled Sentiments*. Berkeley and Los Angeles: University of California Press.

Adedeji, J. A. (1969a) 'The Alarinjo Theatre: the study of a Yoruba theatrical art from its earliest beginnings to the present times. ' Ph. D. thesis, University of Ibadan.

Adedeji, J. A. (1969b) 'Traditional Yoruba Theatre', *African Arts*, 3, 1.

Adedeji, J. A. (1972) 'The origin and form of the Yoruba masquerade theatre', *Cahiers d'Etudes Africaines*, 12, 2 (46).

Adedeji, J. A. (1978) 'The poetry of the Yoruba masque theatre', *African Arts*, 11, 3.

Adeoye, C. L. (1972) *Orúkọ Yorùbá*. Ibadan: Oxford University Press.

Aderibigbe, A. B. (ed.) (1975) *Lagos: the development of an African city*. Nigeria: Longman.

Ajayi, J. F. A. and Smith, R. (1964) *Yoruba Warfare in the Nineteenth Century*. Cambridge: Cambridge University Press.

Ajuwọn, Bade (1982) *Funeral Dirges of Yoruba Hunters*. New York: NOK Press.

Akinjogbin, I. A. (1965) 'The prelude to the Yoruba civil wars of the nineteenth century', *Odu* 1, 2.

Akinjogbin, I. A. (1966) 'A chronology of Yoruba history 1789-1840', *Odu* (second series) 2,2.

Akintoye, S. A. (1971) *Revolution and Power Politics in Yorubaland 1840-1893*. London: Longman.

Amadiume, Ifi (1987) *Male Daughters, Female Husbands: gender and sex in an African society*. London: Zed Books.

Ardener, Edwin (1975) 'Belief and the problem of women', in Shirley Ardener (1975).

Ardener, Shirley (ed.) (1975) *Perceiving Women*. London etc. : J. M. Dent.

Asuni, J. B. (1987) 'Changing Patterns of Ẹgba Childrearing'. Ph. D. thesis, University of Birmingham.

Atanda, J. A. (1973) *The New Ọyọ Empire*. London: Longman.

Austin, J. L. (1962) *How to Do Things with Words*. Oxford: Clarendon Press.

Awẹ, Bọlanle (1964a) 'The Rise of Ibadan as a Yoruba Power 1851-1893'. D. Phil thesis, University of Oxford.

Awẹ, Bọlanle (1964b) 'The ajẹlẹ system: a study of Ibadan imperialism in the 19th century', *Journal of the Historical Society of Nigeria* 3, 1.

Awẹ, Bọlanle (1974) 'Praise poems as historical data: the example of the Yoruba oriki', *Africa* 44, 4.

Awe, Bọlanle (1975) 'Notes on oriki and warfare in Yorubaland', in Abimbọla (1975b).

Babalọla, S. A. [Adeboye] (1966a) *The Content and Form of Yoruba Ijala*. Oxford: Oxford University Press.

Babalọla, Adeboye (1966b) *Àwọn Oríkì Orílè,* Glasgow: Collins.

Babalọla, Adeboye (1973a,b) *Akójọpọ̀ Àló Ìjàpá,* Apa Kinni, Apa Keji. Ibadan: Oxford University Press.

Babalọla, Adeboye (1989) 'A portrait of Ògún as reflected in Ìjálá chants', in Barnes (1989).

Babayẹmi, S. O. (1968) 'Ọyọ ruins', *African Notes,* 5, 1.

Babayẹmi, S. O. (1971) 'Upper Ogun: an historical sketch', *African Notes* 6, 2.

Babayẹmi, S. O. (1988) *Content Analysis of Oriki Orilẹ.* Ibadan: Institute of African Studies.

Bakhtin, Mikhail (1981) *The Dialogic Imagination,* ed. Michael Holquist, trans. Caryl Emerson and Michael Holquist, Austin, Texas: University of Texas Press.

Bakhtin, Mikhail (1984a) *Problems of Dostoevsky's Poetics,* ed. and trans. Caryl Emerson. Minneapolis: University of Minnesota Press.

Bakhtin, Mikhail (1984b) *Rabelais and his World,* trans. Helène Iswolsky: Bloomington: Indiana University Press.

Banton, Michael (ed.) (1965) *Political Systems and the Distribution of Power,* A. S. A. Monographs 2. London: Tavistock.

Barber, Karin (1979) 'Oriki in Okuku town', Ph. D thesis, University of Ifẹ.

Barber, Karin (1981a) 'Documenting social and ideological change through Yoruba personal oriki: a stylistic analysis', *Journal of the Historical Society of Nigeria* 10, 4.

Barber, Karin (1981b) 'How man makes god in West Africa: Yoruba attitudes towards the orisa', *Africa* 51, 3.

Barber, Karin (1984a) 'Yoruba oriki and deconstructive criticism', *Research in African Literatures,* 15, 4.

Barber, Karin (1984b) 'Difference, Dissent, and Contradiction in Yoruba Oral Literature', paper presented at DALL seminar series, University of Ifẹ, Nigeria.

Barber, Karin (1990a) 'Discursive strategies in the texts of Ifá and in the "Holy Book of Odu" of the African Church of Ọrunmila', in Farias and Barber (eds.) 1990.

Barber, Karin (1990b) '*Oríkì,* women and the proliferation and merging of *òrìṣà',* *Africa,* 60, 3.

Barber, Karin and Farias, P. F. de Moraes (1989) *Discourse and its Disguises: the interpretation of African oral texts.* Birmingham: Centre of West African Studies.

Barnes, Sandra T. (1986) *Patrons and Power: creating a political community in metropolitan Lagos.* Manchester: Manchester University Press for the International African Institute.

Barnes, Sandra T. (ed.) (1989) *Africa's Ogun.* Bloomington, Indiana: Indiana University Press.

Barthes, Roland (1975) *S/Z,* trans. Richard Miller. London: Jonathan Cape.

Barthes, Roland (1979) 'From work to text', in Harari (1979).

Bascom, W. R. (1942) 'The principle of seniority in the social structure of the Yoruba', *American Anthropologist* 44.

Bascom, W. R. (1951) 'Social status, wealth and individual differences among the Yoruba', *American Anthropologist* 53.

Bascom, W. R. (1969) *Ifa Divination: communication between gods and men in West Africa.* Bloomington: Indiana University Press.

Bauman, Richard (1977) *Verbal Art as Performance*. Illinois: Waveland Press.

Bauman, Richard (1986) *Story, Performance and Event*. Cambridge: Cambridge University Press.

Bauman, Richard and Sherzer, Joel (eds.) (1974) *Explorations in the Ethnography of Speaking*. Cambridge: Cambridge University Press.

Beidelman, T. O. (1986) *Moral Imagination in Kaguru Modes of Thought*. Bloomington, Indiana: Indiana University Press.

Beier, H. U. [Ulli] (1956) 'Oloku Festival', *Nigeria Magazine* 49.

Beier, H. U. [Ulli] (1958) 'Gẹlẹdẹ masks', *Odu* 6.

Beier, Ulli (1982) *Yoruba Beaded Crowns*. London: Ethnographica.

Belasco, Bernard (1980) *The Entrepreneur as Culture-Hero: preadaptations in Nigerian economic development*. New York: Praeger.

Belsey, Catherine (1980) *Critical Practice*. London/New York: Methuen.

Ben-Amos, Dan (1975) *Sweet Words: story-telling events in Benin*. Philadelphia: ISHI.

Ben-Amos, Dan and Goldstein, Kenneth S. (1975) *Folklore: performance and communication*. The Hague: Mouton.

Berger, Peter, and Luckmann, Thomas (1967) *The Social Construction of Reality*. Harmondsworth: Penguin.

Berry, Sara S. (1975) *Cocoa, Custom and Socio-economic Change in Rural Western Nigeria*. Oxford: Oxford University Press.

Berry, Sara S. (1985) *Fathers Work for their Sons*. Berkeley: University of California Press.

Biobaku, S. O. (1960) 'Madame Tinubu', in Dike (1960).

Biobaku, S. O. (ed.) (1973) *Sources of Yoruba History*. Oxford: Oxford University Press.

Bloch, R. Howard (1983) *Etymologies and Genealogies: a literary anthropology of the French Middle Ages*. Chicago: Chicago University Press.

Bloom, Harold *et al.* (1979) *Deconstruction and Criticism*. New York: Seabury Press.

Bonte, Pierre, and Echard, Nicole (1976) 'Histoire et Histoires. Conception du passé chez les Hausa et les Twareg Kel Gress de l'Ader (République du Niger)', *Cahiers d'Etudes Africaines* 16, 61-2.

Bourdieu, Pierre (1977) *Outline of a Theory of Practice*, trans. Richard Nice. Cambridge: Cambridge University Press.

Brooks, Cleanth (1947) *The Well-wrought Urn*. New York/London: Harcourt Brace Jovanovich.

Buckley, Anthony D. (1985) *Yoruba Medicine*. Oxford: Clarendon Press.

Clark, Katerina, and Holquist, Michael (1984) *Mikhail Bakhtin*. Cambridge, Mass. and London: Harvard University Press.

Clarke, R. J. M. (1979) 'Agricultural Production in a Rural Yoruba Community. ' Ph. D. thesis, University of London.

Cope, Trevor (ed.) (1968) *Izibongo: Zulu praise poems*. Oxford: Clarendon Press.

Cosentino, Donald (1982) *Defiant Maids and Stubborn Farmers*. Cambridge: Cambridge University Press.

Cox, C. B. and Hinchliffe, Arnold P. (1968) *T. S. Eliot: The Waste Land*. London: Macmillan.

Culler, Jonathan (1975) *Structuralist Poetics*. London: Routledge and Kegan Paul.

Culler, Jonathan (1981) *The Pursuit of Signs*. Ithaca: Cornell University Press.

Culler, Jonathan (1983) *On Deconstruction*. London: Routledge and Kegan Paul.

Cunnison, Ian (1951) *History on the Luapula: an essay on the historical notions of a Central African tribe*. Rhodes-Livingstone Papers 21.

Damane, M. and Sanders, P. B. (1974) *Lithoko: Sotho praise poems*. Oxford: Clarendon Press.

Derrida, Jacques (1976) *Of Grammatology*, trans. Gayatri Chakravorty Spivak. Baltimore: Johns Hopkins University Press.

Derrida, Jacques (1979) 'Living on', in Harold Bloom *et al* (1979).

Dike, K. O. (ed.) (1960) *Eminent Nigerians of the Nineteenth Century*. Cambridge: Cambridge University Press.

Drewal, Henry John (1978) 'The arts of the Egungun among Yoruba peoples', *African Arts* 11,3.

Drewal, M. T. and Drewal, H. J. (1978) 'More powerful than each other: an Egbado classification of egungun', *African Arts*, 11, 3.

Drewal, H. J. and Drewal, M. T. (1983) *Gelede: art and female power among the Yoruba*. Bloomington: Indiana University Press.

Eades, J. S. (1980) *The Yoruba Today*. Cambridge: Cambridge University Press.

Eagleton, Terry (1983) *Literary Theory*. Oxford: Blackwell.

Fadipe, N. A. (1970 [1939]) *The Sociology of the Yoruba*, ed. F. O. Okediji and O. O. Okediji. Ibadan: Ibadan University Press.

Faniyi, Dejo (1975) 'Ekun iyawo: a traditional Yoruba nuptial chant', in Abimbola (1975b).

Farias, P. F. de Moraes and Barber, Karin, (eds) (1990) *Self-assertion and Brokerage: early cultural nationalism in West Africa*. Birmingham: Centre of West African Studies.

Fernandez, James W. (1982) *Bwiti: an ethnography of the religious imagination in Africa*. Princeton, NJ: Princeton University Press.

Fernandez, James W. (1986) *Persuasions and Performances*. Bloomington: Indiana University Press.

Finnegan, Ruth (1970) *Oral Literature in Africa*. Oxford: Oxford University Press.

Finnegan, Ruth (1988) *Literacy and Orality: studies in the technology of communication*. Oxford: Blackwell.

Forde, D. and Kaberry, P. (eds) (1967) *West African Kingdoms in the Nineteenth Century*. London: Oxford University Press.

Fowler, Roger (ed.) (1966) *Essays on Style and Language*. London: Routledge and Kegan Paul.

Francis, Paul A. (1981) 'Power and Order: a study of litigation in a Yoruba community. ' Ph. D. thesis, University of Liverpool.

Furniss, Graham (1989) 'Typification and evaluation: a dynamic process in rhetoric', in Barber and Farias (1989).

Gbadamosi, Bakare (1961) *Oriki*. Ibadan: Mbari Publications.

Geertz, Clifford (1973) *The Interpretation of Cultures*. New York: Basic Books.

González-Wippler, Migene (1989) *Santería: the Religion. A Legacy of Faith, Rites and Magic*. New York: Harmony Books.

Götrick, Kacke (1984) *Apidán Theatre and Modern Drama*. Stockholm, Sweden: Almqvist and Wiksell International.

Grice, H. P. (1975) 'Logic and Conversation', in *Speech Acts*, eds. Peter Cole and Jerry L. Morgan, Syntax and Semantics Vol. 3, New York: Academic Press.

Gutkind, Peter C. W. (1975) 'The view from below: political consciousness of the urban poor in Ibadan', *Cahiers d'Etudes Africaines* 15, 1 (issue 57).

Guyer, Jane I. (1972) 'The Organisational Plan of Traditional Farming: Idere, Western Nigeria. ' Ph. D. thesis, University of Rochester.

Hafkin, N. J. and Bay, E. G. (eds) (1976) *Women in Africa: studies in social and economic change*. Stanford, Calif. : Stanford University Press.

Harari, Josue (1979) *Textual Strategies*. Ithaca: Cornell University Press.

Henige, David (1982) *Oral Historiography*. London: Longman.

Hoch-Smith, Judith (1978) 'Radical Yoruba female sexuality: the witch and the prostitute', in Hoch-Smith and Spring (1978).

Hoch-Smith, Judith and Spring, Anita (eds) (1978) *Women in Ritual and Symbolic Roles*. New York and London: Plenum Press.

Houlberg, Marilyn H. (1978) 'Egungun masquerades of the Remo Yoruba', *African Arts* 11, 3.

Ifeka-Moller, C. (1975) 'Female militancy and colonial revolt: the Women's War of 1929, Eastern Nigeria', in S. Ardener (1975).

Iṣọla, Akinwumi (1970) *Efúnṣetán Aníwúrà*. Ibadan: Oxford University Press.

Iṣọla, Akinwumi (1973) 'Ṣàngó Pípè: one type of Yoruba oral poetry.' M. A. thesis, University of Lagos.

Jackson, Michael (1982) *Allegories of the Wilderness*. Bloomington: Indiana University Press.

Johnson, Samuel (1976 [1921]) *The History of the Yorubas*. Reprint: London: C.S.S.

Kenyo, E. Alademomi (1964) *Yoruba Natural Rulers and their Origin*. Ibadan.

Kermode, Frank (1967) *The Sense of an Ending: studies in the theory of fiction*. London and New York: Oxford: Oxford University Press.

Krapf-Askari, E. (1969) *Yoruba Towns and Cities*. Oxford: Clarendon Press.

Kunene, Daniel (1971) *Heroic Poetry of the Basotho*. Oxford: Clarendon Press.

LaPin, Deirdre (1977) 'Story, Medium and Masque: the idea and art of Yoruba story-telling.' Ph. D. thesis, University of Wisconsin.

Law, R. C. C. (1970) 'The chronology of the Yoruba wars of the early nineteenth century: a reconsideration', *Journal of the Historical Society of Nigeria* 5,2.

Law, R. C. C. (1977) *The Oyọ Empire c. 1600-c. 1836*. Oxford: Oxford University Press.

Lewis, I. M. (ed.) (1968) *History and Social Anthropology*. London: Tavistock.

Lloyd, P. C. (1954) 'The traditional political system of the Yoruba', *South-Western Journal of Anthropology* 10, 4.

Lloyd, P. C. (1955) 'The Yoruba lineage', *Africa* 25,3.

Lloyd, P. C. (1958) 'Local Government in Yoruba Towns.' Ph. D. thesis, Oxford University.

Lloyd, P. C. (1960) 'Sacred kingship and government among the Yoruba', *Africa* 30, 3.

Lloyd, P. C. (1962) *Yoruba Land Law*. Oxford: Oxford University Press.

Lloyd, P. C. (1965) 'The political structure of African kingdoms' in Banton (1965).

Lloyd, P. C. (1968) 'Conflict theory and Yoruba kingdoms', in Lewis (1968).

Lloyd, P. C. (1971) *The Political Development of Yoruba Kingdoms in the Eighteenth and Nineteenth Centuries*. London: R. A. I. Occasional Paper 31.

Lloyd, P. C. (1974) *Power and Independence: urban Africans' perception of social inequality*. London: Routledge and Kegan Paul.

Lloyd, P. C. *et al* (eds) (1967) *The City of Ibadan*. Cambridge: Cambridge University Press.

Lord, Albert B. (1965 [1960]) *The Singer of Tales*. Reprint: Cambridge, Mass. : Atheneum.

Lucas, J. O. (1948) *The Religion of the Yoruba*. Lagos: CMS.

Macherey, Pierre (1978) *A Theory of Literary Production*, trans. Geoffrey Wall. London: Routledge and Kegan Paul.

McCaskie, T. C. (1989) 'Asanteṣẹm: reflections on discourse and text in Africa', in Barber and Farias (1989).

McClelland, E. M. (1982) *The Cult of Ifa among the Yoruba*. London: Ethnographica.

Miller, J. Hillis (1979) 'The critic as host', in Harold Bloom *et al* (1979).

Miller, Joseph 1980 *The African Past Speaks*. London: Dawson.

Moore, Henrietta L. (1986) *Space, Text and Gender*. Cambridge: Cambridge University Press.

Morton-Williams, Peter (1956a) 'The Atinga cult among the South-Western Yoruba',
    Bull. IFAN 18, 3-4.
Morton-Williams, Peter (1956b) 'The Egungun Society in South-Western Yoruba
    Kingdoms', WAISER Proceedings, Ibadan.
Morton-Williams, Peter (1960a) 'The Yoruba Ogboni cult in Ọyọ', Africa 30, 4.
Morton-Williams, Peter (1960b) 'Yoruba responses to the fear of death', Africa 30, 1.
Morton-Williams, Peter (1964) 'An outline of the cosmology and cult organisation of
    the Ọyọ Yoruba', Africa 34, 3.
Morton-Williams, Peter (1967) 'The Yoruba kingdom of Ọyọ in the nineteenth century',
    in Forde and Kaberry (1967).
Murray, K. C. (1950) 'Oloku', Nigeria Magazine 35.
Norris, Christopher (1982) Deconstruction, Theory and Practice. London and New York:
    Methuen.
Oduyoye, Modupẹ (1972) Yoruba Names: their structure and their meanings. Ibadan:
    Daystar Press.
Okonjo, K. (1976) 'The dual-sex political system in operation: Igbo women and
    community politics in Mid-western Nigeria', in Hafkin and Bay (1976).
Ọlafimihan, J. B. (1950) Iwe Itan Offa. Ibadan.
Ọlajubu, Oludare (1972) Akójọpọ̀ Iwì Egúngún. Ibadan: Longman.
Ọlatunji, Ọlatunde O. (1973) 'Yoruba oral poetry: the feature types', Spectrum 3.
Ọlatunji, Ọlatunde O. (1979) 'The Yoruba oral poet and his society' Research in African
    Literatures 10,2.
Ọlatunji, Ọlatunde O. (1984) Features of Yoruba Oral Poetry. Ibadan: University Press.
Olukoju, Ebenezer O. (1978) 'The Place of Chants in Yoruba Traditional Oral
    Literature. ' Ph. D. thesis, Ibadan University.
Olusanya, G. O. (1983) Studies in Yoruba History and Culture. Ibadan: University Press.
Ong, Walter J. (1982) Orality and Literacy: the technologising of the word. London and
    New York: Methuen.
Opland, Jeff (1983) Xhosa Oral Poetry. Cambridge: Cambridge University Press.
Oroge, E. Adeniyi (1971) 'The Institution of Slavery in Yorubaland with particular
    reference to the nineteenth century. ' Ph. D. thesis, University of Birmingham.
Ottenberg, Simon (1989) 'The dancing bride: art and indigenous psychology in
    Limba weddings', Man 24, 1.
Oyelaran, O. O. (1975) 'On rhythm in Yoruba poetry', in Abimbọla (1975b).
Peace, Adrian (1979) 'Prestige, power and legitimacy in a modern Nigerian town',
    Canadian Journal of African Studies 13, 1-2.
Peel, J. D. Y. (1978) 'Ọlaju: a Yoruba concept of development', Journal of Development
    Studies 14, 2.
Peel, J. D. Y. (1983) Ijeshas and Nigerians. Cambridge: Cambridge University Press.
Peel, J. D. Y. (1984) 'Making History: the past in the Ijesha present', Man 19, 1.
Pemberton, John (1978) 'Egungun masquerades of the Igbomina Yoruba', African
    Arts 11, 3.
Poynor, Robin (1978) 'The egungun of Ọwọ', African Arts 11, 3.
Pratt, Mary Louise (1977) Toward a Speech Act Theory of Literary Discourse. Bloomington
    and London: Indiana University Press.
Ranger, Terence (1975) Dance and Society in Eastern Africa 1890-1970: the Beni
    Ngoma. London: Heinemann.
Richards, Alan (1983) 'The Effects of Early Firearms on Some African Societies from
    the Fifteenth Century to 1900. ' Ph. D. thesis, University of Birmingham.
Sahlins, Marshall (1987) Islands of History. London and New York: Tavistock
    Publications.

Schapera, Isaac (1965) *Praise-poems of Tswana chiefs*. Oxford: Clarendon Press.

Scheub, Harold (1975) *The Xhosa Ntsomi*. Oxford: Clarendon Press.

Schiltz, Marc (1978) 'Egungun masquerades in Iganna', *African Arts* 11, 3.

Schiltz, Marc (1980) 'Rural-urban migration in Iganna'. Ph. D. thesis, University of London.

Schiltz, Marc (1987) 'The Twilight of the Gods and Female Power among the Yoruba', seminar paper presented at CWAS, University of Birmingham.

Schofield, I. F. W. (1935) *Intelligence Report on the Okuku Area of the Northern District, Ibadan Division*.

Schwab, William B. (1955) 'Kinship and lineage among the Yoruba', *Africa* 25,4.

Schwab, William B. (1958) 'The terminology of kinship and marriage among the Yoruba', *Africa* 28, 4.

Searle, John R. (1969) *Speech Acts: an essay in the philosophy of language*. Cambridge: Cambridge University Press.

Smith, Abdullahi (1983) 'A little new light on the collapse of the Alafinate of Yoruba', in Olusanya (1983).

Smith, Barbara Herrnstein (1968) *Poetic Closure*. Chicago: Chicago University Press.

Smith, Robert S. (1969) *Kingdoms of the Yoruba*. London: Methuen.

Şowande, Fẹla, and Fagbemi, Ajanaku (1969) *Orúkọ Àmútọ̀runwá*. Ibadan: Oxford University Press

Stenning, Derrick J. (1959) *Savannah Nomads*. Oxford: Oxford University Press.

Sudarkasa, N. (1973) *Where Women Work: a study of Yoruba women in the marketplace and in the home*. Ann Arbor: Museum of Anthropology, University of Michigan.

Tedlock, Dennis (1983) *The Spoken Word and the Work of Interpretation*. Philadelphia: University of Pennsylvania Press.

Turner, Victor (1967) *The Forest of Symbols*. Ithaca: Cornell University Press.

Turner, Victor (1968) *The Drums of Affliction*. London: Routledge and Kegan Paul.

Turner, Victor (1975) *Revelation and Divination in Ndembu Ritual*. Ithaca and London: Cornell University Press.

Van Allen, Judith (1972) 'Sitting on a man: colonialism and the lost political institutions of Igbo women', *Canadian Journal of African Studies* 6, 2.

Van Allen, Judith (1976) '"Aba Riots" or Igbo "Women's War"? Ideology, stratification and the invisibility of women', in Hafkin and Bay 1976.

Van Zyl, H. J. (1941) 'Praises in Northern Sotho', *Bantu Studies* 15.

Vansina, Jan (1965) *Oral Tradition: a study in historical methodology*, trans. H. M. Wright. London: Routledge and Kegan Paul.

Vansina, Jan (1985) *Oral Tradition as History*. London: James Currey.

Vidal, Tunji (1977) 'The Tonemic and Melodic Character of Yoruba Principal Chants', paper in DALL Seminar Series, University of Ife, Nigeria.

Vološinov, V. N. (1973a [1929]) *Marxism and the Philosophy of Language*, trans. Ladislav Matejka and I. R. Titunik. English ed. : New York and London: Seminar Press.

Vološinov, V. N. (1973b [1927]) *Freudianism: a Marxist critique*, trans. I. R. Titunik. English ed. : New York etc. : Academic Press.

Wittgenstein, Ludwig (1978) *Philosophical Investigations*, trans. G. E. M. Anscombe. Oxford: Blackwell.

Wolff, Hans (1962) 'Rara: a Yoruba chant', *Journal of African Languages* 1,1.

Yai, O. B. (1972) 'Deviation and Intertextuality in Yoruba Oral Poetry' paper presented at 10th West African Languages Conference, University of Ghana.

Yai, O. B. (1989) 'Issues in oral poetry: criticism, teaching and translation', in Barber and Farias (1989).

GLOSSARY

àбà	staple (used in magical charm)
àáfin	palace
abà	farm hut
àbàjà	type of facial mark
àbàtà	type of red kola nut with 2-4 cotyledons
àbíkú	'born-to-die' child
àbísọ	see *orúkọ*
adé	crown
adìẹ	chicken
adìẹ ìdájọ́	'date-setting' chicken given during betrothal
adóṣù	initiated member of cult [one who has applied *ọ̀ṣù*]
agbára	strength
agbe	Blue Touraco bird
agbégijó	see *eléégún ọ̀jẹ̀*
àgbò	ram
àgọ́	temporary camp
àgùntàn	sheep
ajá dúdú	black dog
ajẹ́lẹ̀	representative of a ruling power
àkàlàmàgbò	hornbill
àkàrà	fried bean cakes
akéwì	performer of *ìwì* (*egúngún* chant)
àkìjà	provocative epithet
akíkanjú obìnrin	formidable/courageous woman
àkùkọ	cock
aládàá	'cutlass-carriers' [junior grade of chiefs]
Aláàfin	king of Ọ̀yọ́
alámọ̀	type of *oríkì*-based chant from Èkìtì
alárìnjó	see *eléégún ọ̀jẹ̀*
aláṣekù	ancestors
àlọ́	riddle, folk-tale
àlùkò	type of bird, with red plumage
amọ̀	mud [emblem of an *orílẹ̀*]
àmútọ̀runwá	see *orúkọ*
ànkóò	'& co.': when a group of people all wear the same cloth to show their solidarity
apidán	see *eléégún ọ̀jẹ̀*
ará oko	'bushman', uncivilised person
àrán	velvet [emblem of an *orílẹ̀*]
aró	indigo dye
arọ̀	type of chain-sequence narrative

arugbá	ritual bearer of calabash
asìngbà	part-time bondsman
àtin-ìn	type of mat characteristic of Ìjèṣà area
ayé	the world; ill-disposed people
ayé àtijó	the old days
ayé òde òní	nowadays
baálé	head of a household/compound
babaláwo	divination priest
balógun ilé	head of young men within a compound
bàntẹ́	shorts
bàtá	type of drum
bòròkínní	person of note
dúkíà	moveable property
ebòlò	Gynura Cernua: herb used in stews, has blue flowers (for illustration see Abraham, 1962, p. 721)
èbùrẹ́	type of leafy vegetable used in stews
ègbè (1)	chorus
ègbè (2)	type of bead
ègbo	mashed boiled maize
eégún alágbo	*egúngún* masquerade empowered with charms
eégún ńlá	'great' *egúngún* masquerade
eégún rere	'good' *egúngún* masquerade
egúngún/eégún	ancestral masquerade
eléégún òjè	entertainment masqueraders of *egúngún* cult [also known as *agbégijó*, *alárìnjó* and *apidán*].
eníyaya	type of plant with broad pinnate leaves
epo	palm oil
erin	elephant
ewúrẹ́	she-goat
ewúuyán	rewarmed pounded yam
ẹbu	place where dye or palm oil are manufactured
ẹfun	chalk
ẹgbẹ́	association, club, age-mate, companion
èkọ	solid or liquid food made from corn-starch
ẹkún ìyàwó	brides' *oríki*-based lament [standard Yoruba]
èlú	indigo plant
ẹńlá	small humpless breed of cow
ẹranko	(wild) animal
ẹrú	slave
ẹsẹ Ifá	verse of Ifá
èwà	boiled beans
ẹwẹ	type of bean
fàájì ìyàwó	the 'bride's day of enjoyment' before her marriage
farájọ	family meeting (held monthly)
fùrò	arse
gbẹ́ran-gbẹ́ran	stealer of livestock

gbéyẹ-gbéyẹ	poultry-thief
ìdabọ̀	small plot cultivated by young boys in spare time
idán eégún	stunts or magic pertaining to *egúngún*
ìdílé	'lineage'
igbákèjì ọba	second-in-command to ọba [i.e. most senior chief]
igbó	forest, bush
igbó dúdú	virgin forest
igbó ilé	domestic forest [round the town]
igún	vulture
ìhọ ikin	'thick clump of palm trees' [rare expression, used in narrative of Okuku history]
ìjálá	*oríkì*-based hunters' chant
ìjìnlẹ̀ ọ̀rọ̀	'deep words'
ìjòkùn	plant giving dark green dye
ikàn	egg plant
ìkòrò	type of fish
ilá	okro
ìlàrí	royal messenger
ilé	house, compound, family, lineage
ilé ìyá	the mother's *ilé*
ilée baba	the father's *ilé*
iléelẹ̀	a one-storey house
ìnáwó	spending of money
ìrèmòjé	type of *oríkì*-based hunters' dirge
ìrokò	African teak tree
ìṣákọlẹ̀	money paid for use of royal land
ìsọ̀kọ́	lineage segment defined by descent from a common male ancestor
ìtàn	narrative, history
ìtúfọ̀	formal announcement of a death
iwẹ̀fà mẹ́fà	the 'kingmakers' [top six chiefs]
iwì	*oríkì*-based *egúngún* chant
iwọ̀fà	bondsman whose labour constitutes interest on a loan
iwúre	chant asking for blessings and good luck
ìyá	mother
ìyá ìpẹ̀ẹ̀rẹ̀	head of the younger wives in a compound
ìyáalélé	head of all the wives in a compound
ìyẹ̀rẹ̀ Ifá	type of Ifá chant, performed for an audience, rather than during divination sessions
iyọ̀	salt
jùjú	magic, 'medicine'; modern style of popular music
ké [iwì]	to chant [*iwì*]
kíjìpá	type of coarse cotton cloth
kowéè	type of bird whose cry is thought to be an omen of death
kóbọ̀	penny [unit of Nigerian modern currency]
lékeléke	cattle egret
lílé	solo part in a performance

móín-móín	steamed bean cake
obì Olókukù	type of kola introduced to Òkukù by Oba Oyinlolá
obìnrin	woman
obìnrin ilé	wife of a household/compound
odídẹrẹ	parrot
odù	figure in Ifá divination system
òfi	type of valuable indigenous woven cloth
òfo	emptiness
ògbodò	type of yam
ojú oórì	grave shrine
oko	farm
oko iwájú	'far farm', cocoa farms made at a distance from Òkukù
oko òwò	place where trade or business is conducted
oko ọnà	place where carving is done
òkun	sea
olele	type of *oríkì*-based chant, found in Ìjèsà
olódòóyò	type of herb
olórìsà	devotee of an *òrìsà*
olóyè	chief, title-holder
òndè [=òdèdè]	corridors, premises
oògùn	medicine, charms
òpó	post [an *orílè* emblem]
òré	type of mat
orí	head, luck, destiny, lot
orígun	'corner', lineage segment defined by descent from a common female ancestor
oríkì	appellations, attributions, epithets
oríkì bòròkínní	*oríkì* of notable individuals
oríkì orílè	*oríkì* of a place of origin
orílè	ancient place of origin
òrìsà	god, goddess
òrìsà pípè	*oríkì* chant addressed to *òrìsà*
orò ilé	family ceremony/ritual
orogún	co-wife (wives of same man or same compound)
orúkọ	name
orúkọ àbísọ	name 'given after the child is born', i.e. reflecting circumstances or feelings of family at time of birth
orúkọ àmútòrunwá	name 'brought from heaven', i.e. relating to birth-order or manner of birth
osùn	camwood
òsù	ritual substance applied to initiand's scalp in certain cults [see *adósù*]
òwe	proverb
owó ilé	money paid to ọba for permission to build a house
owó ìsíhùn	money paid during marriage transactions for 'opening discussion'
òyìnbó àgbà	'senior European'
òyìnbó kékeré	'junior European'
ọba	'king', head of town
ọfaasu	bundle of 120 yams

òfẹ́	free of charge
ọfọ̀	incantation
ògà	alternative term for *ọ̀sù*
òkín	king crane [emblem of *orílẹ̀*]
ọlá	honour, high standing, esteem
òlajú	'enlightenment', 'civilisation'
ọlọ́lá	someone of high standing
ọlọ́pàá	'staff-carriers' [senior grade of chiefs]
ọmọ	child, offspring, descendant
ọmọọ baba	children of the same father
ọmọba	child of the ọba, or of the royal family
ọmọ bíbí inú	'true-born child' [poetic idiom]
ọmọ ìyá	children of the same mother
ọmọ olóòkú	child of the deceased [at a funeral]
ọmọ-ọsú	daughters of a compound [married and unmarried]
òrẹ́dẹbí	'friends become family'
òsà	lagoon
òsùn	type of herb used in stew
òtẹ̀	plotting, intrigue
ọtí-òyìnbó	European liquor
òwá	palm-leaf rib [emblem of *orílẹ̀*]
òwẹ̀	communal labour service
pakàá	type of *egúngún* masquerade
parápọ̀	ceremony 'uniting people' in marriage negotiations
pè [òrìṣà]	to perform the *oríkì* of an *òrìṣà*
pélé	type of facial mark
pètẹ̀ẹ̀sì	house of two storeys or more
rárà	royal bards' *oríkì* chant
rárà ìyàwó	bride's lament (local name: see *ẹkún ìyàwó*)
Ṣàngó pípè	*oríkì* chant addressed to Ṣàngó
ṣẹ̀gi	valuable type of blue tubular bead
sun [rárà]	to perform [*rárà/rárà ìyàwó*]

INDEX

English alphabetical order is followed with the additional Yorùbá letters ẹ, ọ and ṣ appearing in separate sections, after e, o and s respectively.